ALVAR AALTO

ALVAR AALTO

A Critical Study

Malcolm Quantrill

Schocken Books
New York

For Reima Pietilä

First American edition published by Schocken Books 1983
10 9 8 7 6 5 4 3 2 1   83 84 85 86
Copyright © 1983 by Malcolm Quantrill
Published by agreement with Martin Secker & Warburg Ltd, London

ISBN 0–8052–3845–X

Library of Congress Cataloging in Publication Data

Quantrill, Malcolm, 1931–
  Alvar Aalto, a critical study.

  1. Aalto, Alvar, 1898–1976. I. Title.
NA1455.F53A237 1983   720′.92′4   82′–61845

Typesetting and origination by Imago Publishing Ltd
Manufactured in Finland

Contents

Acknowledgements

I should never have got to know Aalto's work at first hand if it had not been for the enthusiasm of Anthony J. Walmsley. He was a fellow-student at the Liverpool School of Architecture, and it was he who persuaded me to spend the summer vacation of 1953 with him in Finland, where we worked in the Helsinki City Architect's office. That first trip to Finland was to influence my entire life in the most positive way, and I therefore owe Walmsley a great debt of gratitude.

This study had modest beginnings in 1960, when Henry-Russell Hitchcock suggested that I write a monograph on Aalto's post-war work. I was able to begin that exercise as the result of a grant from the Research Council of Louisiana State University and the generosity of the late Aarne Ervi, who gave me a place in his Helsinki office during the academic year 1959–60. At that time, however, there was a conflict of interests because Aalto had just agreed for an archival edition of his work to be published by Girsberger of Zürich, which appeared in three volumes with Karl Fleig as editor. The presentation of work in the Girsberger (later Artemis) edition is not chronological and there are omissions but it remains an invaluable resource for the student of Aalto. This book is intended as a critical companion volume to that edition.

Although my original project was abandoned in 1963 my interest continued. Then in 1977, a year after Aalto's death, I was encouraged by Professor Reima Pietilä to undertake a critique of the architect's entire output. In January 1978 I met Elissa Aalto again, at the opening of the Aalto Memorial Exhibition in Helsinki. Subsequently I was instrumental in arranging for the transfer of that exhibition to the Royal Academy galleries in London in October 1978. On the occasion of the Royal Academy showing I was invited by the Royal Institute of British Architects to give a lecture on Aalto's work and thought: that paper formed the basis of the first and last chapters of this study. I am therefore grateful to Lesley Murray of the RIBA Programme Office for stimulating that paper and to David Dean, the RIBA Librarian, for his assistance.

I have met frequently with Mrs Aalto since the spring of 1978 and without her kindness and help I could not have completed this work. The Museum of Finnish Architecture, particularly its Director, Juhani Pallasmaa, and Mrs Maija Häivä of the Archives Department, provided me with invaluable support and assistance during my research: I am grateful to them and to their other helpful colleagues. To Reima and Raili Pietilä I am indebted for their generous hospitality without which I could not have afforded so many visits to Helsinki. Both Dr Göran Schildt of the Aalto Foundation and Professor Kenneth Frampton of Columbia University have read the manuscript and made helpful suggestions for the preparation of the final text.

During the academic year 1979–80 I was granted academic leave by the Polytechnic of North London to enable me to complete my overseas research. This was also facilitated by the award of a travel grant from the Phoenix Trust of London.

Many colleagues encouraged me over the years by inviting me to lecture on Aalto's work and I am particularly grateful to the following: Professor Newton Watson of

University College, London; Professor Dewi-Prys Thomas of the Welsh School of Architecture, Cardiff; Professor Guy Oddie of Edinburgh University; Professor Robert Gardner-Medwin of Liverpool University; Professor Yannos Politis of the Arkitektskølen, Aarhus; Professor Douglas Shadbolt and Professor Michael Coote of Carleton University, Ottawa; Professor Richard Whitaker and Dean Bertram Berenson (then) of the University of Illinois, Chicago; Professor Peter Johnson of the University of Sydney; and Professor Gareth Roberts of the University of New South Wales.

In addition, I am grateful for the kindness and help I have received from the Finnish Embassy in London, particularly from the Ambassador, Dr Richard Tötterman; the former Cultural Counsellor, Mr Henrik Antell; and the present Cultural Counsellor, Mr Tom Södermann. I am indebted also to Mrs T. Wegelius, Mrs M. Lomas, and Dr M. Branch who helped me in matters of translation.

In August 1980 I was injured in the Bologna Railway Station bomb atrocity whilst on my way to photograph the Riola Church. This delayed completion of the manuscript, so I am grateful to my publisher, Tom Rosenthal, for his patience; and to my agent, Diana Tyler, for her support during convalescence.

The patient attention to detail of my editor, Sue Moore, was indispensable in preparing this study for publication. In January 1981 Kate Bramley began the typing of the final text in Amman, and this task was completed by Elizabeth Arundale.

Reg Scott of John Donat Darkroom Associates and his printer, John Conaway, deserve special mention for their help in preparing my own photographs for publication.

Finally, I must thank my family for putting up with the demands of the gestation period: my wife for accommodating my moods and irregular hours with good humour, also for her help in proofreading; and my two daughters, Francesca and Alexandra, who daily saw opportunities to play with Daddy consumed by his work.

Malcolm Quantrill
University of Jordan
Amman

1981

Alvar Aalto *c.* 1937

Introduction

My first visit to Finland, in 1953, was set in motion by the desire to see modern Finnish architecture, post-war buildings for the most part, that were in the course of being built or had just been completed. I was particularly concerned with discovering for myself the work of Alvar Aalto. As an international figure he had already established himself on the basis of his work between 1927 and 1935. What I sought, however, was his new architecture, based on the use of natural materials.[1]

Aalto dominated Finnish architecture for almost half a century, until his death in 1976. For most of that period his highly idiosyncratic buildings were difficult to place in relation to the work of other international masters. His use of traditional forms has never produced a simple copy of the original but a development and transformation.

It was this evolution of traditional architecture, rather than the development of an individual style, that concerned Aalto most. This is not to say that external, international influences were not important in his development. But those influences that did come from outside the Finnish tradition were grafted onto his own very deep understanding of that tradition, and then made intensely personal. By accepting his roots in a national idiom, particularly that of the immediate past, Aalto was able to extend significant design attitudes from the National Romantic movement into his own personal interpretation of modern architecture. For him, the traditions of the 'modern' and the 'new' must inevitably be rooted in an understanding of known geometries, the exploration of familiar contexts and the stimulation of vestigial architectural 'sensations'.

Reyner Banham has reminded us[2] that Aalto did not stand alone in the Finnish architectural landscape any more than Eliel Saarinen had done. The fact that his genius has generated certain special vibrations has singled him out, as Saarinen was singled out before him. But in order to understand his unique contribution his work should be considered in the context of what went before as well as what developed in parallel with his own experiments.

Certainly, when one thinks of innovation in modern architecture the name of Alvar Aalto readily springs to mind. Indeed, Aalto might well have echoed the sentiment of Francesco Borromini: 'I would not have joined the profession with the aim of merely being an imitator.'

But Aalto's innovations like Borromini's must be seen within the framework of the traditions, the forms and formulations to which they relate or against which they rebel. My concern here is to discuss his contribution to the evolution of modern architecture, both in terms of his functional exploration of internal/external spatial relationships and his juxtaposition of historical references with statements in search of the new. Much of the difficulty of relating Aalto's work to the central themes of the Modern Movement has stemmed from the fact that he was already anticipating in the mid-30s the mood of post-modernism.[3] His intention was to humanise space and form, his method was to blend modern technology and standardisation with a craftsman's approach to the design and realisation of his buildings.

The history of Finnish architecture is not as complex as that manifested by Central and Southern Europe but its traditions have clearly identifiable components, and it is in the context of these that Aalto's work must be viewed. Firstly, there is the tradition of materials, of stone and brick and wood, which is rooted in Finland's churches. Then there is the formalism of the Neo-classical period, an influence that was brought to bear at a critical stage in the evolution of modern Finland. As a reaction to the external force and character of Neo-classicism, imposed by the Russians and implemented by the German architect Engel, there emerged in Finnish architecture a modern tradition of formal experiment which was brought into being by the National Romantic movement.[4]

Thematically, Finnish National Romantic architecture expresses a strong historical bent, rooted in medieval imagery; but formally it had little academic interest in the past and its characteristic is an almost exotic sense of caprice. The academic discipline of the Polytechnic educational system, with its re-emphasis of the Neo-classical vocabulary, must be considered in relation to these traditions. Interestingly, whilst Aalto was at the height of his powers in the 1950s and 60s, the academic emphasis was once again swinging back to a formalist position under the leadership of Professor Aulis Blomstedt. And now, after Aalto's death, as Reima Pietilä continues the tradition of organic experimentation, so Pietilä's work and philosophy have been vehemently opposed by the students and followers of Blomstedt.

Aalto's uniqueness derived from his ability to extend, modify and blend these different traditions with international and historical themes, achieving a design approach that combined recognisable elements in new and original forms. It was in this way that he anticipated recent reactions to functionalism. Although he often presented himself as being functionally oriented, there is embedded in his approach to functionalism a conscious irrationality, a softening and humanising touch which keeps the functional intention of the plan or section concealed beneath the building's surface. An Aalto building does not simply materialise in terms of the present: it links us with established traditions of architecture.

Nor does the evolution of Aalto's work from the 1920s to the 1970s present a consistent or continuous development of one image or expression. Rather we find that, as with many great artists, certain distinct themes and directions are established in the early period – in Aalto's case the 1920s and 1930s – which provide the basis for later variations on those earlier statements of intent. The seeds of innovation were planted early in Aalto's career; much of his later work was, however, rather backward looking. His early innovations are clearly set within the decade between the late 20s and the close of the 30s. In his second major period, that of the 1950s, he combined a desire for refinement on the one hand with a new experimental approach on the other. The first period saw the transition from the internationalism of the Turun Sanomat building and Paimio Sanatorium to the expressionism of the Villa Mairea and the New York World's Fair pavilion. The second period was characterised by the Säynätsalo

Town Hall, the Muuratsalo summer house, the Imatra Church, and in Helsinki the House of Culture and the National Pensions Institute.

If we seek evidence of further development in the late 60s and early 70s we shall be largely disappointed. The sheer amount of later work, and in some cases its essential monumentality, seems to have militated against the experimental spirit of Aalto's earlier, smaller-scale and more intimate buildings. For example, although the National Pensions Institute is one of Aalto's largest buildings it nevertheless retains a small scale: this is consistent with the role of the building, since it has no public ritual function comparable with that of an important civic or cultural edifice.

Certainly, the contemplation of his most important unrealised project, the Essen Opera House, changed Aalto's fundamental attitudes about the nature of public buildings and civic scale. The first scheme for Essen dates from 1958–9, when he entered and won the original competition. There was a further new design produced over the period 1961–4 and work on the project continued to occupy Aalto throughout the 60s. It must have been an enormous disappointment to him that this, his most important international commission, was not realised. That sense of disappointment, coupled with the sheer amount of work involved in such a vast undertaking, clearly had its effect on the man and his creative resources.

It has to be remembered, furthermore, that Aalto was already sixty when work on the Essen competition began. Thus, during a period of his life when most senior partners in British and American practices would have been 'put out to grass', Aalto was still hard at it, attempting to bring his international career to its summit. There is also no evidence that his drinking was ameliorated with advancing years.[5] In addition, there was a mounting sense of frustration that yet another of his major competition successes was to be thwarted. For the Essen Opera House promised all that was outstanding in Aalto's previous achievements, bringing interest and quality to the detailing of the interior whilst not becoming pedantically fussy about the massing and expression of the exterior.

The simple external form of the Essen project suggested that he had mastered the art of translating the fine sense of scale he demonstrates at Säynätsalo and in the House of Culture into the larger context of the metropolitan urban framework, just as many of his house plans succeed in miniaturising his statements of urban form.[6] However, the workload in the office during the 60s, together with the other consequences of his advancing years, suggest that the extra pressures and burden of the Essen project began to exhaust Aalto's fertile imagination. Certainly, when he had the opportunity with the building of Finlandia Concert Hall and Congress Centre in Helsinki (1967–75) to achieve the qualities promised by the Essen project he was only able to demonstrate these developments in the interior of the main auditorium.

There are exceptions to the general deterioration of Aalto's performance during the last decade of his life. Consistent with his early interest in church design, beginning with the restoration work at Kauhajärvi (1918–19) and Äänekoski (1924), the Jämsä competition (1925) and the Muurame Church (1926–9), these exceptions include churches. They are the church and parish centre for Riola, near Bologna, begun in 1966 and completed posthumously in 1978, and the unrealised project for a Protestant Parish Centre at Altstetten in Zürich. Their interest is that they extend Aalto's long preoccupation with the fan-shaped plan motif (which dates back to the Enso-Gutzeit weekend house competition entry of 1932) into the section of the building. The last incidence of this third-dimensional reference to the fan shape was to occur in the abortive project for an art museum for the Shah of Iran at Sheraz of 1970.

In his book *Meaning in Western Architecture*,[7] Christian Norberg-Schultz wrote:

> In the works of the younger generation of modern architects, the wish for the individual characterisation based on a pluralism of patterned spatial organisation is ever more felt. We may therefore conclude that modern architecture has liberated itself from the fetters of general types and basic principles and is in the process of realising a true synthesis of order.

My study of Aalto's work has convinced me that, through the range and variety of his architectural experiments, he has probably contributed more than any other modern architect to this 'liberation', or what I would prefer to think of as a true understanding of the principles of order and freedom within our inherited traditions.

The first chapter of this study is devoted to an examination of influences upon him and an analysis of some of his own pronouncements on the nature of architecture. There follows a discussion of the background of Aalto's thinking that exists in the National Romantic movement. Finally there is analysis of the evolution of his work, with a detailed critique of all the significant buildings. This analysis traces the development of Aalto's ideas in terms of planning themes, and formal and technical preoccupations. A further strand is woven through this analysis, that of environmental control in relation to spatial organisation, underlining the fact that Aalto's concerns to bring natural light into the interiors of his buildings was central to his design process from the introduction of the first roof-light in the Turun Sanomat building. As an extension of this concern, the contrast of interior and exterior qualities is also considered, as well as Aalto's approach to detailing and finishes. Thus, I have tried by moving from the architect's general ideas through specific building concepts to their actual realisation, to come to grips with the totality of Aalto's philosophy and its formal expression.

It is my hope that this study will promote further discussion and understanding of Aalto's genius and of Finnish architecture in general. If it succeeds in this respect then I shall have repaid a small part of my enormous debt to Finnish architecture and Finnish architects for the contribution they have made to my own thinking about design and my teaching.

MALCOLM QUANTRILL
Amman, Jordan 1981

CHAPTER I

Inner Process – Outward Form

A proper understanding of Aalto's work within the context of either European architecture as a whole or the evolution of the Modern Movement in particular has always presented considerable difficulties. There are a number of quite obvious reasons why this should be the case. In the first place, Finland is not culturally part of Europe, although, during its long history as a subject nation, it came under the influence of both the Swedes and the Europeanised Russians. As a consequence of this there is a largely Neo-classical overlay on much eighteenth- and nineteenth-century Finnish architecture, so that some of its surface features have an immediately recognisable character within the context of the classical ideal.

Alvar Aalto was brought up within the wider and more westward-looking framework of a Swedish-speaking family. This background had a deep and lasting influence upon his own personal view of Finnish architecture within the broader European architectural context. At the same time he exploited what were and remain peculiarly Finnish characteristics, which belong to a large extent within a category summarised by Eliel Saarinen's view that architecture should be a reflection of the nature of materials.[1] These characteristics also have their roots in Finnish folk culture, with its distinctly mystical, eastern elements, which are consequently more difficult for the westerner to understand. The Finnish National Romantic movement also had a profound influence upon him.

The memorial exhibition of Aalto's work which opened in Helsinki in January 1978 stimulated renewed interest in the architect and raised some interesting questions about the evolution of his formal ideas. Instead of providing a chronological catalogue of works to accompany this exhibition, Aarno Ruusuvuori and Juhani Pallasmaa offered a thematic documentation that ranged across Aalto's work and his thinking.

Of the four introductory essays included in the documentation to the 1978 Aalto Exhibition, those by Göran Schildt and Carlo Ludovico Ragghianti were the most significant, whilst Nils-Erik Wickberg's contribution is also of some interest. Indeed, Wickberg's *Empire Stadier*,[2] which I saw for the first time early in 1960, has been of considerable influence in stimulating my interest in the two main paths of modern Finnish architecture – the one deriving from Italian Renaissance sources and Neo-classical derivatives, and the other stemming from the vigorously independent spirit of the National Romantic movement.

Early in his essay Schildt says of Aalto:

He dreamed of an architecture quite without style, buildings determined

1

only by the diverse needs of the people using them and conditions dictated by the building site, the materials available and financial considerations. He expressed this dream clearly in an article written in 1941 on the architecture of Karelia. In it he speaks of a completely autonomous architecture, influenced by no formal conventions of foreign culture, created by local master-builders to be a perfect instrument in the harmonious life of the people of the Karelian wilds.

In other words, he makes a strong plea for Aalto to be considered as a romantic expressionist.

But we should not be misled by this attempt, albeit a felicitous one, to present Aalto in too simple terms. It is important to remember that in 1941 all things Karelian had a particular topicality for Finland. There is therefore in Aalto's dream of an autonomous architecture as much a hint of 'political man' and of a revival of National Romantic principles. For Aalto was one of the most complex figures ever to work in the sphere of the creative arts.

The autonomous, indigenous line in Aalto's approach was therefore only one aspect of an architectural philosophy that turns out to have many cultural complexities and contradictions. And what is closer to the truth is Schildt's later suggestion that to Aalto:

> ... the art of building was an art only in the sense that medicine and cooking are arts. He conceived it as a humanistic activity based on technical knowledge which can only be pursued successfully by people with a capacity for creative synthesis.

In terms of the concept of both national and autonomous expression in Finnish architecture Aalto's genius lay in part in his realisation that far from cultivating the cultural isolation of Finland to the exclusion of all external influences he wanted both to have his cake and eat it. For, unlike painting or poetry, the art of architecture cannot be pursued in private, introspective detachment. It is precisely because Finnish painters and sculptors continued from the 1920s through to the 1950s to depend too much on perpetuating the spirit of National Romanticism (rather than responding to the invigorating freshness of, say, Helena Schjerfbeck or the equally accessible influence of Edvard Munch) that fine art in Finland remained 'frozen' for half a century.

In contrast it was largely as a result of Alvar Aalto's success in making cross-cultural connections on a highly selective basis that Finnish architecture has, over the past half-century, become internationally significant by any standards. Finnish painting on the other hand has remained far from the centre of contemporary debate. Aalto's work began with references to the Neo-classical but he quickly moved on to show himself as a master of the international rationalist style, then decisively re-emphasised Eliel Saarinen's theory that 'the nature of the materials decides the nature of the form'. At the same time he reverted frequently to classical principles, but more in the spirit of Alberti, Brunelleschi and Palladio.[4] There are also substantial references to the Baroque idiom which may well be derived from Borromini.[5]

This is precisely the measure of the man and for this reason even his reference to Karelian culture, made in 1941, should not be read at only one simplistic level. It was in Karelia, after all, that the vestiges of Finno-Ugric 'tribalism' were inseparably mixed up with the rituals and practices of the Orthodox Church.

Certainly, the fact that Aalto's grandfather, Hugo Hamilkar Hackstedt, gained his certificate as a 'senior forester' firmly roots Aalto in the lineage of Saarinen's 'nature of materials' tradition. Those beautiful and truly fantastic wooden constructions, experiments which spanned from 1930 until 1947, which were central to the inspiration of all his furniture designs of the 1930s and which crop up again in modified forms in the project for the Essen Opera House (1961–5), in the Kauffmann Rooms of the Institute of International Education, New York (1963–5) and at the Finlandia Hall, Helsinki (1962–71), were precisely conjured out of an innate sensitivity to the forms of the forest in general and the unique nature and potentialities of wood in particular.

Not only that, but Hugo Hamilkar Hackstedt was, as Schildt points out:

> . . . a survivor of the eighteenth-century intelligentsia who combined an interest in the humanities and natural sciences in the manner of Goethe or Linnaeus . . . knew his classics, invented useful mechanical devices [and] designed industrial buildings.

The family's interest in teachnology and construction was further reinforced when one of Hackstedt's daughters, the middle one of three and reputedly the most beautiful, married a surveyor, J.H. Aalto – *aalto* meaning, in Finnish, 'wave'. But, as Schildt reminds us, the Hackstedt family was entirely Swedish-speaking, and thus:

> . . . Alvar Aalto shared the liberal Scandinavian tradition. This saved him from the narrow nationalism and authoritarian social views held by a large part of the Finnish-speaking educated classes during the inter-war period.

Aalto, however, being a Finnish name, the mixture was compounded; and although he was christened Hugo Alvar Henrik (giving him the initials H.A.H.A.!) he himself became essentially Finnish-speaking. So that, although his background was Swedish and therefore culturally 'westward-looking', he thought of himself first and foremost as a Finn. Furthermore, his extreme interest in things Karelian meant that he stood in the very centre of two cultures, seeking his cultural wavelengths from both east and west.

At the same time he drew very directly from the central resource of the immediate past, upon the sense of craftsmanship that was an essential feature of the National Romantic movement. It is Aalto's attention to detail that allows the tuberculosis sanatorium at Paimio to remain an outstanding example of rationalism.

His sheer craftsmanship in joinery detailing is evidenced by the fittings and furniture of the Woodberry Poetry Room he designed for the Lamont Library at Harvard University, while the formal and rhythmical influence of the National Romantic movement is readily seen in all aspects of his work, from the design of the handles for the external doors of the Rautatalo (the headquarters building of the Finnish Iron Dealers' Association) and Kansaneläkkelaitos (the National Pensions Institute) to his plans, sections and massing.[6]

J.H. Aalto's influence upon his son stemmed from two basic characteristics: firstly, as Schildt observes, through the surveyor's conscientiousness and capacity for hard work; and then in his highly developed sense of professional pride linked with an awareness of public responsibility. Schildt draws our attention to the fact that:

> The white table at which his father and his collaborators worked at their drawings became for the son a symbol...
> As a small boy Alvar used to play under that white table, but when one of the surveying students was away on business he was allowed to move up and make his own childish drawings at his father's side.

This would appear to indicate one direct origin of those persistent white elements, which not only characterise much of Aalto's furniture but also crop up frequently in many of his architectural details. Indeed, one of the seemingly permanent influences that Aalto exercised upon modern Finnish architecture is through the prevalence of this characteristic 'whiteness' which was to be adopted by Aarne Ervi and Viljo Rewell (both of whom were young assistants in Aalto's office) as well as recurring in the work of Reima Pietilä and Timo Penttilä, to give but a few main examples. Of course, in parallel with this apparent influence, one has to consider the functional necessity of achieving the maximum reflection of light within the interior spaces of Finnish buildings. The Finnish winter is long – at least six months – and the winter days short, with only four hours of daylight at their briefest. Yet those short winter days are often fantastically illuminated by the intensity of brilliant sunlight playing on the snow.

All of Aalto's work demonstrates that he had an acute awareness of the quality of light, not only as it occurs in the Finnish landscape and is reflected in his interiors but also as it relates to the cultures of the Mediterranean and the Southern Hemisphere. I recall one of his typical expressions of this awareness when I visited him in his office in January 1960. He knew that it was the first time that I had spent more than a few weeks, during summer, in Finland and he asked me: 'Well, and how do you like the Finnish winters?' Without giving me a chance to answer him he said: 'I can tell you, they are truly wonderful. Because they are so long, and you can spend them in India or Africa or South America.'

It is through the play of light and shade on forest forms, and in and around those thousands of lakes, that Nature provides yet another source of Aalto's inspiration. Schildt observes that:

The curved lines often appearing in his architecture, reminiscent of the Finnish sea coast viewed from a plane, are in fact the familiar contours used by the surveyor.

Schildt means, presumably, the celluloid profiles we call 'French curves', which were developed to assist the post-Renaissance architect in coping with the complexities of geometric design. It is obvious from Aalto's whole approach to drawing that it is the *inner process* of feeling out the shape of a wall or determining the relationship of parts that is the dominant force in his designs. Certainly the famous 'Savoy' glass vases, originally designed by Aalto with his wife, Aino, and first manufactured for the Savoy Restaurant in Helsinki in 1937, took their form, at least in part, from the shoreline configurations of the Finnish lakes rather than those of the sea coast. But it is puzzling that Schildt mentions viewing them from a plane. Surely, Aalto would have been aware of the patterns formed by the lake shores directly from his excursions into the Finnish landscape. An even more obvious source of reference would have been the surveyor's maps he would have found on his father's desk, and over which he must have pored as a young boy.

It was precisely Aalto's capacity for creative synthesis that made him (in Robert Venturi's phrase) not so much an *either/or* kind of architect but rather one of the *both/and* variety. In one of the most direct revelations of his working method, Aalto described his own approach to creative synthesis in this way:

> When I personally have some architectural problem to solve, I am constantly . . . faced with an obstacle difficult to surmount, a kind of 'three in the morning feeling'. The reason seems to be the complicated, heavy burden represented by the fact that architectural planning operates with innumerable elements which often conflict. Social, human, economic and technical demands combined with psychological questions affecting both the individuals and the group, together with movements of human masses and individuals, and internal frictions – all these form a complex tangle which cannot be unravelled in a rational or mechanical way. The immense number of different demands and component problems constitute a barrier from behind which it is difficult for the basic idea to emerge...
> [First] I forget the entire mass of problems for a while, after the atmosphere of the job and the innumerable difficult requirements have sunk into my subconscious. Then I move on to a method of working which is very much like abstract art. I just draw by instinct, not architectural synthesis, but what are sometimes childlike compositions, and in this way, on this abstract basis, the main idea gradually takes shape, a kind of universal substance which helps me to bring innumerable contradictory component problems into harmony.[7]

What Aalto describes bears an uncanny resemblance to William Gordon's synectic method.[8] Gordon's dictum was that whereas 'ultimate solutions to problems are rational – the process of finding them is not'. His equation for determining the most elegant solution was:

$$\text{elegance of solution} = \frac{\text{multiplicity of variables}}{\text{simplicity of solution}}$$

Moreover, Gordon's work was started at about the same time Aalto described his own working method, in 1946 in fact. Indeed there was a great deal of interest in Gordon's work in Finland and he himself was the guest of Armi Ratia, founder and owner of the Marimekko fashion and textile business, in the early 60s.

Earlier, in 1938, Aalto had already described the importance to him of Nature both as a source of inspiration and as a basis of his process of abstraction, viz:

> ... the best standardisation committee in the world is Nature herself, but in nature standardisation occurs mainly – in fact almost solely – in connection with the smallest possible units, cells. The result is millions of flexible combinations ... Another result is that there is immense richness and an endless variation of organically growing forms. Architectural standardisation must tread the same path.[9]

One persistent aspect of Aalto's approach to architecture was to see it 'as part of the struggle between man and nature'. Viewed like that, he maintained that we would discover 'its clearest inner character' and what he called 'its systematic constant variability'.[10] He described his own departure from the narrow confines of the rationalist style in the following way:

> There is an everlasting increase in the number of problems and, with them, basic architectural elements in its inner process, and at the same time a reduction in the significance of questions which have previously played a dominant role. The resultant 'natural variability of theme' is thus one of the basic characteristics of architecture, and it is of fundamental importance that we make room for it in our everyday work, too.[11]

For Aalto, therefore, the underlying requirement in any approach to standardisation was a resultant 'natural variability' in use. In 1941, already looking ahead to the vast planning and building programmes that would have to follow the devastation of the war, he published a paper entitled 'The Reconstruction of Europe Reveals the Central Architectural Problem of our Time'. And the very heart of this problem to Aalto was, that:

> Architecture should always offer a means whereby the organic connection between a building and nature (including man and human life as an element of greater importance than others) is provided for. This is also the most important thing in architectural standardisation. But this presupposes the

development not only of building components but of a whole new architectural approach for this purpose.[12]

Such an approach, for Aalto, would be systematic only in the comprehensive way that Nature is systematic, the reason for this being that the system must offer freedom rather than rigidity, because, in Aalto's own words:

> After all, nature is a symbol of freedom. Sometimes nature actually gives rise to and maintains the idea of freedom. If we base our technical plans primarily on nature we have a chance to ensure that the course of development is once again in a direction in which our everyday work and all its forms will increase freedom rather than decrease it.[13]

Thus Aalto, writing in 1949, on the theme of 'National Planning and the Goals of Culture'. The importance of nature as our guide and teacher, our natural resource for inspiration, remained one of his recurring themes. Nature, through its vocabulary of warm colours, sympathetic textures and subtle, undulating forms, is the great softener. The theme of nature is reiterated in his 1955 Vienna lecture entitled 'Between Humanism and Materialism', where he says:

> It seems to me that there are too many situations in life in which the organisation is too brutal: *it is the task of the architect to give life a gentler structure.*[14]

But nature, of course, also possesses its own theatricality, those powerful dramatic elements which reflect the struggle that goes on within its own organic and formal systems. It was in the Baroque period that the most dynamic aspects of this conflict emerged into architecture through the forceful geometry of its curvilinear forms. In this sense the architects of both the High Gothic and Baroque embodied the dramatic vocabulary of the natural landscape into their structures.

As a serious student of nature and the organic models its systems provide for building forms, Aalto was acutely aware of this *embodiment* and its extensions. His view of nature as 'a symbol of freedom' and his suggestion that we should 'base our technical plans primarily on nature' in order to 'increase freedom rather than decrease it' connects him directly to the spirit of National Romanticism and the formal experimentation in modern Finnish architecture which had its beginnings in the early years of the twentieth century. In the National Romantic movement, with its free interpretation of historical forms, and its agglutinative anti-academic planning, Aalto found totally sympathetic echoes. For him the juxtaposition of the past with the present, the combination of the classical ideal with the romantic allusion was simply 'doing what comes naturally'. It was Aalto's ability to absorb both classic and romantic elements into his own innovative designs that gave his mature work its authenticity.

CHAPTER II

Modern Finnish Architecture – Background and Evolution

The climate in which Finnish architecture emerged into the twentieth century is well demonstrated by the April/May 1903 issue of Finland's new professional journal, *Arkitekten* (later *Arkkitehti*),[1] which began publication in that year. In that issue the feature article 'Den Nyare Engelska Byggnads Konsten' ('The New English Architecture') was devoted to a discussion of the work of William Butterfield, James Brooks, John Pearson, Norman Shaw, John Sedding and G.E. Street.[2]

This attention to English work clearly indicates not only that the profession in Finland in 1903 was confident enough to produce its own critical journal but also that Finnish architects at the turn of the century were eager to look beyond the boundaries of the then Russian Grand Duchy of Finland.[3] From the beginnings of the National Romantic movement in the 1890s the architectural profession had been dominated by practitioners coming from the highly educated and outward-looking Swedish-speaking community, whose domination of Finnish cultural life goes back to the colonisation of Finland by the Swedes in 1362. Until the 1890s, the most important architects practising in Finland had received their training either abroad or at least with a foreign architect. So that a tradition of overseas influence was clearly established in Finnish practice by the time the new generation, led by Lars Sonck (1870–1956), Herman Gesellius (1874–1916), Armas Lindgren (1874–1929) and Eliel Saarinen (1873–1950), trained in Helsinki at the Polytechnic Institute.

The originators of the Finnish National Romantic movement in architecture were undoubtedly the architect Lars Sonck and the painter Akseli Gallen-Kallela. As early as 1894 Sonck was the winner of a very important architectural competition. This was for the Church of St Michael in Turku,[4] the building of which was finally completed in 1905, with the rear gallery clearly anticipating the planning of Tampere cathedral.

To undertake the Turku commission, Sonck was compelled to abandon another project that was dear to him. This was an excursion to Karelia, Finland's easternmost province, that he had been planning to undertake with two fellow artists. Nevertheless, he remained a keen student of Karelian folklore and the Karelian tradition of wooden construction. In fact, in 1894–5, and perhaps in part compensation for the loss of the Karelian journey, he designed and erected his first two villas, which were clearly influenced by his study of Karelian wood detailing. The chalet-like character of these early villas, with their knotty log construction and bold, jutting cornices, left little doubt about the origin of their inspiration.

8

Right: Traditional wooden farmhouse of the Karelian type: detail of an example re-erected by the late Madame Armi Ratia at Bökars, south-west Finland

Below left: Neo-classical wooden church at Tampere: south doorway. The same simple geometry was to become characteristic of Aalto's early designs

Below right: The cathedral at Tampere by Lars Sonck: detail of the main west door

At the same moment in time, Akseli Gallen-Kallela, who was one of the very first European artists to travel in Africa, paint there and collect African tribal art, was busily engaged in the design and construction of his studio home, *Karela*. This building provided an early model of the new freedom of plan and formal expression that was to characterise National Romantic architecture, and was itself, in turn, clearly influenced by late-nineteenth-century English domestic architecture.

Sonck went on in 1902 to win the competition for the cathedral in the fast-growing city of Tampere.[5] In his design for Tampere he developed the concept already advanced in St Michael's, Turku, and produced a lastingly important monument in the realisation of the new Finnish architecture. The simple hall plan of Tampere cathedral is modified by the vaulting form of the gallery supports, achieving an original and sophisticated solution.

The stonework of Sonck's Tampere cathedral owes an unmistakable debt to the inspiration of the East Coast American architect, H.H. Richardson, while the detailing of the metalwork gives fairly obvious hints of his interest in the models provided by Louis Sullivan's mastery of the medium in Chicago. Indeed, as the true Finnish spirit began to exert its influence on a vital new expression in the arts and crafts, Sonck and his colleagues were quite clearly determined to be fully aware of international developments and make the appropriate connections with their own experiments. Thus, the stonework and metalwork detailing that Sonck created for Tampere cathedral provided the emerging generation of young Finnish architects with a brilliant example of style and craftsmanship. It also had a superbly ambitious scale, so eminently fitting to the spirit of Finnish independence and a Finnish national expression that was being born in their intensely romantic minds.

Sonck's handling of form, mass and detailing at Tampere has remained unexcelled in the evolution of modern Finnish architecture.[6] This cathedral church was one of Alvar Aalto's favourite buildings and its influence upon him is unmistakable. In Aalto's handling of granite and bronze there is a clear obeisance to the grand old master of Finnish architecture who, after all, did not die until 1956, at the very height

Järvenpää: detail of Lars Sonck's villa 'Ainola', built in 1904 for Sibelius. A similar rustic use of timber was to feature in many of Aalto's designs

of Aalto's own career. But Aalto's most direct debt to Tampere cathedral is to be found in the prevailing freedom of his lines which indicate a profound dependence upon the north gallery window depicting the 'Horseman of the Apocalypse'.

Irregularity of form, massing and fenestration became one of the characteristic imprints of Aalto's mature expression, and the spirit of this idiosyncratic playfulness can be readily traced to those inventions which characterise the evolution of the National Romantic style. For example, the 'Sampos' Polytechnic Student House in Helsinki, designed by Thomé and Lindahl, and completed in 1903,[7] exhibits the kind of door patterns and window arrangements which Aalto clearly found so attractive as models for his own formal experiments, while Lars Sonck's private hospital in the Eira district of Helsinki is an interesting precursor of Aalto's approach to plan forms.[8] Sonck's design combines an agglutinative plan form with a free association of geometrical organisation in order to build up a formal muscularity that flexes itself against the shape of the site, yet conforms to the domestic character of the Eira neighbourhood.

Plan of Lars Sonck's Eira hospital, in Helsinki

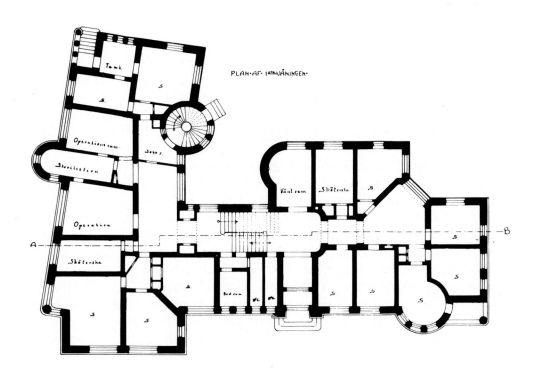

The Villa Tötterman, Kirkkonummi, built by Saarinen in 1902. A clear expression of the architect's theory that 'the nature of materials decides the nature of form'

Indeed, it was Sonck's propensity for the agglutinative plan and his skill in handling the resultant massing which make him such a significant figure in the establishment of the National Romantic style. His entry for the State School Building in Helsinki,[9] also of 1905, literally shows Sonck dismembering the conventional tightly closed plan and creating in its place a number of linked 'pavilions', three of which have boldly rounded corners. And in that same competition the entry with the pseudonym 'SOL' has a similarly agglutinative approach to the plan form.[10].

At the beginning of their partnership, and in their early work, Gesellius, Lindgren and Saarinen looked not to their compatriot Sonck for inspiration but rather sought it in the models of the German *Jugendstil*. Their residential building at No. 7 Satamakatu in Helsinki (1897) certainly reveals this influence, as does their Finnish Pavilion for the Paris World Fair of the following year. The Finnish Pavilion, however, was an amalgam of *Jugendstil* elements with clearly recognisable derivatives from the tradition of Finnish mediaeval stone church architecture, while the overall approach to ornamentation suggested a move towards a distinctly new Finnish flavour on the part of these three architects. And two years later, in their imposing headquarters building for the Pohjola Insurance Company (1900–1901), Helsinki, Gesellius, Lindgren and Saarinen successfully introduced the National Romantic style

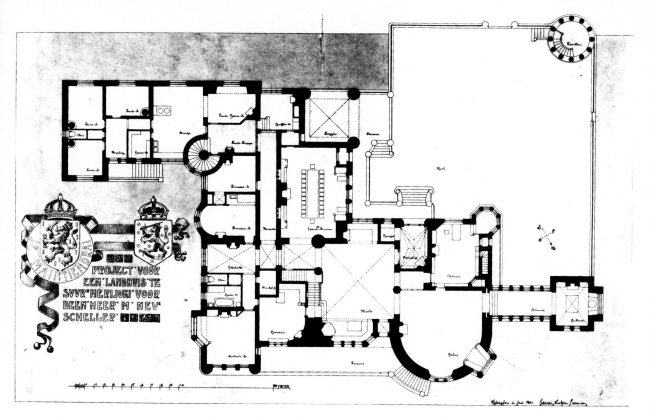

Plan for the manor-house known as 'Suur-Merijoki', built by Gesellius, Lindgren and Saarinen near Viipuri in 1901–3

into Finnish commercial architecture.

In the same year that the Pohjola offices were finished the partnership's design for the manor house of Suur-Merijoki, near Viipuri, arguably the finest example of National Romantic domestic architecture, was already under construction. This house, built for a wealthy manufacturer, was unfortunately destroyed in 1941. Bertel Jung, editor of *Arkitekten – Arkkitehti*, has left us this description of its fine central hall:

> The impression one gets upon entering the hall defies description, but it is equally impossible to forget it. One is immediately aware of many finely executed and colourful artefacts, all of which have been designed by the architects or made under their supervision. Painters and sculptors, as well as craftsmen in every field, have worked together . . . to create a work of art which is a credit to our country and brings glory to the understanding patron who financed all this activity. Here is one of the major achievements of our young art . . .[11]

The destruction of Suur-Merijoki during the Second World War was a great loss to

Gesellius, Lindgren and Saarinen's villa of Hvitträsk, built in 1901–3 at Kirkkonummi, near Helsinki

Finland's architectural heritage, although there is, happily, another good example of the partnership's domestic style remaining in the studio villa of Hvitträsk, located close to Helsinki.

Hvitträsk was built by the partners to serve both as their studio and their home. There the three lived and worked together, sharing not only the accommodation but also their domestic life. The buildings are grouped dramatically on a wood bluff rising up from Lake Hvitträsk. They are planned to range rather freely in responding to the lie of the land, producing a characteristically irregular massing of the elements around a main courtyard.

The lower walls of Hvitträsk are built of natural granite, plastered over in parts, while above, the facing of many of the upper surfaces is of timber. In the roofing there is a mixture of pantiles and shingles. The original, square, timber-faced tower at one end of the house, complete with a capping turret, was not replaced when part of the building was destroyed by fire. Hvitträsk developed the natural stone and wood elements of the Karelian building tradition into a large-scale and sophisticated villa architecture. The buildings are immaculately sited and today have a natural charm and picturesqueness in the landscape. Originally, with its turreted wooden tower, Hvitträsk would also have had something of the romance of a mediaeval castle and, in consequence, a heightened sense of drama.

The first part of Hvitträsk was constructed in 1902, consisting of a studio and workshop, with a flat above in which the three young architects lived at the outset. It is this first stage which draws most directly upon the traditional forms and detailing of Karelian vernacular architecture.[12] Gesellius remained in this flat when the main part of the house was built across the courtyard. The new pavilion had a central, single-storey studio for the three partners, with an L-shaped two-storey dwelling at either end. Lindgren lived in that portion adjacent to the entrance and the original tower, whilst Saarinen occupied the other end of the building, where he provided an additional, attic storey in the roof. After Hvitträsk became entirely his own residence and office[13] Saarinen added the gardens and other external features, including the loggias.

From the outset it was Saarinen who controlled the character and detailing of Hvitträsk, designing most of the furniture and many of the fittings. His second wife, Loja, was a skilled weaver, and she assisted Eliel with the design of the soft furnishings. As at Suur-Merijoki, the best contemporary artists and craftsmen collaborated under Saarinen's guidance to create the unified and harmonious effect of the interior. The painted decorations are by Gallen-Kallela, and his 'Flame' *rya*[14] has a central position in the interior. There are tiles from Louis Sparre's Iris factory at Porvoo, as well as some chairs designed by Sparre[15] himself; while Gallen-Kallela's pupil, Eric Ehrström (1881–1934), contributed some of the metalwork, with the remainder being executed under Saarinen's direction by the local blacksmith.

The interior design of Hvitträsk reflects many influences absorbed from the partners' contemporaries; the metalwork, for example, derives from Sonck, some of the furniture owes a debt to Henri van der Velde (an influence also to be absorbed by Aalto), while the nursery has distinct echoes of Charles Rennie Mackintosh. But the organisation of the plan, with its ingenious changes of level to orchestrate the spatial continuity of the interior, is a highly original contribution, even anticipating Frank Lloyd Wright's evolution of the open plan.

Among the external features added by Saarinen, after he became the sole owner, were the terraces and loggias. He continued to adapt the form and style of Hvitträsk to his own taste, and lived and worked there until he emigrated to the United States in 1923. Aalto was certainly influenced by Saarinen's use of materials and attention to details. The covered ways of Aalto's Finnish Pavilion for the Paris World's Fair (1937), the Villa Mairea at Noormarkku (1938–9), the town hall at Saynätsalo (1952) and the House of Culture in Helsinki (1958) would all seem to owe their origin to the loggias at Hvitträsk.

In 1902, as the first wing of Hvitträsk was being completed, Gesellius, Lindgren and Saarinen were beginning work on a major commission which was to focus public attention on the National Romantic movement. Their design for the National Museum for the display of the national archaeological, historical and ethnographical collections was deliberately derivative of elements from the Finnish heritage of art and architecture. As a whole the building most closely resembles a large mediaeval church but there are also distinct reminders of fortified architecture. Again, the emphasis is upon a picturesque irregularity of form, with a high, granite-faced tower capped by a copper roof and brick spire as the focal point of the composition. The museum has granite walls, with the carved decorations executed in sandstone.

The interiors were designed to provide environments appropriate to the objects

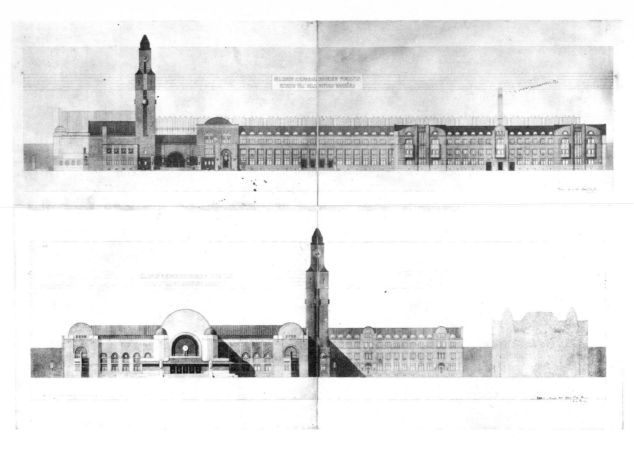

Project number 1 (1904) for Helsinki railway station, by Gesellius, Lindgren and Saarinen

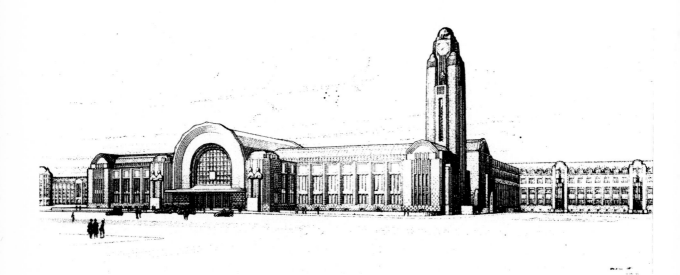

Final design (1904) for Helsinki railway station, by Gesellius and Saarinen. The administrative section was completed in 1909, the main building and the tower in 1914 and 1919

displayed in them; so that there is a church-like room for the ecclesiastical collection, whilst weaponry is accommodated in a room reminiscent of a castle tower. On the exterior this approach is carried through in the great gable end complete with geometrical decorations that are the characteristic feature of the great Finnish mediaeval churches, for example Porvoo and Hattula. The main bronze entrance door and the stained glass of the great staircase are by Ehrström, while Gallen-Kallela contributed the frescoes, executed at a later date.

In the National Museum the partnership reached the high point of its National Romantic style. And, interestingly, although this was a determinedly urban building sited in the very centre of Helsinki, the outlying walls and planting were designed to provide associations with the Finnish countryside and landscape. This treatment provides another clear precursor of Aalto's frequent confusion of the urban with the rural. In this connection it is also relevant to note that the original competition drawings show both the south-east and south-west façades partly obscured by creepers.[16] Aalto's inclination to allow climbing plants to modify the external form of many of his buildings led George Baird to go so far as to suggest that one of Aalto's romantic streaks was to cultivate the architecture of ruins.[17]

Gesellius, Lindgren and Saarinen followed the National Museum with two commissions that were, originally, both designed in the National Romantic style. These were the Northern Joint Stock Bank at No. 32 Unioninkatu (since demolished) and the Helsinki railway station. Both designs underwent substantial revisions before they were built, resulting in a new, transitional style. This was in part due to the fact that Lindgren left the partnership in 1905 to become the Director of the Central School of Applied Art, with Gesellius going two years later. The original railway station design, from the three hands, dates from 1904, while the revised drawings were published in February 1905.[18] Although these revised drawings still carry the name of all three partners, Saarinen was clearly responsible for coordinating these

Sigurd Frosterus' entry of 1904 for the Helsinki railway station competition

revisions. Significantly, the character of the main entrance and the tower, which in the original design echoed the forms established a couple of hundred yards away in the National Museum, were substantially modified in the new design to reflect the more radical, but unsuccessful, design submitted in the competition by an architect who was later to become prominent, Sigurd Frosterus.

In his entry for the Viipuri railway station competition, which was held later in 1904,[19] Saarinen already adopted the general features and character derived from the Frosterus drawings for the Helsinki station which he was later to incorporate in his own revised design. He was probably using the opportunity afforded by the Viipuri competition to try out the new, transitional style that he was in process of evolving for Helsinki. But in doing so he successfully established the new Finnish railway station format for three decades. There was not another competition for a new station in Finland until that for Tampere, held in 1934 and entered unsuccessfully by Aalto. In a similar way, Aalto was later to develop distinctly recognisable characteristics in the civic centres he designed, not only in Finland but also for Marl and Wolfsburg, in West Germany.

Lindgren submitted a separate entry for the Viipuri station competition, which offered a more lively and inventive approach to the design than Saarinen's adaptation of the Frosterus style.[20] His capacity to be bold in his innovations was particularly evident in the combination of the arched main entrance with the clock tower over it. In the light shed by this design and other examples of his work there is evidence that Lindgren may have been the greatest innovator of the three.

Certainly, Saarinen's work went on to become increasingly formalist and often

Viipuri railway station (1908–13), by Gesellius and Saarinen

Viipuri railway station: Saarinen's original competition perspective, showing the use of tiling as a means of emphasising the basic architectural forms – a detail that was to become characteristic of Aalto's mature work

turgid. And had not Lindgren chosen to concentrate his energies into an academic career he may well have become the most prominent designer of the three. For example, the house he designed and built for Mr Pietinen in Viipuri[21] offers much more anticipation of the Modern Movement than we find in Saarinen after Hvitträsk. And this capacity for originality in Lindgren's work was maintained in the Wanemuine theatre, concert hall and clubhouse complex at Dorpat, where he continues the progress from the National Romantic towards more simplified forms and massing without the monumental pretensions of Saarinen.

Before Saarinen embarked on his more monumental and oppressive style, and whilst he was still in partnership with Herman Gesellius, he created one of his most stunning designs, again interestingly for a country house, in the Villa Remer, which was built at Altrupp near Berlin between 1905 and 1907.[22] The Remer house had especially fine interiors, and some of the furniture was, once more, clearly indebted to Mackintosh. Immediately after Gesellius left the practice, Saarinen designed another, much smaller, villa for a Dr G.J. Winter to be built at Sordavala.[23] The Winter house appears to be Saarinen's last truly expressionist work, and it is extraordinary in his *opus* for its extreme plasticity of form. It explores the limits of tile-hanging and provides a clear precedent for Aalto's own experiments in merging roof and wall to achieve a plastic continuity of building form. Soon after the publication of the design for the Winter house, *Arkitekten – Arkkitehti* again discussed Hvitträsk and illustrated Saarinen's recent modifications.[24]

For more than a decade, from 1894 when he won the Turku church competition until 1905, Lars Sonck contributed a number of major building designs. These, taken with the work of Gesellius, Lindgren and Saarinen, provide the core of Finland's National Romantic architecture and the very substantial foundation on which the later developments in Finnish architecture, with their distinctive national characteristics, were based. Of these main works, Tampere cathedral and the Eira hospital have already been discussed; there remain the Helsinki Telephone Exchange in Korkeavuorenkatu and the former Private Bank.[25]

Sonck was a man steeped in the tradition of mediaeval architecture; his buildings of this early period reflect this preoccupation. But Sonck's adaptation of mediaeval forms and motifs was no mere superficial exercise in geometry or draftmanship; his early buildings are totally convincing statements which exude that most elusive of architectural qualities, *authenticity*. His total command of the language of mediaeval precedents offered by churches and castles allowed him to assimilate these influences into a completely original expression that was entirely his own. Unfortunately, when Sonck decided to move on, together with the other founding fathers of modern Finnish architecture, to that streamlining of forms which characterised the spirit and expression of Modernism, he was unable to achieve either a successful transition or further development. For what was important to Sonck's architecture was the sheer weight and massiveness of a building, and thus for him the process of streamlining involved only the shedding of the mediaeval vocabulary of strength through detailing rather than a heartfelt desire to embrace the lightness and transparency offered by the exemplar of industrial refinement.

Whereas Tampere cathedral and the Eira hospital provide cultural and social interpretations of the National Romantic style, whilst also offering the contrasts of the monumental and domestic scales, the Helsinki Telephone Exchange and the Private Bank contribute statements that epitomise the movement's value in terms of the exterior and interior expression of the commercial environment. In the Private Bank, where the banking hall had to be fitted into the volume of an existing Neo-classical

Project (1909) for the Villa Winter, by Eliel Saarinen

building, the emphasis is upon interior qualities. This accounts for the low ceilings, and the heavy arches and columns. But this sense of weight and strength is complemented by the uncluttered space between the columns. Walter Jung's furnishings, together with his carved and painted motifs and coloured glass, which greatly enriched Sonck's design, have, unfortunately, been removed. What remains, however, following Aarno Ruusuvuori's restoration,[26] confirms Sonck's command of the quality and character of the bank's interior. It combined the strength and dignity of its function with great richness of materials and careful restraint in its detailing.

The exterior of the Telephone Exchange is equally restrained in the detailing that gives the façade the superficial image of a long-standing military bastion. But Sonck's use of mediaeval forms and motifs in this building is far from being a simple historical catalogue. There are as many as eleven different window types employed in this elaborate composition; but their combination is not just aimed at achieving a sense of mediaeval *authenticity* by the irregularity of their form and arrangement. In fact, the fenestration is grouped in a way which, at first glance, appears to give an overall sense of order to this complex façade. But this order is merely present in the basic geometrical division of the elevation. Within this overall gridding of the façade the elements take on a dynamic expression of their own. Also, some of the carved decoration is an abstraction of telegraphic equipment components. And the result is not at all expressive of the weighty stability of a mediaeval castle.

The elements themselves may be mediaeval in inspiration but their organisation within the elevation sets up conflicts stemming from apparent contradictions in architectural intentions. In the case of the turret at the left extremity of the elevation, which is superficially a powerful element, its-qualities as a *tour de force* are diluted by the playful decoration of the cylindrical piers of the windows in the upper storey immediately below the great, elongated pyramidal roof. This playfulness is repeated in the motifs immediately beneath the semi-conical roof of the semi-circular oriel bay that relieves the massiveness of the stonework below the upper gallery. And the oriel bay itself has an astonishingly contrasting scale compared with that of the turret which it embellishes, in fact a thoroughly domestic scale. This turret, it should be noted, is located as far as possible from the main entrance doorway to the Exchange.

The other principal feature in the upper storeys is a bold oversailing bay supported on two great undecorated corbel stones. This feature, with its decidedly Art Nouveau use of a large, airy circular window within its massiveness, is also not related to the entrance below, but is set off on the building's right extremity as a conscious counterweight to the turret at the other end. The entrance itself occupies an apparently arbitrary position in the organisation of the façade. It is not simply that it is off-centre; it is also by its smallness relatively insignificant. Although the shallow projection of the steeply pitched frame to the semicircular-headed door actually cuts through the string-course located at first floor sill level, the scale of the doorway itself consciously denies the importance of its function. Rather than giving an impression of strength and importance, the ashlar doorframe with its comparatively delicate decorations appears to be attached to the string-course like the travelling marker on a slide-rule; it seems a movable feature that could occur anywhere along the façade.

These apparent contradictions of architectural intention occur by *design* in Sonck's Telephone Exchange. This is not the accidental composition of the amateur but the confident and fluent contrivance of an architect who was both master of the mediaeval vocabulary and a man well read in contemporary international developments. And just as Sonck apparently owes a debt to H.H. Richardson, it would seem that he was also aware of Frank Furness's handling of mediaeval elements in his public buildings for Philadelphia.[27] For the Helsinki Telephone Exchange shows Sonck confidently achieving a very sophisticated exercise in personal mannerism at the age of thirty-five. And the determinedly anti-rationalist elements[28] of this key work in the National Romantic style provides yet another interesting comparison with Aalto's formal preoccupations and solutions. The highly mannered expressionism of Sonck's Telephone Exchange was a readily available source of just the sort of contradictions in scale and emphasis that characterise Aalto's work from the mid-30s onwards.[29]

In January 1908 Sigurd Frosterus took over the editorship of *Arkitekten – Arkkitehti*. The following month the journal published the competition designs for the Landtdaghus (Local Government Headquarters) in Helsinki. Saarinen took first prize with a scheme that was determinedly monumental and anticipates the form of the Adam, Holden and Pearson design for the Senate House of London University. His former partners, Gesellius and Lindgren, entered a much more interesting design that followed the line of the original partnership, with particular reference to the original Helsinki railway station proposal. They were awarded the second prize. Fourth prize went to Sonck for a design that blended monumentality with plasticity and certainly had the most interesting plan form. In his editorial published in the March 1908 issue of *Arkitekten – Arkkitehti*, Frosterus compared Saarinen's solution with Sonck's and made his preference for the latter quite clear.[30]

The atmosphere in the architectural world of Helsinki in the first decade of the twentieth century was keenly competitive. Both the social and professional worlds were small and tightly prescribed, and the sense of close friendships combined with

Frosterus's 'Taos' block of flats, built in Helsinki in 1913

Eliel Saarinen: Lahti town hall, 1911–12

clear expressions of envy and enmity which were born then still characterise relationships between architects in the Finnish capital today. Saarinen's position as leader of the profession was always a vulnerable one which he constantly strove to defend in his efforts to develop a new post-Romantic style. Certainly, in his design for the department store Helsingfors Magasins[31] he once again put himself ahead of his colleagues, and this project clearly anticipates Frosterus's later design for the Stockmann department store.

Indeed, Saarinen and Frosterus learned a great deal from each other in the period that followed. For example, in his 'Taos House' block of flats in Helsinki[32] Frosterus developed a simplified plasticity of modelling in the façade which looked towards Modernism; and the oriel windows over the ground-floor openings in his design were emulated by Saarinen in the Lahti town hall;[33] while the Kajana Folkskoletävlan[34] (Adult Education Centre competition) shows Frosterus leaning on the inspiration of Saarinen's 1911 Magasins design while creating a stepping-stone towards his approach to the Stockmann store. K.S. Kallio was also influenced by the simple dignity of the modified Saarinen design for Helsinki railway station in his church at Alavo,[35] which has nave vaulting reminiscent of John Soane.

Project for Lahti town hall, by Eliel
Saarinen

Frosterus's Stockmann department store, in Helsinki

By 1915 the emphasis in much new Finnish work was strongly eclectic. This element had already been present much earlier in, for example, the work of Professor G. Nyström. He had shown his predilection for the Italian Renaissance style, with his Föreningsbanken (Cooperative Bank) in Helsinki (1899) having a strong Palladian influence, while his Finnish Bank in Turku (1901) follows the design of Florentine *palazzi*. But in his Församlingarnas (Congregational Centre) Walter Jung adopted a complete mixture of styles, with a National Romantic doorway fitting into a Florentine *palazzo* ground floor, while the cornice is also Florentine but the windows between are a hybrid of Italian and English Renaissance; the interior is, however, Greek, with Doric columns in the entrance hall.

The pattern of Finnish architectural competitions results frequently in an architect other than the winner getting the actual building commission. This was the case with the Stockmann department store project, where Valter and Ivar Thomé got the first prize, while Frosterus got second prize and the commission. Interestingly, Saarinen's entry, which was awarded the third prize, seems once again to be more progressive with its large areas of glass on both the ground and first two upper floors, giving a much lighter appearance to the building volume. But Frosterus's design was distinguished by its bold internal arrangement which had an atrium in the centre with galleries on the upper floors looking down upon the open-plan ground floor. The National Romantic influence was no longer evident in the entries to this competiton, and the design by Oiva and K.S. Kallio showed a distinct Neo-classical preoccupation, both in the symmetrical, blunt 'arrowhead' plan form and the fenestration.

Later in 1916, Frosterus wrote a leader in *Arkitekten – Arkkitehti*[36] illustrating a Saarinen project for a commercial building on Keskuskatu ('Central Street') which is

Project by Eliel Saarinen for commercial buildings on Keskuskatu, Helsinki

Saarinen: project of 1917 for Turku town hall

a variation on Saarinen's design for the adjacent Stockmann site. And yet a further variant of this design appears in Saarinen's drawings for the town hall in Turku,[37] demonstrating that the architect was confident in this new mode of expression. With his design for the Kalevala Insurance Company Building,[38] Saarinen returned for the last time to the National Romantic idiom, with a great mediaeval-style tower that recalls the Hanseatic architecture of the Baltic region;[39] while his Cinema Palace,[40] also in Keskuskatu, continues the new urban style in brick established by Frosterus's Stockmann building across the street, but with a new boldness in the *piano nobile* and a definite attic of two storeys. Brick was to become an important element in Aalto's post-World-War-II urban statements.

With the staging of the Regional Museum competition for Vaasa on the Gulf of Bosnia[41] a new mediaeval romantic style emerged briefly. Borg, J.S. Siren and Åberg received the first prize, with Eino Forsman second, and Arnold Erickson and Uno Moberg third. The new romantic revival of Ragnar Ostberg's Stockholm town hall was clearly experienced in Finland too. Entries for the Chicago Tribune Tower were illustrated in the same issue of *Arkitekten – Arkkitehti*, with Saarinen's second prize entry obviously pandering to the American sense of historicism through mediaeval imagery, just as the Jarl Eklund and Einar Sjöström entry was modelled on the traditional stepped-gable Danish church form.

By this time *Arkitekten – Arkkitehti* was in its twentieth year of publication and one of its avid young readers was Alvar Aalto. He was clearly impressed by issue No. 2 of 1923, entirely devoted to Italy, and particularly by the article 'Italia la Bella',[42] which included travel sketches of the Italian landscape and architecture by Hilding Ekelund and Erik Bryggman. But one wonders how he must have reacted to the following issue of *Arkitekten – Arkkitehti*, which included illustrations of Sonck's competition entry for a church on the island of Suomenlinna.[43] Sonck's design was clearly modelled

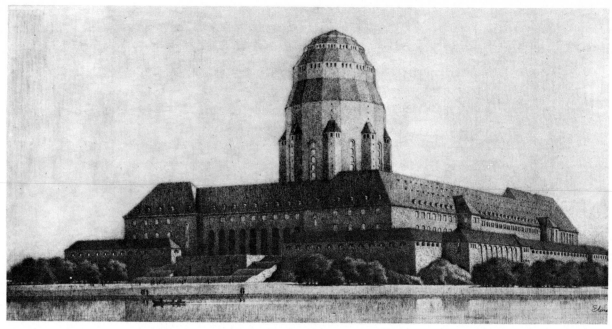

The Kalevala building, in Helsinki (1921); project by Eliel Saarinen

upon the Neo-classical architecture of Leningrad and, in particular, the distinctive silhouette of the church on the fortress island of St Peter and Paul, although his plan form is reminiscent of Engel's Great Church in Helsinki.[44] Sonck eventually incorporated this tower into his design for the St Michael Agricola Church in Helsinki, which was completed in 1935.

Nineteen twenty-three brought Saarinen's fiftieth birthday and his emigration to the United States. Issue No. 7 of the 1923 volume of *Arkitekten – Arkkitehti* was designated as Saarinen's fiftieth birthday tribute, but it was in fact mostly devoted to Swedish architecture, particularly the work of Ragnar Ostberg.[45] For Finnish architects the most notable thing about 1923 was the competition for the Finnish House of Parliament.

By 1924, with Saarinen safely in America, *Arkitekten – Arkkitehti* could devote a long section to his designs for the Tribune Tower and the Lake Shore development, including Grant Park, Grant Plaza and the Grant Hotel.[46] The Parliament competition was formulated to allow the entrants to propose their own ideal site, and Alvar Aalto entered with a design for the harbour site immediately below the Russian Orthodox cathedral, the location which was, eventually, to accommodate his design for his Enso-Gutzeit headquarters. Aalto's design was mentioned with the three first stage winners and purchased. G.H. Eklund won the first prize but once again it was the second prizewinners – Borg, Siren and Åberg – who were eventually given the commission to build this important national symbol.[47] And the design selected for execution represented a real setback to the evolution of modern architecture in Finland.[48] Rather than being an expression of the new freedom of the Finnish people it represented a return to the classical formality of Helsinki's origin under the Czar, but without the freshness and charm of Engel's originals.

In strong contrast to the outcome of the Parliament competition, the designs entered for consideration by the Viipuri town hall jury later in 1923 showed a marked influence from the Stockholm model of Ragnar Ostberg. This influence can be especially observed in the entries of Jussi and Toivo Paatela, Hilding Ekelund and Uno Ullberg.[49]

Meanwhile, in Finland, the strong spirited designs that had characterised the development of a new national architecture at the beginning of the century faded more and more into the background. In his 'Arena' buildings, a block of offices and flats on the corner of Hameentie and Siltasaarenkatu, Helsinki, Sonck deteriorated into a bland formula of Neo-classical massing,[50] while Oiva Kallio's wooden church was based upon traditional Finnish models combined with an open-posted, wooden, pyramidal tower that seems to derive from Norwegian examples.[51]

The second Parliament competition only served to confirm the dead hand of Siren, with the second prize going to Hilding Ekelund's Italian Renaissance design, and Armas Lindgren carrying off the third prize with an extremely pious Neo-classical solution.[52] Jussi and Toivo Paatela clearly thought it prudent to back two horses and, whilst adopting the general style and character of Ostberg's Stockholm town hall, managed to combine this with a distinctly Neo-classical portico. But by far the most astonishing design was by Einar Wikander, who produced a cruciform plan with an octagonal drum and a dome in the Persian style. And, as if this were not enough evidence of eclectic propensities and talents, he added two untapered obelisks to his design at the foot of which were copies of the equestrian sculptures by Michelangelo at the top of the approach ramp on the Capitoline Hill.

It was in 1926–7 that Aalto began to make his mark in Finnish architectural competitions, with his first published work being his entry for the Jämsä church competition.[53] In the Jyväskylä 'Suojeluskuntatalo' competition,[54] for a building to house members of Finland's volunteer civilian reserve force of men and women (1918–45), Aalto actually gained second prize. It is useful to compare his design with P.E. Blomstedt's two entries, both of them monumental in character and Neo-classical in style and one of which gained the third prize. All this is quite helpful evidence against those ardent simplifiers of the evolution of modern Finnish architecture who have argued that its strength and uniqueness stem from the twin sources of national cohesiveness and an essential likemindedness in matters of style and taste.

Aalto's entry for the 'Suojeluskuntatalo' is interesting for its use of a circular staircase which projects its cylindrical form into the courtyard. This feature, when it recurred in his design for the Turun Sanomat newspaper building (1928–9) in Turku, is often quoted as indicating his early anticipation of what was to become a standard motif of Modernism. In fact it is a common and familiar feature in the courtyards of late-nineteenth-century Helsinki apartment blocks. And in the case of the 'Suojeluskuntatalo' project Aalto clearly introduced this feature in response to, and to complement, the existing staircase across the courtyard in just such a context.

The first recorded appearance of the horizontal strip window in Finnish architecture seems to occur in Antero Pernaja's entry for the Viipuri town hall competition.[55] But the entries for the 'Pohja' Insurance Building competition[56] in Helsinki indicate the rapid transition to Modernism that took place in Finland in the mid-20s. In this connection the designs submitted by Oiva Kallio and Lasse Björk are of particular interest; while Hilding Ekelund, who it must be remembered had offered an Italian Renaissance solution for the second Parliament competition of 1924, prepared the most sophisticated modern entry. And Ekelund maintained his Modernist approach in his entry for the Vallila church competition.[57] Ekelund's plan had a stepped form which narrowed the nave from the altar to the west end, with vertical windows between the 'steps' admitting light directed towards the altar. His design also had a glass dome and a tower with a glazed top. Amongst the other entries, 'No. 1', and 'Glas, Beton, Eisen' displayed similar Modernist tendencies.

But these steps to bring Finland into line with the most advanced architectural trends in Europe were, nevertheless, tentative when compared with Aalto's rapid and sure advance. His entry for the Paimio Sanatorium competition (1929), which gained him the first prize, demonstrates how very quickly he had mastered both the plan form and expression of functionalism.[58] Amongst the other entries, only Erik Bryggman's design, with its simple, curved plan form and clear horizontality of expression, is comparable. In fact, the radical transformations in Aalto's work from the simplified Neo-classical block of the South-West Finland Agricultural Cooperative Building (1927–9)[59] (see pp. 41, 43) and the designs for Paimio and the Turun Sanomat newspaper premises (see p. 50) are quite extraordinarily bold and uncompromising. The Turun Sanomat building was already under construction by August 1928, while the first Paimio competition drawings were made between the end of 1928 and the beginning of 1929.

There is little doubt that Bryggman was something of a midwife in the birth of Aalto's radically new expression. In the first place Aalto had assisted Bryggman in the preparation of the latter's competition entry for an office building in Vaasa, which was submitted at the end of 1927.[60] Then, the following year, Aalto found himself together with Uno Ullberg and Armas Lindgren on the jury for the Suomi Insurance Office (Helsinki) Extension competition. In fact, Aalto quarrelled with his fellow jury members on that occasion, and went on record as giving his vote to the Bryggman design as the outright winner.[61]

Within the span of these two projects Bryggman himself achieved a remarkable transition of expression. The Vaasa drawings still evidence an uncomfortable marriage between the near-strip windows of the three upper storeys with the ground floor fenestration which is interrupted by a double-height doorway. These vestiges of refined Neo-classical volumetrics are, however, no longer present in the rhythmically ordered composition of horizontal and vertical elements in the Suomi Insurance design. Because of his involvement on the Vaasa project and the opportunity afforded him, as a jury member, to study closely Bryggman's design for the Suomi project, it is clear that Aalto was able to monitor these important developments in his colleague's work. Of course, the Turun Sanomat building was designed by the time Aalto was involved in the Suomi project jury, but it is entirely possible that Aalto either saw Bryggman's scheme on the drawing board or discussed with him the obvious similarities of their two different tasks.

What is clear is that, by 1930, Aalto had put himself decidedly in the lead of those Finnish architects who were following the course of functionalism. The maturity shown in both the Turun Sanomat and the Paimio designs gave him this undisputed position.[62] But close behind him at that time were Hilding Ekelund with his Sports Institute[63] and Oiva Kallio with his Pohja Insurance Building in Kaiseniemenkatu.[64] At the same time, however, it is interesting to note that Kallio managed to keep alive the romantic strain in Finnish twentieth-century architecture with his sauna at Villinge,[65] which sowed the seeds of a further revival of interest in vernacular sources. Indeed, it is easy to understand in this context why Aalto always insisted that he was a functionalist, because in the evolution of modern Finnish architecture differing building functions have always been open to a number of interpretations when it comes to their formal and material expression.

CHAPTER III

The Formative Years in Jyväskylä and Turku: 1923–33

Aalto's work in the 1920s reveals how quickly he shook off the immediate influence of his education at the Helsinki Polytechnic in the continuing tradition of Romantic Classicism and evolved statements in the Turun Sanomat newspaper building (see p. 50) and Paimio Sanatorium (see pp. 52–3) that placed him at the very centre of the Modern Movement. This rapid transition more or less coincides with the removal of his office, with his first wife Aino as his partner, from the provincial centre of Jyväskylä to the more cosmopolitan city of Turku (the former Swedish capital of Åbo). Although Aalto's career began in the established mode of Romantic Classicism, it was from the earlier period of National Romanticism that he was to draw much of the inspiration for his mature work.

The spread of Romantic Classicism in Scandinavia derived from a revival of interest in Neo-classicism that originated in Denmark under the influence of such writers as Vilhelm Wansher, who began to publish articles on Neo-classical art in 1907. What interested Wansher and other writers who contributed to the establishment of the movement, for example the German Paul Mebes, and the Danes H. Kampmann and E. Thompsen, was not however the historically correct philosophy or aesthetic of Neo-classicism. It was rather an elemental approach based on an interpretation of Doric architecture in its simplest volumetric terms, focusing on the work of the Danish Neo-classical architects, Gottlieb Bindesbøll and Christian Frederick Hansen. Carl Petersen's Faaborg Museum (1911) is generally regarded as the first product of this Romantic Classical revival. In Sweden its impact was first felt in Carl Westman's Stockholm Law Courts (1915), which also contains National Romantic elements, and culminated in Gunnar Asplund's Stockholm Public Library (1920–28). It was finally exhausted, as we have already seen, in J.S. Siren's Finnish Parliament Building (1926–31), which substitutes a heavy neo-Egyptain formalism for the 'Doric sensibility' that had been initiated in Denmark two decades before.

In 1923, the year that Aalto opened his office in Jyväskylä, there were two important architectural competitions in Finland. The first, for the Finnish Parliament Building, brought a Romantic Classical result in Siren's design; while the outcome of the second, for Viipuri City Hall, showed a dramatic swing towards a revival of the National Romantic style in emulation of Ragnar Ostberg's Stockholm City Hall. Although Aalto himself had demonstrated the eclectic variety of his interests in his designs for the 1922 Tampere Industrial Exposition, his work from 1923 until 1927 showed him almost entirely preoccupied with the Romantic Classical vein. The main pavilion for the Tampere Exposition uses modular panels that resemble Otto Wagner's design for the Karlsplatz station in Vienna of 1899; but it could also have been inspired by Asplund, Bergsten or Markelius. In either case it reveals Aalto's early interest in the standardisation effected by industrial production. Nothing could have been less industrial in expression or provided a greater contrast to the main pavilion than Aalto's design for the Craft section, which was an extremely vernacular, thatched-roof kiosk for the display of Finnish handicrafts. But even the radically different approach to the two buildings offers the seeds of Aalto's attachment to his personal interpretation of the functionalist *credo*, namely that each and every building has its own functional *esprit* and expression.

Aalto opened his Jyväskylä office early in 1923 and in May participated in the first stage of the Parliament Building competition, to determine the building's location, with a proposal for the Helsinki harbour site. The significance of Aalto's original proposal is that he saw the Parliament Building as the 'missing link' in Engel's composition for the centre of the new Finnish capital. In Engel's plan it was the 'Great Church', now the cathedral, that dominated the grouping of civic and university buildings in this provincial seat of government. Aalto quite rightly saw the Parliament competition as the means of revising and completing Engel's design by the addition of what should be the main political symbol of the new nation. His design, appropriately entered as 'Piazza del Popolo', because it was intended to provide a focus in Helsinki for the new national spirit, maintained Engel's scale and simple massing in a single building presenting a giant classical order. This building would have 'closed' the harbour frontage at its east end, framed Engel's City Hall, and provided the major focus of civic activity that is still missing from Helsinki.

By the simple expedient of extending Engel's composition right down to the harbour front and increasing the complexity of this public space, Aalto's design offered the possibility of bringing together the functions of City Hall, Parliament and Presidential Palace, creating in the process that essential ingredient of the urban framework 'the sense of downtown'. The decision not to use the harbour site was a major contribution in the irrevocable process of destroying the central magnetism of Helsinki. By selecting the Mannerheimintie site, and attempting to create a new urban focus based on Saarinen's railway station and, later, the Central Post Office, an essentially provincial approach to planning, the opportunity to capitalise on Engel's original statement of urbanity was lost at one fell swoop. And, although Aalto subsequently built the Enso-Gutzeit 'palace' (see p. 161) on his original Parliament Building site, neither the scale nor the function of this office building could provide the grandeur of his original concept.

Ironically, much of his later career was spent in planning exercises intended to generate, in the area framed by Saarinen's National Museum and railway station, and Siren's Parliament Building, some of the complexity and significance that were already extant in Engel's framework to the harbour setting. Significantly, when Aalto submitted a design in the second stage of the Parliament competition in 1924 he abandoned the single building concept and cohesive framework demanded by the context of Engel's buildings and produced instead a loose assymetrical grouping of individual 'pavilions' centred on the meeting chamber. In doing so, he demonstrated even at this early stage in his career that, although one generator in his design *gestalt* had a distinctly classical basis, this was very much associated with the requirements of particular sites. This complementary approach had its origins in the informal courtyard groupings found in Finnish vernacular architecture and the more freely expressive planning and geometry of the National Romantic movement. These two forces, a complementary interest in Neo-classical formality and the informality of the Finnish farmyard (or the irregular Italian piazzas), remained central to Aalto's design approach throughout his mature career and account for much of the elusiveness and sense of conflict in his later work.

The Parliament competition provided Aalto with a unique opportunity early in his career to demonstrate his precociousness and depth of perception. His design for the second stage of the competition received no mention from the jury and there were no opportunities on a similar scale during the remaining years of the Jyväskylä office. There is a certain Italianate charm about his design for the Railway Workers' apartments in Jyväskylä of 1923–4 but they do not display any remarkable quality other than the delicacy of the detailing. This concept for the Railway Workers' housing was essentially a utilitarian building, with everything reduced down to essentials. Aalto's concentration of decorative emphasis on the arched doorways, balconies, the eaves corbel brackets and rainwater downpipes is consistent with the treatment of similar workers' housing projects in England at the same time. The commission for the Jyväskylä Workers' Club, which also dates from 1923, did however provide Aalto with considerably more scope to develop his design vocabulary in the Neo-classical idiom.

The planning and detailing of this building established the standard for Aalto's design approach within this mode that continued through to his original entry for the Viipuri Library competition in October 1927. Whereas the Railway Workers' housing had involved a stripping down to the barest of architectural essentials, the Workers' Club gave Aalto an opportunity to provide a civic symbol, albeit on a small scale. His response was to look towards the Greek model of Neo-classicism as developed in the nineteenth century by German architects; and this again links back to his own training and the Helsinki Neo-classicism of German origin. It was designed as a free-standing pavilion, with windows on all sides. The accommodation had a basically simple functional division, with the ground-floor housing the club restaurant and coffee bar; whilst the double-storey theatre was at first-floor level. Simplified Doric columns, with windows between, gave an open, light and airy character to the ground floor.

Internally, Aalto used a skilful arrangement of the ground-floor plan with most of the columns absorbed in the circular wall of the coffee bar to disguise the problem of supporting the wide span of the theatre above. Aalto approached this problem and its

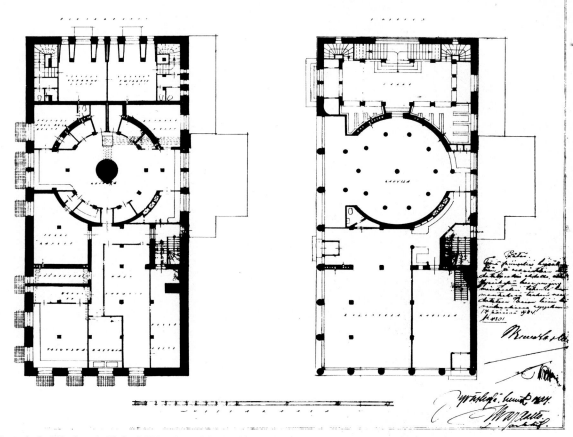

Jyväskylä Workers' Club (1923–4): original plans, showing the basement and ground floor (right), with the circular café that links the entrance lobby with the lower foyer of the theatre

solution in terms of the dual axiality of entry from the street and internal function. Half of the coffee shop wall is repeated as a semi-circular drum in the first-floor foyer to the theatre, as one of Aalto's attempts to retain classical purity and axiality in this design. On the other axis, however, he was unable to place the 'Palladian' window motif centrally both inside the theatre and on the long façade.

There is clearly a conflict between the functional programme of the Workers' Club and its Neo-classical expression. It is equally obvious that Aalto learned many fundamental lessons involved in axial planning in arriving at the solution to this building. His detailing of the interior, in particular the fine plaster panelling to the curved rear wall of the auditorium that projects into the foyer, and matching panelling of the entrance doors to the theatre in their semi-circular-headed arched frame, recalls Roman and Romanesque detailing. There is certainly nothing provincial about Aalto's handling of the classical forms in the Workers' Club. In this one design he showed himself equal to his Helsinki colleagues in connecting Finland with the prevailing international mode of expression. The Workers' Club also established a hierarchy of

Workers' Club, Jyväskylä: exterior view of Aalto's bold Neo-classical treatment of this corner site, with the main entrance on the left beneath a neo-Palladian balcony motif

design problems in the classical idiom which Aalto went on to tackle in his entries for two church competitions as well as that for the South-Western Agricultural Cooperative Building, in Turku (see pp. 41, 43).

The first of these was in 1925, a limited competition, in which Aalto was invited to participate, for the design of the parish church of the Jyväskylä suburb of Jämsä. His design was based on a basilican plan, an unusual plan form in the context of post-eighteenth-century Finnish churches, and was decidedly Italianate in form and character. He proposed a flat coffered ceiling to the nave, with vaulted aisles and an arcade between on columns with Corinthian capitals and pew-height bases. To complete the Italianate style of the interior, even the aisle vaults were to have iron tie-rods. The west front showed a rectangular composition, a little longer than a square, with a design of large rectilinear panels that is reminiscent of San Miniato al Monte, Florence.

Consistent with his axial approach to the design of the Jyväskylä Workers' Club, Aalto provided a counter-axis to that of the nave in the organisation of the piazza along the west front of the church. This piazza is located, in a manner familiar from Assisi, on a hilltop, and is reached by a monumental flight of steps.

Certainly Aalto's interest in things Italian would have been stimulated by the 'Italia la Bella' issue of *Arkitekten – Arkkitehti* at the beginning of 1923,[1] with its travel sketches by Hilding Ekelund and Erik Bryggman. Also, a year later, in the spring of 1924, Aalto married Aino Marsio, another architect four years his senior who had begun work in his office only a few months before. It is significant that the couple decided to spend their honeymoon in northern Italy. Some of the travel sketches Aalto made on that excursion were included in the *Sketchbook* published by Göran Schildt in 1972,[2] and clearly established the connection between this, his first trip abroad, and the design attitudes he formulated immediately following that important visit.

Aalto's admiration of the qualities of Italian architecture, particularly those of the Romanesque, Renaissance and Baroque periods, had begun in earnest and was to continue throughout his long career. Ekelund had set out to indicate the promising sources offered by Italian architecture to the younger generation of Finnish architects who were seeking a new and fresh expression that had more elegance and lightness than the models of Neo-classicism. Aalto certainly demonstrated in his Jämsä competition entry his enthusiasm for the rediscovery of the true Renaissance spirit. His interior perspective for the church, which was boldly featured in the *Arkitekten – Arkkitehti* review of the competition, shows Aalto's interpretation of the Italian basilica as the warm and vibrant alternative to Scandinavia's cold and austere versions of the Neo-classical theme.

It must be remembered that he had taken part in this competition by invitation. In his design he showed himself to be not just a willing follower of Ekelund's lead but in possession of first-hand knowledge of the Florentine tradition and the work of Alberti. For, although the plan has some similarities with Saarinen's Emmanuel Church, Helsinki (1904–5), its spirit is more original, Aalto confidently calling upon a variety of original sources, including the upper portion of the façade for Alberti's Sant'Andrea at Mantua. Also, one of the interesting features in terms of Aalto's own progress as a designer was the introduction of the plastic quality of the nave arcade and aisle vaulting. From all these points of view, the Jämsä church design represents a tremendous advance in confidence and freedom of expression over the difficulties Aalto had encountered in resolving the conflicts of style and function presented by the Jyväskylä Workers' Club.

From the very beginning of his career, even as a student, Aalto had been involved in the problems of church design. As early as 1918–19 he had been commissioned to add a belfry to the church at Kauhajärvi, and in 1924 he had undertaken the restoration of another church, at Äänekoski. Also, at the same time as he was completing the Jämsä design he was remodelling yet another church, at Viitasaari. And there is little doubt that, with this considerable amount of experience under his belt at the age of twenty-seven, he began to see a role for himself as an important theorist in church design. In fact, he did not build a church of his own until the one at Muurame (1926–9) (see p. 39), which incorporates salient features of his earlier designs. But, curiously, in two interim designs he abandoned the elegant Italianate approach which he had pioneered at Jämsä, and returned to the more formalised elements of the Neo-classical vocabulary.

His entry for the Töölö (Helsinki) competition (1927) provided for another hilltop composition, with the four elements of the design – the church, the campanile and associated facilities – grouped around a piazza, recalling his Parliament House entry. But, although the compositional source of the Töölö design was Italian, the elements themselves were certainly more Neo-classical in their massing and detail. Similarly, his design for the Viinikka church (Tampere) competition (1927) shows in the perspective Aalto's predilection for an Italian hilltop composition; but once again the elements are only superficially Italianate in form. Whether the campanile is square, as in the Töölö design, or cylindrical, as for the Viinikka church, they indicate more of the simplified massing of the Romantic Classical revival than the richly decorated surfaces and more plastic volumes of the Jämsä design.

In site planning terms, however, both the Töölö and Viinikka designs represent further developments of the courtyard approach which Aalto first introduced in his entry for the second stage of the Parliament competition. The Viinikka design, in particular, balances the formal character of church, campanile, social centre and presbytery with an informal grouping around the court. Nevertheless, the resultant impression conveyed by these two interim designs is one of confusion between the conceptual intention and the formal expression, with a prevailing horizontality introduced into both church and campanile by decorative mouldings. This horizontal emphasis was also carried into the interior of the Viinikka church design. Significantly, both designs provided for a simple hall church, rather than an aisled basilica.

To a certain extent, the church at Muurame resolves these stylistic conflicts and offers a more coherent and unified design. In his design for this building Aalto returns, on the whole, to the Italian inspiration of Jämsä. This is particularly evident in the organisation of the west front which, in its use of the central triumphal arch motif, once again recalls Sant'Andrea, Mantua. There is also a finely detailed arcade in the return of the administrative wing at the east end. The interior, as well, returns to an Italianate simplicity, with the painted decoration concentrated into the small apse behind the altar which is filled by a distinctly Florentine-style fresco; while in the ceiling treatment, the coffered panelling Aalto suggested for Jämsä is replaced by a design that cuts away the flat panelling to expose truss ties with a simple, boarded vault revealed beyond. Although there were further church projects for Vallila, Helsinki (1929), and Lahti (1950), it was to be another thirty years before Aalto had another opportunity to express his theories of church design, when he built his most accomplished piece of ecclesiastical architecture in the Vuoksenniska church at Imatra (1956–9) (see pp. 199–201).

The Muurame church has a fine stucco finish outside and a simple, plastered interior. Apart from the simple mouldings introduced at door height and at the line of the springing of the west front arch, the exterior is free of elaboration. Even the campanile has only a simple frieze, similar to that used on the Jyväskylä Civil Guards Building (1927–9), which occurs just beneath the belfry with its square-headed opening, the whole being capped by a low-pitched pyramidal tile roof in the Mediterranean tradition.

Church at Muurame (1926–9): exterior view, showing Aalto's bold Italianate design

Muurame: interior view of the church, showing the transition in Aalto's work by the completion of this building, the simple treatment of the basic volume contrasted by the detailing of the ceiling and organ loft

Although the first designs for Muurame church date from 1926, it was not completed until 1929. The exterior therefore represents the realisation of Aalto's Italianate aspirations dating from 1924–5, whilst the interior, which was the last part of the building to be designed, combines two modes of expression – the Italian tradition on the one hand and a new functional vocabulary on the other. This new vocabulary expresses itself most strongly in the opening up of the ceiling, which provides a modern interpretation of the 'tied' aisle vaults of the Jämsä design; while from the flat soffits that are left along the side walls (perhaps vestiges of the Jämsä aisles) hang Poul Henningsen's light fittings, the type of direct/indirect fixtures that were to provide the inspiration for Aalto's own later pendant designs. The rear choir loft is also determinedly modern in that it stands free from the walls, being supported on its own posts. Within this loft the organ-pipes are arranged in three rows, one central and two flanking, that rise up above the side soffit panels and penetrate through the ceiling slot into the open vaulted loft beyond. Passing from Aalto's perfectly synthesised Italian Renaissance church exterior into the interior we therefore become aware of the architect's transitional mode of expression, a state of being between the historical, formal organisation of the exterior volume, and the functional, structural interpretation of the interior.

This flurry of church design activity coincided with the move of Aalto's office from Jyväskylä to Turku, and whilst the Muurame church was being built he produced two designs that were to place him in the very centre of the Modern Movement: those for the Turun Sanomat newspaper building in Turku and the Tuberculosis Sanatorium at Paimio. But the opportunity of moving his office from provincial Jyväskylä to Finland's second city was presented to Aalto by the commission to build the headquarters for the South-Western Agricultural Cooperative.

In spite of its demotion by the Russians in favour of Helsinki, Turku had remained the cultural and commercial centre of Finland throughout the nineteenth century, as well as retaining its position as the country's principal port. The largely wooden city had been destroyed by fire early in the nineteenth century, and had been replaced by a design based on broad, straight streets with low classical-style buildings. As the new city of Helsinki was dominated by the architecture of Carl Ludwig Engel, so the new Turku bore the imprint of the Turin-born, Swedish-trained architect Carlo Bassi. When Aalto arrived in Turku in 1927 it had already given up its cultural pre-eminence to Helsinki, but it was still Finland's commercial centre and major port, and as such it remained a bustling city with a vigorous programme of new building to which Aalto was to contribute. Four years before his arrival there the Turku-born architect Erik Bryggman (1891–1955) had returned from Helsinki, where he had gained experience in the offices of Frosterus, Lindgren and Walter Jung. Aalto was to share with Bryggman the dominance of the new work in Turku at the end of the decade, both in responding to the Neo-classical framework of Bassi and as a pioneer of the new functionalist architecture. It was especially valuable for the young Aalto to have the experienced and open-minded Bryggman available as *confidant* and collaborator.

Given Aalto's relative success in handling his Neo-classical solution for the Jyväskylä Workers' Club, the challenge of fitting the South-Western Agricultural Cooperative Building into the Bassi framework of Turku would not have appeared to present him with great difficulties. His winning solution for the Turku building was certainly the simplest in detailing, but there was otherwise little to distinguish the overall concept of Aalto's design from the second prize solution of Ekelund or that of Bryggman who was awarded third place. All three architects offered a five-storey office block with a large central courtyard; and the exterior articulation of openings, with large shop windows at street level and regularly stacked rectangular windows above, was similar in all three designs. There seemed to be substantial agreement amongst top Finnish architects about what should be built on that site, in that city at that time, and the fact that Aalto came out on top is a tribute to his ability to excel at that consensus view.

Interestingly, Aalto modified the extreme rectangularity of his design between the competition and construction and further reduced the differences between his original scheme and the entries by Ekelund and Bryggman. These modifications did not substantially vary either the plan form, circulation, or spatial characteristics of Aalto's design. But he did incorporate more circular and semi-circular forms at critical points in the organisation of the plan and, in doing this, he seemed to be reflecting a desire to fit in more closely with the local tradition. Certainly, after his arrival in Turku, his revised design reflects his response to Bryggman's two recently completed buildings, the Atrium apartment block (1925) and the Hotel Hospits Betel complex (1927), although Aalto's final design continued to dispense with the wide projecting eaves detail that characterised both of Bryggman's buildings.

The South-Western Agricultural Cooperative Building, Turku (1927–9): detail of entrance to apartments, with shop fronts and canopies

If Aalto's plan revisions and the exterior still reflected the prevailing mode of Romantic Classicism in Turku, there is evidence behind the façade, however, of Aalto's transitional explorations. Pearson has drawn our attention to the balconies and service ladders in the south-west corner of the internal courtyard;[3] these, together with the pipe railings on other balconies in that court, combine a sense of the utilitarian with hints of the international style drawn from ships' railings and gangways. Both the theatre and the restaurant have elements indicative of his new direction in design. In the theatre these have a volumetric emphasis. The original staircases leading into the auditorium were converted into vomitoria in the form of stepped ramps like ships' gangplanks which were enclosed for their full length, with the exception of a large porthole on either side close to the top which gave views back into the foyer. These ramped 'tubes' provide linking rooms between the two worlds of the foyer and the theatre and were, with various modifications, to become an Aalto hallmark in treating important internal staircase elements. The sense of transition from the outer world of the foyer to the interior of the theatre was further heightened by the grey and rose coloured plush used to line the walls of the vomitoria; while the unadorned walls of the auditorium itself were painted in a deep blue, giving the effect of a dark, magical box.

The treatment of the ticket booth in the entrance to the theatre foyer also has an interesting volumetric form. For, although the elements themselves, a rectilinear mass and a half cylinder, are familiar from the classical canon, the way in which the curved transparent ticket window and its solid base are slotted into the wall opening reveals a new elemental purity that is decidedly nautical and akin to those tubes which form the theatre vomitoria. The studding to the corners of the base is also reminiscent of ships' detailing – the riveting used to join steel plates. Aalto would not have been short of such inspiration in the busy port of Turku, where the architecture of the ships would have stood out in contrast to that of the town. Also, it was not possible for Aalto to visit neighbouring Sweden without experiencing the functional detailing of naval architecture.

The Itameri restaurant, in the Cooperative Building, Turku, which dates from 1930, exhibited a distinctive nautical flavour, with its clean lines, tubular steel furniture and an upper gallery with two-person tables that looked down onto the main dining area. These clean lines combined with the tubular steel balconies were to characterise Aalto's next step towards the realisation of a truly functionalist expression. But his ability to undertake that next step had been assured by his success in winning the Cooperative Building competition and the greatly enhanced reputation in Turku which the construction of this multi-functional project was to bring him. For it was while the Cooperative Building was being built in the latter part of 1927 that Aalto was asked by Juhani Tapani to design a row of apartments, utilising the Tapani method of precast concrete units (which had been introduced in 1913) for the structural system.

The idea of linking theory with practice, of using the means of factory production combined with a functional standardisation of a building, clearly appealed to Aalto at that time, and his resultant design is acknowledged as the first functionalist work in

The South-Western Agricultural Cooperative Building: foyer and ticket booth, and staircase to the theatre

The Association of Patriots Building, Jyväskylä: interior of cinema, showing the projection booth treated as a pure sculptural element

Finland. In fact the Tapani apartment block is an exercise in rationalisation rather than standardisation. It is based on three structural entities, i.e. spaces between cross-walls, and each of these has its own staircase and contains two apartments. But each of the three is of different bay width and contains quite different accommodation. Only in the central unit are the two apartments identical but mirrored on the other side of the staircase. The result is that of the six units on each floor there are five different apartment types. This means that even the fenestration, based on horizontal organisation of windows made up of one, two or three vertical casement units, is irregular in its distribution along the façade.

Aalto provided lettable commercial units at ground-floor level on the street side, some with large almost square windows subdivided by glazing bars and a separate door with clerestory light over, while others combined the two elements by wrapping an 'L'-shaped display over the top of the door. The fenestration of the rear elevation is much more regular, having only the one type of three-light window above the ground floor, with a vertical slit door and window ensemble expressing the staircase element, linking the wide cantilevered mezzanine balconies with their tubular steel guard rails. This building was completed in 1929 and its design clearly connected Aalto with the mainstream of the Modern Movement in Europe.

It was whilst he was working on the design of the Tapani housing that he took part in a competition sponsored by the popular household magazine *Aitta* in the spring of

1929. This was in two parts, with Part A calling for a small family vacation cottage and Part B posing the problem of a three-bedroom villa. Aalto won both sections of the competition with decidedly functionalist designs, although in the case of Part A he played it safe by entering an alternative design which was very conventional and traditional. The programme for the vacation cottage, based upon a central living area for the family plus a kitchen and two separate sleeping spaces, had a tight budget and called for a combination of compact and informal planning. In both Aalto's entries, 'Konsoli' which won him the prize, and the alternative 'Kumeli', he combined the same basic arrangement of the kitchen and one two-bed space at one end of the plan with the living area in the middle and the other bedroom at the further end behind the living room fireplace, the major difference in the interior arrangement being the use of a cylindrical fireplace element in the winning design, while the other solution offered a square element. But this use of a cylindrical form within the rectangular plan, together with a flat roof to replace the low pitch of 'Kumeli', a verandah recessed under the flat roof to produce a deep horizontal slot along most of the length of the cottage, with a strip window beneath the roof overhang, and the pronounced articulation of the kitchen chimney on the end wall with a window on either side, means that in external appearance 'Konsoli' has little in common with 'Kumeli'. One feature the two designs did share, however, was an earth roof, retaining the romantic image of the traditional Finnish country vacation cottage that was familiar to Aalto from his childhood.

Summer house design for the *Aitta* competition (1927): Aalto's first-prize entry, 'Konsoli'

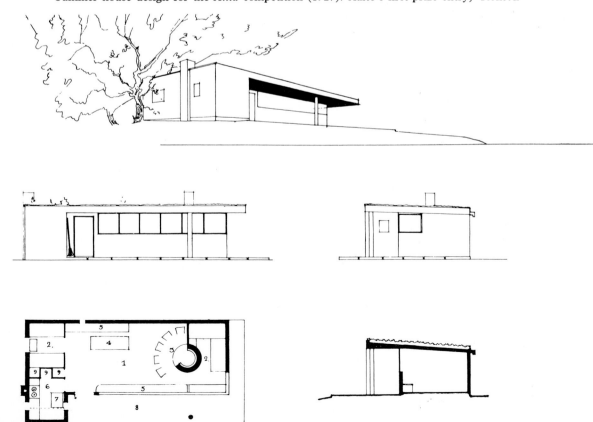

The more precise functions of the larger house required by Part B of the competition did not permit the same degree of informality in planning. Aalto's solution placed the living room at one end, once again using the open fireplace as a means of defining the internal functions. Behind the fireplace, the kitchen and bedrooms are located off a short corridor. But the whole of this compact plan is then bent in the form of two thirds of a circle, so that the living room and corridor look out into a central paved courtyard. In fact, the plan of this entry, which Aalto titled 'Merry-Go-Round', is exactly the same form as that he used for the fireplace included in the 'Konsoli' design. Although this part-cylindrical form could be seen as deriving from Neo-classical models, its use in both designs is entirely modern. In fact, both 'Konsoli' with its cut-away verandah, and 'Merry-Go-Round' with its segment of a drum, show Aalto exploring the destruction of the Neo-classical ideal by an interpenetration of space and volume that is reminiscent of Ledoux. Both designs show him breaking down the conventional building volumes and letting fresh air into his designs. The verandah of 'Konsoli' is partially enclosed within the building volume by the kitchen wall, just as the plan of 'Merry-Go-Round' is wrapped around the greater part of a circular central court. Aalto was to develop the use of the partially enclosed courtyard throughout his career, and the 'confusion' of the outside and

Design for the *Aitta* competition: Aalto's entry for the larger house section, 'Merry-Go-Round'

inside elements in the planning of these two units was also to remain a hallmark of his spatial relationships in his mature work. In this connection, it is interesting to note that Aalto included a rail carrying a curtain (shown fastened back in the competition perspective) which could be drawn to complete the circular form of the external 'room' provided by the central court.

The years 1927 and 1928 were critical ones in the development of Aalto's career. Not only did they involve the removal of his office and home from Jyväskylä to Turku, but they saw the launching of his reputation as a master of modern architecture. With the Cooperative Building he had proved himself to be more than competent in the conventional style of the 20s. He had gone on to learn the basic lessons of rationalisation in the Tapani apartment block. Then, in the *Aitta* competition, he had begun to flex his muscles, albeit on small-scale elements, in his exploration of new plan forms and volumetric expression. All that was required now was a project of sufficient size and prestige to allow him to develop his new experience into a coherent exercise in the new idiom. This opportunity presented itself in the commission to design the new premises for the foremost newspaper in Turku, the *Turun Sanomat*.

The commission, which dates from January 1928, was a direct result of Aalto's growing reputation in Turku, based both on the buildings in progress and on his increasing confidence in promoting himself and his ideas amongst professional colleagues and business associates. But before he undertook the design of the Turun Sanomat building Aalto was involved in yet another significant and formative exercise in the new expression. For, late in 1927, he assisted Erik Bryggman in preparing an entry for another competition, the subject of which was an office block in Vaasa. Superficially, this entry, entitled 'Waasas' and disqualified by the conservative jury led by J.S. Siren of Parliament Building fame, is not as advanced a solution to fenestration as the rear elevation of Aalto's Tapani block designed at much the same time. It should be remembered, however, that the Tapani block was not actually completed until 1929, by which date the Turun Sanomat premises were also finished and Aalto was already engaged in the design of the Tuberculosis Sanatorium at Paimio. More importantly, Bryggman's entry raised two design problems in relation to the expression of the modern commercial building: (1) the continuous slit window indicative of the upper office levels; and (2) the double-storey entrance at ground level and its relation to shopping units there.

Aalto's first use of the continuous slit window motif on any building would appear to date from the Konsoli cottage design submitted in the *Aitta* competition. The precise dating of the different developments in Aalto's expression in the period 1927–8 is difficult to arrive at, but there would appear to be no evidence of the continuous horizontal window motif as early as 1927. His original competition entry for Viipuri Public Library (see pp. 60, 62) had no hint of it: it was conceived in the Romantic Classical manner of an earlier city library, Gunnar Asplund's for Stockholm. Although Aalto would have been aware of the published designs for Asplund's library, final ones of which date from 1923, the building was not completed until 1928 when he actually saw it. Aalto's first design for Viipuri includes an exaggerated form of the monumental Egyptian entrance to Asplund's library, as well as the same basic pattern of classical fenestration – double-square windows at the *piano nobile* – as employed by Asplund in the Stockholm design. In fact, Aalto's one concession to modernism in the elevations of the first Viipuri submission was the full-height glass-brick window indicating the subsidiary staircase on the north-east end of the building.

The similarity of Aalto's design to Asplund's includes a variation of the same principle of staircase approach to the main reading area, its control and the natural lighting of this area. These features were functional innovations within the conservative framework of a Neo-classical architectural box. Aalto's approach, however, even in this first rather traditional presentation, is further innovatory in his use of a change of axis from the entrance to the reading level, rather in the manner that he had used this change of axis in transition from the entrance level to the upper foyer of the theatre in the Jyväskylä Workers' Club. Even in his earliest following of the examples of other architects Aalto manages to implant his own personal variation or twist. Within the framework of architectural expectations he was always seeking an element of the unexpected, the environmental surprise. But to return to the finer points in the emergence of Aalto's new mode of expression.

The vertical entrance feature, of two storeys or more, which was not employed by Aalto in his Jyväskylä Workers' Club (1924) or by Bryggman in his Turku 'Atrium' apartment block (1928), makes its first appearance in an Aalto design in the Cooperative Building (1928), although it is, of course, delineated in the Alberti-inspired entrance frame of the Muurame church. Interestingly again, however, in the Cooperative design Aalto takes the fascia above the shops, which in Bryggman's 'Atrium' block is deep and flush with the main wall, and draws it out into a projecting canopy which clearly cuts off the larger elements of the shop fenestration from the smaller windows above. Furthermore, this canopy element extends into the two-storey entrance recess on either side, which has the effect of increasing the horizontal bond of the composition and diminishing the vertical break effect of the entrance. This same double-storey entrance feature then reappears in the Bryggman 'Waasas' design but without the horizontal interruption, as Bryggman still retains his flat fascia but pushes it up to span over the recessed entrance opening and provide a continuous horizontal element on which the three upper floors of almost continuous office windows sit.

In this complex process of transition, it is important to examine again the chronology of these designs. Although the original designs of the Cooperative Building antedate his arrival in Turku in the summer of 1927, the final design, including the canopy variation, would have been more or less contemporaneous with Aalto's collaboration with Bryggman on the 'Waasas' project. In the interim period, however, Aalto undertook and completed the preliminary design for the Viipuri library. This is confirmed by the fact that the Viipuri competition conditions were not available until 27 June and competitors were required to submit their entries by 1 October. That also does much to explain the tentative and highly derivative external character of Aalto's original design for the library. The move from Jyväskylä would have placed him under considerable pressure during those four months and he almost certainly sacrificed the traditional Finnish month-long holiday of July that summer. It also shows us how he was able to utilise the complexity of his experience in those early months in Turku once he had adjusted to the pressures upon him.

The vertical staircase treatment of the Tapani block, for example, is clearly anticipated by his first proposal for the similar problem posed by the Viipuri Library. Also, we can see how he reacted in two quite contrasting modes to the two-storey entrance solution of Bryggman's 'Waasas' design: (1) in the Cooperative frieze that he converts into a canopy treatment; and (2) in the solution he evolved for the two lower storeys of the Turun Sanomat design. Clearly, the collaboration between Bryggman and Aalto on the 'Waasas' project generated quite a lot of interaction between the two men and affected the design approach of both in the coming months. Bryggman's entry for the Extension of the Suomi Insurance Helsinki Headquarters competition in the autumn of 1928, on the jury of which Aalto served, includes a vertical staircase window similar in design to that first used by Aalto in his Viipuri entry the previous autumn. Aalto was also probably influenced by Bryggman's 'Waasas' design in his use of virtually continuous strip windows in the upper floors of the Turun Sanomat building. But it was equally clear to him that he could neither use Bryggman's elevated fascia motif nor adapt his use of the canopy from the Cooperative Building.

The problems of the Turun Sanomat street elevation were entirely different, stemming from the fact that there were three points of access rather than one – the newspaper's own public office at street level, an entrance giving access to the offices above and a service entrance to the courtyard behind. Aalto wanted to give emphasis to the public office – his design incorporating a two-storey display window to accommodate a large-scale projection of the daily front page – and suppress the minor entrances. His solution was to remove the display window from a central position, creating a striking asymmetrical composition; he then matched the double height of this and the office staircase element by expressing the first-floor offices over the shops as a 'clerestory' to the shop windows. Doubtless the two architects were constantly in and out of one another's offices and meeting socially to discuss their common problems in the creation of the new architecture. And Aalto was undoubtedly influenced by Bryggman's approach; but, equally clearly, Aalto's Turun Sanomat street elevation was a highly original design. Its boldness of organisation, particularly the use of the giant projection of a newspaper front page as a banner, a concept first employed by the Vesnin Brothers in their project for the Pravda offices in Leningrad in 1924, has more confidence and clarity than any of Bryggman's contemporary designs.

The complexity of the design problems confronting Aalto was greatly increased

The *Turun Sanomat* newspaper building, Turku (1928–9): original perspective of street elevation, showing display window with proposed front-page projection

Turku, the Turun Sanomat building: the street elevation as built

when he won the first prize in the Viipuri Library competition. He can hardly have imagined that his hurriedly conceived entry would have brought him this success; but the strength and originality of his planning gave him the edge over Hilding Ekelund, who took second place. So, at the end of February 1928, within weeks of being commissioned to design the Turun Sanomat building, Aalto found himself with two new major projects on the drawing board whilst the Cooperative Building was still under construction. He had been extremely industrious during the previous year; but he had also been lucky and, although he was to have some setbacks in the next decade, he had succeeded in firmly establishing himself just after his thirtieth birthday.

The implementation of the Viipuri Library was, however, to prove a lengthy affair, with the revised designs for the original Aleksanterinkatu site not presented to the building committee until May 1929, and the final design for the new site adjacent to the cathedral not put forward by Aalto until 14 December 1933. Following its acceptance by the City Council at the end of December, work finally began on site in mid-April 1934. This delay of more than six years between winning the original competition and the commencement of construction brought many frustrations for Aalto. At the same time, however, it allowed time for his interpretation of the functionalist idiom to mature, so that the Viipuri Library remains a masterpiece in this mode. Also, the timing of its construction programme allowed him to move his office to Helsinki in December 1933. In the meantime he had entered the competition for the Tuberculosis Sanatorium at Paimio, carried off first prize with a daring design and completed the construction of this work. The Turku period, therefore, bridged not only the last three years of the 20s and the first three of the 30s but witnessed the complete evolution of Aalto's international style from these first steps in the Tapani block and Turun Sanomat building to the complete mastery of Paimio and Viipuri.

The competition programme for Paimio was yet another one of incredibly short duration, spanning only from its announcement in November 1928 to the submission in January 1929, and providing the competitors with even less time than they had been given for the Viipuri Library. Of the published designs it is not surprising to find that Bryggman's was the only other entry to interpret successfully the functionalist approach; its simple, curved plan form was given a comparably clear horizontal expression. Bryggman's entry was unplaced, although his design clearly impressed the jury, because it was purchased.

During his travels in the summer of 1928 Aalto saw not only the new architecture of his Swedish colleagues but also visited Holland and, in particular, Hilversum. There he would have seen outstanding examples of brickwork by the Dutch follower of Frank Lloyd Wright, Wilhelm Dudok, including that architect's Rembrantlaan School of 1919, the Minchelers School of 1925 and his recently completed Town Hall. A strong reference to Dudok's massing and use of detailing seems evident in Aalto's later expressionist work, especially in his Säynätsalo town hall (see pp. 129–32) and at the University of Jyväskylä (see pp. 188–90). But it was the work of another Dutch architect that was to have a more immediate impact on Aalto's development. Johannes

Duiker had also been a follower of Wright but after 1926 he moved away from Wright's influence and went on to produce two buildings in the constructivist vein. The first of these, the Zonnestraal Tuberculosis Sanatorium in Hilversum, had been completed just before Aalto's visit in 1928; the other, and until recently better known, example of Duiker's constructivism was the Open Air School he built in Amsterdam in 1920. In the Zonnestraal Sanatorium Aalto was able to see a perfect model of functionalist planning on an open site combined with constructivist expression that was the logical extension of concrete construction.

Within a few months of his return to Finland Aalto was to find himself involved in the Paimio competition, in an almost identical architectural programme. Pearson has drawn our attention to the fact that Aalto not only adapted Duiker's plan for his Paimio entry but also depended very substantially upon the Dutch architect for the details he used in the building's reinforced concrete frame construction.[4] Indeed, Aalto's adaptation of the Duiker plan consisted of simply compressing two of the patients' wings on the Zonnestraal design into one long one. The fact that Aalto was later required to increase the number of beds by forty per cent meant that his original nursing wing was increased in height from four to six storeys. This had the effect of changing the essentially horizontal stress of the original design but had the advantage of heightening the dramatic impact of the approach to the building.

Superficially, therefore, the similarity of Aalto's design to Duiker's is not now as evident as it would have been in the original drawings. Aalto cleverly disguised the considerable length of his own patients' wing from the entry court by placing the

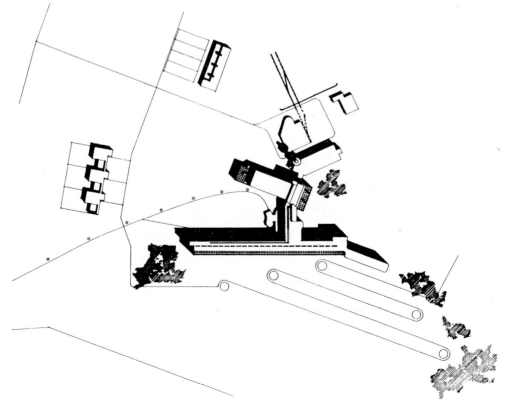

Tuberculosis sanatorium, Paimio (1929–33): site plan, showing the main hospital and the residential units for doctors and staff

Paimio: view towards main entrance (showing original *porte-cochère*), with main ward block on the right

nursing access at the midpoint rather than at the end as in Duiker's design. Originally, also, Aalto's borrowing of the Zonnestraal water tower motif, combined at Paimio with the boiler flue, stood out more prominently. In the completed building Aalto's treatment of the entrance canopy, together with the other plastic elements he introduced on the rear of the building, diminished the overall effect of a constructivist building. Another element that linked Paimio with Duiker's influence, the 'L'-shaped windows that characterised the patients' wing and gave Aalto his entry motto of 'Piirretty ikkuna', a feature that had appeared in the Duiker and Bijveet Aalsmeer house of 1924, were replaced in the final design by square windows. So we must conclude that Aalto's visit to Hilversum in 1928 made it possible for him to win the Paimio competition and detail its design and construction; but this in no way diminishes his skill in doing so or the outstanding contribution to modern architecture made by the result.

Indeed, Aalto developed a great number of original details for this building, including specially designed washbasins for the patients' rooms, light fittings, door furniture and the mechanical ventilation system for the main kitchen. Also, the reinforced concrete frame supporting the wing with the cantilevered sun-traps had no precedent in Duiker's design. The employees' housing in the grounds, however, sited so as to look away from the sanatorium, again appears to look to a Dutch inspiration, with seemingly clear references to the work of J.J.P. Oud in the Hook of Holland and Rotterdam. This influence upon Aalto is also an important one: the terraced housing designs which he first adopted at Paimio were to prove the model for all his later housing of a similar type. The examples he saw in Holland of two-storey terraces, the upper floor having a continuous balcony divided at party walls by screens or walls, clearly provided the inspiration for the workers' housing not only at Paimio (1933) but also at Sunila (1937–8) (see p. 73).

With the design of Turun Sanomat already finalised, Aalto had set off on his travels in the summer of 1928 intent upon expanding his grasp of modern architecture in Western Europe. It is significant that he went to Holland at that time, because this experience allowed him to extend considerably his experience of the modern idiom which until then had, in terms of first-hand knowledge at least, been confined to the new work in Sweden and the experiments of his compatriot Bryggman. There seems to be no record of this visit in Aalto's sketchbooks,[5] but Paimio, Viipuri and his later housing developments in the 1930s, as well as his mature expressionism of the 1950s, show how well he retained what he saw in his mental notebook.

To return for a moment to the Turun Sanomat design. We have already noted that one of the unique features of Aalto's design for Paimio was the asymmetrical cantilevering of the sun-terracing system from a single spine column. This vertical structural member was designed rather like the main trunk of a tree, substantially thicker at its base than at the top, supported by great tapering foundation pads that spread out into the ground like roots. But this structural emphasis in Aalto's interpretation of constructivist expression had its origin in the design of the giant

View at Paimio from upper window showing roof and rooflights of surgical theatre block

Paimio: exterior view of sanatorium

columns that support the building over the cathedral-like press hall of the Turun
Sanomat design. In their form, these columns adopt the reverse profile of the Paimio
structure, tapering from top to bottom in order to open up the maximum amount of
space at floor level for the printing press machinery. Although the image of the
cathedral springs readily to mind, with aisles on either side of the columns and light
pouring in from the adjacent paper storage area with its down-to-earth mushroom
columns, this modern industrial space probably owes more to the influence of a ship's
engine room. The sheer elegance of the original columns, their junctions with the
floor slab above taking the form of flattened bell capitals was, even more than the
street façade, Aalto's unique contribution in this building. Regrettably, this feature
and therefore the pure quality of the press room has been lost in the remodelling
necessitated by the introduction of larger and heavier machinery. Spatially, Aalto had
allowed for this consequence of development but he had not anticipated the need to fix
the new machines to the columns. They have now been squared off and covered with
white ceramic tiles.

But the importance of the Turun Sanomat columns, and the sun-trap wing and
grand piano-like entrance canopy at Paimio, is in Aalto's early interest in extending a
minimal structural solution to a functional programme in the direction of a plastic

The Turun Sanomat building: in the newsprint storeroom Aalto applied Maillart's mushroom
construction (originally used in Zürich, 1910); and in the press hall, seen here, he develops
Maillart's approach to produce an asymmetrical column and cap design

interpretation. The introduction of these carefully articulated sculptural forms is in direct contrast to the main elements of basic plan and expression of the building, and represents Aalto's early revolt against the more puritanical constraints of constructivist and functionalist geometry. For him the Cubist masses of a rationalist architecture were, like the stripped-down volumes of Neo-classicism, merely points of departure in his search for life-giving forms.[6] Standardisation, either of elements (as in the Tapani system) or formal expression, could never be an end in itself for Aalto. Whilst the international style and many of its practitioners were to become known by their uniformity, Aalto was beginning to seek out diversity.

For Aalto architecture was not a box for accommodating functions but a living organism, a life-force to be experienced and enjoyed in the variety of stimuli which it had to offer. This attitude is typified by his concern in the design of Paimio to pay particular attention to the limited environment that confronts the long-term non-ambulatory patient in a hospital.[7] The Turun Sanomat building also contains Aalto's first use of a lens roof-light, which he went on to develop at Paimio. He was able to make the introduction of natural light into interior spaces one of his major pre-occupations in the achievement of interior environmental quality, and the design of roof-lights was to become one of the most sophisticated elements in Aalto's architecture.

His little-known competition entry for the University Hospital at Zagreb of 1930

On the Turun Sanomat building, Aalto tried out the rooflight lenses that were to become such a salient feature of his designs

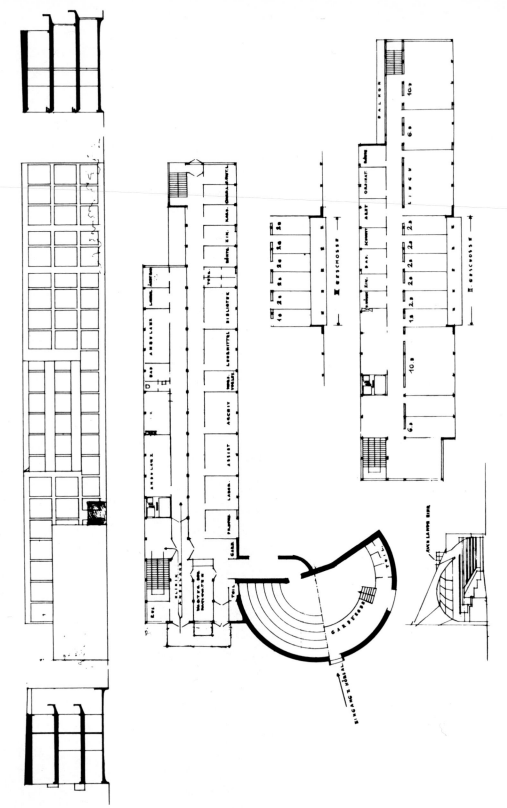

Hospital for Zagreb project (1930): plan, section and elevation of typical teaching block (original competition drawing). The section through the auditorium shows Aalto's first use of an indirect daylight system in the rooflight treatment for this function provides an early example of this sophistication. In response to the vast programme of this building Aalto provided a main hospital block around five interior courts. But the smaller clinics for Surgery, Internal Medicine, etc., were given separate pavilions. Each of these had its own lecture theatre, and Aalto adopted the ingenious solution of using the space under the stepped auditoria as the main entrance to these clinics. Equally ingenious was the natural lighting of these auditoria, by two systems of roof-lights, one placed at the rear to give a hidden light source for the student audience while the other, separated from it by the dome-like ceiling of the auditorium, gave light from a second hidden source which was directed onto the lecturer's demonstration area. The basic plan form of the auditoria was, like the 'Merry-Go-Round' design, slightly more than half a circle, with the external volume a partial cylinder that was truncated at a slight angle. But this deceptively simple exterior concealed a highly plastic interior form of great complexity. This was also Aalto's first exercise in lecture auditorium design but, in its truncated cylinder form and the introduction of complex natural light sources in the ceiling, it already anticipates his post-1950 designs, culminating in the main auditorium for the Technical University at Otaniemi (1955–64) (see pp. 124–5).

The three design stages of the Viipuri Library occupied Aalto for more than six years, from the summer of 1927 until the end of 1933. During that period his approach to its design went through radical changes. Originally, both in the competition entry and its revision of 1929, it was based on a site located on the north-west side of Viipuri's main shopping street, the Aleksanterinkatu, and it was proposed to build a House of Culture on the opposite corner of the street at a later stage. Aalto's original design provided for a public open space in front of each of the two buildings, effectively creating a piazza that spanned across the Aleksanterinkatu, cutting across the axis of the tree-lined street at that point by setting both the library and the House of Culture back into the trees of the city centre park-belt. This competition entry was, as we have noted, heavily influenced by Asplund's design for the Stockholm City Library and it consisted of a main high rectilinear block with a low entrance wing at right angles to it. The reading room and principal public accommodation was to be first-floor level, the *piano nobile*, reached from the entry wing by an imposing staircase. In the revised design the building retained its basic original form, although the entrance wing now went the full height of the building and embraced a fully transparent staircase hall, with its glazing wrapped around the corner of the entrance wing at its junction of the main block with the open forecourt. The general organisation however was completely changed. Apart from the new feature of the glazed main staircase lobby which, together with the retention of the original glazed service stair 'slot' at the end of the building, struck a thoroughly functionalist note, there was neither the overall cohesion nor the convincing modernism that characterised the precisely contemporary design of the Turun Sanomat. Admittedly the Asplund-inspired fenestration had gone but this had only been replaced by the rather uncertain pairing of three-light steel-framed windows at the *piano nobile* with smaller two-light ones above.

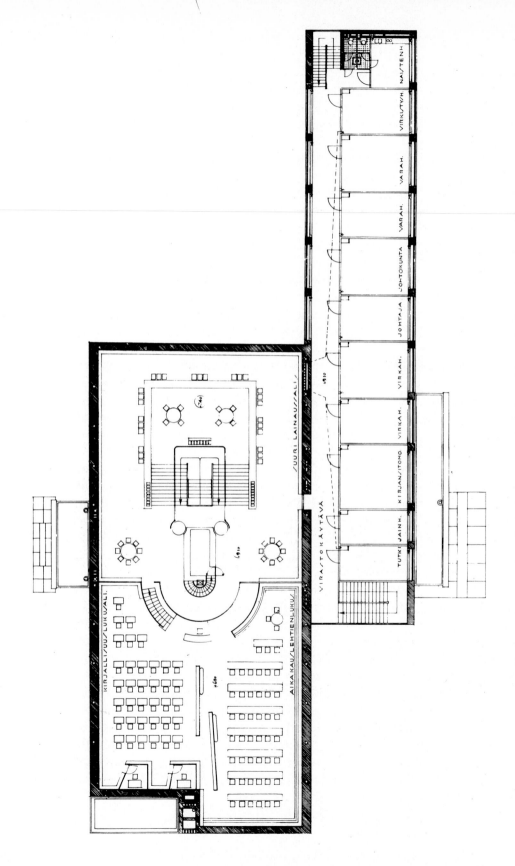

Municipal library, Viipuri (original competition 1927: built 1933–5): plan at upper level, showing the reading room, with first use of a sunken area

This design was accepted by the committee but fortunately not built. For the City Council, when asked for its approval, found itself in the midst of a controversy about the site. This centred upon a dispute between the commercial interests that favoured the original choice, probably their own, and a group led by the City Architect, Uno Ullberg, and the Chief Architect in charge of planning, Otto Meurman, who wanted the library to be built adjacent to the cathedral. This 'professional' group argued that the use of the original site, which involved cutting into the tree belt of the city park, would spoil its line and effectiveness. Meurman's group eventually won the day and Aalto was therefore given the chance to start again.

He must have been pleased to have this new site, without the artificial constraint of the projected House of Culture, which almost certainly would not be built or, even worse, might be designed by another architect. Now he could design a free-standing pavilion in the park, within the shadow of the cathedral, with each building having its own clear territorial prerogative. His response was to undertake a fundamental reorganisation of the plan. No longer confronted by the formality of a large public anteroom, a piazza, Aalto reduced the scale of his new design to conform with its garden setting. The monumental entrance staircase was no longer called for. Instead he contrived to get people into the library with as little fuss as possible, evolving three separate entrances – access to the main library on the north side, access to the separate children's library on the south side and the entrance to the periodical room from the east. On the north the main entrance is framed by trees, while to the south the children's library adjoins the playground.

Once inside the main entrance the visitor found the garderobe and lavatories to the right with the lecture room beyond, while ahead a short flight of steps gave access to the reference room on the right and through it a quadrant stairway, which changed the axis through ninety degrees, led to the main reading room. The interior scheme of Aalto's original competition design had adapted Asplund's solution of bringing the public up into the main reading space by means of a central stair well. He retained the concept of this central stair well with a high interior volume by providing a sunken well, containing a segregated reading area, within the main reading room. Thus, the general plan form and massing of the Viipuri Library, based as it is upon two overlapping horizontal volumes, is determinedly modern, a fact reflected in the free flowing of the stacks between the two volumes at ground level; while the interior organisation of the main public area has distinct vestiges of Neo-classicism in its symmetry, its contrast of rectilinear and semi-circular forms and its use of level changes along the strong central axis. In the statement of the inner sanctum of the reading room as a sunken pit Aalto presented a feature that was to become common to all his subsequent library designs. This feature is far from functional from a staff point of view and is criticised by professional librarians to whom the additional work load imposed by level changes in a reading area is anathema. But this is only another example of Aalto's concern to meet overall environmental needs, in this case those of the reader, rather than treat the functional programme of a building as a management

Viipuri: exterior view of main entrance, showing glazed staircase wall

Interior view of main entrance to Viipuri municipal library, showing braced doors and glazed staircase lobby (Aalto, centre, with Aino, right, and Aarne Ervi)

exercise. His use of level changes, particularly in the feature of the reading 'well', allows the retention of a large, well-lit comprehensive interior volume that avoids a sense of claustrophobia but at the same time achieves a variation in ceiling heights and a variety in the character of individual areas that is never monumental and sometimes intimate. And the advantage of the comprehensive interior volume is focused, in Aalto's approach to library design, on the possibility of introducing natural daylight into the different reading areas by means of his carefully designed roof-light system.

It is this concern with lighting, and with an overall lightness and airiness, beginning with the entrance hall and its transparent connection to the staircase that goes up to administrative offices (that traverse the access of the entrance at first floor level), through to the top lighting of the reading areas, that makes the Viipuri Library a truly modern building. The concept of the library as a civic symbol, which had dominated Aalto's first two designs, had given way to the idea of a library as 'an invitation to read'. Aalto's use of glass in the Turun Sanomat design, at Paimio and in the Viipuri Library is centred on the achievement of an inviting quality, to ensure that the *ethos* of a building – whether it be a commercial building, a social service or a cultural symbol – is *both* functional *and* enjoyable. It was in this spirit that he addressed himself to the problem of the lecture room at Viipuri. And in its design he established one of the characteristics of his unique architecture.

In Turun Sanomat and at Paimio, Aalto had demonstrated his command of the new materials of modern architecture, reinforced concrete and metal-framed windows. At Viipuri he introduced that quintessentially Finnish material – wood. Its use in the ceiling of the library's lecture and discussion room is highly original and represents an extension of his earlier interest in the design of wood furniture. Thus, the final form of the Viipuri lecture room, which dates from 1935, has to be seen in the context of those earlier furniture designs and his other experiments in wood of the early 30s.

Aalto's earliest furniture designs, one-off pieces for family and friends, were Neo-classical. In 1928 he made a dramatic switch in his designs for furnishing the sacristy of Muurame Church and various rooms of the South-Western Agricultural Cooperative Building in Turku. The manufacture of these designs brought him into contact with Otto Korhonen, of Huonekalu-ja-Rakennustyötehdas Company, Turku. One of the results of this association was the design and production of a stacking chair, an amalgam of traditional solid wooden elements and plywood, which Aalto used in the auditorium of the Association of Patriots Building, Jyväskylä, in 1929 (see Appendix, p. 251). He went on to extend his use of bent plywood in another stacking chair, commissioned by Korhonen for the Huonekalu-ja-Rakennustyötehdas pavilion in the Turku 700-Year Exhibition of 1929. In this design Aalto adapted a plywood seat form, originally pioneered in Estonia, for use on public transport, by the Luterma Company as early as 1908,[8] so that it was supported by a tubular steel cantilever frame (his first experiment with a cantilevered support of laminated wood having been discarded as too heavy in section). To describe its characteristics Aalto dubbed this model 'the word's first soft wooden chair'. Finally, in the 'Paimio' chair of 1930–33, originally designed for the sanatorium, Aalto managed to overcome his earlier difficulties with the wood support systems by abandoning the cantilever frame

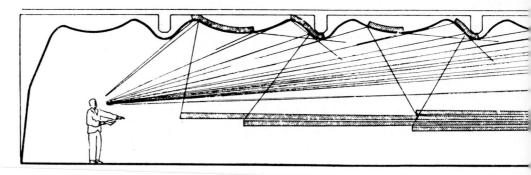

Viipuri: transverse section of ground-floor lecture room, showing its exaggerated length and the corrective wooden acoustic ceiling

in favour of continuous support and arm members between which spanned an elegant 'spring' of bent plywood. And by 1935 he was able to adapt the 'Paimio' design in the first of a successful series of cantilevered armchairs based on the same principle but using the basically 'U'-shaped arms also as 'springs'. Some of these armchairs were used in the Viipuri Library lecture room.

Aalto's interest in furniture design, together with his good fortune first in being commissioned by Otto Korhonen and subsequently his involvement with Maire Gullichsen in the formation of the Artek Company for the manufacture and distribution of his own designs, permitted him to achieve one of the unique qualities of his architecture, namely the cohesion between the forms of his interior spaces and their furnishing. This is yet another feature of his work that places him directly in the tradition of Saarinen's National Romanticism as well as connecting him with Frank Lloyd Wright's concept of an *organic* architecture (see Appendix). And the important discovery that Aalto made in his experiments at the end of the Turku period, the link which enabled him to develop the warm, personal architecture that he made his own, was his realisation that wood offered two complementary yet contrasting attributes that lent themselves to the creation of a distinctive architectural quality. For wood was capable not only of being subjected to new industrial processes, to responding to mass production in the creation of anthropometric sculptural forms, but it also remained by its very nature, its warm colour and texture, a vestigial source of tactile experience in a world that was, already in the 30s, promising an increasing harshness and brutality. It was to provide Aalto with an important key in his philosophy of creating an architecture with which Man can connect, 'to give life a gentler structure'.

Thus, in a very practical way Aalto was involved from the end of the 20s in the search for a humane machine aesthetic, and this search was being conducted on the factory floor. But his choice of material in this search allowed him to continue to see furniture in National Romantic terms, a means of both extending and softening the architectural quality of an interior. The *raison d'être* of the ceiling of the Viipuri Library lecture room has, in common with all Aalto's designs from the Turku period onwards, a number of sources. In its simplest, functional terms he argued it as the

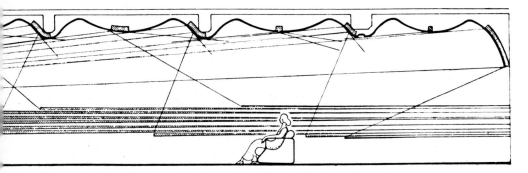

logical solution to the acoustical problem of the space. But the space itself, a long and narrow room, is hardly the ideal form for lectures and discussions. Clearly this attenuated form gave him the opportunity, one might say the excuse, to combine an experiment in acoustical correction with his by then extensive experience in the handling of wood forms.

Although the ceiling is essentially a hand-made element, using small, flat wooden members to build up the contours which reflect and concentrate sound waves, its form is clearly inspired by the results of his recent bentwood experiments. Just as the

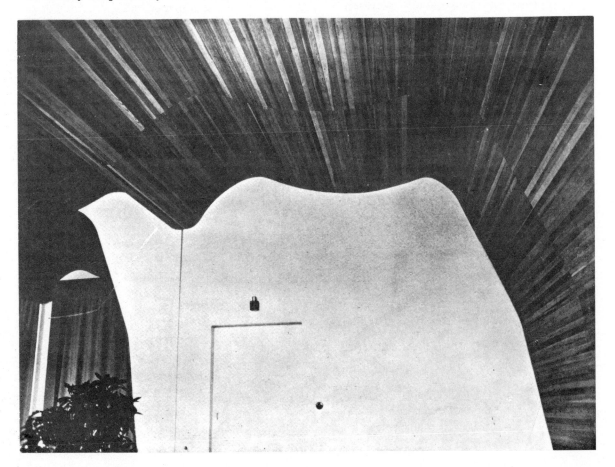

Detail at Viipuri of wooden batten ceiling treatment to front of the lecture room

ceilings of the reading areas had the functional requirement of letting in daylight and therefore were perforated by lenses, so the ceiling of the lecture room was required to convert an unfunctional shape into an acoustically comfortable environment. Aalto's solution of *furnishing* the ceiling with a wooden lining[9] had, of course, been anticipated at Muurame, and the Viipuri treatment can also be seen as a development of that simple wooden vault he used in his church design. The Muurame vault is, however, quite clearly within the established tradition of wooden barrel vaults in Finnish churches.[10] A more direct connection can be seen in Aalto's unsuccessful competition entry for the Tehtaanpuisto (later Michael Agricola) church in 1930, where the section of his simple hall design resembles a modern concert auditorium. There is a distinct shell form over the altar and apse, while the body of the church has a series of shallow vaults spanning its width. These vaults are all identical in section, imparting a regular rhythmical interruption of the directional emphasis of the plan. They appear to owe their origin to Aalto's earlier acoustical designs, namely that of the wooden bandstand for the Tampere Exhibition (1922) and the choral shell for the Turku 700-Year Fair (1929), rather than to his wood experiments of the late 20s.

The contour of the Viipuri ceiling, however, develops a plastic, free-form quality that marks the watershed between Aalto's mastery of the international functionalist, rationalist and constructivist mode and the emergence of his own personal expression. By the time the Viipuri ceiling was put up Aalto had successfully transferred his office from Turku to Helsinki and, after establishing himself in the Finnish capital, was on the threshold of the first stage of his international career.

Turku 700-Year Fair (1929); timber choral platform and shell – a transitional design connecting Aalto's earlier Neo-classical designs with his later free-form wooden constructions

CHAPTER IV

Helsinki, and an International Career: 1933–9

Aalto's professional progress from Jyväskylä to Turku and, in the summer of 1933, on to Helsinki, had so far left an imprint only in provincial centres, for he had spent the first ten years of his career without a commission in the Finnish capital. Indeed, he was not to receive one until 1937, and even that was only an interior design project for the Savoy Restaurant. Having grown up in Jyväskylä he was well known there, and on his arrival in Turku he had quickly established his reputation both within the architectural profession and the business community. In a similar way, over the period of the various designs submitted for the Viipuri Library between 1927 and 1933, he had made his mark in Finland's easternmost province of Karelia. Outside Finland, however, his designs for the Turun Sanomat building and for Paimio had already given him a distinctive reputation amongst other European architects, not least because of his own promotion of his work at the CIAM (Congrès Internationaux de l'Architecture Moderne) conferences in Frankfurt (1929) and Brussels (1930). But he still needed someone, a client, or better still a patron, to discover him and make him known in the Finnish capital itself. The person destined to fulfil this role was the industrialist Harry Gullichsen; or rather it was the special combination of Harry and his wife Maire.

Mrs Gullichsen had been born into the Ahlström family. The large Finnish timber and wood-pulp business of Ahlström had been established by her grandfather and developed by her father. This influential undertaking was centred on the port of Sunila and, at the time when Harry Gullichsen met Aalto, although the Ahlström family no longer retained the financial control of the company, it was very much under the personal influence and direction of Gullichsen in his role as Chairman of the Board of Directors. Gullichsen was an avowed modernist: he was determined that his company should be up to date and able to compete on equal terms in the international markets. Furthermore, his interest in modern thinking was not confined to the industrial sphere. He lived in a country with strong folk traditions that had only recently gained its political independence, and Harry Gullichsen's attitudes to his work also spread into the way he lived and the style he wanted to see reflected in his own personal surroundings and those of his workers. Maire Gullichsen combined her family background and wealth with her training as an artist. The result was that she had an eye for what was good and innovatory in the world about her. Their marriage brought together her inherited and educated sense of discrimination with Harry's determination and ability to put new ideas into practice.

Popular legend had it that Gullichsen met Aalto soon after the architect's arrival in Helsinki. One version of their meeting was that Maire encountered the young architect between 1933 and 1934, whilst she was searching for furniture for the Gullichsens' Helsinki flat; and that Harry, at much the same time, spotted an Aalto chair in a Helsinki shop window. Even Pearson, in his *Alvar Aalto and the International Style* (1978), gave credence to something along these lines. In fact, Aalto did not meet the Gullichsens until 1935, when Artek was founded; but the interim period was certainly not uneventful, especially from the point of view of Aalto's furniture. And those events did centre on contacts Aalto made soon after he moved his office to Helsinki in 1933.

Shortly after the move he attended the most celebrated of the CIAM meetings, held at Athens in August of that year. He was accompanied by a young Finnish devotee, the art critic Nils Gustav Hahl, and there he met and formed a life-long friendship with the English critic Morton Shand. The outcome was Shand's promise to organise an exhibition of Aalto's furniture in London. That it was possible to arrange such an event at all was something of a miracle, especially bearing in mind Aalto's inclination to forget agreements, to which was added the fact that Huonekalutehdas was unable to correspond with London in English! But Shand, who was on the staff of the *Architectural Review*, worked expeditiously to stage a display of Aalto's furniture under that journal's sponsorship. He was so successful in this undertaking that the exhibition opened at the Fortnum and Mason department store in Piccadilly less than three months later, on 13 November 1933, with Aalto himself designing the display.

The emphasis of the exhibition was on Aalto's new all-wooden furniture; and the experimental reliefs he had produced in collaboration with Korhonen's workshops were also included. Aalto's furniture offered a marked contrast to the cold, tubular designs that had characterised much of the modern idiom in furniture: also, it was inexpensive. In response to the enthusiastic reception accorded the Fortnum and Mason exhibition and Aalto's designs, Shand founded Finmar Ltd to import and market his friend's furniture. This business developed rapidly, selling successfully not only in Britain but also in the USA and Australia, and keeping Korhonen and his modest factory more than busy. Korhonen was naturally cautious and unwilling to expand his manufacturing plant: he was unsure how long this seemingly freak demand could be sustained. Also, Aalto was not only forgetful about contracts; writing and answering letters was anathema to him. The joint consequence of Korhonen's limited production and Aalto's unbusinesslike methods was a crisis for Finmar and the Swiss company Wohnbedarf, in the summer of 1935, when it became impossible to meet obligations to customers.

It was during this crisis that Morton Shand remembered Aalto's young companion at the Athens CIAM meeting two years before. Nils Gustav Hahl was a confidant of the Gullichsens, advising them on modern art. One subject of his correspondence with Maire was a project for an avant-garde art gallery in Helsinki. When Shand drew

Hahl into the problems between Huonekalutehdas and Aalto the young critic arranged a meeting between Maire, himself and the architect. Hahl suggested a company be formed to promote new ideas in housing which would be centred on Aalto's furniture, and also to sell works of modern art. Maire was to be the financier and promoter, Aalto would be the creative force and Hahl himself the executive director. Thus, Artek was born and the Aaltos met the Gullichsens on Hahl's initiative. The new company commenced business in December 1935 and the first Artek shop was opened in Fabiankatu on 1 March 1936.

Harry Gullichsen was intrigued by the fact that he had not heard of Aalto until then. Here was an architect who had been producing outstanding modern buildings in Finland for almost a decade, yet he was a prophet virtually unknown in his own country. Gullichsen was impressed by Aalto's design talents and he became determined to help the young architect and promote his ideas. The sudden appearance of Aalto in the capital was something of a gift for Gullichsen. In his campaign to reform and modernise the conservative Ahlström company what better ally could he have than this energetic and native-born genius? Also, the perceptive and entrepreneurial Gullichsen would have been aware of his opportunity to provide a new image not only for his company but also for Finland. One imagines that when the Chairman introduced the young Modernist to his Board of Directors they must have felt as though he were tossing a hand-grenade into their midst. Gullichsen insisted that he would take full responsibility for Aalto's performance. Aalto's close working relationship with Gullichsen, and Harry's continuing faith in him, a faith that was translated into a steady flow of industrial commissions, allowed him to keep his office open and continue with his experiments when other more challenging design work was denied him.

Aalto's first involvement in industrial architecture had been in the design of the Toppila wood-processing plant at Oulu in north-west Finland in 1930. In response to the rapidly increasing demand for paper which began in the early 30s there was a substantial programme of expanding Finland's important industry of converting timber into wood-pulp for paper-making. The Enso-Gutzeit Company, Finland's largest paper and wood-product manufacturer and later one of Aalto's important clients, had brought in the Finnish government as its principal shareholder soon after Finland's independence. Buildings put up in response to this expansion in the mainstay of Finland's economy therefore became symbols of her independence, her development and her future. By their very size these complexes of log plants, sawmills and production mills, with supporting facilities that included their own power plants and housing, were bound to make their mark on the new Finland.

As a dependency of Russia, Finland experienced no industrial revolution in the nineteenth century and the form and character of these industrial cathedrals was dramatically to change the nature of the Finnish landscape in the 20s and 30s. In the 20s their basic characteristics were established by the fact that brick was the only material easily transported to the remote sites on which these plants were built, and it was used in rectangular volumes with little detail other than the arches over the window openings. They were essentially utiliarian structures with little effort to coordinate the groupings of windows or achieve other architectural refinements.

Aalto was to gain little experience in the planning and design of cellulose sulphate production at Oulu, where he was employed only to effect some improvements in the appearance of a plant already under construction. But at Sunila, adjacent to the Baltic harbour of Kotka, where he was responsible for the overall planning as well as the detailed design, he had to face up to the complex technical problems of the whole production process. Significantly, Aalto adopted his standard approach to the new challenges that confronted him at the beginning of his career. In other words, he derived his design from other contemporary examples, particularly Väinö Vähäkallio's mill for Enso-Gutzeit at Kaukopää, but he added his own distinctive features, notably the clear articulation of tall vertical and long horizontal strip windows, and the contrasting of the sober brick masses with the introduction of bow-string trusses to support the roof of the central building. Regrettably, Aalto's crisp interpretation of the established convention, with his clear and confident solution in relating the great masses of brickwork to the rugged, rocky shoreline, has now largely been lost in the subsequent profusion of additional buildings. There is no doubt that Aalto contributed at Sunila to a fundamental reform in the design of Finnish industrial buildings, and the benefit of this reform is to be seen in the power stations by Aarne Ervi and Timo Penttilä.[1]

More significant, from our point of view here, is the employees' housing which Aalto designed for Sunila, which was built in 1937–8. Work commenced on the workers' 'village' close after the completion of the main plant buildings. Access from the village to the plant is by way of a bridge, with the housing for the senior managerial, technical and executive staff located closest to this bridge and that for the mill workers organised in a fan shape up the adjacent hillside. It is the housing form rather than the 'village' that is of interest. In fact, there is no planned village as such, simply several terraces of houses. The two house types that are of most importance in terms of Aalto's development are the engineering staff residences of 1937–8 and the three-storey terraced apartments that were added in 1938–9. In the residences for the engineering staff we see the first consequent development of the fan motif in the planning of Aalto's buildings, although this was anticipated in the broken cylinder of the 'Merry-Go-Round' summer house project for the *Aitta* competition and in the wedge-shaped sauna built for the employees at Paimio in 1932.

The gentle splay in the arrangement of the houses for the engineering staff ensures that no two units in the terrace of five has exactly the same orientation. To achieve this benefit the units are stepped, with the three central houses having one party wall that is not parallel to that at the other end of the house. Two of these units are handed symmetrically in relation to the central party wall, with a third unit of the same plan stepped back from it. The two end units, the one being the largest of the five and the other the smallest, have similar 'L'-shaped plans but with both end walls parallel.

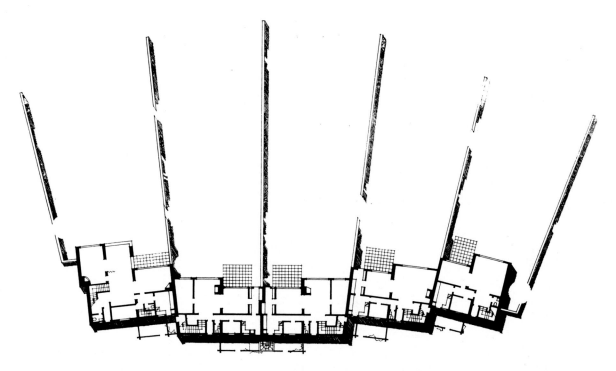

Housing for pulp-mill engineers at Sunila (1935): plan, showing slight fanning to increase privacy

This arrangement also provides optimum privacy on the garden side, with each of the units having a terrace tucked in under the balcony above. Thus, the 'L'-shaped plans are linked together and drawn out into a form that produces considerable plasticity of effect with economy of means. While the form of the terrace has a functional basis – the achievement of maximum privacy and environmental quality – clearly, Aalto's objective on these wooded slopes across from the pulp mill was to build in a charm that is no part of the functionalist *credo*. This element of charm is emphasised by the introduction of a large-grid rectilinear pattern of trellises, providing forecourts on the entry side of the terraces. These trellises are made up of the natural trunks of small trees and saplings, complete with bark, on which plants and vines are trained to soften further the white linear mass of the terrace, with painted brick at ground level and stucco above. This technique of adding elements to building exteriors, frequently rough natural elements, has already been traced back to the agglutinative plan and mass syndrome of the National Romantic period, with particular reference to Hvitträsk and the National Museum. It was to characterise Aalto's mode of expression in this new transitional phase, and we shall discuss this important phenomenon in detail shortly. Meanwhile, let us return to the later Sunila housing, the three-storey units of 1938–9.

This later development was of white-painted brick terraces of six units, consisting of three pairs each mirrored about their common party wall. It is to be noted that all the housing, like the plant itself, is of brick, with superior red brickwork used for the industrial buildings and the inferior quality of brickwork of the housing either painted or stuccoed, thus observing the two basic traditions of European brickwork practice. Entrance to the flats at ground level is by doorways paired about the party wall. At ground level this party wall projects a few inches between the two doorways, while above it is set back. Balconies at first- and second-floor level then span between these wing walls, again for reasons of privacy. As the ground level is built into the slope of the ground, access to the two upper levels is on the other side of the terraces at the middle floor level. Again the doorways are paired, with the one giving direct access to the first-floor flat alternating with the second door to a stairway that leads to the top-level flat. Although there is some privacy at the upper levels, the ground-floor flats have only a small planted area, without the trellis screening provided for the engineering staff units. Furthermore, the units are very cramped internally and, because of ineffective site planning, not protected from the nuisance of vehicular traffic on all sides. The principal interest of these units is that they appear to owe their exterior configuration, particularly the treatment of the balconies between the screen walls, to similar compact terrace housing by J.J.P. Oud that Aalto would have seen in Holland in 1928.

In overall terms, however, Aalto's work at Sunila established his reputation as an industrial architect not only with the Ahlström group but many other leaders of Finnish industry. Harry Gullichsen's gamble had paid off and in consequence Aalto was to become involved in a steady stream of projects for factories and industrial housing that were to provide the backbone of his practice until the mid-60s. The other significant long-term development to come out of the Gullichsens' patronage of the Aaltos was the formation in 1935 of the Artek Company, with the aim of promoting the manufacture and distribution of well-designed items of home and office furniture. Aalto was able to exploit this venture as the outlet for his own designs of furniture, furnishings and glassware. It became in consequence an important source of revenue. Artek continues to flourish and the controlling interest in the company remains in the hands of the Gullichsen and Aalto families. Through the agency of Artek many of the designs which Aalto originally prepared for individual building commissions became available to the public.

Aalto's reputation as a furniture designer was so well established by 1933, when the architect transferred his office to Helsinki, that his first exhibition abroad during the same year was entirely devoted to this aspect of his work. In fact, all Aalto's celebrated furniture designs, as well as most of the principles that were developed in his later designs, date from the period 1929–35, that is from the beginning of his work on Paimio until the completion of the Viipuri Library (see p. 248ff.).

We have already noted how this intensive period of experimentation with bentwood forms influenced Aalto's solution for the ceiling of the lecture room in the Viipuri Library. The experience he gained in the intimate scale of detailing involved in furniture design, combined with the informality of the Sunila trellis motif, was to

Sunila: engineers' housing from garden side, showing use of creepers to achieve organic statement

provide a source of inspiration for all his important transitional designs between 1936 and the outbreak of the Russo-Finnish War. This transition from the international style of Turun Sanomat, Paimio and Viipuri, to the unique combination of the romantic tradition with the principles of functionalism that we have come to recognise as his own mature mode of expression, can be traced in five designs.

These are: (1) his own house and studio in Helsinki (1936); (2) the Finnish Pavilion for the Paris World's Fair (1937); (3) the Villa Mairea (1937–8); (4) the stepped housing for Ahlström at Kauttua (1938) and (5) the Finnish Pavilion for the New York World's Fair (1939). During this brief period of intensive activity, spanning only four years, and also including four major competition entries – for the Finnish Embassy in Moscow and the State Alcohol Monopoly (ALKO) Headquarters in Helsinki in 1935, and the Tallin Art Museum and the Helsinki University Library extension in 1937 – Aalto showed the world a new architectural expression that was not only modern but also every bit as Finnish as the work of Saarinen and Sonck. The quintessential elements of this new expression comprise (1) the prevalence of the courtyard plan, (2) the agglutinative form of both plan and massing, and (3) the addition of external features, frequently made up of rough natural timber members as a means of softening or blurring basic architectural forms.

An understanding of Aalto's planning strategies as they evolved at this critical stage of his career is therefore essential in our efforts to grasp the underlying forms and principles of all his later expressionist work. Normally when we speak of the plan as a form-generating force we are inclined to subscribe to the classical system whereby structures are 'built up' upon the outlines of the plan, extending the horizontal profile vertically, as in the case of the Parthenon or the Tower of the Winds. This approach to the plan-form relationship corresponds in part to the modelling technique of the sculptor, with material being added to achieve a 'positive' form in space. But in extending and manipulating his forms in space the sculptor is not limited to the additive process of modelling: he also carves. An architect does not actually *create* space: he works within a given volume dictated by an area of the Earth's surface, just as a sculptor would be limited by the finite dimensions of a block of stone. Unlike the stone-carving sculptor, however, the architect is free to both model and carve. This interest in both modelling and carving is quite clear in Aalto's experimental wooden structures as well as in his rough study models of building forms.

I believe we must therefore consider Aalto's mature work both from the point of view of classically constructed volumes – the positive forms – and the carving out of 'negative' spaces within volumes. This negative side, the 'destruction' of plan-generated volumes, the hollowing out of new spaces within the total volume dictated by site limitations, offers a counterpart to the classical *parti*, a romantic or organic antithesis that Aalto calls 'autonomous' activity. By considering Aalto as both modeller and carver the apparent contradictions of his plan forms may be seen to offer simultaneously the erosion of conventional spatial volumes and the establishment of new entities which have both functional and ritual components. In this sense, at least, Reima Pietilä may be seen to continue the Aalto tradition.

Even in some of his earliest designs, certainly by the time he was thirty, the external courtyard and a centralised ritual feature which served as a complementary internal focus, had made their appearance. His competition entry for the design of the *Aitta* holiday cottage (1928) is planned around a courtyard that is a segment of a circle, while the interior space has a centrally located fireplace. Within the context of a holiday cottage the fireplace provides the focus for evening gatherings, a 'ritual' centre for the roasting of sausages and for conversation; it reflects internally the daytime focus of the courtyard sun-trap. At the same time, we can view the form of the *Aitta* cottage both as (1) the modelling of a rectangular plan around the circular form of the courtyard, and as (2) the destruction of the classical cylinder by carving away part of the total enclosure.

The focal internal space had already been introduced in Aalto's earlier Neo-classically inspired Jyväskylä Workers' Club (1924–5). There the circular central space, the café, created the true focus of the club's social life. In form it is reminiscent of the entry atrium of Engel's main University building in the Senate Square,

Helsinki. This atrium in Engel's design is on a quasi-mezzanine between the external approach steps and the internal corridors and main staircase. Thus, on entering the front door one finds oneself in a courtyard that is apparently sunken, with monumental steps on three sides forming a stylobate for the imposing Doric columns that provide the gateways to the internal circulation of the building. This use of a sunken space to provide an internal focus was, as we have seen, adapted by Aalto to become a standard feature of his library interiors from Viipuri onwards.

Aalto's design for the Tallin Art Museum (1937)[2] bears a strong relationship to his reorientation of classical planning axes in the final design for the Viipuri Library (1933–5). But in the Tallin competition design the internal court of the stepped main reading room at Viipuri is replaced by an open courtyard intended for the display of sculpture. This open court also admits daylight to the adjacent main circulation area which in turn gives access to the stepped display areas that are themselves top lit. As we shall see, the top-lighting that Aalto used for the stepped reading room at Viipuri is later incorporated into the design of internal courts. This development of the naturally lit internal court became a central feature in Aalto's work. It was a direct functional response to the Finnish climate, particularly the winter, much of which has to be spent indoors with only a few hours of daylight. In his later designs the roof-light

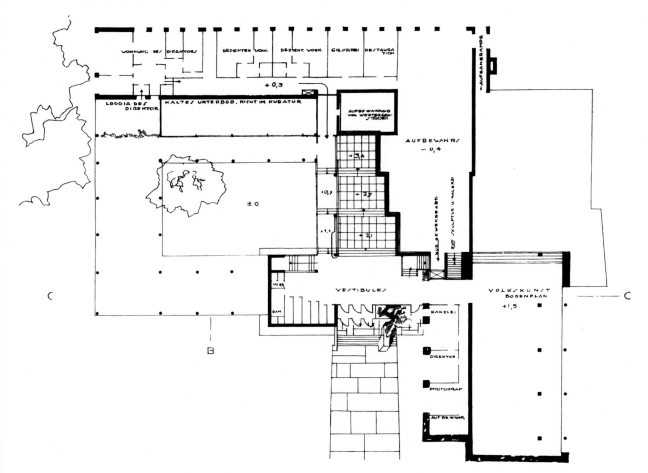

Art museum project for Tallin, Estonia (1937): original competition plan, showing stepped plan form of gallery adjoining the entrance vestibule and courtyard

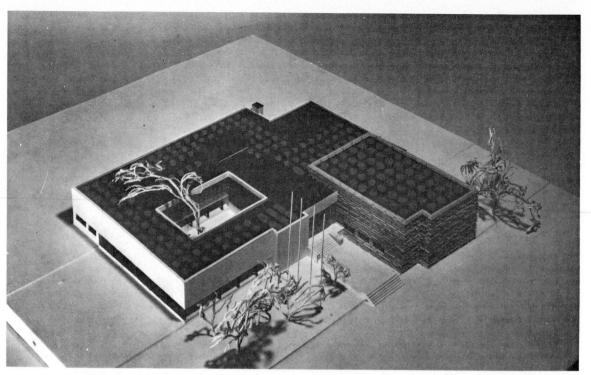

Tallin art museum project: original competition model, showing entrance platform, heavily rusticated stone treatment of the administrative wing, and the courtyard and rooflights

lenses were augmented by a light fitting suspended above the opening to simulate daylight when this was not available.

In his design for the Tallin Art Museum the circulation space links the external open space with the top-lit galleries, a solution that would have achieved a subtle transition from the open air of the courtyard to the artificial environment of an indoor art display. The Tallin plan contrasts strongly, therefore, with that of a Neo-classical museum; in the latter the preoccupation with the externalisation of the building form to fit a classical mould normally achieves ill-lit approach and circulation areas that give access to the glass-roofed internal atria of the actual galleries.

It is immediately clear from the form of Aalto's house and studio in Munkkiniemi (1936) that the simple volume generated by the 'L'-shaped plan has been carved away to reveal a much more complex building. The basic 'L' form of the plan is made up of a main residential wing that is two rooms thick at ground level, with a thinner studio wing placed at right angles to it at one end. There is a separate entrance for the studio at the rear: it is a two-storey volume with a gallery on two sides at first-floor level. Even at ground level the residential wing is eaten into by a terrace placed at the opposite end of the house from the studio for privacy; while at first-floor level there is a deep stepped cut into the volume to provide a partially covered terrace that separates the sleeping area from the upper level of the studio.

This plastic treatment of the basic rectilinear volume is, however, only the

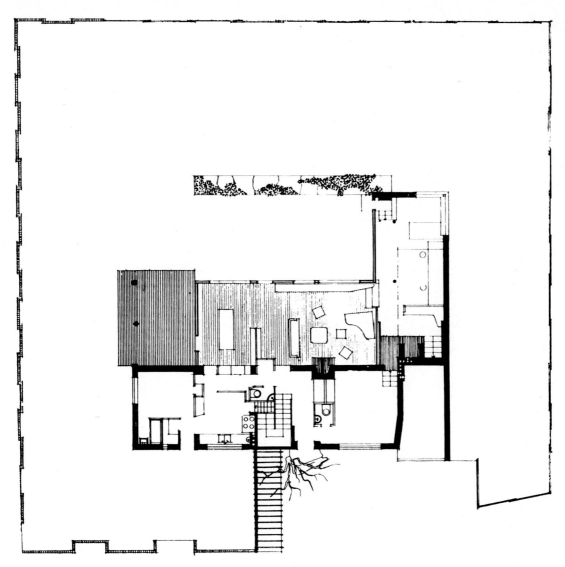

Aalto's own house and studio at Munkkiniemi, Helsinki (1934–6): the ground-floor plan

beginning of Aalto's re-statement of the building's exterior expression. On the one hand, a direct contrast of functions is drawn in this expression with white painted brickwork being used for the full height of the studio wing and a large eight-light studio window placed at the upper level; while in the residential wing the upper projecting portion is wrapped around with vertical wood-strip cladding. Thus, one part of the volume, the two-storey studio, is apparently unified; the residential wing, in contrast, is divided and fragmented both volumetrically and in the use of materials. But even in the studio wing there is an element of tension, imparted by the different levels and character of the three windows. Clearly in this, his own house, Aalto had

Munkkiniemi: view from the stepped and staggered boundary wall, showing timber cladding to first floor

the opportunity to experiment with his new ideas about form and materials that were uppermost in his mind at that moment. And it must be remembered that the Aaltos had just arrived in Helsinki from Turku. What better opportunity would there ever be to demonstrate those ideas to his clients? For this was not only the architect's private home, it was also his public office. This building was to Aalto, therefore, what an exhibition is to an artist.

What is evident and important in this the first building Aalto was to build in the Finnish capital is that the high functionalism which had characterised the lineage of Turun Sanomat, Paimio and Viipuri had disappeared almost entirely. Only in the organisation of the fenestration on the north-west wall of the studio wing are we reminded of the canon of functionalism, and even there we find a certain ambiguity, deriving from rough rail fencing immediately adjacent to it. It fact, this fencing detail picks up the textural reference established by clear-finish birch boarding used to clad the first floor of the residential wing. Indeed, the purity and clarity of Aalto's earlier functionalist line has given way in this building to the expression of functions in form and detail rather than subjugating all functions to a discipline of formal expression. Even so it is difficult to account for the introduction of that birch cladding *except* as a reflection of the nearby woods, confirming that this is not an urban house but a suburban villa.

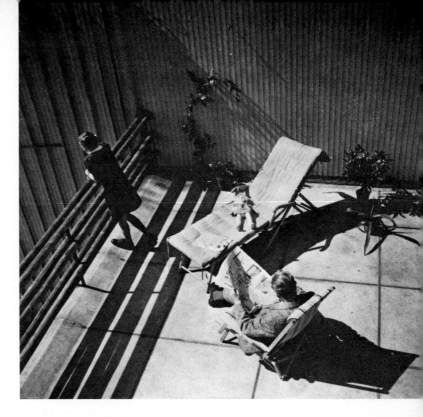

Roof terrace at Munkkiniemi, showing un-stripped pine saplings used as balcony rails (Aalto seated in foreground)

The choice of a site in Munkkiniemi corresponds with Aalto's family background in Middle Finland and the projection of his new, personal interpretation of a romantic functionalism. After all, the aggregation of Finnish farmhouse complexes can be argued on the grounds of function. So also can the treatment of the terrace balcony detail in Aalto's house, varying as it does from a solid treatment with pergola over in front of the bedroom to the open horizontal framework or rails screening the deeper, more public balcony. In this detailing Aalto distinguishes between privacy and semi-privacy; he also breaks down the rectilinear formality of the bedroom balcony, which is a timber variation on the cubist forms of international functionalism, into a woodland expression evoked by three pairs of rough saplings acting as the railing to the remainder of the balcony area.

This railing detail also occurs, as we have seen, in the trellising to the engineers' houses at Sunila (1935). Two years after he completed his own first home in Helsinki, Aalto used a composite variant of this treatment in the balcony rails and trellises on a group of stepped apartments for Ahlström employees at Kauttua (1938). He proposed to build four such blocks around the knoll of a steep hillside. Its outline form suggests the influence of Italian hillside housing; its detail form again shows Aalto breaking down the harsh profiles of functionalist massing to achieve a montage of building with environment. But in addition to their antecedents at Sunila and Munkkiniemi the rough pole railings in the Kauttua group were anticipated in another little-known design of 1935.

Pearson has drawn our attention to Aalto's entry for the competition in 1935 to

Stepped housing at Kauttua (1937): exterior view, showing unstripped saplings used as balcony rails

design a Finnish Embassy in Moscow.[3] His design avoided any functionalist excesses; yet it is clearly an exercise in the international style. Indeed the elevation he proposed for the public side of the building, whilst it is clearly indebted to Le Corbusier, owed more to the Frenchman's domestic rather than public building style. Aalto's entire treatment of the Embassy was in a low key, reflecting a restrained but correct modernity in all but one detail. On the garden side, where the Embassy banqueting and conference suites formed a wing projecting forward on *pilotti*, Aalto contrasted the flat, smooth gable wall with the return elevation to the courtyard. There he again introduced the rough pole trellis along the upper level of the façade, indicating that the clarity of this wall was to be further dissolved by training creepers onto these rough wooden elements.

Thus, we find in the Sunila housing, the Moscow Embassy project, and his own house and studio a definite departure in 1934–6 from the purism of the international style. It makes its first appearance in 1934–5. Pearson asserts that the additive elements first appear in the Embassy project drawings but they were first realised at Sunila and may well have been first conceived in the design of the balcony handrails and column elaboration for the Munkkiniemi house. We know for certain that by 1936, when he designed his entry for the Finnish Pavilion at the 1937 Paris World's Fair, these additive elements had become an established part of Aalto's new vocabulary. The Pavilion design is, however, interesting not only from the point of view of these details – the further development of the Munkkiniemi cladding, the lashed columns in the garden and the fins added as column guards – but because it establishes precedents of plan form that were to continue to dominate Aalto's thinking well into the 50s.

In his design for the Paris World's Fair Pavilion Aalto returned to his earlier preoccupation with the courtyard plan. The competition gave him an opportunity to present his latest ideas to the world. A Finnish Pavilion was the perfect vehicle for Aalto at that moment in time. The whole idea of a national pavilion is to synthesise the qualities of national products and *esprit* in both the building and the displays. The national pavilion designer is in a unique position to translate the characteristics and aspirations of his country into a provocative form. Aalto had been grooming himself to fulfil this role for a whole decade. Even the motto he adopted for his main entry[4] made his intentions abundantly clear. 'Le Bois est en Marche' literally implied the movement of the woods of Finland, and Aalto himself, towards Paris. It was clearly inspired by Shakespeare's image of the march of Birnam Wood to Dunsinane. To Aalto it expressed the hope that the new Finnish spirit, in the person of himself, was about to make an international début of great significance. The pavilion design offered him the chance to plant the concept of a new Finland in the French capital. As we have seen, this spirit in Aalto's terms, as evidenced by his experiments from 1927 onwards, was inseparably tied up with a concept of the indivisibility of modern Finnish architecture and wood. Thus, the image of 'Le Bois' had a double meaning for Aalto in the context of the Paris pavilion.

The informal courtyard arrangement Aalto evolved for this design owes something to the loose organisation of farm buildings in Middle Finland and the grouping of the separate houses on the Harjukatu site in Jyväskylä where the architect grew up from the age of seven. On the sloping triangular site Aalto brought in the public at the highest point. From the entrance they progressed into the interior under covered walks that led them around a garden court. The roofs of these walkways were supported by columns, some of which were made up of four separate vertical members that were lashed together. In addition to this column detail, Aalto also used here for the first time shaped projecting fins that were attached to the rough tree-trunk columns that supported the remaining walkways. After passing around the garden court under these walkways the visitors arrived in a preliminary exhibition area; this was in the form of another, enclosed court with skylights. This court, with its dominant feature of thirty-two wooden poles grouped under the central opening, was redolent of the Finnish forest.

Thus, by the time the visitors reached the main hall they had passed through a variety of external and internal spaces that provided a superb introduction to the idea of Finland as a country of forests; in the process they would have been aware, also, of the underlying romantic connection between Man and Nature.

This main hall was also timber clad. Having worked their way down to the lowest point of the site, the visitors entered a rectangular building with rounded corners,

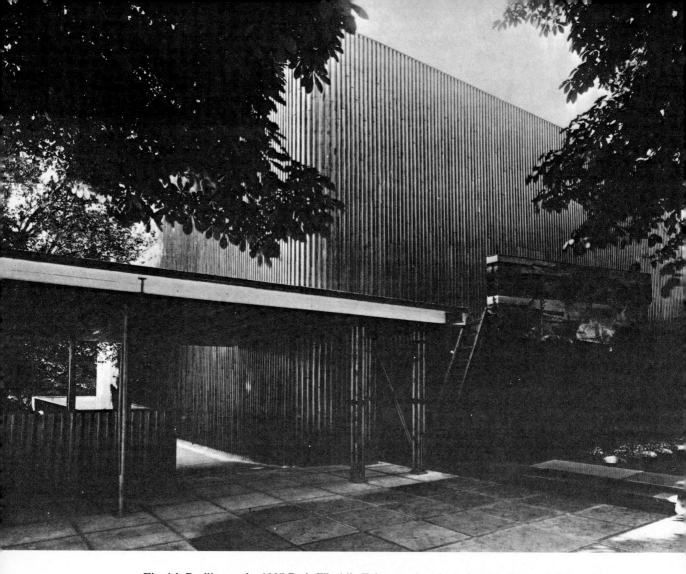

Finnish Pavilion at the 1937 Paris World's Fair: exterior view, showing double-height volume and the two treatments of the columns supporting the canopy – with applied "fins" (left) and a cluster of "poles" bound together with cane (right)

entirely covered in a close-board and batten system, with the boards given a distinctive and emphatic concave form. The main hall had the two-storey height that had become a characteristic feature of Aalto's designs for this type of space, and it was entirely top lit. There was a gallery on all sides at first-floor level, similar to that of the Itämeri Restaurant in the South-Western Agricultural Cooperative Building at Turku, while the skylights above were almost identical to those used in the Viipuri Library. Coming immediately after the Munkkiniemi house it showed how Aalto's new planning strategies were beginning to be supported by a certain degree of standarisation of volumetric treatment and the external detailing of building forms.

Throughout the Paris Pavilion, Aalto's first overseas building, there was an immediate sense of the liveliness and originality of his new Finnish architecture. The importance of this pavilion and that for the New York World's Fair of 1939 cannot be over-estimated, for they brought Aalto's work before an international public that was knowledgeable and discriminating about the new directions of architecture and design.

The influence of traditional Middle Finland structures is also apparent in his designs (1938) for another Gullichsen commission, the 'A. Ahlström System' cottages (sometimes referred to as 'the growing house'), where the whole concept is based on the principles of the additive approach that Glanville has identified in Finnish vernacular farmhouses.[5] The aim was to meet the expanding needs of the growing family both in terms of space and economic stages. The method was to offer a range of separate cabin 'cells', giving a variety of both size and type of accommodation. Significantly, the first set of these designs, Mark I, provided for the grouping of these separate units, which would ultimately give distinct spaces for sleeping, cooking, washing and general living, around a central courtyard which has a strong resemblance to the morphology of both the Harjukatu site of Aalto's Jyväskylä home and vernacular Finnish farmhouses.

The alternative 'Ahlström System' designs, which group the packages' 'cells' under a common roof, are much less interesting, the result being more conventional than the method. But the first proposals, with their dependence upon an open courtyard as the planning core, demonstrate the persistence of this central theme in Aalto's spatial thinking. From the further development of this mode of thinking it is also clear he viewed architecture as a bridge that serves to connect the world of the external environment, upon which Man makes his symbolic mark, and the internal cosmos which caters more to our functional and ritual needs. One is always able to detect classical influences, even distinct classical elements, within Aalto's planning. The reason for this seems to be connected with Aalto's personal interpretation of functionalism, an approach based on the belief that if form was to follow function then functions must be properly defined. In other words, functions must have distinct representational or symbolic meaning. If there is a difference, therefore, between Aalto's functionalism and the functionalism of other masters of modern architecture it is this: *for Aalto the function itself should have a ritual basis so that the form which derives from that function can have a symbolic meaning.* This helps to explain why there is in Aalto's architecture a great deal of sheer formality of effect in spite of the apparent informality of his plans.

The Villa Mairea (1938–9) is another of Aalto's courtyard solutions and bears a very close relationship to his design executed for the Finnish Pavilion at the Paris World's Fair of 1937. In the pavilion the main hall is a high, rectangular element off which leads a stepped wing of low display rooms – itself a domestic image that appears to relate directly to the 'Ahlström System' designs – with the high hall and the lower rooms all grouped around a central court.

The commission to design the Villa Mairea allowed Aalto, before the long freeze effected by the Second World War, to summarise several of his principal preoccupa-

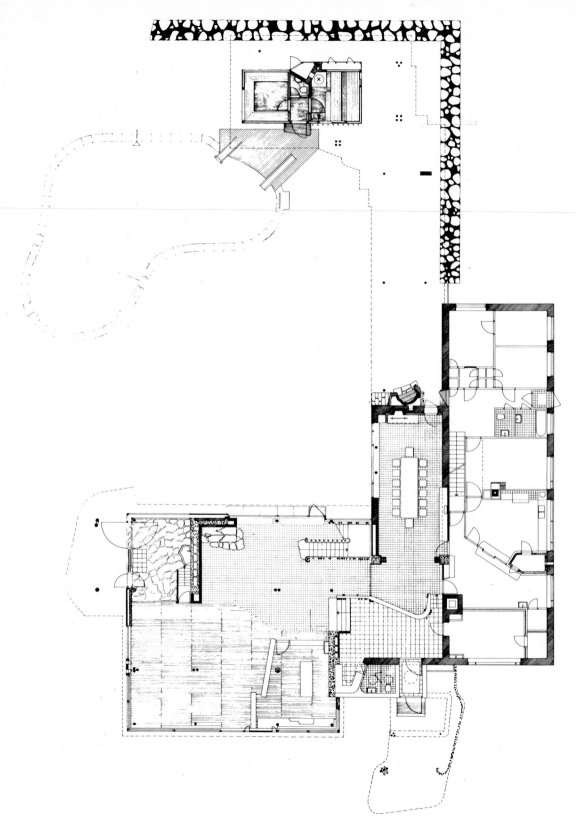

Villa Mairea at Noormarkku (1937–9): ground-floor plan, showing free-form *porte-cochère* (right) and the sauna (left: built after World War II)

tions of the 20s and 30s, bringing these together in both the planning and the formal expression of the Gullichsen's Noormarkku home. For, although he did not speak of an autonomous architecture, free from foreign influence, until 1941, the Villa Mairea is already an anticipation of the full range of Aalto's mature expression.

No other building by Aalto succeeds in merging so completely with the landscape. The irregularity of the plan form serves in particular to diminish the total volume as perceived. Then the *porte-cochère* belongs in its construction more to the surrounding forest than to the automobile, the roof supports being young saplings complete with bark. And finally, on the garden frontage, the detached sauna and the loggia which links it back to the house proper, are roofed with turf. Viewed from the air, therefore, these outbuildings, representing the most essential of Man's ritual activities, the bath, are completely assimilated into the landscape of the garden, becoming virtually invisible.

The design of the Villa Mairea is precisely contemporary with those for the Ahlström System cottages. It sits in forested parkland belonging to the Ahlström family. Its additive planning form reflects that of the Ahlström System cottages Mark I and in turn that of the Finnish vernacular farmhouse. Of course, the *villa* presents a more sophisticated resolution of the accommodation problems but the characteristic 'cell' elements are nevertheless there. They were to crop up again in the Maison Louis Carré (1956–8) in a more compacted form (see pp. 148–52).

Although the Villa Mairea is a rather large residence the family's accommodation on the ground floor is relatively simple, comprising only an entrance vestibule which leads up three steps into the main living area, a separate study, a garden room and a long thin formal dining room off the living area; the main staircase also rises out of this area to give access to the upper bedroom floor. At right angles to this family wing is a narrow service wing containing the kitchen and the servants' quarters. This basic form of the plan can be seen to have a superficial resemblance to Aalto's own house. But in the Villa Mairea this basic form is modified by the dining room which steps out against the service wing, and by the plastic character of both the *porte-cochère* and the projecting outline of Mrs Gullichsen's studio at the first-floor level.

The living area, if the study is included, comprises a large square which opens for most of one wall directly onto the garden, looking towards the sauna. Consequently, the Villa Mairea is not simply an open-plan arrangement; the openness of the interior is extended through to another 'room', the outer room of the garden itself. Also, the garden intrudes into the house, admittedly not a piece of Finnish landscape, but a formalised architectonic one of large-leafed tropical house plants. And this interior garden element is combined with the vertical 'trellis' formed by the extended balustrade of the main staircase to form a subtle screen that has two functions. First, it literally merges the interior and exterior space as the screen of plants acts as a daylight filter. Then it also acts as a spatial fulcrum, the element upon which the living room turns the corner into that long, narrow dining room. Thus, we experience an interior court, which is the living room itself, approached by way of the *porte-cochère* and the

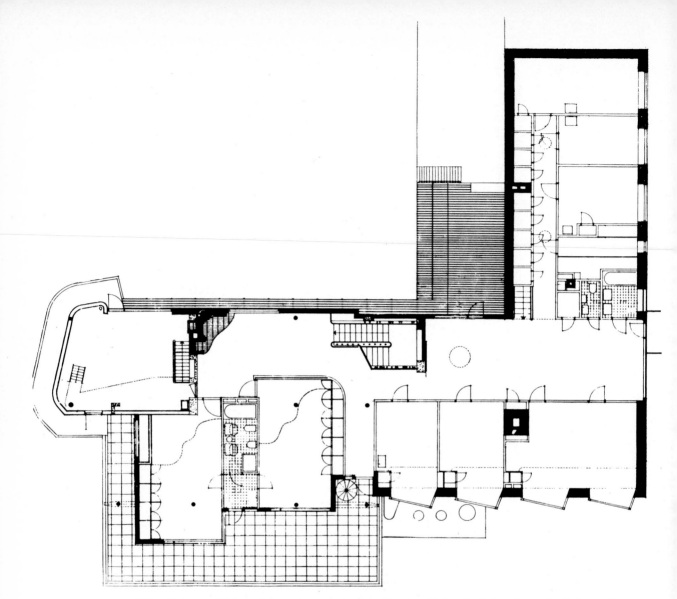

Villa Mairea at Noormarkku: upper-level plan, showing Maire Gullichsen's studio (left), and roof terrace

entry vestibule, both of which are umbrageous areas reflecting the semi-tamed forest rhythms by means of those familiar vertical wooden elements. As we climb from the *porte-cochère* into the living room we are reminded of the plan of the Paris Pavilion.

The living room in turn looks out onto the tamed garden, a garden that has a distinctly Japanese flavour, and that is partially screened by the more refined 'forest' elements of the staircase balustrade. This progression from the forest clearing at the front of the house through the *porte-cochère* and the vestibule, past the staircase screen, all with their architectural vestiges of the forest, conveys the impression of being suspended, both conceptually and symbolically, between the two worlds of outdoors and indoors. Although completed when he was only forty-one, it represents

Exterior view of Villa Mairea: junction of studio balcony with roof terrace, with vertical wood boarding and external Venetian blinds

Interior of Villa Mairea from entrance lobby towards living room and open fireplace, showing the repetition of forest rhythm in vertical members on right-hand wall and staircase beyond

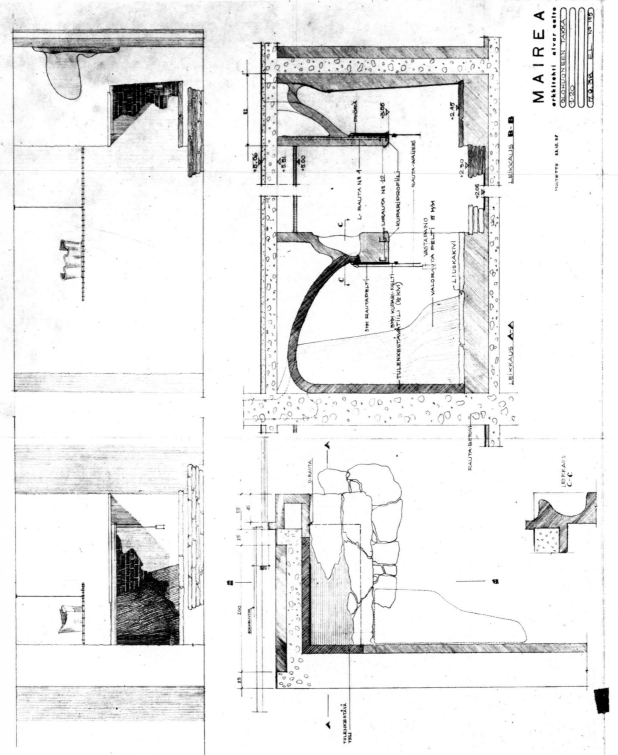

Villa Mairea: original working drawing of the living room fireplace, showing the open corner
and sculptural treatment of the side wall

Interior view of seating area in music room (adjacent to living area) at Villa Mairea, showing internal planting and looking out towards the forest beyond

Villa Mairea: detail of sauna door and external cladding to the bath-house

one important summit of Aalto's planning and spatial genius. The sauna was not built until after the war in 1946.

In addition to the interest of its plan, the Villa Mairea also presents an almost complete vocabulary of Aalto's unique architectural language, a language that depends for its expression upon what he himself describes as the 'simultaneous reconciliation of opposites'. The complete vocabulary might be categorised as having the following characteristics: (1) a deliberate informality, or inverted formality, of the main entrance; (2) apparent freedom of planning that runs counter to classical axiality although the building form itself may be reminiscent of the classical *parti*; (3) a complexity of massing or skyline that does not derive directly from the 'footprint' of the plan; (4) the establishment of a deliberate conflict between the apparent geometrical system of ordering the façade and the overall rhythms or total 'structure' of the façade as a whole; (5) a deliberate blurring of boundaries within both plan and three-dimensional form, so that the containment of an element is dissolved or destroyed; and (6) the conscious confusion of parts of the building with the surrounding landscape, the architecture being built up in a manner that reduces its formal presence, implying a *raison d'être* of self-effacement in which the forms present or induced in nature determine the formal expression within the site, or parts of it, while the building itself becomes virtually expressionless.

Four of these characteristics are to be clearly observed in the Villa Mairea, viz.: (2) apparent freedom of plan (although the plan is in fact constructed upon two intersecting axes at right angles, disguised in the plan by stepping the spatial elements); (3) complexity of massing and skyline that does not directly reflect the plan; (5) deliberate blurring of boundaries in plan and form (in the inter-relationship of the internal living area and the planned garden room); and (6) the conscious confusion of parts of the building with the surrounding landscape (viz. the *porte-cochère* and the sauna). Also, the entrance is informal (1) and there is a conflict between the apparent geometric ordering and its actual rhythms; but these elements are less obtrusive since in those respects the Villa Mairea conforms to the character consistent with the relaxed atmosphere of a country house. Interestingly, Professor Kenneth Frampton informs me that some of his students found the *square* to be the ordering principle of this apparently irregular work.

Baird describes my fourth category as 'the ironic fragmentation of ostensibly rational building geometries'[6] in his suggestion that, at one level, what Aalto intended was not the realisation of coherent forms of architectural statements of a conventionally rational nature but an erosion of the formal architectural landscape by the creation of a self-effacing morphology of 'ruins'. Certainly, the amalgamation of seemingly irreconcilable fragments of geometries from the classical vocabulary on the one hand and aspects of indigenous architecture on the other (N.B., his sketchbook records include both the theatre at Delphi and Spanish vernacular buildings) suggests a *Museumslandschaft* of the various influences to which he responded. Yet, of all the buildings selected by Baird (Säynätsalo town hall, Jyväskylä University, the National

Glass vases designed for Scandinavian Glass Competition (1936) and first made for use in the Savoy Restaurant, Helsinki (1937)

Pensions Institute and the Enso-Gutzeit headquarters) to fit his designation of designed 'ruins', Aalto's own house in Munkkiniemi and the Villa Mairea, perhaps the most natural candidates, are not mentioned in this connection.

Aalto's first Helsinki commission dates from 1937. The opportunity to design the interior of the Savoy Restaurant allowed him to concentrate the newly evolving characteristics of his design vocabulary in a completely relaxed way. Two features occur here that were to be included in the Villa Mairea: there is a low, perforated plywood screen at the end of the back wall of the Savoy dining room which recurs in the Villa at the top of the main staircase as the balustrading; while the free-form cold buffet table in the centre of the restaurant anticipates the shape of the swimming pool located next to the sauna at the Villa Mairea, Noormarkku.[7] The tables, chairs and light fittings were specially designed, while the so-called 'Savoy' glass vases and bowls were an adaptation of an unsuccessful competition entry of the previous year. Along the back wall of the dining room, which is located on the top floor of a commercial building, Aalto introduced a false ceiling sloped to suggest that the restaurant was carved out of an attic storey. This element, another use of his close-boarding motif, is in fact simply a louvred screen hiding ventilation windows placed high up in the wall behind. Ivy was trained along these louvres, introducing the feature of an internal trellis that is still a common feature in Finnish restaurants and coffee shops to this day. But there was little, apart from the important introduction of those vases, that makes this interior exceptional. It is really only a sketch design for later developments although, interestingly, this is one of the few designs jointly credited with his first wife Aino. (Another is that of the Woodberry Poetry Room, in Harvard's Lamont Library, which also has a distinctive wooden screen, and was completed in 1949, the year of Aino's death.) Most importantly, it was to Helsinki what the Paris and New York pavilions were to the world, a shop window for Aalto's ideas.

More significant was Aalto's entry for the competition to extend Engel's library for the University of Helsinki. In this unsuccessful project, which also dates from 1937, Aalto was again confronted with the problem of the reading room. He located the main reading room at the same level as the principle floor of Engel's building. In this project the scale was, of course, very different from that of Viipuri. Aalto's plan solution was uncompromising. Although he maintained Engel's axis through the front of the building to the main circulation area at the rear, he then set the main reading room off to one side with the new stacks at right angles to it along the rear of the site. In the design of the reading room he projected the first truly monumental use of his new mode. The three-storey-high volume offered a vast top-lit space that was free of any internal structure. His treatment of the ceiling derives from the Viipuri reading and lecture rooms. Its perspective shows close boarding that is perforated at the top by closely packed roof lights and sweeps down in a curving incline through the two upper storeys of the north wall. Then, supported and broken only by the great splayed concrete frames at the lower floor, it dips over these and flattens out as the ceiling of the single-storey extension of the reading room on the north side, eventually curving again to meet the windows on the external north wall.

It was to be a long time before Aalto had the opportunity to build on such a scale but in his design for the New York World's Fair Pavilion he was able to interpret the monumentality of the Helsinki University Library project and achieve a sense of Baroque grandeur in what was a relatively small space. Aalto's success in winning in 1938 the competition for the Finnish Pavilion to be built in New York for the 1939 World's Fair, following immediately on the heels of his success with the Paris Pavilion and the construction of the Villa Mairea, was his crowning achievement for the second half of the 30s. This intense period of building activity between 1936 and 1939 came in stark contrast to the lack of success in competitions that characterised his early years in Helsinki. In 1934 alone, for example, he entered three competitions with the following disappointing results: (1) Tampere railway station – unplaced; (2) National Exhibition Hall, Helsinki – third prize; (3) Helsinki Central Post Office – unplaced.

Originally, the New York pavilion had to be fitted onto a rectilinear site that would allow only a windowless solid form sixteen metres in height. The programme required a restaurant for light Finnish snacks and a cinema to show Finnish documentaries. Aalto entered three separate schemes, namely: (1) 'Maa, Kansa, Työ, Tulos' – 'Country, People, Work, Product'; (2) 'Kas Kuusen Latvassa Oravalla' – 'The squirrel has a nest in the spruce tree's top'; and (3) 'USA 39'. Not only did he win the first prize with (1) but also the second and third prizes with (2) and (3) respectively. Obviously, it was helpful to the Aaltos that they had just completed the Paris Pavilion, for their experience in that building was invaluable in preparing the New York designs. Also the continuity of challenging commissions had given Aalto greater confidence. By 1938 he had assumed the mantle that had been Eliel Saarinen's: he was recognised as being Finland's most interesting architect both at home and abroad. With the Paris Pavilion he had made his mark in Europe; the New York competition presented the opportunity to establish himself in America. The United States represented to Aalto at that time the essence of all that was modern and progressive. He looked favourably upon many American trends and the theme of the 1939 Fair emphasised those aspects of modernity that appealed to him most. Winning this competition was therefore to Aalto the greatest challenge in his career to date.

But from his selection of entry mottoes and the designs themselves the emphasis is decidedly upon a modern Finnish image. In fact, the third prize design, entitled 'USA 39', was the weakest in this respect, being by far the most conventionally functionalist of the three designs. Interestingly, this entry was credited solely to Aino Aalto, and the interior perspective shows a marked debt to the drawings of Le Corbusier. The concept behind 'the squirrel's nest' second prize entry was a literal expression of the motto, with the cinema apparently suspended among the by now familiar vertical poles like a nest in the treetops. In all three designs the cinema and restaurant were combined, with both Aalto's first and second prize entries placing these functions behind the main display wall. The revised winning design separated these elements out, putting the cinema-restaurant opposite the display wall as had been proposed in the third prize submission. This revised form allowed Aalto to move his open vertical volume into the centre of the pavilion on an axis that was almost diagonally across the length of the building.

The arrangement of free form that had characterised the winning design became, as a result, more disciplined. Also, the clear use of the diagonal gave greater apparent length internally. And the relocation of the cinema-restaurant meant that this could be given a more straightforward functional wedge-shape that presents a straight balcony to the central 'court'. This in turn gives greater impact to the gently undulating battened wall that rises the full height of the interior, leaning out over the spectators. The wall leans out for a functional reason, to allow the giant photographs displayed on it to be seen more easily from below. But once again this functionalism is freely interpreted by Aalto, and the result, a sensuous curving wall that leans out almost threateningly as it soars upwards in horizontal bands of increasing projection, is reminiscent of Bernini and Borromini. This is not surprising when we consider that the *function* of Aalto's plan form is to distort the diagonal axis, thus increasing the apparent lateral dimensions, and that this is combined with the technique of splaying the wood wall outwards as it goes up.

In the functionalist canon there is no licence for such spatial manipulation. But we

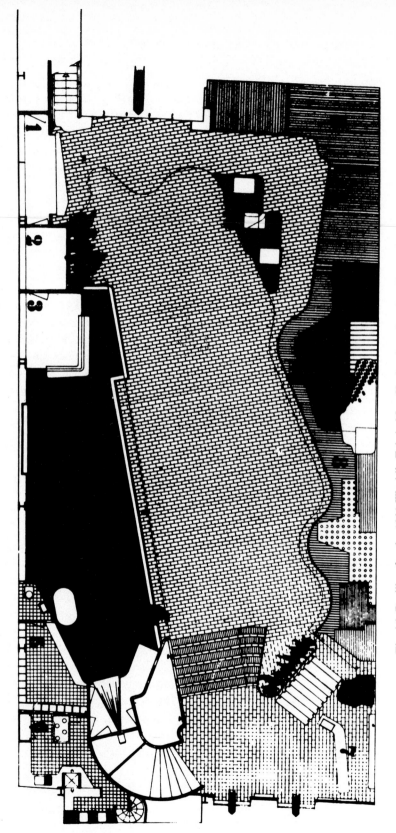

Finnish Pavilion for the 1939 World's Fair in New York: plan, showing diagonal arrangement with serpentine display wall

Interior view, Finnish Pavilion, New York, showing the serpentine display wall

may account for the pulsating and dramatic qualities of the New York Pavilion by reviewing the progress of Aalto's strategies in the Viipuri Library and the Villa Mairea. At Viipuri Aalto modified the Neo-classical *parti* and produced a counter-axial plan; he also introduced the free-form space-modifying ceiling. The Villa Mairea offers the same counter-axiality, but the exterior volume and spaces are substantially modified by the plastic forms that are added to the basic plan format – the *porte-cochère*, the projecting first-floor studio and the swimming pool. In the Villa Mairea these elements are still essentially additions in the National Romantic tradition of agglutination. But in the New York Pavilion the diagonal axis, and the undulating wall with its heightened sense of drama deriving from its threatening angle,[8] are the actual generators of both plan and section.

The mature grasp of volume, scale and movement which Aalto demonstrates in the New York Pavilion was not to be repeated until the Essen Opera House project of twenty years later. Even his organisation of movement through the exhibition, a development of the pattern he used in Paris, to ensure the greatest variety of spatial experiences as one progresses around the one-way system, has Baroque planning origins. This pavilion was truly a 'magic box' from a spatial point of view on the inside, whilst it remained a simple functional box on the outside. The only 'decoration' on the exterior is the addition of vertical wood strips to screen the restaurant window that was made possible when a new site was allocated after the competition. These strips seem to have no other function than to deny the functionalism of the otherwise bare box forms.

CHAPTER V

Urban and Academic Challenges: 1939–48

Nineteen thirty-eight had been a particularly busy year in the Aaltos' office, so much so that Alvar was compelled to forego a visit to the United States in March. Thus, he was denied the pleasure of attending the opening of the first major international retrospective exhibition of his work at the Museum of Modern Art in New York. In fact, the announcement of the competition to design Finland's Pavilion for the 1939 World's Fair in New York was actually made whilst Aalto would have been in America for the exhibition opening, and clearly he was aware that such an announcement was imminent. Aalto was to become involved not only in the World's Fair Pavilion competition but was also appointed as a jury member of an important planning competition for the Kemi district of Finland as well as being commissioned to design a small pavilion for the forestry section of the national agricultural fair held at Lapua. This last commission is of special interest because in the design of the pavilion's undulating external wall Aalto employed his most direct emulation of forest rhythms up to that time.

The irregular, squeezed-in box of the pavilion has a completely *plastic* free form. Its external wall of slender sapling poles, complete with bark, resembles, in its sense of movement induced by the plan form, the quality of a dense forest. Quite unlike the free-standing poles of the Paris Pavilion, this dense enclosing wall synthesizes the forest rhythms of the *porte-cochère*, entrance and stair balustrade of the Villa Mairea into a complete architectural form. The shaping of the bandstand for the Itämeri restaurant, the buffet table of the Savoy restaurant, and the Villa Mairea swimming pool is brought to life.

The Lapua pavilion would have been on Aalto's drawing board at the same time as the New York competition. In both material and form it provides an important link between the domestic experiments with plasticity in the Villa Mairea *porte-cochère* and studio wing and Aalto's bold final solution for the New York pavilion. When we observe that Aalto had employed a similarly bold curvilinear treatment in the wooden acoustic ceiling of his entry for the Helsinki Library competition (1937) it is easy to understand how, in the New York design, he achieved such a perfectly coherent form. Aalto had been preoccupied with plastic forms at least since the Paimio sanatorium and chair (1929–30) and there are references even in 1928 in both the form of the columns in the Turun Sanomat machine hall and proposals for the musicians' dais in the Itameri Restaurant, also in Turku. His entry for the Michael Agricola Church

Forestry Pavilion for the Agricultural Exhibition at Lapua (1938): view of entrance, showing serpentine wall of unstripped pine saplings

competition (1930) further extended this preoccupation, and he had employed the forest image persistently since 1935. His exercises at the Villa Mairea, at Lapua and in the Helsinki University Library extension entry clearly put him in first-class condition to bring off the stunning originality and total competence of the New York World's Fair Pavilion.

The real success of this pavilion building lies in Aalto's achievement for the first time of an architectural quality of which he had little first-hand experience, namely *urbanity*. His commissions for the South-Western Agricultural Cooperative Building, the Turun Sanomat building and the Viipuri Library had hardly given him an adequate canvas of urban scale and complexity. Indeed his first design for the Viipuri Library on the original Aleksanterinkatu site reveals quite clearly this lack of experience in the grouping of urban elements. Even Paimio, probably the most important commission during his first fifteen years of practice, had a woodland setting, while the domestic scale of the Moscow Embassy project entrance façade combined with its somewhat bucolic garden elevation does not suggest confidence in handling the urban motif in a cosmopolitan setting. This leaves only one commission of the 20s and 30s that was sufficiently large and monumental to allow him to escape the constraints of provincial scale; and that, ironically, was his pulp mill complex for Sunila.

We shall see that a consistent expression of urban from remained absent from Aalto's work, even in his latest projects, right up to the very end of his career.[1] But in his handling of the interior of the New York Pavilion he achieved a sense of continuity of form that is absolutely urbane. This confidence with the handling of complex forms was to be carried through into the design of the Baker Dormitory for MIT at Cambridge, Massachusetts (1947–9), where he also successfully combined domestic character with urban scale (see pp. 109–13).

It is interesting to speculate here on how Aalto's work might have developed had he won the Finnish Parliament competition of 1923, based on his own choice of the Helsinki harbour site, and thus begun his career with the problem of measuring up to Engel's command of scale and urbanity. Unfortunately, none of the other problems of urban design which confronted him in the Finnish context were able to offer the challenge of the Helsinki harbour site combined with that major national building and symbol. For this reason we might also ask what may have happened to him had he, after his success with the New York Pavilion, followed Eliel Saarinen in emigrating to America. The laws of probability denied to him the first course whilst war, which affected so many Finnish careers, tipped the balance in the second case.

Aalto's long involvement with America can be traced back to the summer of 1937 when the West Coast architect William Wilson Wurster and the American landscape theorist Richard Church came upon the Aaltos' house in Munkkiniemi and rang the doorbell. Wurster's deep interest in natural materials, particularly wood, created a ready bond between himself and Aalto. The two architects soon struck up a firm friendship, and their correspondence stimulated Aalto's connections with the architectural profession and universities in America. Within little more than a year of this first meeting with Wurster, Alvar and Aino paid their first visit to the United States. This was in October 1938, when they had to sort out on site important questions concerning the construction and detailing of the New York World's Fair Pavilion.

At that time Aalto still spoke little English. American architects were, however, as curious about him as he was about America and he was invited to lecture not only in New York but also at the Cranbrook Academy of Arts, which had been designed by the director of its arts and crafts school, Eliel Saarinen. He gave simple talks, showing slides of his own work, and explaining his ideas and feelings as much by sign language as by words. Wurster also arranged for the Aaltos to be invited to exhibit their furniture and fabrics at the 1939 Golden Gate Exhibition in San Francisco.

Aalto realised that he would have to communicate more effectively if he was to take advantage of a foothold in America and during the winter of 1938–9 he actively prepared himself for his next visit by attempting to improve his English. Thus, when he returned to New York in March 1939, to supervise the final details of construction on the Pavilion, he was able to explain his ideas more clearly. Taking advantage of this new confidence and seeking to gain as much publicity as possible from his presence on American soil he immediately set about promoting the idea of a lecture tour of the United States. Wurster invited him to lecture at Berkeley but, although the Aaltos subsequently went to San Francisco to see their display in the Golden Gate

Exhibition, Aalto did not give any lectures there at the University of California. Before he left for the West Coast, however, he gave several talks at Yale University as a follow-up to the opening of the New York World's Fair. These presentations of his ideas during 1938 and 1939 formed the beginnings of Aalto's new interest in discussing the philosophical basis of his work. These lectures also launched him on a new phase of his international career, that of the visiting professor.

Aalto took advantage of the contacts he made as a result of these lectures to do two things. The uncertain situation in Europe in general and Finland in particular prompted him to look to America as a future base for his professional career. Also, his increasing popularity as a lecturer stimulated in him a return of his earlier interest in establishing himself as a prominent architectural theorist and thinker.

We have already observed[2] how Aalto's philosophy of architecture and design was inclined towards oblique and even whimsical ideas. His architecture may have sometimes been deficient in its urban expression but his wit was always urbane. Also pragmatism and functionalism in Aalto's design equation were inevitably modified by the more elusive element of *feeling*. For Aalto the environment was not only a question of science but also of poetics. Then, in his own terms, he had been concerned both at Paimio and at Viipuri with the social consequences of his design decisions. The sheer functionalism of the sanatorium and the library had been tempered by his interest in people's reactions to his architecture. His concept, formulated in San Francisco in 1939, to form an Institute for Architectural Research was, however, bold and original. It was probably the first attempt to bring scientific research techniques into play in the assessment of architectural performance, although there is little evidence after the Second World War of Aalto's interest in following up this early initiative. In fact, it is abundantly clear from his preoccupations from 1935 onwards that those architectural qualities which were most important to him were precisely those that are most difficult to assess on a rational basis. It is essential to understand in this context, therefore, that Aalto's design coherence did not develop consistently on the basis of any concept of a generally applicable method but rather from a system of highly personal responses to architectural programmes.

The very nature of Aalto's broad and diverse approach to design would not allow him to adopt a simplistic attitude to a hierarchy of practical problems. But it was precisely those specific practical problems that occupied the minds of the majority of his American colleagues in 1939. Aalto's view that much of the technical research and development in progress in America was neither being absorbed nor evaluated by the architectural profession places him a good twenty years ahead of his time. It seems, moreover, that he wanted his proposed Institute to tackle broad philosophical issues confronting the profession; in other words to ask questions rather than find specific solutions.

But it appears that their fundamental pragmatism made it difficult for his American colleagues to grasp the benefits of such a generalised approach. To them there were more immediate problems to be tackled, for example those posed by the competition

I Typical small Finnish country stone church with wooden interior (note use of stripped sapling as a hatstand)

II Tampere cathedral by Lars Sonck (1905): 'Horseman of the Apocalypse', detail of stained-glass
    window on the north wall

III Villa Mairea: exterior detail of sauna (completed 1946)

IV Muuratsalo, 'experimental house': view towards the kitchen/bedroom wing

V 'Experimental house' at Muuratsalo, looking across the courtyard towards the living area

VI Maison Carré (1956–8): view of the garden side from the swimming pool

VII Technical University at Otaniemi: view of main auditorium block (completed 1964)

VIII House of Culture, Helsinki (1955–8): end detail of the roof to the covered way, with brickwork of the main auditorium block beyond

of the speculative developer. Faced by such real threats they must have found Aalto's arguments too abstruse, possibly even smelling of aesthetics in disguise, and concluded that Americans could not afford his level of abstraction. It would seem equally evident that Aalto had misjudged American enthusiasm for his ideas. It was one thing for him to describe what he had done, or his personal architectural intentions, but it was quite another to attempt to convert them to his philosophy of how to put the architectural world to rights. Americans were interested in Aalto as an architect, not as an architectural Messiah.

Aalto returned to Finland from the United States in the summer of 1939. He had devoted nearly five months to his American visit and, compared with what he had managed to achieve between 1935 and his departure for America, he must have regarded those months as rather lacking in success. It was the first time that he had been really lionised. Also, the whole period had been leisurely by Aalto's standards, including the necessary double crossing of the Atlantic by boat. He had experienced some of the strong contrasts in the pattern of American life, from the somewhat frenzied pace of the East Coast to the relaxed informality of California. America must have been seductive to Aalto at forty-one and at the very height of his creative powers and energy. But he had neither succeeded in establishing a professional base in the United States nor in creating an architectural research institute. Yet how could he have achieved either objective satisfactorily on the basis of such a short acquaintance with the New World? The most positive support for his ideas he was able to muster were suggestions that he canvas them with one or two of the wealthy American foundations. But he had little time to reflect on any sense of disappointment or frustration, however, for within a few weeks of his return to Helsinki Russia had invaded Finland and the so-called Winter War between the two countries had broken out.

That war was of rather brief duration. Peace was signed in Moscow on 13 March 1940 and by the end of that month Aalto was back in New York, this time to effect some modifications to the Pavilion before the World's Fair reopened for a second season. Although it was only a short war it had cost Finland heavily in terms of human lives, and property damaged and destroyed, and perhaps more importantly, in emotional terms, following Russia's annexation of the Karelian isthmus. Quite apart from the problems posed by war damage and reconstruction Finland was faced in addition with the difficulty of rehousing half a million Karelian refugees.

As a consequence of that refugee problem and Aalto's experience of the Kemi district planning competition he soon became involved in the planning of Finland's reconstruction strategies. He was appointed as a visiting professor at the Massachusetts Institute of Technology, commencing in the autumn of 1940, and this appointment was with specific reference to his experience with Finland's reconstruction. The Alfred J. Bemis Foundation was responsible for sponsoring his engagement and it reflected the Foundation's bias towards prefabricated, modular, low-cost housing as an integral part of such a reconstruction process. Aalto was the main advocate in Finland, following the Winter War, of the advantages of standardisation in low-cost and temporary housing and pioneered these developments in the Association of Finnish Architects (SAFA) from 1940 onwards.[3] His attitude towards standardisation, a reflection of his industrial experience in designing furniture first with Korhonen and subsequently in collaboration with the Gullichsens, represents an important and frequently overlooked aspect of Aalto's design philosophy. In simple terms, he wanted high-quality straightforward furniture and basic well-planned housing to be within the reach of every Finnish worker.

In fact he was never given the direct opportunity to develop his early housing ideas for Sunila and Kauttua or enable these to make a substantial contribution to the general standard of Finnish housing. There is no doubt, however, that his ideas permeated the profession, particularly through his participation in SAFA standardisation committees during the 40s and 50s. Also, he did produce designs for low-cost, single-storey, single-family wooden houses, examples of which were erected near Helsinki in the early 40s; and these follow some of the ideas he incorporated earlier in his designs for the Ahlström System houses. In addition, Aalto not only planned a factory at Varkaus to produce low-cost houses in 1945 but also designed examples that went into production: yet another Ahlström commission.

It did appear that he might have a chance to demonstrate his housing ideas on a large scale, however, when the HAKA (the Social Democratic building society) competition for 580 apartment units was announced in the late summer of 1940. The advent of this competition and the opportunity it afforded to put his ideas into practice must have been frustrating to Aalto since he had to remain in the United States until after the submission of entries in October. He finally arrived back in Helsinki on 21 November. His entry was unsuccessful, and the competition was won by a new firm consisting of Hugo Harmia and Woldemar Baeckman. His failure to win this important competition should not surprise critics of post-war housing towers, for Aalto's solution consisted of four twelve-storey blocks. Such a design was clearly out of tune with prevailing thought in Finnish housing at that time; also it is a somewhat surprising development in relation to Aalto's housing attitudes of the 30s. But it is interesting from two points of view. First, it once again looks towards European developments, this time of Modern Movement housing in the 30s,[4] which had never found sympathy with Finnish architects during that period; then it introduces a planning motif that was to be of major significance in Aalto's later repertoire. For in his HAKA towers Aalto uses a single-loaded corridor plan for the first time, developing it into a segmental or 'fan' shape. This development was to influence his planning of the Baker Dormitory for MIT and ultimately to be perfected in the housing tower he designed for the Neue Vahr district of Bremen.[5] This fan motif had, of course, already been anticipated in the previous decade, in for example the radial site planning of the Sunila 'village' of 1934 and the plan arrangement of the engineers' apartments at Sunila of 1936 (see pp. 71–3).

Aalto commenced his duties at MIT in the first week of October and was scheduled to reside in Cambridge for three months. But early in November he left for Finland again as the result of increased tensions between Germany and Russia, and his desire to be with his family in Helsinki. Soon after his return home the Finnish President, Kallio, resigned, on 19 December, and Aalto was then caught up in the consequences of the Second World War. Although references have been made to his subsequent involvement at MIT in 1941 it has been established that he was not in fact able to return to the United States until after the end of hostilities.[6]

It is therefore an indication of Aalto's energy that, during the few weeks he spent at MIT during the autumn he initiated a sketch design for an ideal new town based on the needs of Finland's programme of reconstruction. This design was completed by Aalto and his students during his brief stay and again includes two items of interest. These are: (1) perspective drawings of terraced housing that is based on the stepped terraces of apartments designed for Sunila and Kauttua, both dating from 1938; and (2) single-storey, single-family wooden houses, with the roof continued as a porch supported by angled posts, of exactly the same type he was to construct outside Helsinki after his return home.

War broke out on Finland's borders again in June 1941 when Germany invaded Russia. Almost immediately Russia began air attacks on the civilian populations of cities in southern Finland. But the Finns were now better prepared, as a consequence of German advice and aid, and they launched a counter-offensive with the aim of recapturing the Karelian isthmus as their first priority. They achieved this objective during the summer of 1941 and then prepared for a long war. This involved plans not only to protect citizens from future Russian aggression, especially from the air, but also the reconstruction and rehabilitation of Viipuri and the rest of Karelia following their recapture. Industry had to be relocated and expanded, new hospitals built and adequate air-raid shelters provided. And associated with these needs was an overall planning policy to relocate and rehouse the population, a policy that resulted in the design of new towns.

With such pressures upon the Finnish government and people it seems an absurdity that the problem of providing a major public air-raid shelter for the important intersection of Erottaja in Helsinki was made the subject of an architectural competition. This does not say much for the perception of reality in the Finnish capital in May 1941; but it does demonstrate the strong influence that Finnish architects have continued to have on their society since their involvement in helping to shape the nation's image began at the turn of the century. Aalto confirmed his pre-eminence amongst Finnish architects by winning this competition, with the jury that made this award including three of Finland's other leading architects – Erik Bryggman, Hilding Ekelund and Uno Ullberg. It was Aalto's first essay in the mechanics of town planning, since the intersection of Helsinki's three main streets – Mannerheimintie, Bulevardi and Esplanadi – involved a sophisticated traffic engineering solution, with the separation of trams from other vehicles and also the pedestrian access to the underground shelter. In the event Aalto's winning design was not realised, and a more austere subterranean facility was constructed instead by the City.

For the remainder of the war period Aalto's output was limited and consisted mainly of planning and development projects for the government and industry, which he managed to achieve in the brief periods of relative calm. His industrial work during this period was mainly for his friend Harry Gullichsen, beginning in 1941 with the preparation of the master-plan for the Kokemäki River valley. This area of Finland, which surrounds the city of Pori, is one of the country's best agricultural regions; it adjoins the western coast and its fertility derives from the fact that it was formerly under the sea. It also centres on Noormarkku, an operational centre of Ahlström industries, where of course Aalto had already built the Villa Mairea. The problems of the Kokemäki River valley introduced Aalto to the fundamentals of regional planning. Through this first war-time strategic exercise he came to grips with both the theoretical and practical aspects of a mixed agricultural and industrial community. This particular blend of characteristics allowed him to call not only upon his own personal experience of growing up in a rural area but also upon his early professional career in both Jyväskylä and Turku.

The experience of the Kokemäki master-plan in turn gave Aalto a good background for his participation in a limited competition for Oulu. There was only one other competitor, Bertel Strömmer, and the two architects also submitted proposals for a related project, that of the Merikoski power station. Designs had to be submitted in December 1942 and the result was announced in January 1943. Strömmer won the subsidiary project for Merikoski, but this was in reality only an exercise in restyling. Winning the main Oulujoki competition, however, gave Aalto the opportunity to become involved in one of Finland's most interesting planning projects since the country's independence. The development of the Oulujoki valley, especially in the area immediately adjacent to Oulu, was an integral part of the creation of Finland's major concentration of hydro-electric power generation. This scheme, which had its origins in the establishment of the Oulujoki Company in 1941, was eventually completed in 1958.

Aalto was able to build on his experience of the Kokemäki River plan in his approach to the Oulu River project, and his command of town and regional planning, as well as his reputation in this field, emanates from his proposals for the development of Oulu. These involved the use of land on and between a group of islands in the Oulu River in the very heart of Oulu itself. He proposed the creation of zones for residential, recreational and educational development, projecting a plan for the University of Oulu.

Aalto had no formal training in planning techniques but at Oulu and in various industrial development projects for the Gullichsens he gained invaluable experience in the planning field. Nevertheless, his planning exercises, being limited to Finland, were necessarily small in scale and he never really developed an international reputation as a town planner. His emphasis was rather on urban design and even in this area his limited experience of scale and magnitude is all too evident in his later work at Seinäjoki and Rovaniemi. But there is no doubt that his proposals for the Oulu River, and later for another major hydro-electric development and its consequences at Imatra in eastern Finland, were an essential component of Finland's strategic planning towards industrial and economic recovery from the ravages of the Winter War.

In Aalto's submission for the Merikoski power station we can trace a line of design thinking that originated in his entry for the Tampere railway station and culminated in the industrial character he evolved for the Sunila pulp mill. Although this line was subsequently abandoned by Aalto it was faithfully developed by one of his former assistants, Aarne Ervi,[7] when he designed one of the Oulujoki upstream power plants in the mid-50s. Unlike Rewell, Ervi never emerged as a strongly individual designer and whereas he always acknowledged the master's influence in his work he was much too close in age to his former employer to ever have a chance of succeeding him as the leader of the profession in Finland. Instead Ervi concentrated in his later years on planning work. In recognition of this he was invited to the Chair of Town Planning at the Technische Universität in Stuttgart and, although he did not accept this position, ended his career as the chief planner to the City of Helsinki.

Between 1943 and 1945 Aalto initiated two other planning studies which were to provide significant components of his later career. The first of these was the design of a new town for the government-controlled Enso-Gutzeit Company at Säynätsalo, on a wooded island in the lakes immediately south of Jyväskylä. His project for this 'forest town' was similar to his entry for the 1949 competition for the town hall and town centre, which he won and subsequently executed. The original proposal provided for the town hall to be placed on the southern base of a large, triangular open space or 'clearing' which was framed on the other two sides by apartment blocks that are stepped in relation to the open area. In the executed design of 1952 the town hall was moved to the other end of the site to stand on the highest point at the apex of the triangle. The stepping of the parallel blocks of apartments has its origins in Aalto's earliest site-planning concepts and is a variation of the stepped and *fanned* layout of the Sunila village. It remained one of his favourite planning motifs and was avidly followed by his disciple, Aarne Ervi, in the housing layouts, for example in the new town of Tapiola just outside Helsinki. In the realised project for the town hall Aalto made the central courtyard a completely enclosed element, isolated from the external surroundings by its location at first-floor level. The original Säynätsalo project of 1942–4 was thus another watershed of Aalto's career: it was mainly based on earlier concepts of spatial relationships and site layout and it marked the end of Aalto's loose frameworks of spaces other than those he produced for Seinäjoki and Rovaniemi after the war (see pp. 182 and 187).

German withdrawal from Lapland in the autumn of 1944 presented another challenge for Aalto. His proposal for the replanning of Rovaniemi, the capital of this area of Finland, dates from 1945 and depends on a low-density development with

The Enso-Gutzeit village at Säynätsalo: perspective view of the original plan (1942–4), taken from the proposed administrative centre at the base of a triangular space. The arrangement of this space was changed when the centre was built (1950–52), so that it was placed at the apex of a proposed triangular open space

many open spaces for recreational purposes. Although it is often quoted as one of his most successful and authoritative planning exercises it is, in fact, more evidence of his provincial attitudes to town planning. It even includes the distinctly suburban element of detached one-family houses, no longer grouped as were the Helsinki wooden examples but spread out along the lines of the American subdivision pattern, with individual driveways and garages.

The development of the Rovaniemi centre at the end of Aalto's career confirmed this 'loose-weave' of new-town suburbia that had its origins in Saarinen's proposal for the decentralisation of Helsinki and the design of Munkkiniemi (1950). It can be argued that Aalto's desire to humanise was at the root of this loose-fit design. And the image of the suburban house may also have derived from his visit to California before the outbreak of war, when he had seen Frank Lloyd Wright's Hanna House at Palo Alto.[8] But Aalto's work was never to achieve, in the conventional sense, that density and complexity essential to the rhythm of life in a true urban locus.[10] Saarinen had already begun to destroy Finland's urban imagery with his plan for Helsinki, while Aalto's work at both Rovaniemi and Seinäjoki offers, in essence, the 'forest town' without the forest.

Just before the end of the war, in late 1944, Aalto received a commission of less

Sawmill extension for Ahlström Company at Varkaus (1944–5): sculptural forms used to mask an industrial function

seriousness than these strategic planning studies. Once again his clients were the Ahlström Company and the project was an extension to the top of the Varkaus sawmill, the problem being to enclose the incoming log conveyors. This commission gave him an opportunity for free play, a chance to have some small-scale fun after all the responsibility attached to those master-plans. The penthouse structure he evolved has an essential sculptural quality, creating an interesting skyline in the Baroque sense by combining traditional board and batten construction in abstract geometric forms that recall both the Villa Mairea and the New York World's Fair Pavilion. It was an opportunity to combine his awareness of the needs of industrial architecture with that element of playfulness which characterises much of his best work. Also, the Varkaus extension marks another watershed in Aalto's design thinking; it was, after all, a backward-looking gesture; and from 1946 onwards his work begins to map out new terrain.

Britain declared war on Finland in December 1941, although no fighting ever took place between the two countries. This declaration was occasioned by the Japanese attack on Pearl Harbour and the fact that Finland, as an ally of Nazi Germany, was linked with the Axis Powers. Curiously, the United States never actually issued a declaration of war against Finland and throughout the war period Aalto continued his correspondence with Wurster and his good relations with MIT. As a result of these continuing links arrangements were made immediately following the cessation of hostilities for Aalto to return to MIT in the autumn of 1945 as a visiting professor.

He apparently had a much grander idea of his academic role in relation to MIT and the United States Office of Information than either body was prepared to substantiate. It was his proposal to prepare himself for his new appointment by undertaking a tour of war-ravaged Europe at his hosts' expense. Clearly, he still had in mind the unfulfilled terms of reference of his original 1940 appointment with its support of the Bemis Foundation. But MIT no longer seemed to be in a frame of mind receptive to Aalto's exploration of the strategies for post-war reconstruction. MIT's interest was not in Aalto as a theorist or a director of research but as a distinguished practising architect from Europe; what they wanted and expected from him was simply to teach design in the architectural studios.

In any case, after the war Aalto's time in the United States no longer provided for continuous periods of three months. Instead he undertook to make two visits to MIT during the academic year, each of only four to six weeks' duration, and with this pattern of working he became one of the first European visiting professors to commute to American universities in the post-war era. In the circumstances Aalto's ambitions for his American programme were obviously quite unrealistic. This was especially so since, following the war period of 1939–45, he was committed to the development of his career in connection with Finland's struggle to re-establish the image of its national sovereignty.

Finnish independence had once again been threatened by Russia in 1939 and the decision, albeit involuntary, to become the ally of Nazi Germany in 1941 had certainly lost her a lot of Western sympathy. In addition, the Karelian isthmus and other parts of Karelia, totalling more than ten per cent of pre-war Finland and some of its vital transportation arteries in terms of the timber trade, had been successfully claimed by Russia before the end of the war. These valuable lands, together with an enormous amount of financial 'compensation' were, to our lasting shame, awarded to Russia by the Allies as war reparations during the infamous carving up of Europe agreed at the Yalta Conference. In the circumstances, within the limitations of Aalto's commitment to MIT, it was important that his efforts should be concentrated to achieve maximum impact. There was also another significant development early on in his appointment. By the autumn of 1946, only a year after his acceptance of the visiting professorship, Aalto was commissioned to design a new dormitory for senior students at MIT.

From that time onwards he spent less and less time on teaching and devoted most of his six-monthly visits to supervising the planning and construction of the building which was to become known as the Baker Dormitory. In this project Aalto was required by American law to work in association with a local office, and the Boston practice of Perry, Dean and Shaw became his collaborators.

The design of the Baker Dormitory advanced Aalto's development as a designer in a number of significant ways. In the first place it was his largest commission since the Sunila pulp mill of 1934–5. Secondly, it provided Aalto, following the change of site for the Viipuri Library, with his first actual challenge in urban design. Thirdly, it allowed him to further explore in its undulating plan form, his earlier preoccupation with the 'fan' motif. Then, it introduced him to the possibilities of brick expression, a characteristic that was to be so important in his architecture of the 50s and 60s.

The Sunila mill was, of course, also an exercise in brick expression but in that complex Aalto was merely adhering, as we have noted, to the European tradition, largely of nineteenth-century origin, of using brick for industrial buildings such as warehouses, factories and breweries. But in his use of this material on the Baker Dormitory, Aalto followed more closely the examples offered by red-brick buildings conceived during the previous half century for the campuses of Harvard, Yale, Princeton and Pennsylvania universities, members of the so-called Ivy League of American colleges. This Ivy League element is of some significance since the appellation derives from the image presented by the ivy-clad brickwork on those campuses. We have already noted Aalto's earlier interest in the use of vines and creepers to promote the breaking down of the boundaries between buildings and landscape. In this context it is easy to see that the ivy image had a strong appeal to him. Both the fourth and final stages of the Baker Dormitory design show, in the perspective sketches, how trellises and vines were incorporated into the façade facing the Charles River to soften further the effect of the seven-storey curvilinear wall from the river-front.

Another influence that almost certainly came to bear on his use of brickwork in the Baker Dormitory probably derives from his earlier interest in the brick buildings by Dutch architects he saw on his visit to Hilversum in 1928. This earlier stimulus, and indeed the whole Baltic tradition of brickwork, would almost certainly have been revived in Aalto's mind as a result of his visit to Wright at Spring Green, Wisconsin, during the Christmas vacation of 1945. For what would have been more natural than for Aalto to look up Wright's work in publications in advance of that visit and, in so doing, to come upon the Robie House in Chicago and the Larkin Building in Buffalo amongst the American architect's brick buildings.

The size of the commission was of great significance to Aalto, as was its location on the north bank of the Charles River, facing that important Cambridge thoroughfare, Memorial Drive. From the outset, Aalto responded to this site in his characteristic way, grouping the accommodation into a number of stepped pavilions that echoed the path of the river even in his earliest sketches. As the design developed he converted the rectilinear geometry of those early drawings, which still conformed to the site planning of adjoining sites with its parallel blocks of buildings, into a more free and appropriate interpretation of the site in relation to the Charles River. Thus, he created a serpentine wall that faces onto the river, reflecting its path. This he did by changing the angle at which his building composed itself upon the site, going against the regular rectangularity of the adjoining buildings and their layout, so that his serpentine form,

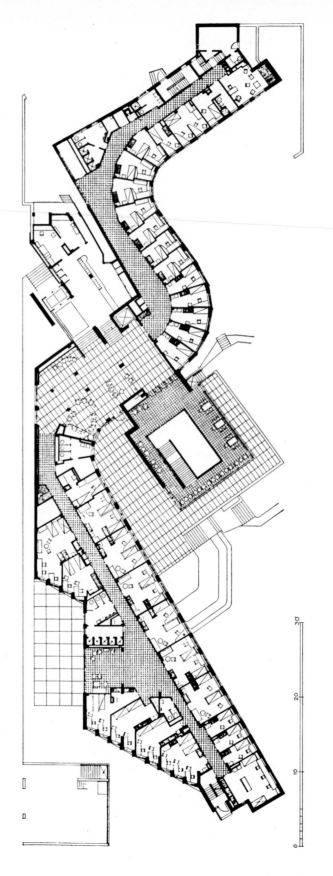

The Baker Dormitory, Massachusetts Institute of Technology, Cambridge, Massachusetts (1946–7): plan, showing most student bedrooms facing onto the Charles River, with the cafeteria on the river side

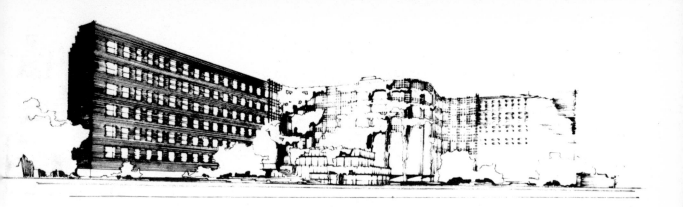

The Baker Dormitory: perspective view from the Charles River, showing the serpentine block with the cafeteria in the foreground

although contained within a parallel grid of its own, was shifted to allow the outline of the plan to follow the course of the river.

But this curvilinear treatment of the plan was only partly in response to the nature of the site; it also, of course, echoed the curvilinear form he had already employed in the New York World's Fair design of 1938–9. In doing so it reflected as well Aalto's sense of the basic functionality of the plan. For, by curving the plan and 'fanning' the arrangement of the students' rooms, the occupants of the study-bedrooms were given a wide variety of views across the river frontage. Even the boldly expressive, cantilevered staircases on the rear, north wall, with their seemingly Mannerist inspiration, were considered by Aalto to be part of this functionalism in direct response to the Fire Marshal's ordinances.[11]

In fact the cantilevered form of these staircases serves a double *function*. Since they descend from the east and west in a downward arrow shape they point directly to the main entrance of the dormitory, an indication that is clearly visible from Memorial Drive and the main buildings on campus. Thus, the *function* of this element was used by Aalto to serve as *expressive* of another, a device which was to become typical of his double standard in approaching a building's functional performance. By making the subsidiary element of the staircases into a main design feature Aalto emphasises the importance of vertical circulation in dormitory design. This importance was further emphasised by his radical treatment of the fenestration within this staircase element. Of course this treatment can be traced to Aalto's functionalist approach, in that the windows are stepped to follow the line of the stairs. But the actual organisation of the sash elements and the triangular fixed casements that make up the staircase fenestration is highly irrational in the irregularities and inconsistencies it develops. These anomalies are particularly noticeable from the inside as one ascends the stairs. However strongly one is struck by the radical design of the north elevation, especially in the treatment of the staircase, one is nevertheless reminded in using the stairs of the possible sources of this design. The long straight flights, for example, recall the office stairway in the Turun Sanomat building, whilst the window detailing is highly reminiscent of sash details that occur on the summer verandahs of Eastern European villas, particularly along the Baltic coastline.

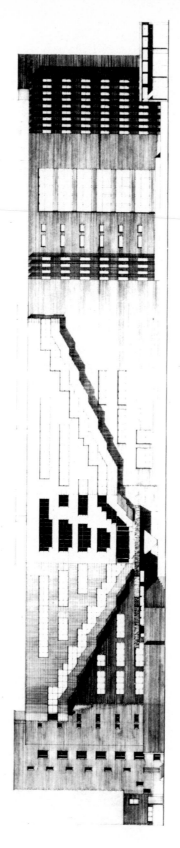

Elevation of the Baker Dormitory from Massachusetts Avenue, showing the cantilevered fire-escape stairs

To many the Baker Dormitory remains as an American anomaly in Aalto's *oeuvre*; but in its bold use of apparently conflicting geometries and an equally confident handling of the fenestration, both towards the river and Memorial Drive, it clearly outlines the programme for Aalto's direction in the next two decades. Also, in the way in which the cafeteria is placed to nestle into the corner curve on the river front, with its overhead, external artificial light fittings, it takes Aalto's interest in the top-lighting of the principal internal function a stage further.

It is difficult to imagine how he would have tackled the design of his Helsinki brick buildings of the 50s without the experience he gained at MIT. By accepting an invitation to teach there he put himself in line for the important Baker Dormitory commission, and with that design Aalto's urban architecture began to realise its mature expression.

CHAPTER VI

The Mature Expression: 1948–66

The Baker Dormitory was under construction by October 1948 when Aalto arrived back at MIT, but he was not able to stay on for the autumn semester to make final decisions about the remaining items of detailing and materials. A cable, informing him of Aino's illness with cancer, summoned him home to Helsinki again in mid-November. He remained with her in Helsinki until her death in January 1949. In October 1950, after the completion of the dormitory, he returned to MIT as a visiting critic for a few weeks only, finally resigning four months later. He left his mark on America not as a teacher and research professor, as had been his original intention, but with a forcefully expressive piece of architecture. Indeed his return to MIT in the autumn of 1950 seems to have served little other purpose than allow him to make a final inspection of the completed building. MIT must have realised that they had got the best value out of their visiting professor in the Baker Dormitory. Also, by 1950, Aalto was too busy for continuation of an overseas teaching commitment.

This intensive activity really began in the closing years of the war with the Rovaniemi master-plan and the Varkaus sawmill extension, both of 1944–5. There were a number of industrial projects dating from this period and the years immediately following the war. These include a machine shop for Ahlström at Karhula (1944–5), and a meter factory and housing estate for the Strömberg Company at Vaasa (1944–7), as well as the house and sauna for the chief engineer at Kauttua (1945) and a one-family housing development at Varkaus (1945–6), both for Ahlström. Following the opening of an Artek factory to produce Aalto's furniture at Hedemora in Sweden, he designed an adjacent exhibition pavilion, in 1945. This, derivative of the Villa Maired, the Lapua pavilion and the New York World's Fair building, was a minor masterpiece of Aalto's 'autonomous architecture'. It combined a tough timber exterior with an elegant bridge on a steeply sloping site.

Nineteen forty-six was a particularly busy year; for not only was Aalto involved in the Baker Dormitory design for MIT, but he entered three separate but linked competitions with the Swedish architect Albin Stark. These were for the new Swedish town of Nynäshamn and comprised: (1) the master-plan, (2) the town hall, and (3) a housing development of seven-storey apartment blocks knowns as 'Heimdal'. He was not successful in any of these competitions, and that for the town hall, entered under the motto 'Song of the Pines', is quite undistinguished. In 1946 he also completed the Villa Mairea, by the addition of the sauna that was left unbuilt at the outbreak of war, and designed a one-family house for a site in Pihlava which was also unremarkable.

Nineteen forty-seven saw him involved in the preparation of another regional plan, this time for the area around the city of Imatra on Finland's new eastern border with Russia, a project that was to continue to demand his attention until 1953. Also in 1947 he added a laundry and sauna to the Strömberg meter factory at Vaasa and was commissioned to design a research institute for the Johnson Company at Avesta in Sweden. This project did not come to fruition and I have been unable to trace the drawings in the Aalto office.

Nineteen forty-eight was an important year in Aalto's career in the first place because it saw him getting his first major commission in the Finnish capital, that for the headquarters building of the Institute of Engineers. In addition, he participated during that year in two major Helsinki competitions, both of which were undertaken with the assistance of his wife Aino. These two competition entries constitute their last collaborative works. Aino was not to see the development and completion of these projects, which by their size, scope and importance were to ensure the security of Aalto's Helsinki office and therefore confirm him in his resolve to give up American aspirations.

The first of these competitions was to provide the headquarters for the National Pensions Institute (or Bank). This project was both by size and social significance of major importance in Finland's programme of reconstruction and new building and it attracted a large field of entrants, forty-two in all. In this competition proposals were originally asked for on a site located on the west side of the Mannerheimintie, opposite Töölö Bay on raised ground, immediately to the north of Saarinen's National Museum, where the Intercontinental and Hesperia hotels are now located with the Helsinki air terminal. The jury included Professor Aulis Blomstedt, the teacher who was to have such a strong influence on the post-Aalto generation of Finnish architects, and Yrjö Lindegren.[1] Aalto won first prize with his main project, the motto for which was 'Forum Redivivum', while his former assistants Viljo Rewell, Heikki Siren and Aarne Ervi also shared in the awards.

This original site was entirely bordered by streets and essentially triangular in shape but blunted at its southern end. The main frontage was to the Mannerheimintie itself and Aalto's main entry reflected this alignment, presenting two principal elements to this major thoroughfare. At the southern end of the site was a thirteen-storey slab office block, with four storeys of offices around an internal, top-lit court at the northern end. These two elements were located on a podium of more than one storey, which formed an open courtyard between them. This raised courtyard was reached from the Mannerheimintie by two flights of steps – a monumental one ran parallel to the street up to the lower block, while the subsidiary one gave direct access to the tower. It was Aalto's first use of the monumental external staircase since the second Viipuri Library design of 1930; but whereas the Viipuri proposal was for an unbroken flight, the 'Forum Redivivum' design of 1948 reflects the Baker Dormitory fire-stair motif by the introduction of major landings. The podium was used in this design in the mode of the classical *parti* as the circulation link between the office elements. Unlike the use of the podium in Asplund's Stockholm Civic Library, however, Aalto used the 'bridge' of the podium between the staircases as the principal entrance to the complex, thus advancing an anti-classical thesis by reducing the dominance and significance of the main entry. This treatment of the main staircase and main entrance was retained in Aalto's final built design on the revised siting farther north along the Mannerheimintie.

With his entries for the Paris (1936) and New York (1938) World Fair pavilion competitions Aalto had established a pattern of hedging his bets with alternative designs. He continued this practice by submitting a 'Forum Redivivum B' entry. This alternative proposal embraced an additional plot of land to the south which allowed Aalto, by bridging the intervening street, to re-align his elements in relation to the Mannerheimintie, creating in the process his characteristic split-axis or fan-plan motif. By lowering the accommodation to be built upon the podium at the southern end of the site and opening up the space between this and the tower, he achieved a wedge-shaped deck at first-floor level which opened out towards the lower, top-lit element at the northern end of the site.

Aalto's main idea in both entries was to conceive the building not as one entity but as a *reconstruction* of the urban environment in relation to the functions of the architectural programme. His 'concept' therefore is not of a single building but a number of separate buildings that are linked together by a podium. This podium serves literally as a 'base' building, a single-storey structure that is perforated by courtyards around which the internal circulation within the site is accommodated. The 'Forum Redivivum' designs thus provide an important key to Aalto's post-war architecture. In them we see his technique of eroding forms and masses, which we have already observed in his own Munkkiniemi house (1936) and the Villa Mairea (1938), combined with a new interpretation of his earlier use of the Neo-classical *parti* in the Viipuri Library Stage II design (1930). These 'Forum Redivivum' competition entries, particularly 'B', also return to an even earlier preoccupation, that of the organisation of Italian piazzas as evidenced by his Parliament Building competition entry (1923–4) and that for the Viinikka church competition (1927). In this approach he was following precedents he had established early in his career, with the entries to the second stage of the Parliament competition (1924) and the Töölö Church competition (1927), where a number of separate buildings are grouped around a piazza. A variation of this urban aggregation is to be found in the Paris World Fair Pavilion (1936–7) and the Tallin Art Museum project (1937), where the grouping is compacted so that the courtyard replaces the piazza. And we shall see that the Säynätsalo town hall (completed 1952) was to become the ultimate expression of this urban intention. In the 'B' solution, for which he was awarded the first prize, he not only shifts the axis of the piazza adjacent to the Mannerheimintie but also creates a further *piazzetta* in the north-west corner of the site enclosed by the public concert hall (dropped from the final building programme) to the south, with an apartment block along the northern edge and returning partway on the east flank. The disjointed, almost casual relationship of these two spaces recalls the non-alignment of many Italian piazzas.

National Pensions Institute (Bank), Helsinki: perspective view of the interior court at upper level (original competition drawing, 1948)

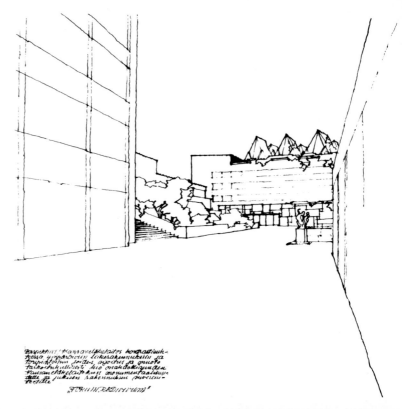

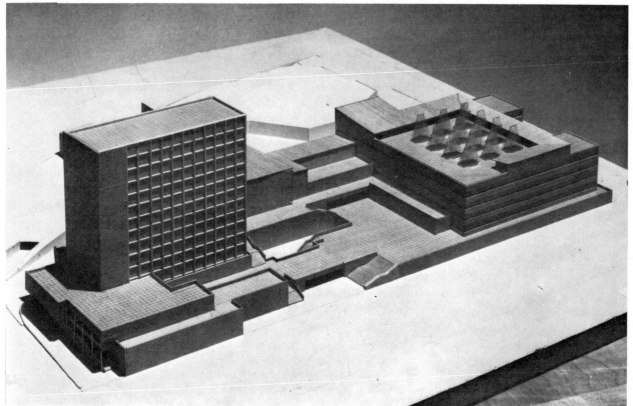

National Pensions Institute, Helsinki: model for the first site, showing upper-level piazza treatment (refinement of original competition design)

These entries for the National Pensions Institute competition enabled Aalto to work out a strategy of his larger-scale post-war buildings. As we have observed, it was in his design for the Baker Dormitory that he began to grapple with the problems of urban scale and complexity. It was also at MIT that he first used red brick as an external finish on an urban building, and it is his red-brick buildings that form the core of his important post-war work. The guidelines he established for the organisation of urban sites with the 'Forum Redivivum' entries provide the yardstick by which his subsequent exercises succeed or fail. His understanding of the essential complexity and variety that make up urban space and form, creating in the process that elusive sense of urbanity, is nowhere more apparent than in the 'Forum Redivivum B' design. He was able to retain much of its original quality, and even add others, in the executed design on the larger, more northerly site; but the building as realised is very different in form and profile if not in essence.

The site for the National Pensions Institute was changed to provide for the increased office accommodation that was to be generated by this new bureaucratic function of the Finnish state. At the same time it was decided to concentrate solely on this administrative function and not to confuse the state's programme of social benefits with its cultural ones; the concert hall was therefore omitted. The new site is some thirty metres from the Mannerheimintie, and is more trapezoidal in form. It was infinitely more difficult to plan, as its triangular wedge form pointing towards Mannerheimintie with its base backing onto the linear axis of a park behind, offered a long rear (minor) elevation, considerable exposure to the sloping side streets and almost none to Mannerheimintie itself. Although Aalto's site plan shows its location as the arrowhead of a spinal development to the west (rear) the change of levels along this axis cancels out any such effect. Certainly the site is an extension of the Mannerheimintie set back. But it is important to realise that once this principal artery reaches the north shore of Töölö Bay and the National Exhibition and Olympic Stadium, it ceases to be a truly urban thoroughfare, as it suffers the impact of residential suburbia albeit in large apartment-block form.

Aalto's solution to the new site was to retain the two linked courts but to reduce the overall scale by eliminating the tower form in favour of a cranked 'L' shape of office accommodation. This accommodation is then wrapped around the two (one square and one rectangular) courts, with the single-storey cafeteria block given the pivotal corner position in place of the dominance allotted to the concert hall in 'Forum Redivivum B'. The executed building is thus much more compact. Without the dominant axis offered by following the line of the Mannerheimintie (or setting against it as in scheme 'B') in the competition designs, the realised scheme has less interaction between the external environment and the interior of the site. Also, of course, the external environment, the view of Töölö Bay no longer available, is not of a quality that admits to interaction. Aalto therefore excluded it and concentrated on the internal environment, which takes on the form less of a public *piazzetta* and more of a private garden in the sense of London's Bloomsbury and Pimlico squares.[2]

National Pensions Institute, Helsinki (1952–6): model of revised design for final site, in which the rooflight element has been reduced and the piazza extended (although now more as a continuation of an adjacent garden layout)

The change of arrangement for the office accommodation also reduced the significance of the internal court, which became the heart of the Institute as it serves to house the interview cubicles of the case-workers where individual problems may be discussed in private. But the whole emphasis on the court/piazza system is sacrificed for a lower-key, more homogenous scheme. In other words, with its transfer to the final site 'Forum Redivivum B' became domesticated. This is not to suggest that the building lacks variety and complexity, however. From the exterior the main item missing is the tower, with the panelled curtain wall expression that was indicated on the original model being reserved for later Aalto buildings. The National Pensions Institute remains as one of Aalto's most successful buildings, and is certainly his most original solution to the problem of both site planning and expression in the urban context.

This originality is manifested in the treatment of the difficult junction of the

Helsinki, National Pensions Institute: pensioner waiting at the main entrance for the building to open

building with its set-back connection to Mannerheimintie. Aalto's solution was to step the façade, giving importance to the massing, with its horizontal bands of windows, whilst the entrance is de-emphasised as it was in the concept for the original site. Since the staircase to the left of this entrance gives access only to the courtyard at first-floor level the main entrance can be seen as having remained within the podium, and this fact is emphasised by the oversailing of the upper four storeys above the entrance. As though to give the lie to the uniformity of the office 'wrap around', Aalto introduces a unique detail at the internal corners all round the building, both on the street and the courtyard sides. This involved a 'slipping', up or down, of the copper band that serves as a string course or head mould along the tops of the window bands. The effect is curious, even alarming, because what at first sight appears to be a uniform horizontal banding of the fenestration is in fact thrown out of true at these internal junctions. Yet there is a certain logic in this 'overlapping' of the fascia strip, partly because it indicates a slotting in of these 'trays' of offices, but more because it derives from the corners of rough-hewn log structures. In other words it could be seen as what we might refer to as Aalto's 'Middle Finland' or 'Jyväskylä' syndrome.

Coupled with this *slipping* or *slotting* in detail of the internal angles is the treatment of the external angles, where the whole depth of the window on the front is returned to announce its presence on the side in the form of a copper profile. The head of this profile is above the string course that runs into it on the return deviation, thus reflecting the disjunctive condition of the internal angles. As we have seen, it was common for Aalto to carry parts of a vocabulary from one building to another; but this treatment of the internal and external angles on the upper floors of the National Pensions Institute is without precedent in his work and he did not use it subsequently.

Four years elapsed from the competition result at the end of 1948 and the commencement of construction, and the National Pensions Institute took another four years to complete. The competition for the design of the new Technical University at Otaniemi, a wooded area just outside Helsinki, was announced whilst Aalto was at MIT, in November 1948. When he returned to Helsinki to be with Aino during her terminal illness he worked on the Otaniemi competition, involving her as much as possible in discussions of the design, which was submitted in their joint names. The award of first prize, in April 1949, three months after her death, was made to both Alvar and Aino Aalto.

The competition was for the master-plan of the Otaniemi campus and the design of its central teaching complex. Although the layout reflects the more open woodland site of Otaniemi, Aalto's design of the central administrative teaching facilities comes closest of all his projects to the concept he developed for the National Pensions Institute. This transference of an urban imagery to a truly suburban site is achieved by the creation of an 'acropolis', a concentration of buildings conceived as strips but organised round courtyards that are grouped around the high point of the site. In the original competition submission the main auditorium block was used as the fulcrum of the layout, with a formal forecourt or piazza held between the stepped, parallel blocks of the different institutes (around their courts) and the formal entrance through a *piazzetta*, which was flanked by the two parallel buildings of the library and administration, both set at a sharp angle to the axis of the teaching elements.

Thus the scheme had the formality of the Pensions Institute in its arrangement around a piazza, but also its own informality of the subsidiary areas in the overall organisation about this central, focal space, for which the stepped arrangement of the institutes formed a backdrop. The plan form of the main auditorium itself was originally given a wedge shape and, interestingly, its elevation as revealed in the competition drawings anticipated the profile of the council chamber tower of Säynätsalo town hall, the competition for which also dates from 1949 (see pp. 129–32).

Both of these focal elements were substantially modified in the final design, with the emphasis on the one being exchanged for that on the other. This revised design, which dates from 1955, reduced the piazza element to a number of insignificant pedestrian areas, with the terracing of the natural landscaping taking over from the original large public space. At the same time Aalto brought the main auditorium out from its previous position behind the linear blocks of the institutes and transformed its simple wedge plan into a quadrant form. This auditorium element now dominates the entire composition because it is not only a quadrant in plan but resembles in section and volume half of the seating arrangement of a Greek amphitheatre, the form of which was familiar to Aalto from his visits to Delphi and Epidauros as recorded in his sketchbooks.[3] In its total form of raked lecture theatres within and partial amphitheatre without – complete with a small stage sunk into the pedestrian area – it represents the culmination of Aalto's experiments with lecture auditoria, which began, a quarter of a century earlier, with his lecture theatres in the competition project for Zagreb Hospital (1930).

This final design for the teaching and administration centre was built between 1961–4 and its use of red brickwork with copper facing details links it in expression with the National Pensions Institute, which was built a decade earlier, i.e. 1952–4. The emphasis on the more plastic shape of the auditorium reflects also Aalto's preoccupations in two designs of the late 50s – the church at Vuoksenniska, Imatra (designed in 1956 and built between 1957 and 1959: see pp. 200–201), and the so-called House of Culture, the headquarters of the Finnish Communist Party (commissioned in 1955 and completed in 1958: see pp. 174–5) – as does the brickwork detailing, particularly of the curious, ventilator-like ribbed and slotted windows, reminiscent of mediaeval detailing, that relieve the monotony of large expanses of brickwork.

The only institute in this complex which does not conform to the red-brick aesthetic is, perhaps not surprisingly, the School of Architecture. This was the last part of the scheme to be built and reflects Aalto's preoccupation with a new material, white Carrara marble. His involvement with this Italian marble began with its introduction into the entrance of the church for Seinäjoki (1956–60) and gained momentum when he used it exclusively for the cladding of the Enso-Gutzeit 'palace', designed in 1959 and built between 1960 and 1962 (see pp. 161–4); this use of marble cladding was illogical in Finland's severe climate, especially since the material he used for this purpose was only approximately twenty millimetres in thickness.

It was fortunate that, following Aino's death in the January, 1949 proved to be a busy and productive year for Aalto. In addition to entering the Otaniemi competition

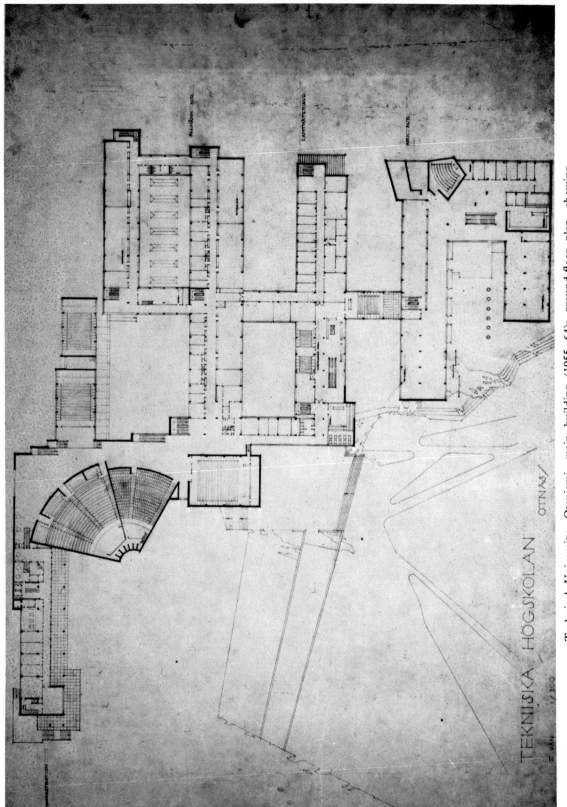

Technical University, Otaniemi, main building (1955–64); ground-floor plan, showing auditorium complex, with courtyard grouping of various institutes (School of Architecture, bottom)

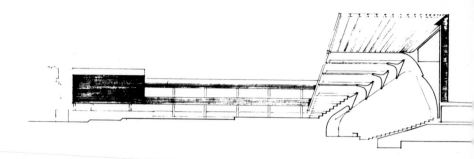

TEKNILLINEN KORKEAKOULU
OTANIEMI /

LEIKKAUS   1/200

Otaniemi Technical University: section of main building showing lecture theatre amphitheatre

Technical University, Otaniemi: exterior view of main building, showing the lecture theatre/
amphitheatre complex

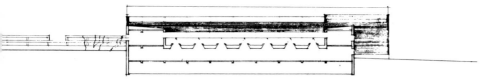

10/8 1/40 ALVAR AALTO, ARKKIT

treatment, the ultimate statement of the section initiated in the Zagreb Hospital project

Interior of main lecture theatre in main building of Otaniemi Technical University

Otaniemi, main university building: detail of brickwork and light fitting

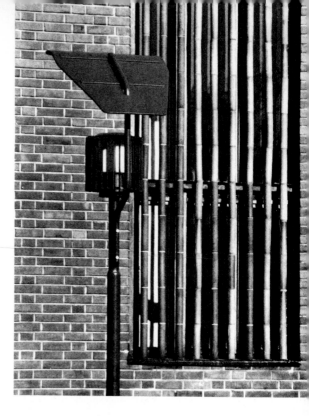

Otaniemi, Sports Hall: interior of athletics hall, showing wide-span wooden trusses. In this design Aalto established the structural expressionism of timber forms that was to influence Pietilä, for example in his design of the Brussels World's Fair Pavilion

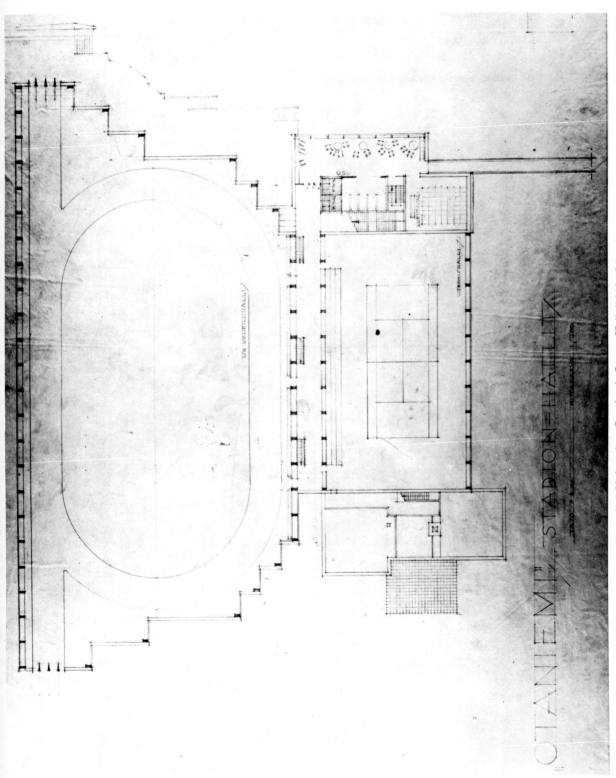

Technical University, Otaniemi, Sports Hall (1949–54): plan

he made submissions for two others. The first of these was the so-called 'Sea Harbour Facilities Competition', to provide a passenger terminal for those arriving in Helsinki by sea; Säynätsalo town hall was the other. Aalto's entry for the sea passenger terminal was undistinguished and he received no mention in the awards. His opportunity to build on the sea front was not to come until a decade later, when he designed the headquarters for Enso-Gutzeit on the site he had originally proposed for the Finnish Parliament House. We know that he already had a special interest in the Säynätsalo town hall, having already prepared a village plan for this community at the invitation of Enso-Gutzeit during the war (1942–4).

Aalto's design for the Baltic passenger terminal was thoughtfully given the motto 'Entrez en Paradis'. It contrasted strongly with his design philosophy as developed from the Villa Mairea, through the New York World's Fair Pavilion and the Baker Dormitory and emerging in the confident statements for the National Pensions Institute and the Otaniemi Technical University, a line with strong romantic, historicist and antirationalist characteristics. Instead it repeated his earlier rationalist canon of the late 20s and early 30s but more particularly reiterated the structural expressionism which originated in the machine hall of the Turun Sanomat building, was echoed in the cantilevered balconies of Paimio and came to a climax, at least in terms of elevational treatment, with the design for the state alcohol monopoly ALKO (competition project 1935). This 'structural expressionism' had none of the flamboyance of Turun Sanomat or Paimio, however, and offered a low-key, and for Aalto virtually anonymous, solution which failed to attract the attention of the jury. Ironically, an equally low-key and undistinguished building by Hytönen and Luukkonen won the competition and was built. Aalto was thus cheated of the prospect of having buildings on opposite sides of the harbour approach. There is little doubt that his harsh massing with somewhat crude post and beam expression, relying heavily on a terraced garden as the softening agent, would have been modified had he won.

'Entrez en Paradis' is frankly an unimaginative design and probably reflects the fact that Aalto simply had too much on his plate in 1949, especially now that Aino was no longer there to support him. But the pressure was to increase rather than lessen, for he was to become involved in two further competitions that year. The Imatra plan, commenced in 1947, continued to occupy his attention and would do so until 1953; he also designed and built a warehouse for the Ahlström factory at Karhula; and he was involved in a housing project for Tampere. In addition, as a consequence of winning the Otaniemi Centre competition he was commissioned that year to design the University Sports Stadium (see pp. 123–7). But more importantly it seems, because the two competitions more or less coincided, he put his main creative effort into the Säynätsalo project. For this competition provided him with an opportunity that was to prove unique in his career and he must have realised it. Säynätsalo offered the programme of an administrative building, a social focus and a cultural symbol all wrapped in one; and furthermore it was in miniature.

The challenge at Säynätsalo was to create a building for the inhabitants of this forest village that was, to them at least, of comparable significance to that of the Pensions Institute or the Technical University. For Aalto this challenge must have held several attractions. It would provide an opportunity of scaling down his new urban imagery to the context of this forest village. At the same time it was his first opportunity since the Kauttua housing (1937–9) of relating his work so directly to nature. Such a context clearly held the key to significant shifts in his architectural expression. Aalto was also very familiar with the site from his village plan studies. These factors must have combined in his determination to win the competition and produce a masterpiece of architecture. He succeeded in doing both. The unexpected bonus of the Säynätsalo design was that it brought him into close contact with a young architect in his office, the striking Elissa Mäkiniemi, who was to become his second wife in 1952.

They spent their honeymoon in Sicily, touring; and they would have visited the Roman site of the Piazza Armerina and seen some of the finest mosaics in the West, as well as Morgantina, the only known example of a polygonal Greek agora, which would have been of considerable interest to Aalto.

It is important to understand that Säynätsalo is a rather rugged island in Lake Paijänne. At the time of the competition for the town hall it had a population of about three thousand, all supported by the company industry of Enso-Gutzeit. Appropriately, the town hall is a small building, with a total volume of little more than 380,000 cubic feet which includes the accommodation for the local government

Säynätsalo: view into the upper level courtyard of village centre from beneath the pergola at the head of the formal staircase

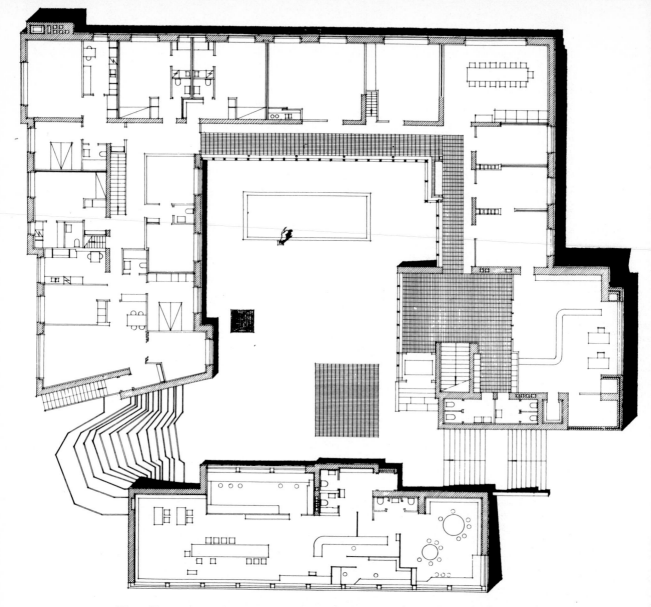

The village centre, Säynätsalo (1950–52): plan at the entrance (upper) level, showing the formal approach staircase leading into the courtyard, with the administrative accommodation grouped in a "U" around three sides of the court and the library arranged along its base

offices, and the Council Chamber, the community library, some staff flats and some shops which, at a later stage, were intended to become additional offices for the municipality. The provision of a municipal building for such a small community emphasises, of course, the economic importance of Säynätsalo. This importance, out of all proportion to its mere size and population, conjures up images of mediaeval precursors in the field of urban design, and examples like Dinkelsbühl and Montpaizier and King's Lynn. The responsibility for designing this small building was also disproportionate to its volume.

Säynätsalo village centre: exterior view of library block (left) and Council Chamber (right) framing the formal staircase to the courtyard

Aalto's solution was for an essentially two-storey building which was set into the ground at the head of a triangular open space flanked on its long sides by housing in blocks angled towards the streets. This of course exactly reversed his layout in the master-plan of 1942–4, where the town hall was at the base of that triangle. Also, the building, being set into the sloping site, presents its dominant mass culminating in the second-floor corridor which is expressed running around the council chamber tower that rises above it against a background of the forest. The ground floor of the façade facing the open space is devoted to shops, with a formal granite staircase giving access to a courtyard at first-floor level. This courtyard is semi-formal and almost domestic in scale, containing a pool and fountain, and a small paved area, within a garden setting. It is approached under a pergola that bridges the space between the entrance to the council offices and that of the library (running over shops) at the head of the formal staircase.

We climb this staircase from the unpaved street below. Stepping onto the first tread already removes us from the casual world of the forest village. And as we proceed up the first flight the quiet dignity of another, more ordered ethos becomes quickly apparent. Already at the first landing we have become drawn in between the flanking

Exterior view of Säynätsalo village centre: the boarded earth "steps" with the courtyard, and the Council Chamber beyond

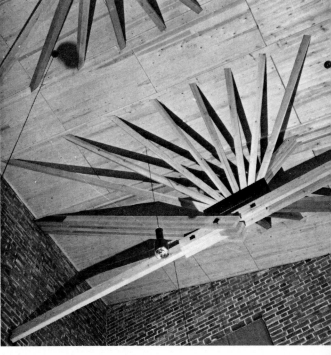

The village centre, Säynätsalo; two interior views: the brick staircase leading up from the entrance hall to the Council Chamber, and the fan-shaped three-dimensional timber trusses supporting the Council Chamber roof

Aalto's studio at Munkkiniemi (1955): plan, showing relationship of the general drawing-office, with Aalto's own studio (curved wall) looking into the garden court with its amphitheatre treatment

walls of an entrance of imposing but not forbidding consequence. The second flight, although in fact longer, seems shorter as we are invited into the intimate enclosure of the pergola portico. Once under its shelter we are confronted not by a grand doorway but by the small garden landscape of the courtyard. This is not at all a piazza but, as at the Villa Mairea, an open-air extension of the internal functions of the town hall.

The modest entry to the administrative portion of the building is to the right, whence we are led by the pergola. Even more modestly the library entrance is tucked unobtrusively into the left-hand corner. Once inside the entrance hall, with its low ceiling and warm brick floor, we feel as at home as in any domestic interior. Straight ahead is a plain brick wall, broken by the opening that gives access to the circulation corridor for the offices. The glazed wall to our left faces north and looks out through a 'trellis' of vines onto the grass of the garden court. Ahead, through the narrow opening, we can see the reflected sunlight from the corridor running back along the east end of the court. To our right is the glazed entrance to the enquiry office, whilst tucked behind us and the entrance is the main staircase.

This stairway is another version of the form developed by Aalto in the South-Western Agricultural Cooperative Theatre at Turku of 1928: we are enclosed in a 'tube' that carries us, supported by a simple pine handrail, to the Council Chamber, in two gentle flights. Both the staircase and the upper gallery passage are sparingly top-lit by a strip clerestory window that runs around the top of the second floor just beneath the slightly overhanging eaves. The square Council Chamber is a contrast of subdued elegance in the seating and a large, wooden-louvred west window which, like the staircase, is reminiscent of mediaeval examples. Two fan-strutted pine roof trusses support the pine-boarded ceiling of the monopitch roof above. Whilst clearly modern and idiosyncratically Aaltoan in form, these trusses and the roof they support beyond recall great barns, an entirely appropriate 'umbrella' for this assembly of councillors drawn from farming stock.

The natural temptation is to connect this courtyard plan with classical precedents;[4] but there is obviously nothing classical about the disposition of elements around this informal open space. The access to and egress from this court are in the south-west and north-west corners respectively; but they are not linked by any route. Otherwise the form of the courtyard recalls rather an Italian piazza in miniature, with the pergola and entrance lobby roof cutting into the south-west corner of the rectilinear space, whilst the back wall of the library advances in an irregular profile from the south and, finally, there is an irrational jutting into the north-west corner of a room of the caretaker's flat. The 'landscaped' steps, consisting of sods of earth held in place by stout planks driven into the contours, that lead down in the north-west corner, also suggest an Italian model. But this courtyard feature is not, after all, a pedestrian space; rather it is a landscape element that negotiates the gap between the formality of the entrance and the surrounding forest terrain; it is an internal visual link between architecture and Nature.

The predominant impressions of this architectural composition and its assembly of elements are twofold: (1) there is a repetition of the disjointed unity that characterises the grouping of buildings in the traditional farms of Middle Finland; and (2) there are more than casual references to the massing and compositions Aalto would have seen in Dudok's buildings during his Hilversum visit in 1928. These latter references are particularly noticeable in the treatment of the exterior wall of the Council Chamber approach, with its cantilevered upper storey; the use of the slit window running just

Munkkiniemi: exterior view of Aalto's studio

beneath the eaves; and the relationship of this lower wall to the tower of the Chamber rising above.

With the completion of this building Aalto planted his red-brick expression (born in America at MIT) on Finnish soil. For although the original designs for the National Pensions Institute and the Otaniemi Technical University antedate that of Säynätsalo, both these other buildings were commenced later, in 1952 (by which time Säynätsalo was completed). In both its form and detailing it developed a sophisticated, urbanised expression of the characteristics he had established in his Munkkiniemi house (1936) and the Villa Mairea (1937–9). We have noted how, in those two houses, he began the process of extending the disjuncture of the plan into the erosion of conventional volumetric forms. This process was to be carried to a fine art by Aalto throughout the 50s and into the 60s; but the first post-war manifestation was in the Säynätsalo town hall.

With the completion of Säynätsalo, Aalto confirmed his position as one of the masters of modern architecture. He already had behind him a quarter of a century of outstanding and innovative work, beginning with Turun Sanomat (1928–9) and advancing through Paimio (1929–33) to the Villa Mairea and the New York World's Fair Pavilion (1938), then on to the Baker Dormitory (1946–50) and Säynatsälo (1949–52). Equally important was his contribution to industrial design through his furniture, glassware and light-fittings (see Appendix). As it was, Säynätsalo was to prove only the beginning of his second major creative period, what in Aalto's case we can call the 'mature period'.

It is significant that Elissa Mäkiniemi came on the scene in 1950, from which point in time she acted as job captain on the Säynätsalo project, for this brought her into close contact with Aalto and his approach to design at a time when his mind was at that important transformational stage between the ideas of 1927–39 and those of his mature expression (of the 50s and 60s). The first period was abruptly terminated by the war; the second by the fact that, in the mid-60s, with Aalto already beyond the normal retiring age, he began to run out of creative energy. Of course, Elissa had missed the first quarter century of the master's development; nevertheless for the next twenty-five years she was to share the most intimate moments of his life and work. Yet there is no evidence to suggest that she was any more of a creative partner than Aino had been before her. The fact is that, even after marriage, Elissa remained the right hand, the 'job captain'. As she herself has said: 'The ideas always began with his first sketches'.[5] The fact is that, without his attention to the detailing of the idea *as a totality* it could never advance from those initial sketches into an authentic Aalto statement.[6] Aalto's was, frankly, not the kind of talent that could be absorbed into teamwork; his interest was to conduct the chamber orchestra rather than play string quartets.

Between the time of the Säynätsalo competition and the completion of that building, a period of some two years, Aalto was involved in a vast range of projects. These included (1) the Lahti church and community centre competition (1950), in which he received first prize; (2) the Malmi funeral chapel competition (1950), a further first prize; (3) the Jyväskylä Pedagogical Institute (later University) competition (1950), again the first prize; (4) the Kivelä Hospital competition (1950); (5) the Kuopio Theatre and Concert Hall competition (1951), yet another first prize; (6) the Lyngby (Denmark) funeral chapel and cemetery master-plan (1951–2); (7) the first stage of a regional plan for Lapland (1950–55); (8) a paper factory for Enso-Gutzeit at Kotka (1951) and a paper mill for the same firm at Summa (1951–3); (9) the first stage of the Rautatalo (Iron House) administrative and commercial buildings; (10) a paper mill for Chandraghone, Pakistan (1951–4); (11) the Enso-Gutzeit Club at Kallvik (1952); and (12) the Seinäjoki church competition (1952), in which he again carried off first prize. There is no denying that, from their early working association, Elissa's presence and subsequently her intimate involvement with Aalto had an inspiring and energising effect on the master. As Clara Schumann remarked about her husband's

Fourth Symphony '. . . marriage had a totally positive effect upon the working of his genius'.

The Malmi funeral chapel prize-winning project (1950) was an important one in the development of Aalto's mature work. Like both the National Pensions Institute and the Säynätsalo town hall it offered a courtyard solution, in fact for three chapels, and the most complex and compact organisation of interior and exterior spaces in Aalto's entire *oeuvre*. Once again, as in the original 'Forum Redivivum B' design for the Pensions Institute, he employed the split axis; this slight deviation in the alignment of the building volumes[7] allowed him in that project to link the two main courtyards without permitting those spaces to leak into one another. In the Malmi design this split axis has a more directly functional purpose in that it allows the separation of the approaches to the two main chapels. But the most significant element in the Malmi project is a systematic approach to the ordering of the plan.

This organisation of the plan is quite clearly based upon the use of 'the square' as the module of form and order. Each of the three chapels is basically square in plan, and whereas the main chapel is approached by a colonnade that is open to the landscaped hillside the colonnade to the second chapel passes through a courtyard of three squares in plan, while that to the smallest chapel opens onto a large square court. Aalto said of this design:

> Already, for quite a long time, ever-increasing demands have led to a quasi-industrialised type of operation in the use of funeral parlours. Here, in Malmi, three chapels have been brought together in a centralised group so that the mourners would not be made aware of the technical, functional aspects of the chapel routine. *Each of the three chapels has its own ceremonial court,* so oriented as to prevent the possible occurrence of distracting disturbances when the three chapels are being used simultaneously.[8]

It is therefore apparent that he sought to restore the ritual element of burial in this composite facility, which would quite often be highly programmed in use. Although all the mourners would have used the same car park, once they entered the colonnades of the particular chapel they were attending they would have been in a completely private world of their own ritual, totally unaware of the rituals being enacted in parallel, 'next door'. To achieve this not only was each approach way, each external space, conceived in a different vein; the interior treatment of the three chapels was also intended to be completely individual, with top-lighting being used in the largest chapel only whilst the two subsidiary ones were to have variations of side-lighting from large louvred openings in the walls.

In external expression, however, the Malmi design appears from the competition drawings to have little to do with the complexities that characterise both the Pensions Institute and Säynätsalo. Instead, we find simple barn-like trusses, with gentle dual-pitched roofs; and all the windows were proposed to be straight-forward rectangles without any fussiness. This again was in fulfilment of Aalto's intention to achieve 'natural simplicity' and avoid 'banal effects' and 'pompous formalities' in his concept.[9] This highly articulate, carefully modulated design was to influence Aalto's approach to a number of subsequent projects that form a distinct group in the *corpus* of his mature work.

The first of these was for another funeral chapel, at Lyngby, Denmark, begun at the end of 1951 and submitted in competition early in 1952. This project required the design of the chapel together with the layout of the cemetery. Again Aalto separated the two chapels and their private courts or 'cloisters' but, although this design is disciplined within a strictly rectilinear framework, the square module is not used. The result is therefore of less interest in plan and form than Malmi, for whilst the discipline remains the dynamic is missing. Beginning with the Baker Dormitory (1946–50) and consolidated by the designs for Säynätsalo (1949–52), the National Pensions Institute (1948–56) and Malmi (1950), Aalto established his highly idiosyncratic expression on the basis of this unique blend of discipline and plan form dynamic.

If this dynamic does not exist within the walled courtyard enclosures of the Lyngby chapel, it does however do so in the contrast between the building form and the site treatment. There is a truly Baroque sense of space and scale implied by Aalto's treatment of the crater-like ravines into which the cemetery is terraced. His design sought to exploit the natural terrain, combining the access paths with the existing watercourses, to provide a dramatic foil for the quasi-temple form of the crematorium above, and organising the graves and memorial gardens into twin 'amphitheatres'.

This use of the amphitheatre theme precedes by one year Aalto's visit to Greece in 1952, the year Säynätsalo was completed. After his Greek holiday the amphitheatre motif was to recur at Otaniemi (redesigned 1955) (see pp. 123–5), in the true amphitheatre at the North Jutland Art Museum, Aalborg (first designed in 1958 and completed in 1972: see p. 192), and the project for the Art Museum at Baghdad (1958) (see pp. 190–92). The first built example of this 'Greek experience' was incorporated into his own studio at Tiilimäki 20, which was designed immediately after his return from Greece and completed in 1955, although, as we have remarked, there was the genesis of this form already present in the auditoria design for the Zagreb Hospital competition of 1930.

After Lyngby, in this group, Aalto's summer house at Muuratsalo should be included. Built immediately after the completion of Säynätsalo town hall, this private retreat for Alvar and Elissa was also a honeymoon cottage. Aalto referred to it, however, as his 'experimental house', explaining that: 'An architect must know his materials. It is not allowed to experiment with the client's money. Therefore I have used some of my own to test some materials and effects.'[10]

There are elements at Muuratsalo that are already familiar from Säynätsalo, particularly the dominant central role of the courtyard in the plan and the use of the monopitch roof. But the prevailing effect of this from within the courtyard, which in

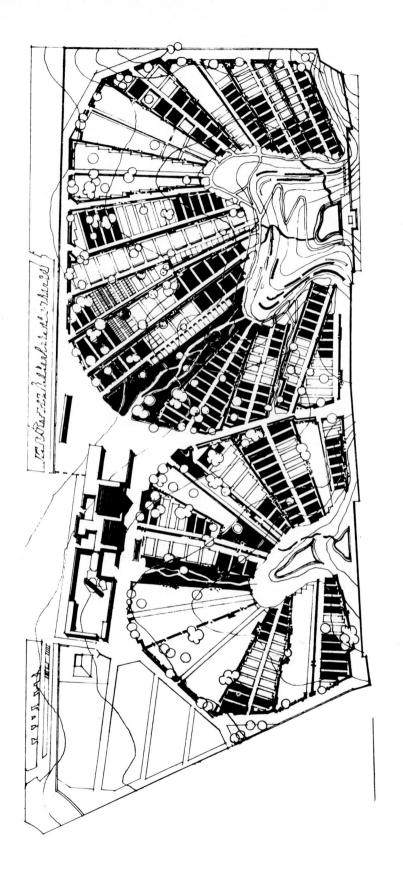

Cemetery and funeral chapel complex for Lyngby, Denmark: site plan of the competition entry (1951–2), showing the fan-plan layout of the cemetery gardens, with the chapel complex (upper left)

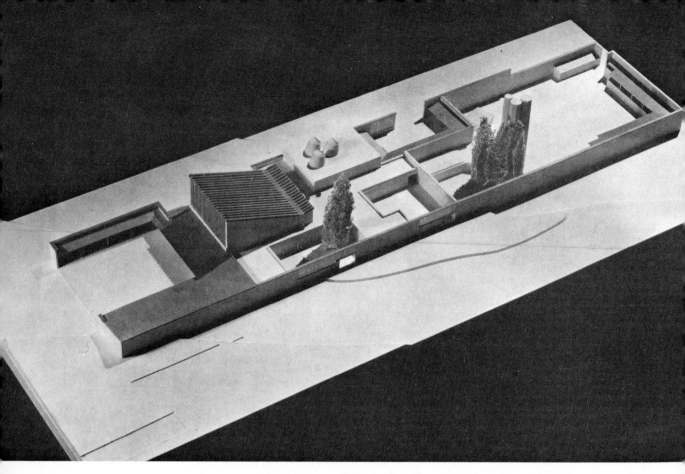

Lyngby cemetery and funeral chapel complex: model of the chapel complex

this Finnish summer cottage is the principal room of the house, is one of geometrical modulation that is quite unknown in the rest of Aalto's entire work. The elaborate patterns which Aalto worked out in the brick 'floor' of the court and the brick and tile treatments on its enclosing walls are, again, very much dependent upon the square. This square motif is clearly established as the central one by the location of the open-air fireplace, which is simply a square hole centrally placed in the brick paving and framed by single rows of bricks, used as stretchers which are lapped at the corners. The notional enclosure sketched in his *Aitta* 'Kumeli' design of 1928 is here replaced by the intimately detailed framework of walls that enclose three of the court's four sides. Indeed, the treatment of the 'floor' in the Muuratsalo court can be seen as more articulate development of the floor patterning and organisation of the main ground floor space in the Villa Mairea, the square formal court now replacing the landscaped court of the earlier design.

One explanation of this decisively modular treatment of both the floor and walls of the Muuratsalo court is that Aalto, whose paintings are strictly notional and expressionist in character, sought here to systematise the architectural expression in a painterly form. If this is so, then his model is clearly that of the De Stijl movement

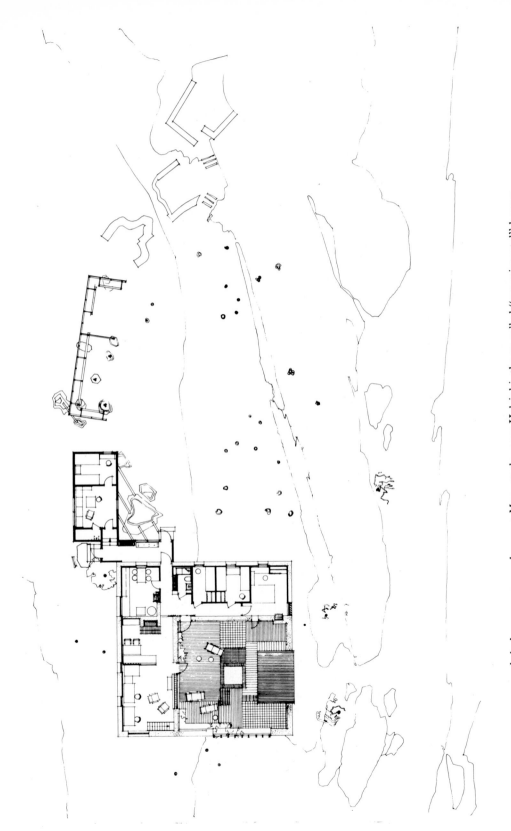

Aalto's own summer house at Muuratsalo, near Helsinki; the so-called "experimental" house: plan, showing main accommodation grouped around the courtyard with subsidiary elements ranging up the granite slope behind

(1917–31), which was at its height when Aalto visited Holland in 1928. The use of raked brick joints is a characteristic of Dudok's work, of course, and Aalto would also have been familiar with it from Wright's houses. But if the neo-plastic use of brickwork at Muuratsalo points directly to the inspiration of De Stijl, the effect he achieves is certainly one of remarkable richness and variety, although it avoids the ornate.

Certainly this effect, which may have originated in the functional programme of demonstrating and testing materials, goes far beyond such mere technical considerations. The modular organisation of the wall surfaces, in particular, emphasises the 'painterly' neo-plastic origins of this design. Only one wall, that which looks out over Lake Päijänne, is not so treated. The reason for this is that it contains the 'window' or open lattice screen that frames the view across the lake, with the pine trees in the foreground. Thus, this wall is left untreated, even unfaced, like an unfinished Italian church façade – such as that of San Lorenzo in Florence – so that the view itself becomes the treatment on that particular wall, recalling in turn the idea of fresco.

In his treatment of the other two walls Aalto adopts a strict hierarchy as we move from the 'natural' view wall, to the living-room/studio wall (with its large three-light window coupled into an 'L' with the pine-slatted partially glazed door) and then, finally, the wall that expresses the bedroom corridor, with its two doors (one slatted and partially glazed and the other diagonally slatted). The living-room/studio wall is the larger of the two treated walls and has appropriately larger, and constructionally more varied, elements. For example the almost uninterrupted brick panels above the window are quite extensive, while the raking of the joints in the horizontal panel immediately over the window is both wide and deep. Also, there are bold projections of smaller areas – brick headers in the case of the upper two – while there is a massive projection of a group of sixteen perforated clay blocks to the left of the window. This 'L'-shaped window-door element is interesting in that it echoes Aalto's original windows for Paimio that gave the motto 'Piirretty ikkuna' to his prize-winning design; and it subsequently became a repeated motif following its reintroduction at Muuratsalo. Although there are small panels of encaustic tiles on the living-room wall – below the window and immediately to the right of it – there are none of the glazed tiles that, following the construction of the National Pensions Institute, were to become such a predominant characteristic of both Aalto's interiors and exteriors.

These glazed tiles are reserved for a small panel on the bedroom wing wall, located between the high-level horizontal slit window and the diagonally battened door. This flattened-square panel is recessed and is divided horizontally just beneath the mid-point. The lower area is filled with large linear-glazed tiles in deep blue and white, arranged in two bands with the blue above and the white below; but the use of joints between the tiles emphasises a counter-rhythm of vertical lines. In the upper portion most of the tiles are of a smaller pattern and, although there is a dominant verticality, the overall design of this portion is decidedly random, with slots of rendering left between the groups of tiles and at the top. Thus, this recessed panel becomes a distinct focus, and more than an architectural feature it suggests a painting. So, as we have the interaction of the geometrical patterning of floor and walls and with each surface itself a composed entity, here in his focal panel of the composition we have confirmation of Aalto's painterly intention, i.e., a picture within a picture. He later commented on these intentions in his work:

> Paintings and sculptures are all part of my working method. So, I wouldn't like to see them separated from my architecture as if they could express something above and beyond it ... We could say that I don't see paintings and sculptures as things in different professional spheres.[11]

Although the inspiration for Aalto's highly articulated treatment of the Muuratsalo courtyard seems clearly to derive from the De Stijl movement, it is very probable that his decision to use it at that particular point of his career was influenced by more immediate events in Finland. For it was at that moment in time Aulis Blomstedt began to emphasise the importance of modular coordinates in his paintings, in his teaching and in his buildings. Aalto was never involved with the new wave of Finnish rationalism, which centred on André Schimmerling's little magazine *Le Carré Bleu* and was to contribute significantly to the development of Aalto's successor, as leader of the profession in Finland, Reima Pietilä.[12] Nevertheless it appears that he was tempted to 'experiment' with a geometrical *gestalt* that is seemingly quite alien to the main line of his development from the Villa Mairea onwards.

Otherwise this delightful summer residence, with its white-painted external walls, monopitch roof with a pantile coping, louvred windows (that recall the New York Pavilion restaurant and Säynätsalo) and the loose scatter of outbuildings that ascend the granite escarpment from the back door, seems to be more of an exercise in refining Aalto's own tradition of the new. This is, until we realise that it sits on that granite slope like a defensive *castelletto*.[13] Also, there is the imagery of the courtyard plan, on which the whole concept is based and which is certainly more akin to a Roman patrician's house than Säynätsalo. From all these points of view, therefore, this tiny house, which turns out to be almost as complex in its expression as Säynätsalo, is truly *experimental*.

Meanwhile in his 'Studio R-S' (1954) project, a combined house and studio designed for the artist R. Sambonet, to be located on a site close to Lake Como and the Swiss frontier, Aalto continued to work in the modular vein. But by 'stripping off' the corners of the squares, converting them into octagons, Aalto moved into a geometrical *gestalt* that he was never to repeat. As in the Malmi design, these octagonal elements are employed as separate cells, rooms with different functions that are completely divorced from each other. Also, as in the Malmi project, he uses a slight change of axis to create a central division which becomes the circulation element. In common with the Malmi solution, Studio R-S has its entrance in the wide end of this wedge that is driven between the cell-like rooms. From this entrance the studio, itself a fan shape, and the *en suite* living/dining areas fan out. This allows the public areas, opening immediately off the entrance hall, to have an open plan. The kitchen, however, is tucked into the 'private wing', off the same wide corridor as the bedroom 'cells' with their own bathrooms, with the maid's bedroom leading off the kitchen and the guest room beyond. The master bedroom for the parents is linked to the children's room by a private corridor with a common bathroom. These bedrooms are screened by the gardens and garden walls that surround them. Access to this garden is from the narrow end of the corridor.

The 'Studio R-S' project had another feature in common with that for Malmi, namely the funnel-like top-lighting that Aalto had suggested for the main chapel. As with the Malmi project, it is a loss that 'Studio R-S' was not realised, although as a planning exercise it is much less happy than that for the chapels. It is as though Aalto quickly became aware of the restrictions which any regular geometrical system would impose upon him, and for this reason he broke the discipline of the octagon in the free-planning of the public areas. But the marriage of the two geometries seems unconvincing. If we did not know for sure that the Sambonet project came from Aalto's hand we might have reason to question its authenticity.

Such reasonable doubt could not exist in the case of the next project in this category: the apartment block for the Interbau Exhibition, built in the Hansaviertel district of Berlin between 1955 and 1957. A number of internationally famous architects were invited to build apartment blocks for the 1957 Interbau as part of Berlin's rehabilitation programme. These included Le Corbusier, Gropius and Mies van der Rohe, the old guard of between-the-wars international modernism. Aalto now joined this distinguished group, and not before time, for in 1955 he was already fifty-seven. More importantly his contribution to the 1957 Interbau was one of the finest, certainly from a planning point of view. Planning was always a strong point in Aalto's functionalist canon, and he never sacrificed 'commodity' for 'delight'; rather he created the one out of the other. What is extraordinary about the external appearance of this building, however, is that it has a distinctly 30s character. There is an uncertainty about the use of the external cladding, which is altogether too uniform to be consistent with Aalto's other work of the mid-50s (with the exception of the uninspiring housing he built for the employees of the National Pensions Institute, 1952–4); but it must be remembered that, other than his entry for the HAKA competition in 1940, the Berlin block was his first exercise in high-rise housing. In reality, at eight storeys it was only medium-rise, with Aalto's use of a strongly horizontal expression and faceting of the block further diminishing its apparent height.

Aalto set himself the problem of bringing to apartment-block living some of the qualities of the private house. Behind the apparent conventions of a neo-30s façade, therefore, Aalto's new humanist functionalism was at work. Of this solution he himself wrote: 'The conventional small corridor-like balconies were here transformed into patios around which the rooms of the apartments were grouped. This grouping around the open-air room created an intimate, private atmosphere.'[14]

He set out to achieve this by grouping the apartments in two 'towers', each with four apartments to a floor, with two further apartments on each floor housed in a link. This link introduced in the party wall between its two apartments the by now familiar slight change of axis. The resulting subtle movement of the mass further reduced its institutional quality. This sense of intimacy was also further developed by locating the entrances at the base of each of the 'towers', opening up completely the ground-floor area of the link, which was carried above on *pilotti*. This columned, open-air entrance court tucked under the building is, of course, yet a further link with the architecture of the 30s. Once within this space, however, we realise that it is Aalto's own, because (1) he has added 'pilasters' to some of the *pilotti* and (2) he has created a 'floating free-form ceiling treatment between the *pilotti*, thus breaking completely with 30s formality as he had already done in the Villa Mairea and the New York Pavilion.

But it is the organisation of the apartments within the 'towers' that makes the Hansaviertel design conform to the present modular group. Basically these towers are planned on the gyratory or 'swastika' principle, except that only selected 'arms' actually project. Aalto's central idea, as we have observed from his own remarks, was to provide a deep balcony for each apartment and group the rooms around this outdoor element. The balcony in the Hansaviertel design is therefore a substitute for the courtyard of his private house designs, and the depth of the balcony varies according to the size of the apartment to which it belongs. There are five large, three-bedroom apartments on each floor, and the three largest of these (in area) have the deepest balconies which are larger than the smallest bedroom in those units. The planning of these three-bedroom units, which form the nucleus of the scheme's *gestalt*, is centred on a large square living area which enjoys the full width of the balcony, while the dining room and master bedroom also have direct access to this open-air focus. With the ancillary rooms grouped around the central living area – part of which, by extension, becomes the balcony – we see that what Aalto has done is extend the patrician atrium plan of the Muuratsalo house to improve the above-ground environment of city apartments. Thus, by introducing the courtyard principle into the design of flats Aalto attempted to combine 'in an ideal manner, the specific advantages of an apartment block with the merits of the individual house'.[15]

Although inclusion in the Interbau *concours* was a significant accolade in terms of his position in modern architecture, Aalto had been receiving important honours in recognition of his contribution to the art since shortly after the war. The first of these was his honorary doctorate from Princeton in 1947; then he was included as a founder member of the Union Internationale des Architectes (UIA) when this was established in Lausanne in 1948. He was to continue his close relationship with Switzerland from this time: his collected works were to be published by Hans Girsberger (later Artemis) of Zürich, commencing 1963, and he and Elissa went there annually from 1960 to 1975 to ski at Davos, a tradition she has maintained since his death. His honorary doctorate from his own university, the Technical University of Helsinki, came in 1950. In 1953, following his own initiative, he was responsible for

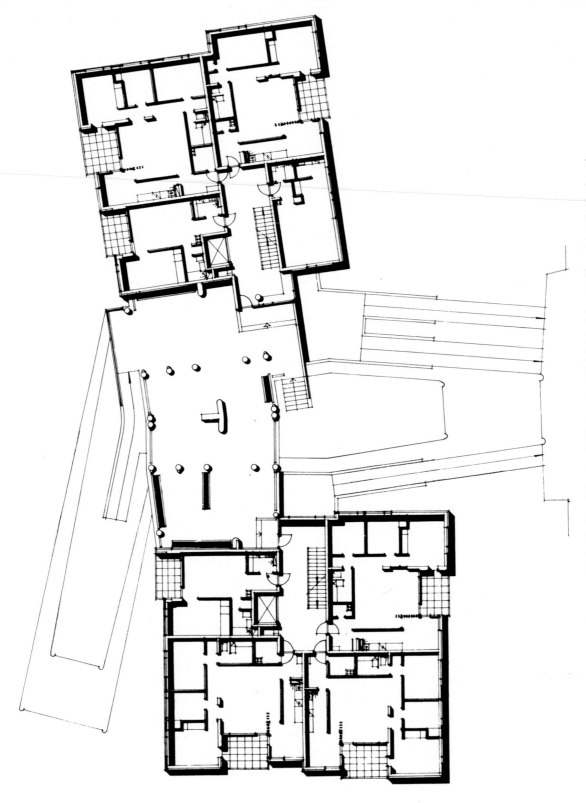

Apartment block (designed for the 1957 Interbau Exhibition) in the Hansaviertel district of Berlin (1955–7): plan at entrance level, showing the approach ramp, covered link and layout of the units with their deep balconies

Hansaviertel apartment block: view towards the approach ramp, showing the rhythmical treatment of the deep balconies within the façade the overall direction of the first 'Finland Builds' exhibition in Helsinki. The following year, 1954, he travelled a great deal, going to Brazil as a member of the international jury for the Matarazzo Prize and staying on for the congress of Brazilian architects, and on this trip of course he met Oskar Niemeyer. Later in the year he was in Vienna on the occasion of his election as an honorary member of the Austrian Artists' Association. He also undertook an invitation lecture tour to Berne and Basel, as well as spending the Christmas holiday period on his first visit to Baghdad. In addition to all these activities in 1954 he succeeded in bringing pressure to bear for the creation of Finland's pioneer institution, the Museum of Finnish Architecture.[16]

In 1955 he was given the distinction of being elected as a Member of the Finnish Academy. Nineteen fifty-six saw an invitation lecture tour to Venice, Milan and Florence, following his visit to the twenty-eighth Venice Biennale, for which he had designed the Finnish Pavilion. Then in 1957 came an invitation to lecture and exhibit his work at Malmö, in Sweden, and what was one of the highest honours of his career, the award of the Gold Medal of the Royal Institute of British Architects, which he travelled to London to receive.[17] During the same period (1956–8) he was also invited to New York to act as a consultant on the setting up of the Lincoln Center for the Performing Arts.

Whilst the Hansaviertel block was being built, Aalto received the commission in 1956 to design a house at Bazoches-sur-Guyonne (close to Versailles) for the French art dealer, Louis Carré, whom he had met at the Venice Biennale. This villa also falls within the group that I have labelled as the 'modular works'. The problem here was in many ways similar to that of the 'Studio R-S', in that it was essential to house a substantial part of Monsieur and Madame Carré's collection of modern art in a house that was primarily a residence; therefore the more public display areas had to be arranged side by side with the private parts of the villa. Aalto structured this 'privacy gradient' by providing a large entrance-hall-cum-gallery that led directly into the major living–reception area, taking advantage of the natural slope of the wooded site. He created the transition between this entrance gallery and the reception room by means of a broad flight of steps. These lead down from the hall, which is lit only by a clerestory over the entrance portico, towards the view across the gently rolling site that is revealed through the reception-room window.

The cell-like rooms (which in the Villa Mairea were contained in a separate wing) lead off the gallery in an arrangement that is familiar from the 'Studio R-S' project. At the front of the house these rooms comprise M. Carré's study and library (leading off the living area), the dining room (tucked behind the entry vestibule and projecting out to enclose the portico), the kitchen, pantry and cook's dining area adjacent (with a staircase leading up to the servants' quarters above); then along the back of the gallery are grouped three double bedrooms, each with their own bathroom, the master bedroom also having its own sauna en suite.

In this plan structure the square is once again the dominant theme, with the study/library and the two largest bedrooms conforming to this shape, as does the

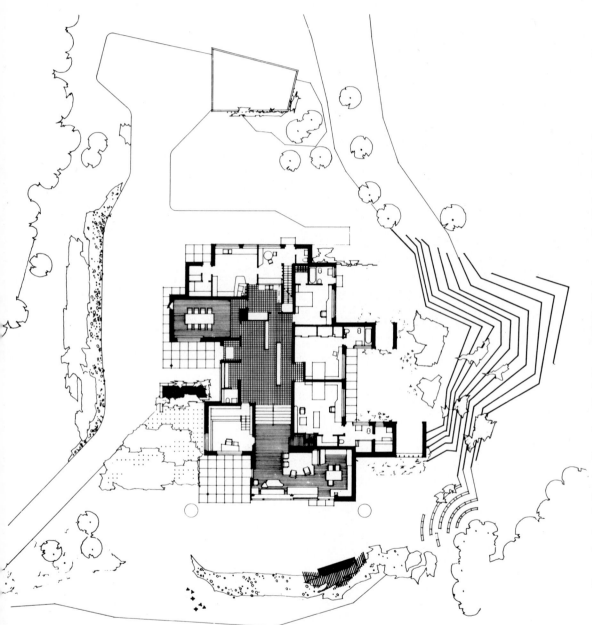

House for Louis Carré at Bazoches, Ile de France (1956–8), known as La Maison Carré: plan at entrance level, showing dining room, gallery and stairs down to the living room and Louis Carré's study

Interior view of gallery and lower level, Maison Carré

entrance portico and the terrace leading off the front end of the living room. The result is a highly articulate interaction of solid and void which, consistently obeying the rectilinear discipline, is much more coherent than the projected 'Studio R-S'. In M. Carré's lifetime one would have entered his small private gallery, moving through it on the way to the reception room then back again through the same space on the way to eat.[18]

A further examination of the plan reveals another significant motif. Superficially, Aalto's overall plan *image* for the Maison Carré may suggest a variation on a plan theme by Frank Lloyd Wright, in that there are clearly two axes which are at right angles to one another, while the elements that relate to those axes do so in a disjunctive way denying the cruciform origin of the axial plan generators. But closer scrutiny uncovers another source. It would, of course, be difficult for an architect to design a 'Maison Carré' without thinking of the original, that charming little Roman temple at Nîmes. But it seems that Aalto chose another source for his plan inspiration, one from the Italian Renaissance. For, by regrouping the two main bedrooms, the kitchen, the reception area and the dining room and study so that these elements

Interior view of Maison Carré from lower level showing the grand flight of steps up to the entrance gallery

Maison Carré: view of entrance façade, showing portico and split-pediment treatment

conform to the crossed axes of the plan generators we have a close approximation to the main plan idea of a Palladian villa; say the Villa Malcontenta, which is a cruciform shape set within a rectangle. That Aalto had such a Palladian model in mind is convincingly confirmed by the geometrical organisation of the entry façade.

Again, at first sight the main line of the roof, a monopitch, recalls Muuratsalo, which as we have seen also has an Italian model for its plan. This main line also follows the gentle up-slope of the terrain from the reception room and lower terrace up over the entrance portico and its clerestory window to the gallery within. And what would be more natural than for Aalto to echo the terrain in this country house? But there are a number of clues that give the lie to the idea of a villa in the bucolic style! First of all the wall supporting the line of the monopitch is not represented as a monolithic entity; instead it is divided horizontally into two, with the lower or podium band faced in a special grey travertine, while the upper triangular slice is finished with white-painted brickwork. But it is not as simple as that either, because the entrance is carved deeply into this mass, with the clerestory window set well back from both the portico and the main line of the white painted brickwork.

This carving into the line of the simple monopitch mass again recalls the form of Muuratsalo and the interruption of the enclosing wall by the 'slot' that gives access to the courtyard. Then we notice, however, as we look closer at this intersection, that there is a counter-direction introduced by expressing the roof to the dining room and the kitchen beyond as a second monopitch running from left to right. This second roof threatens to meet up with the first roof, running up from right to left; but that union cannot actually take place because of the cleavage of the portico and clerestory cutting into the façade and through the forward lines of these two opposing roofs. Had they met, however, these two triangular segments of roof would have formed a pediment over the entrance portico. In his characteristic disjunctive way Aalto has frustrated this eventuality, although the possibility of its having happened is still, tantalisingly, there. And the fact that this 'broken pediment' motif was deliberate is seemingly confirmed by the fact that Aalto's original sketch for this façade showed both roof lines parallel to each other, in complete harmony with the slope of the site. The decision to change the direction of the minor roof and create this discordant expectation on the entry façade, coupled with the realignment of the plan elements about the Palladian cruciform axes, shows his great subtlety as a maker of plans and forms.

On the garden side, however, the Maison Carré reveals the conventional monopitch with the two small bathroom 'pavilions' of the main bedrooms jutting out. But this white-painted rear elevation is not at all indicative of an informal country house either. Although the elevational geometry is informal in massing and detail, it is also crisply modern, and the building (viewed from the swimming pool at the lowest corner of the site) once again suggests the sharp contrast of built form with Nature that is the essential spirit of Palladio's villas in the Veneto.

Regardless of the villa's external form, however, the interior, with its stepped ceiling in the reception area rising up under the monopitch to meet the sharper inclination of the gallery vault, owes more to Aalto's undulating ceiling for the lecture room of the Viipuri Library. This suggestion of acoustic functionalism, which in the Maison Carré is a purely Mannerist gesture, was conceived in parallel with his design for the church at Vuoksenniska, Imatra, which was also begun in 1956 (see pp. 199–201). The re-emergence of this undulating ceiling in the Maison Carré and the Imatra church heralded a new and exciting period in Aalto's work during which he was to abandon and modular discipline in favour of a flowing, free-form, highly plastic approach to design.

He was to return, however, to the modular discipline in three further designs. These are: (1) his competition entry for the British Petroleum Administrative Building in Hamburg (1964); (2) his competition entry for the Pohjola Insurance Company's so-called 'Maiandros' office building in Helsinki (1965); and (3) some of the apartments projected for HAKA, the Social Democratic building society, intended for Gammelbacka, just outside Porvoo. Taking these in reverse order, the Gammelbacka project included a design for one- and two-bedroom apartments with the rooms arranged around large square balconies that 'eat into' the plan in the manner of the Hansaviertel block in Berlin. The Pohjola Insurance Company project is merely an extension of the planning system Aalto evolved for the BP Hamburg competition, so we will concentrate on an analysis of that latter design.

Aalto's design for BP's Hamburg headquarters was, potentially, his most interesting office building after the National Pensions Institute, but he was awarded only the third prize. He described his design strategy for this project in the following terms:

> ... the programme prescribes a horizontal open-plan hall with elastic contact among the different work groups, with a minimum office width of 25 metres being called for. *The author is of the opinion that open-plan expanses have their definite limits.*
>
> Psychological pressures may result if certain limits are exceeded; these limits involve the distances from sources of illumination, both artificial and the window walls, and perhaps also other incalculable factors.
>
> The author has therefore articulated the entire plan into distinct but adjacent groupings, with close interdependence between these groupings...[19]

The limits of the open-plan and his predilection for interaction between groupings led Aalto to select a tower element (as in the Hansaviertel block) which is square in plan – four structural bays in each direction – with these elements overlapping one bay at corner intersections. This permitted him to develop a form of 'domino' plan in the arrangement of the five towers, which were further articulated by having different heights. Thus the apparent working space is only twenty-five metres by twenty-five, while there is free access, through the corner bays, to the adjacent 'tower' which is connected at that point. Each tower was, however, independent from the point of view of access and services, with the lifts, stairs, toilets and ducts occupying approximately one bay: one sixteenth, or less than seven per cent of the floor area. This made his planning system very efficient in terms of the area required for services and circulation. Also, on a tight site, Aalto concentrated on this plan efficiency as a means of achieving environmental quality within the building rather than in external courts or landscaping.

As it happens the Aalto office building which is most memorable after the Pensions Institute is also in Helsinki, in the heart of the downtown area in Keskuskatu, opposite the rear entrance of Stockmann's Department Store. The 'Rautatalo' (Iron House) is the headquarters building of Finland's Association of Iron Dealers and occupies what is basically an 'L'-shaped site adjacent to Saarinen's Cooperative Bank building of 1911 and only fifty metres from the Swedish Theatre at the intersection of Keskuskatu and Esplanadi. In this building (designed in competition 1952, built 1953–5) Aalto employed for the first time the elevational treatment he had originally proposed for the office tower of the 'Forum Redivivum' entries for the National Pensions Institute Building (1948).

The Rautatalo plan is a remarkably simple one, making most efficient use of this

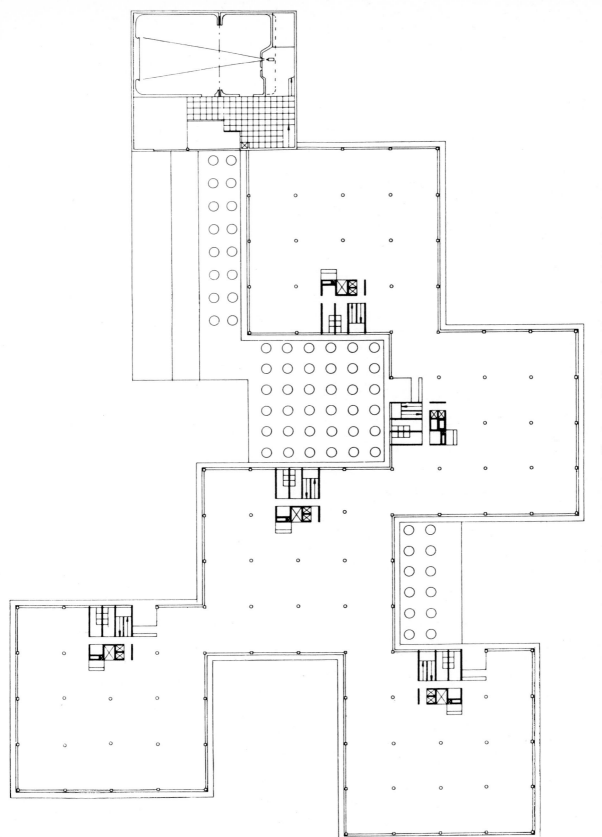

British Petroleum headquarters project, Hamburg (1964): plan, showing interlocking *Büro-landschaft* "towers" (competition entry)

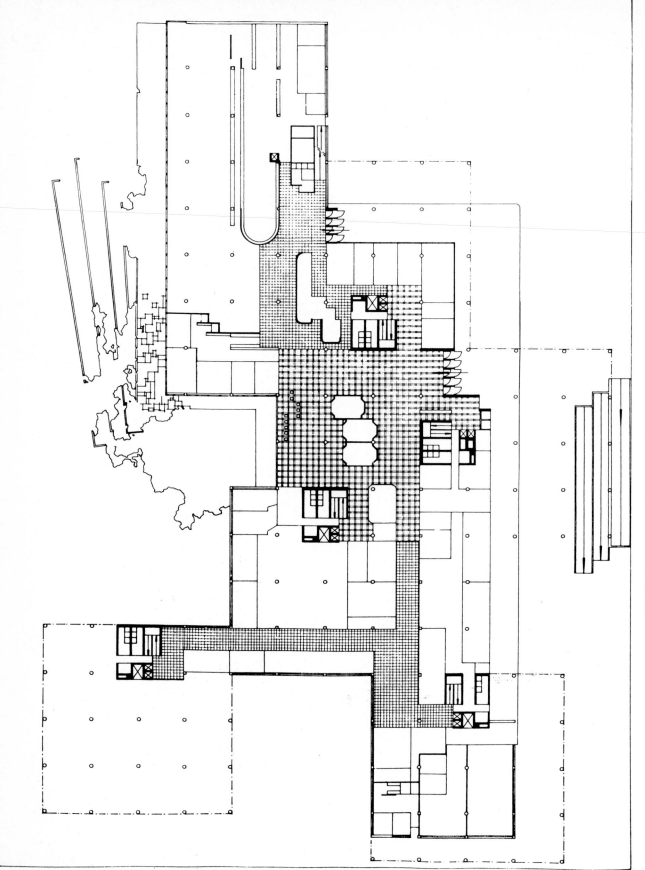

BP Headquarters project: ground-floor plan (competition entry)

cramped city site that measures approximately 120 feet by 150 feet overall. Shops occupy the entire ground floor (with the exception of a small lobby containing the staircase to the mezzanine or *piano nobile*). The basement is also devoted to shopping as is part of the *piano nobile*. Originally Artek occupied the entire basement and the ground-floor shop to the left of the main entrance, with the Artek Gallery occupying the shopping area on the *piano nobile*; but this upper space was taken over by Armi Ratia as a downtown Marimekko boutique at the end of the 60s. This occupancy by furniture, design and fashion firms is an important feature of Rautatalo, which being located between two of Helsinki's principal shopping streets, Esplanadi and Aleksanterinkatu, made it an ideal focus for such mainstream shopping.

In his design Aalto exploited the importance of Rautatalo as a focus of shopping and shoppers by his arrangement of the *piano nobile*. He created an internal court at first-floor level which serves as the main circulation space for the shops at that level as well as providing a spacious entrance lobby for the offices above. This *piazzetta* has an area of about 4,500 square feet, or nearly one third of the total floor area at that level. Aalto justified this internal thoroughfare as a meeting place for shoppers and intellectuals alike. It is, after all, located between the Swedish Theatre and the Finnish National Theatre, which stand at either end of Keskuskatu, whilst it is only a quarter of a mile from the University of Helsinki. To this end he devoted the open area beneath the office balconies to a café which could be patronised by those working in and using the building as well as the general public.

The drinking of coffee in Finland is a habit of great social significance, while the climate makes the use of open-air cafés an event of only brief, seasonal duration. Aalto therefore sought with his Rautatalo covered *piazzetta* and its open-plan cafe to bring to the Finnish capital the social advantages of the Mediterranean climate. The Rautatalo café became an instant success and is always well patronised; in fact it fulfils precisely the function and ritual that Aalto had in mind. But, although the office workers and visitors have to take the lifts from this level to the upper floors, there is not really enough activity generated by the shops and offices to create a sense of downtown bustle in the *piazzetta*. The logical, i.e., shortest, route between the head of the stairs and the cafeteria counter is diagonally across the open space, which rises a further two storeys above with access balconies stepping back and running around this court. Although the court is attractively planted and has a fountain it is generally empty There is a certain amount of traffic between the Marimekko shop and the café, passing across the mid-point of the *piazzetta*; but the environmentally shy Finns[20] avoid the direct, diagonal route to the counter, seeking instead to dodge around the periphery of the space and lose themselves in the 'population' of the café rather than be exposed to view in crossing the open area.

Nevertheless, the Rautatalo *piazzetta* and café comprise an outstanding contribution to the complexity of urban life in Helsinki; and internal shopping malls became the vogue in Helsinki during the 60s, although none is as successful as Aalto's. In his Rautatalo design he succeeded in raising the office and commercial building to the

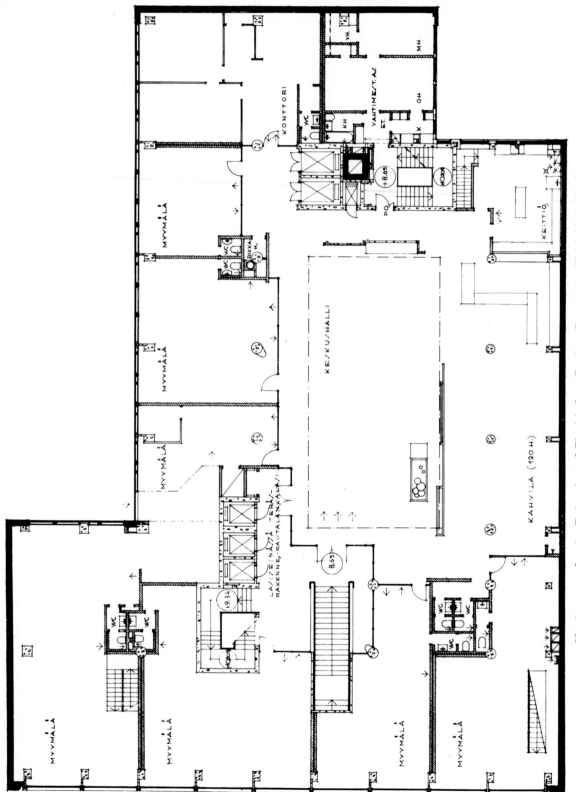

Headquarters for the Federation of Finnish Iron Dealers (Rautatalo), Helsinki (1953–5): working drawing showing the first-floor plan, with the internal *piazzetta*, café and fountain

Rautatalo: interior view, showing the *piazzetta*, fountain, café and stepped galleries to the offices above

level of a social and cultural statement, much of the success of which depends upon the intimacy of its small scale. The interior court is naturally lit by forty roof lenses of the pattern first used at Turun Sanomat and developed in the Viipuri Library.[21] When daylight is not available, and Helsinki has only four or five hours of daylight in mid-winter, light is provided by lamps that are suspended above the lenses.

The façade treatment, as we have already noted, had already been mapped out in the original competition designs for the National Pensions Institute. While the building has a reinforced concrete frame, there is a lightweight metal framing system that carries on the weight of the façade – i.e., the windows and the wind load. This façade is clad in copper over cork insulation.

In execution, the Rautatalo (1953–5) parallels the National Pensions Institute (1952–6) and, whereas the façade system is distinctive for that date, it has various other details in common with the Pensions Institute. These include the stacking bronze door handles, used in pairs, which reflect the elaborate curvilinear designs of the National Romantic period. Their calculated bifurcation is most certainly a post-functionalist statement! It was in this building that Aalto first made extensive use of marble and the parapet walls to the balconies are of travertine, whilst the *piazzetta* floor and fountain are of white Carrara. Mixed with these marbles, and familiar from his 'experiments' at Muuratsalo, are deep blue ceramic tiles from the Arabia factory,

Detail of Rautatalo façade to Keskuskatu, showing the careful treatment of junction with Saarinen's bank

which are used to give a vertical emphasis on screen walls at either end of the atrium; and these tiles, blue, white and buff, are also used in the public areas of the Pensions Institute.

With the Rautatalo, the atrium of Säynätsalo and Muuratsalo, already partially assimilated in the interview hall of the Pensions Institute, is successfully transferred to the very centre of the building, becoming the *pneuma* of the interior. And shortly after Rautatalo was completed Aalto was to apply his atrium principle to the balconies in the planning of the Hansaviertel block.

Following the completion of the Pensions Institute in 1956 Aalto was not involved in another office/commercial building project for two years; then, in 1958, he designed a totally unremarkable administration building for the Post Office in Baghdad. But only a year later, in 1959, came another important office commission, to design the headquarters in Helsinki for the Enso-Gutzeit Company, which was built between 1960 and 1962. This prestigious administrative building is located, as we have already noted, on the site originally used by Aalto for his Parliament Building competition entry of 1923. It was therefore gratifying for him to be invited to place a building of his mature period in this particular location.

Aalto was concerned that it should respond to the Neo-classical discipline of Engel's

The Enso-Gutzeit headquarters building, Helsinki (1959–62), seen from across the harbour, with the Russian Orthodox cathedral in the background

The Enso-Gutzeit building: the original study model, showing the new waterside 'palazzo' in relation to the nineteenth-century framework of the City Hall (left), the Presidential Palace (centre) and the Russian Orthodox cathedral (right)

buildings on the harbour front and his cathedral on the hill behind the Great Square. To this end he prepared a panoramic elevation that spanned the harbour front from the cathedral, past the town hall and the Presidential Palace up to, and including, the Russian Orthodox Church. The Enso-Gutzeit site is immediately below the Russian church, on the very edge of the harbour. Aalto then overlaid this panoramic elevation with a modular grid which showed the dimensional relationship of the different parts of the panorama to the whole.

In fact this modular overlay did not demonstrate a cohesive proportional relationship of the different buildings to each other; this kind of dimensional analysis can of course be used to prove almost anything. Aalto, in his analysis, treated the panorama in the spirit of an Italian Renaissance façade, whereas he was dealing with a disparate group of buildings. Also, the mathematical intentions of Alberti and Palladio had become somewhat diluted in the process of being handed down to Engel. Furthermore Aalto's whimsical view that a module might be anything from 'a brick', to 'a centimetre' to 'a millimetre' does not exactly inspire confidence in his modular exercise on the Helsinki harbour front. In the first place there are altogether too many gaps in the information about what this modular analysis is supposed to convey. But close examination shows that Aalto had several options in arriving at the lowest common denominator within this organizational survey; and it appears that he took the belfry towers of Engel's cathedral (the only element in the entire panorama that appears twice!) and used one third of this for the width of the window bay for the Enso-Gutzeit building.

Having made this decision Aalto then took this window 'module' as the basis of both the horizontal and vertical division of his façades by using square windows. So, from this point of view, the Enso-Gutzeit 'palace' can be thought of as modular; but

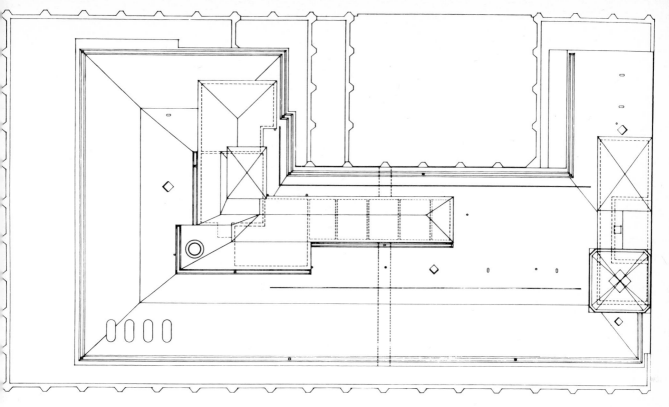

The roof plan of the Enso-Gutzeit headquarters, showing the irregular stepping of floors to the rear court area

this modularity is externally generated and affects only the façades. In fact in the layout of the offices the partitions are deliberately located at the extremities (rather than on the centres) of the window mullions, ranging from left to right extremity more or less arbitrarily. So, we see that Aalto has built up, through the panoramic modular analysis, the whole panoply of a classical formal discipline. Yet, when it comes to the design of the building itself this discipline, as with the modular grid itself, is just a superficial overlay.

Aalto always referred to this building, symbolically, as the *palazzo*. Set on the very forefront of the harbour and seen immediately by every visitor arriving by boat, his *palazzo* appears to actually front onto the harbour, whereas in fact it faces back towards the city centre. And this fact led Aalto to carve out one bay on the end of the harbour façade at street level to provide a *porte-cochère* on the city frontage. This carving away of significant bits of the building's mass is not limited to the exterior elevations. And the result is that what at first sight appears to be a neat little Italian Renaissance palace, lifted from the Ca' Grande in Venice and planted on the harbour's edge in Helsinki, turns out to be a very complex and mannered statement. The interior roof form, although carved away in a similar manner to both the National Pensions Institute and Rautatalo, is in fact much more complex than either. In its elevational treatment the exterior envelope seems to conform to the *raison d'être* of a

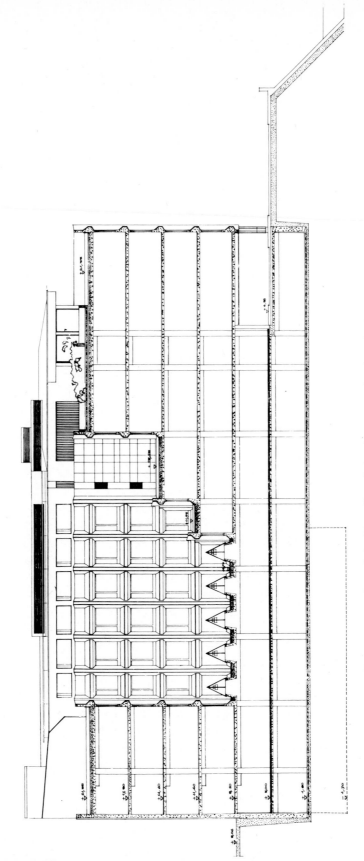

Transverse section of the Enso-Gutzeit headquarters, showing the irregular stepping of the floors from the upper roof terrace down to the lantern lights

free-standing site, where the admission of daylight to all the exterior walls presents no problems. But when we examine the section, on the other hand, we find that its pattern of visually arbitrary setbacks resembles a design proposed to overcome the difficulties of a site left over between tightly compacted office masses in, say, London or New York.

Thus, in the Enso-Gutzeit *palazzo* Aalto has once again prepared us to expect a particular architectural context, in this case one that is all too familiar to the student of Western forms and norms. But the formalism of the façade turns out to be only a cover-up for Aalto's more elaborate spatial preoccupations. He succeeds, however, in momentarily suspending our belief in this façade. It is the façade, after all, that draws the dividing line between the worlds of urban imagery and interior function. In the case of the Enso-Gutzeit *palazzo* it also stands between the worlds of our formal expectations, i.e. not 'what does the plan promise?' but 'what does the façade reveal?' – and Aalto's carving and eroding of the overall volumetric mass.

Aalto's position as a master of modern architecture is very much characterised by his careful selection of formal themes. His variations, his 'constant variability of theme', however, confirm that he did not accept those basic themes as isolated phenomena but sought to interpret both their symbolic content and their application by cutting across the thematic landscape of his formal vocabulary. In this sense Aalto is not only *not* a stylist, he is also *not* a mere formalist either. His buildings possess, therefore, the texture of his formal concerns rather than mere reflections of preconceived formal intentions. Those often ill-fitting, uncomfortable forms are direct extensions of his drawing technique, attempts to solve problems by expressing them in terms that are still fresh. Aalto's consistent struggle in design was to keep architectural language alive by reinterpreting its familiar terms while at the same time inventing others.

Following the Enso-Gutzeit *palazzo* Aalto's next commercial project of note was the original proposal for extending Frosterus's Stockmann department store on the adjacent site at the intersection of Mannerheimintie, Esplanadi and Keskuskatu. The designs for this date from 1962, when Aalto won the competition based on this original adjoining site. In his original proposals Aalto maintained the fascia line of the large display windows on the ground floor of the Mannerheimintie façade in the Frosterus building. Above this line there were to be four floors before the set-back at eaves level, and the fenestration of these floors used the square-window module he had employed in the Enso-Gutzeit *palazzo*. The design, however, expressed the neutrality of the Rautatalo project, with the only relief to this restrained treatment being provided by the entrance canopy projecting out over the pavement on the return façade to Esplanadi. This design was abandoned, however, when Stockmann's acquired an alternative site across the street on the corner of Keskuskatu and Esplanadi.

Although the store subsequently expanded onto the original site it did so in the existing buildings of the National Romantic period which had become protected by a

Extension to the Stockmann department store known as the Academic Bookshop (1966–9): elevation on Keskuskatu (Central Street), Helsinki

conservation order. Aalto was therefore asked to prepare a revised design for the alternative site. The result was that having built Rautatalo on the left-hand side of Saarinen's Cooperative Bank he then completed the rebuilding of that side of Keskuskatu. Like his solution for Rautatalo the new building is restrained on the exterior, which also has a copper-clad window wall. But the detailed treatment of the fenestration is very different in character, resulting from the fact that the Stockmann extension, which houses the famous Academic Bookshop, has large interior volumes which requires air-conditioning.

The Academic Bookshop, with an external regularity and severity that recalls Mies van der Rohe or Eiermann, especially at the street corner, cannot be said to reflect exactly the Neo-classical character of neighbouring buildings. We can appreciate, however, that by the sheer weightiness of the copper-clad window wall (in which the dominance of the glazing is held in check by the dark copper trim), Aalto has followed the tonal quality of the Saarinen bank next door (already continued in the Rautatalo façade). But the carefully prepared modular grid which he had devised for the Enso-Gutzeit *palazzo* (originally designed in 1959), generated the square-window module which was also to recur in the Nordic Union Bank's administrative building

The Academic Bookshop: interior, looking towards Keskuskatu, showing the interior street with galleries and lantern lights above

(competition 1962, built 1962–4). The Nordic Union Bank façade to Fabianinkatu, which bridges between a delicate Neo-classical corner 'pavilion' that returns on to Esplanadi and a dull 20s commercial building, is arguably the most delicate of his series of copper-clad façades.[22] Compared with the earlier, straightforward divisions of the Rautatalo façade, with its deep modelling of the mullion and transom sections, or its later interpretation in the bolder but flatter grid of the Academic Bookshop façade, the Nordic Union Bank has the delicacy of moulded paper rather than metal, with a complex delineation of both vertical and horizontal 'zones' representing floor slabs and columns (and an intermediate vertical division) that again speaks of Eiermann and even Alberti.[23]

In the case of the Academic Bookshop it is once again, as with Rautatalo, the interior volumes that are of greatest interest. Aalto's emphasis on top-lit interior courts, which goes back to the final version of the Viipuri Library (December 1933), was, of course, very much generated by Finland's climatic and daylight conditions. Harsh winters dictate the search for ideal internal environments; the shortage of daylight in mid-winter makes it necessary to extract every lumen from the sun and introduce this light into internal areas that are far from window walls. This is especially so on compact urban sites such as that of Rautatalo. But Aalto sought to exploit this interior court even when the sites for which he was designing did not have these strict urban limitations. We have noted this for example in his original use of the interior court motif (1) at Viipuri, where the library is located in parkland but the interior court is designed to give the reading room optimum privacy in the heart of the building; and (2) the Enso-Gutzeit *palazzo*, where the site has no daylight problems but a section of the ground floor is below street level and top lit. In the case of the Enso-Gutzeit building this 'sunken' portion of office accommodation does not even comprise a distinct unit or function, with the twenty roof lenses appearing quite arbitrarily over the different rooms and corridor. Interestingly, in his project drawings Aalto shows these roof-lights as sharply pointed lanterns (of a similar pattern to those used in the National Pensions Institute) whereas in the executed building these were subdued to the lens and light-fitting design of Rautatalo.

The interior of the Academic Bookshop represents a peak of Aalto's achievement in terms of urban design. Realising that the really usable urban space in Finland can best be achieved inside the building envelope he modelled the Academic Bookshop on Frosterus's original Stockmann store. This, we recall (see Chapter II, p. 26) was in the form of a central void, rising the full height of the building. In other words it was a prototype for Aalto's galleried internal courts in the Pensions Institute and Rautatalo. But both the Pensions building and the Iron House are tentative exercises in this genre since they have a purely visual rather than a completely physical and social interaction between the lower level and the galleries above. In the Academic Bookshop, however, Aalto was able to achieve the perfect marriage between commercial function and urban complexity. What was missing in the Rautatalo *piazzetta* was the sheer intensity of human activity. The Finns are renowned, in spite of the exorbitant price of print in their country, as the world's most voracious buyers and readers of books. When Aalto was commissioned to build the new Academic Bookshop its main rival, the Finnish Bookshop, had already rebuilt its premises in the well-known City Passage across the Aleksanterinkatu from the main entrance to the original Stockmann building. But the new Finnish Bookshop is on one floor and offers only a typical department store atmosphere. Aalto therefore set out to define, delineate and enliven an ideal book emporium for Finland's capital.

The similarity between Aalto's solution for the Academic Bookshop and Frosterus's design for the original Stockmann store may not be immediately apparent. In the Stockmann building the galleried central court extends five floors above the continuous shopping floor on the entry level. Frosterus's Stockmann design still has a sense of scale into which Helsinki, as a city, has only grown since the early 50s and the beginning of Aalto's own career. But in 1916, when it was designed, it formed a prelude to the emergence of Finland as an independent nation. In the wake of Engel's Great Church had come Finland's entry into the twentieth century with Saarinen's Helsinki railway station, while the Stockmann competition of 1916 was evidence of the Finns' commercial ambitions even before they had thrown off the Russian yoke.

Extension to the Stockmann department store: perspective sketch, showing the proposal for the original site at the junction of Mannerheimintie and Esplanaadi

Certainly, in the middle of the second decade of this century, the Stockmann store was a very ambitious project indeed within the context of Helsinki. The interior of Frosterus's Stockmann building has a grandeur that is frankly Roman, for the central court is no modest atrium but a great hall such as we might find in the centre of the Baths of Caracalla. Aalto's atrium for the Academic Bookshop, in contrast, is more in scale with a subsidiary hall, the *frigidarium*, say, of Hadrian's *thermae* at Leptis Magna or, to seek a more modern image, which surely was in Aalto's mind, that of the nineteenth-century market hall.

As in Frosterus's Stockmann store the ground floor is a continuous shopping space, set out with a wide mall, just off centre, that leads from the main entrance lobby through to the rear of the bookshop. Off this circulation are located the numbered and categorised counter islands, with subsidiary aisles giving access from both sides. An escalator also leads up to the other sales area, the mezzanine, at first-floor level. Above this first-floor gallery is another at second-floor level, stepped back from the lower gallery as in Rautatalo, which contains the administrative offices. The floor and gallery parapets are faced in white Carrara marble, and the whole interior is brightly lit. But the *ethos* evoked by the brilliant clear lines of the marble is that of a Venetian *piazzetta* in full sunlight, with the activity visible over the balconies from below confirming this image; and this impression holds good in summer and winter alike. Consistent with Aalto's principle of balancing the lighting so that daylight and artificial lighting are more or less equal, the ceiling over the atrium is opened up to the sky by means of three large lanterns that leave relatively little of the roof slab between them. These lanterns are composed of double glass 'shells', as in the Pensions Institute atrium, to provide a thermal barrier and avoid condensation on the inner skin. But unlike the Pensions Institute lanterns, on which they are clearly modelled, those of the Academic Bookshop have an inner skin that projects down into the atrium below, presenting a sloping faceted pentagonal form that resembles the bottom of a dinghy. Thus, the complete form of these lanterns is an unequal decahedron, with the sharper angled half thrusting up above the roof and the gentler bottom half suspended like a great chandelier in a faceted reveal cut into the deep slab. The delicate way in which these lanterns are subtended by the upper edge of the roof slab offers Aalto's most refined expression of his roof-light treatment. Since construction on the Academic Bookshop began in 1966, the year he was invited to design the Riola church (see pp. 202–4), it also provides convincing evidence that Aalto did not himself detail the crude lantern over the Riola baptistery.[24]

It is to be regretted that England, whose critics were early to appreciate his contribution to the evolution of modern architecture,[25] has no Aalto building on her soil. The real opportunity presented itself with the commission to design St Catherine's College, Oxford, on a site that should have brought out Aalto's best qualities. But this opportunity went unheeded and the commission went to Arne Jacobsen. Vienna came much closer to enjoying the benefits of an Aalto building. This occurred when Aalto won first prize in the 1953 competition to provide a national sports and music centre in the Vogelweidplatz, whilst he was building both the Pensions Institute and Rautatalo. His design for the Vienna centre is, however, in marked contrast to his other work of that period, with the possible exception of the sports hall for the Technical University at Otaniemi, which occupied him from 1949 until 1954.

The Otaniemi sports hall is interesting because it can be seen as a structurally based response to the modular theme in some of his 50s buildings which began with the Malmi funeral chapel design of 1950. Also, the Otaniemi design, which rationalised Aalto's staggered wall plan *gestalt* (that goes back to both the 'Le Bois est en Marche' and the 'Tsit Tsit Pum' entries for the Paris Pavilion of 1936, *and* the Tallin Art Museum entry of the following year) into a structural expressionism, remains an important link between Aalto and his successor as the leading figure in Finnish architecture since the mid-60s, Reima Pietilä. Aalto's structural expressionism was converted by Pietilä into a dynamic exercise in modular planning in 1956. It was appropriately in the context of Aalto's success with the Paris and New York pavilions, that Pietilä should begin his own career by winning the competition for Finland's pavilion at the 1957 Brussels World's Fair. The Vogelweidplatz design, however, shows Aalto returning to the plasticity of the New York pavilion (1938) and the Baker Dormitory (1947). In his Vienna project, however, he exhibits a new, bolder and more simple line. It was to be developed in 1955 in the design of the studio and garden court of his own office in Munkkiniemi, followed by its adaptation to the 'fan' plan in the House of Culture, Helsinki (1955) (see pp. 174–5), then recurring again in a competition project for the Kiruna town hall, Sweden, of 1958 (see p. 176),

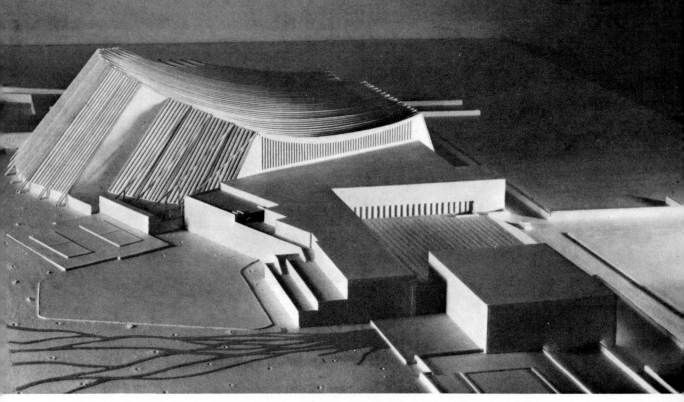

Sports and Music Centre, Vogelweidplatz, Vienna: model of the competition entry (1953)

and culminating in the daring masses of the first Essen Opera House project of 1958–9 (see pp. 195–6). Both Aalto's Vogelweidplatz design of 1953 and Pietilä's Brussels pavilion of 1956 demonstrate the clear lead that Finnish architects had in the new European architecture of the first half of the 50s.

The Vogelweidplatz project would have been Aalto's largest building. Its programme included a combination sports hall and concert auditorium with a maximum capacity of 25,000 people, together with many auxiliary rooms, and halls for tennis, boxing and gymnastics. It was intended also to serve as an exhibition building. Aalto grouped most of the principal functions, including the main 'arena' and tennis and sports halls, into a variation of his 'wedge' or 'fan' plan, with the roof structure, conceived on the model of suspension bridges, spanning this vast conglomerate in a series of catenaries that dip down towards the centre of the arena. Acoustical control for musical performances was to have been effected by a series of automatically movable baffles suspended from these catenaries. Considering the large scale and complexity of this project Aalto's solution has an elegant simplicity, which he was to achieve again at the end of the 50s in his design for the Essen Opera House.

It was clearly Aalto's intention to emulate these simple volumetrics in his project for the Oulu Theatre and Concert Hall of 1955. But the success of the Vogelweidplatz design was to achieve simplicity from a complex equation, whereas the Oulu plan itself has a banality that is unworthy of Aalto in the mid-50s. Of course, 1955 was again a rather busy year in Aalto's office, with the Pensions Institute still under construction and the first stage of Jyväskylä Pedagogical Institute (later University)

Oulu theatre and concert hall project: original competition perspective view from the river, showing the massing of the stepped fan-form foyer to the auditorium

already under way, while he also had the revised designs for Otaniemi on the board as well as the competition for a new town hall at Gothenberg. In addition he was involved that year in building and moving to his new studio and office at Tiilimäki 20, as well as commencing the designs for the House of Culture in Helsinki.

So with all these important activities occupying him in major centres he cannot have had much time for the Oulu project. Even the signed perspective drawing conveys none of the flair or panache of an Aalto concept. One can only conclude, therefore, that this design was turned over to an assistant at a very early stage. The stepped treatment of the outer sweep of the 'fan' plan, the foyer, is simply unconvincing as a mature Aalto gesture.[26] The Gothenburg city hall and municipal offices competition project, for which Aalto was awarded first prize in 1955, with the design revised in 1957 but remaining unbuilt, is also a curious design for the mid-50s. There is no question, however, that Aalto was anything but deeply involved in this project and ensuring its success. His many theoretical sketches as well as details of various elements and the basic layout[27] confirms his presence throughout the entire design process. But, although the overall planning concept seems to follow the rectilinear block and court form he used at Otaniemi, the elevations and massing return to the functionalist spirit of the Tampere railway station competition entry of 1934 and the State Alcohol Monopoly (ALKO) competition entry of 1935. The Gothenberg design projected a crisp semi-classical design, with a vast ramped rectilinear agora that was visible from the city centre and flanked by two long stoa that reached out from the parkland site towards the centre. Although construction work actually began on this vast undertaking it never rose above ground. The municipality had second thoughts, called for revised designs and then indefinitely postponed its continuation.

Without doubt, the most important project to begin and take shape in 1955 was the headquarters building for the Finnish Communist Party, known as 'The House of Culture' or 'Kultuuritalo'. Again it is perfectly clear from studying the evolution of its complex plan form that Aalto must have lost interest in the Oulu project at an early stage. It is equally clear that in working out the highly original, mediaeval-fortress-like contours of the auditorium massing, with its distinct annular banding or zoning in the 'fan' plan, he anticipated the organic plasticity of the Vuoksenniska church in Imatra, which was begun a year later, in 1956.

The Kultuuritalo realises a number of breakthroughs in Aalto's design language. It is the first of his brick buildings to abandon a rectilinear or angular discipline in favour of a full curvilinear form – although this seems to be implied in a simpler way by the Oulu theatre perspective and was developed also in the revised Otaniemi main auditorium building of the same year. Secondly, it shows Aalto in the interior of the auditorium experimenting both with structural column and acoustical ceiling forms that were to provide dominant themes for his interior treatments of the next decade. The columns, basically simple rectangles but with elegant triangular fins fanning up towards the ceiling, recall his earlier interest in this splayed form in the machine hall of Turun Sanomat, while the irregular cusping of the acoustic tiled ceiling onto the walls has many Renaissance and post-Renaissance models, of which the Capella degli Scrovegni in Padua (which appears in Aalto's sketchbook for 1924) is a possible source. Thirdly, the use of specially made bull-nosed headers to allow him to achieve an optimum negotiation of curved brick surfaces, and the delicate modelling of the cantilevered projectionist's booth thrusting out at eaves level like a mediaeval gun turret, showed Aalto's plastic geometry as being highly romantic in origin. Interestingly, he was never again to attempt this same impeccable quality in brickwork. The Kultuuritalo is thus the ultimate refinement of those brick experiments begun at Muuratsalo in 1953; but after its completion in 1958 Aalto turned, for most of his major buildings to be completed in the 60s, to the use of marbles and ceramic tiles as the principal external facing material.

Aalto's design for the Finnish Pavilion at the Venice Biennale of 1956 is a small one-roomed structure, with none of the grandeur or complexity of either the Paris or New York designs.[28] Its external timber structure of lapped triangular frames, that recall the expressionism of the Otaniemi Sports Hall (1953), supports the small pavilion which is suspended between them. Internally, the ceiling has a split level within the roof trusses to bring in daylight from an indirect, semi-concealed source. Aalto was to use this ceiling technique in a number of buildings, including the main auditoria at Otaniemi. But its most direct application is in the Central Finland Museum (1959), the North Jutland Art Museum (1958–72) and the Seinäjoki Library (1963).

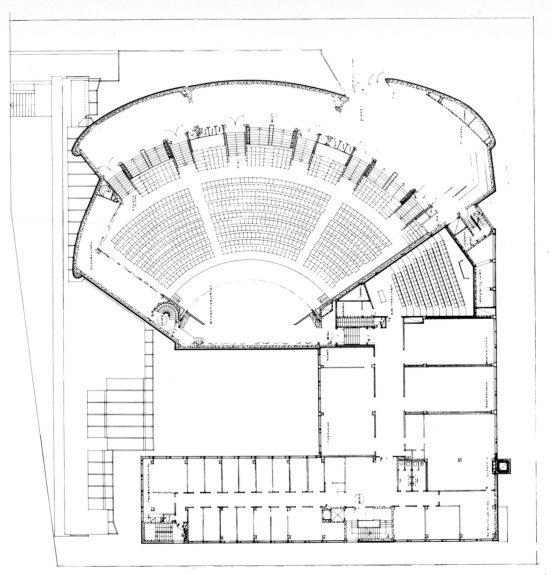

Headquarters for the Finnish Communist Party, Helsinki (1955–8), known as the House of Culture: plan at first-floor level, showing the irregular fan-shaped plan of the auditorium and the outline of the pergola roofs that span the front of the building and close the entrance courtyard

In Germany Aalto's first attempt to develop his reputation by building there was his entry for the Marl town hall competition in 1957. This design has its origins in two earlier ones – that for the Pensions Institute ('Forum Redivivum B') of 1948, and the Malmi funeral chapel project of 1950. The Marl project had a large *Innenhof* or piazza at first-floor level whilst the split axis of the planning composition centres on the grouping of the assembly hall council chamber and small meeting room with the wedge-shaped council chamber acting as the fulcrum. There is a main administrative wing that stretches out towards the neighbouring park, while the three other office elements fan out like fingers. Aalto's sketches show that he drew the analogy of the

Finnish Communist Party Headquarters: interior of the main auditorium, showing the undulating forms of the acoustic ceiling and the fan-shaped columns

Finnish Pavilion for the Venice Biennale (1956): view of exterior, showing triangular bolted wooden truss structure and lantern lights on roof

branching of a plant form; but the image of a 'hand' is nevertheless clearly present in this design.

He received no award for this project, although the competition drawings promised a much more interesting building than the later Wolfsburg Cultural Centre (1958, 1959–62), which was clearly based upon the Marl concept. By taking the vehicular traffic underneath the podium level Aalto was able to offer an external urban space of interest. The steps up to it are reminiscent of those he proposed in the original Pensions Institute design, while the handling of the relationship of the three 'finger' blocks to that space – creating in the process a *piazzetta* that nestles between the three blocks – owes something both to the Malmi design and the irregular pattern of streets leading into an Italian piazza; and in this case those flowing into Il Campo in Siena suggest themselves. This loosely knit design is disciplined but open-ended, offering an acceptable scale for what was after all a very substantial bureaucratic centre. In contrast, as we shall see, the Wolfsburg Cultural Centre is monumental in spite of its apparent informality. Also, Aalto's competition drawings indicate a red-brick building rather than the marble of the Wolfsburg centre. There is something explicit in Aalto's conceptual geometry which often demands an open-ended plan form. The more closed courtyards of the final Pensions Institute design and Säynätsalo town hall are, of course, his other main theme.

Nineteen fifty-eight was another of those frantically busy, momentous years in Aalto's office, and no fewer than five major projects were set in motion during the course of it. These were the town hall for Kiruna (Sweden), the Wolfsburg Cultural Centre (Germany), two art museums – one for Baghdad (Iraq) and the other for Aalborg (Denmark) – and finally, at the end of the year, the Opera House for Essen (Germany). In addition, he was still in the midst of building another important commission, the Vuoksenniska church at Imatra, while work on the Maison Carré was drawing to a close. And he also found time to prepare designs for the Central Post Office Administration Building in Baghdad.

The competition project for Kiruna town hall, with which Aalto won first prize, saw him still working with the curvilinear, plastic masses that originated in the House of Culture (1955) and which achieved the peak of their development in the Vuoksenniska church (1956–9). Kiruna is the centre for iron-ore mining in Sweden. The landscape of the immediate area is therefore an artificial one, produced by man in the process of extracting the ore and depositing mounds of slag. Aalto sought to reflect these special characteristics of the Kiruna region in his design. There was also the climatic factor: Kiruna has severe winters with heavy snowfall and powerful blizzards, resulting in considerable problems with drifting. Taking the steeply sloping slag mounds as the image for his solution Aalto developed a quasi-symmetrical plan form consisting of an angled administrative block which turned its 'cliff' face to the north. Behind this protective, virtually windowless wall nestles the council chamber, linked by a roof terrace that faces south. The angled, faceted cliff-face treatment is reminiscent of the outer walls proposed for the Vogelweidplatz project in Vienna

Town hall competition project for Kiruna (1958): Aalto's original *Ideenskizze*, showing the basic plan shape

(1953) and was intended to shed the driving snow, keeping it from the main office windows. Most of the office accommodation was therefore arranged at the back of the cliff wall, facing south over the terrace towards the council chamber. This plan form is unique in Aalto's *oeuvre*; it was a direct response to local conditions and bears no relationship to his other designs of this period for municipal centres.

The Cultural Centre for Wolfsburg, 'the Volkswagen town', was conceived as an intellectual counterpoint to the otherwise monotonous life of an industrial community. Although this building has a closed form, and the structure itself is entirely enclosed (i.e., without the characteristic open courtyard of his 50s designs), Aalto took as his image for this building the Greek agora.[29] In other words he conceived it as a social 'magnet' in response to the four-part programme of (1) library and adult education centre; (2) a vocational 'hobby' centre; (3) a club and social centre; and (4) additional community facilities (grouped around a roof garden).

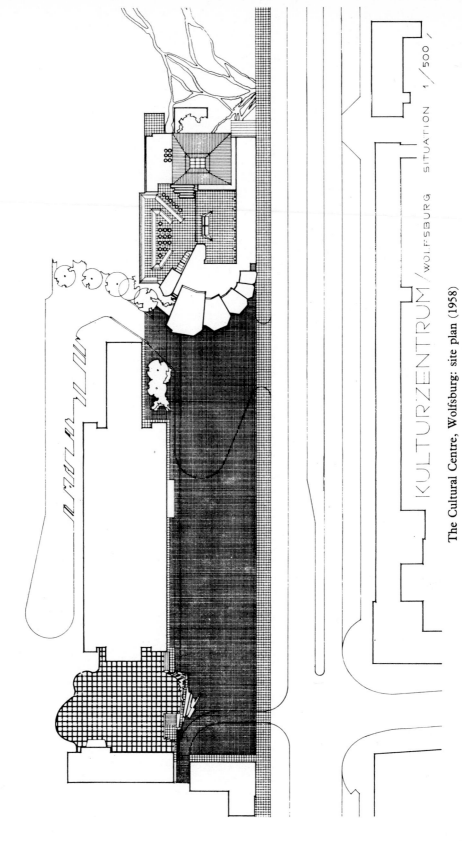

KULTURZENTRUM/WOLFSBURG SITUATION 1/500

The Cultural Centre, Wolfsburg: site plan (1958)

Wolfsburg Cultural Centre, seen from the revised piazza, with car parking intervening between the mass of the fan-plan and the public space

Aalto's stepped 'fan' arrangement of the main auditorium and meeting rooms is a familiar feature, although the way in which this element is carried on columns, to provide an ambulatory under its periphery, contributes a unique treatment to the dominant outer edge of this building (constructed 1959–62). Indeed, in view of Aalto's reference to the Greek agora, this ground-floor colonnade can again be construed as a stoa. The fan shape having been assigned to the auditoria, the library at Wolfsburg was given a similar and closely related plan form, that of the wedge. At ground-floor level the accommodation is tightly packed on either side of a 'spinal' corridor, which leads off the generous circulation beneath the auditoria. The library is the main element at ground-floor level, with a separate children's library (which originated at Viipuri) associated with a small outdoor court. In the centre of the library is a sunken reading area (also initiated at Viipuri) which is top lit. The other large rooms are also grouped on the other side of the corridor spine at ground-floor level, with the auditoria above. At first floor the roof terrace, which forms an open court in the heart of the building, where it is well protected from traffic noise, provides the focus for the upper foyer of the auditoria and the remainder of the accommodation. These smaller rooms are ranged along a glazed corridor, in the manner of Säynätsalo, so that there is a covered circulation on three sides of the terrace with continuous views from it of the external open space. At the far end of the complex from the auditoria the other principal rooms at first floor are again grouped around an internal top-lit court.

Thus, the Wolfsburg centre presents in its plan form a compact and seemingly

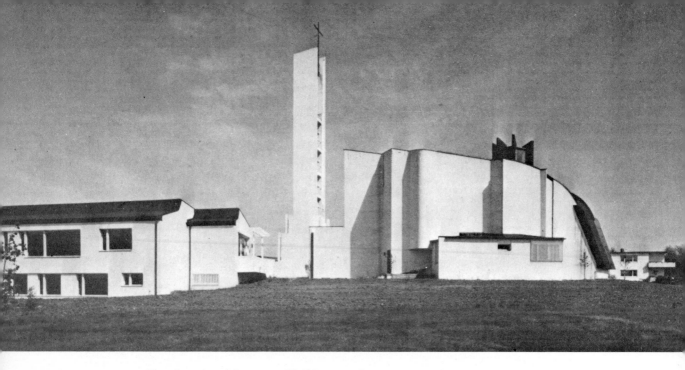

Church and parish centre, Wolfsburg (1959–62): general view of the grouping

Wolfsburg: detail of the east end of the church, and window treatment

regular volume, with the exception of the auditoria treatment. But within this tight organisation it is the court motif, either internal or external, that provides the plan dynamic. It becomes apparent that this is not one building but a number of separate structures that have been shunted together in this tight-packing arrangement. The agora is not one simple space, either, but a number of related spaces. Thus, the Wolfsburg centre becomes a highly articulated exercise in regulated irregularity.

It is rich in both the variety of forms and detailing. The use of banded stonework on the auditoria element, alternating Carrara marble and syenite Pamit, is probably Aalto's most successful use of this material and is reminiscent of Tuscan and Sienese examples – a rich image for bringing *Kultur* to German factory workers! Also, the variety of scale from the urban formality of the colonnade beneath the auditoria to the more intimate secondary entrances and children's library court, is graduated from one end of the building to the other. To emphasise this intimacy when one is close up to the building and beneath the colonnade, Aalto uses ceramic tile facings for those recessed walls, already suggesting that one is within the building's envelope. In contrast, from the distance, it is the marble masses that announce this civic symbol for Wolfsburg. (An interesting feature of the interior is the treatment of the main auditorium, which recalls Aalto's competition project for the Helsinki University Library extension, 1937.)

It is unfortunate that Aalto abandoned this discipline of 'tight-packing' when he came to design the town centre for Seinäjoki in Finland. He had already won the competition for the design of the church in 1952 and this was under construction (1958–60) when he won the competition for the town centre plan in 1959. He made the church, located on high ground at the east end of the site, the focus of his urban composition in a long attenuated axial design, which places the theatre (as yet unbuilt) at the far end of the axis. Between these two theatres, the sacred and the profane, he grouped the town hall and administrative offices to the north, creating an artificial mound between them and the central axial space, with the municipal library closing the framework of the group to the south.

This framework, in complete contrast to the Aalto urban 'tradition' of the Pensions Institute, Säynätsalo and Wolfsburg, and even to the campus designs for Otaniemi and Jyväskylä, is too loose adequately to contain the space which it frames. In this matter Aalto's design has not been helped by the construction of a main arterial road between the ecclesiastical 'acropolis' and the secular buildings at the other end of the site; the centre is thus cut in half. But it fails in any case at the visual level. The separate sites for the church and the civic centre always allowed for this split. Aalto's strong interest in Italian urban containers equipped him to understand the need for the visual linking of 'church' and 'state' in this composition, and evidence of his competence to do this is well demonstrated by the 'Forum Redivivum B' design. Yet the grouping of town hall, library and theatre at Seinäjoki gives a distinctly suburban flavour, with the wide open space between the administrative block and the library allowing the space to drain out into the main road precisely where it should *contain* the

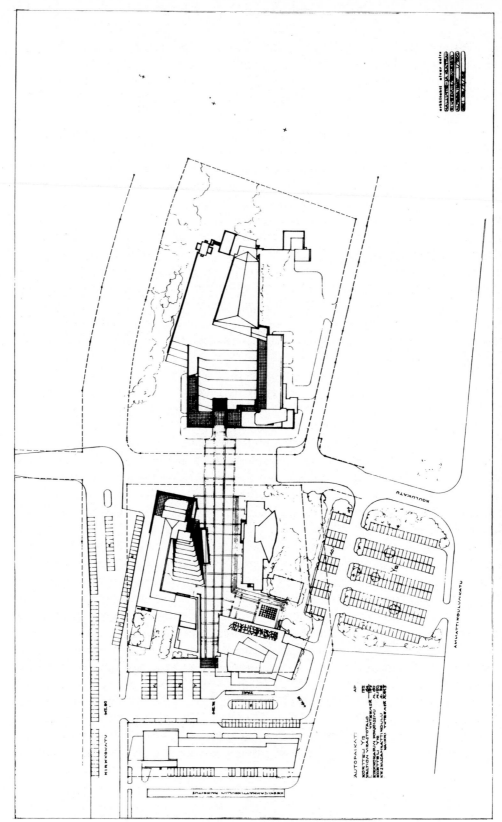

Town centre plan for Seinäjoki (1959), showing the civic centre with town hall, library and theatre (left), and the church and parish centre (right)

Seinäjoki town centre: view towards the church, with the town hall (left) and library (right). An unharmonious arrangement

secular functions and *frame* the campanile of the church. Aalto's church design for Seinäjoki is also his weakest for this building type. Its simple hall form presents a boringly bland west front, the whole of which is seen, without interruption from the great tract of space between town hall, library and theatre. When we recall Aalto's subtlety in the 'Forum Redivivum B' design, we are entitled to ask 'Whither the piazza?'

In a situation where the utmost tightness and coherence of space and volume was required to breathe into Seinäjoki, a fast developing 'expanded' town, the spirit of urbanity, Aalto provided a loose collection of buildings that simply do not connect either spatially or visually. His parkland solution for Seinäjoki, without the benefit of a park, seems peculiarly out of keeping with the town's needs. He was to repeat this error of judgement in the context of urban space when he came to design the centre of Rovaniemi in 1963.

The most interesting building in the Seinäjoki town centre is the municipal library (1963–5), which takes the precise 'fan' shape of the reading-room plan from two housing designs – the high-rise block in the Neue Vahr district of Bremen (designed in 1958 and constructed 1959–62), the plan of which was repeated in part of the student hostel at Otaniemi (designed in 1962 and built 1964–6). Both of these are refinements of the profile introduced in the auditoria block at Wolfsburg (also designed in 1958). The relationship of the fanned reading room to the control desk in the Seinäjoki Library repeats that of the Wolfsburg model, as does that of the fan

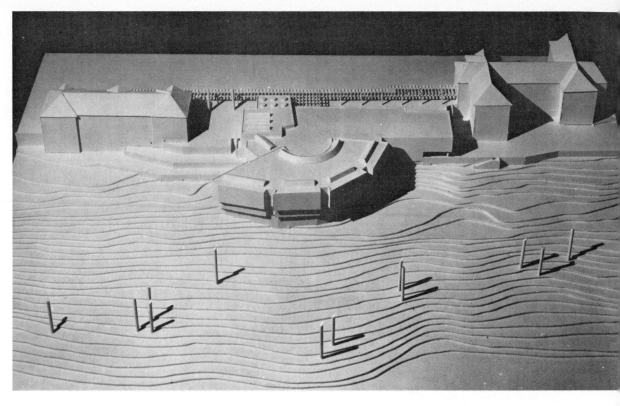

Library for the Mount Angel Benedictine College, Mount Angel, Oregon (1965–70): model showing the project in relation to existing buildings adjoining

shape to the spinal corridor. In the case of the Rovaniemi Library, which was also designed in 1963, the fan motif returns to the more fragmented, cellular model of the Wolfsburg auditoria arrangement, as does the plan of the library for the Mount Angel Benedictine College in Oregon (designed 1965–6 and built 1967–70). Also, both the Rovaniemi and Mount Angel plans abandon the direct relationship with a spinal corridor in favour of a freer connection with this linear element of accommodation.

Whilst still on the theme of town design, it should be noted that next to the plan for the Otaniemi campus that for the University of Jyväskylä probably provides the most cogent example of urban form in Aalto's work. It is, in the best sense of the term, a 'forest town', nestling as it does on a thickly wooded hillside above Jyväskylä. This quality is well demonstrated by the original buildings Aalto designed for this project, particularly the main auditorium block. Aalto won the competition for the overall planning of the University (then the Pedagogical Institute) in 1950 and the first stage, including the auditorium block, was built between 1952 and 1957. In this block Aalto already began to develop the fan motif on a large scale by thrusting the wedge-shaped auditorium itself hard against the rectilinear lecture theatre block. This gave the two elements a common, party wall, which has openings to allow the circulation between the two parts of the building and shared use of the garderobe which occurs at this juncture. Inside the building Aalto exploits two urban motifs that were to become a

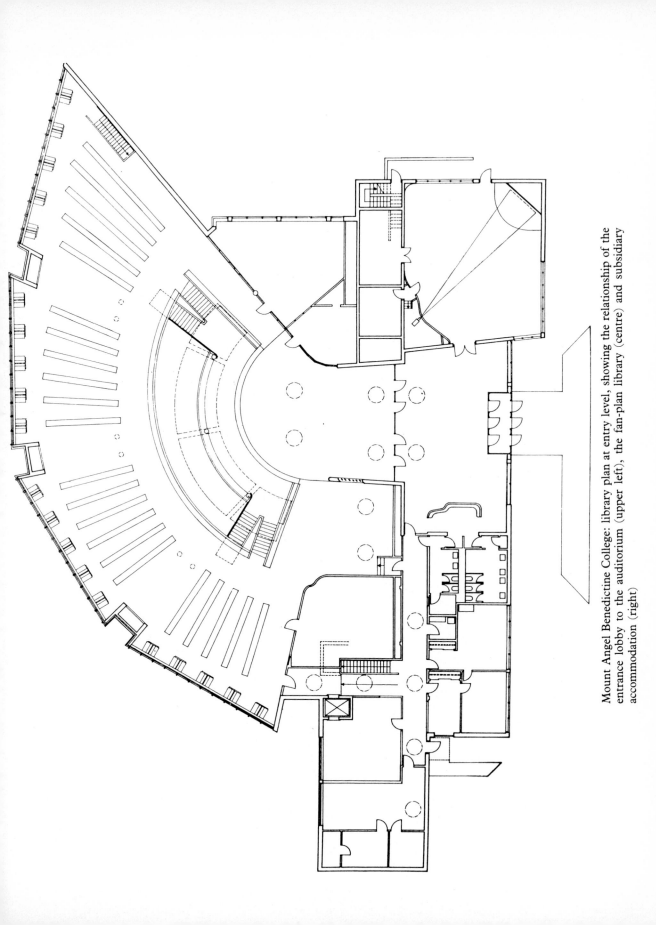

Mount Angel Benedictine College: library plan at entry level, showing the relationship of the entrance lobby to the auditorium (upper left), the fan-plan library (centre) and subsidiary accommodation (right)

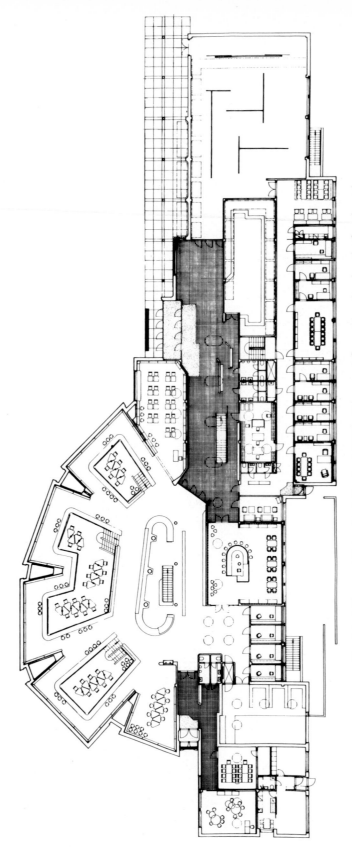

Municipal library at Rovaniemi, Lapland (1965–8): ground-floor plan, showing the fan-shaped reading room with its three sunken areas

Rovaniemi municipal library: interior view of reading room, with sunken area and clerestorey windows that provide natural light for the upper level

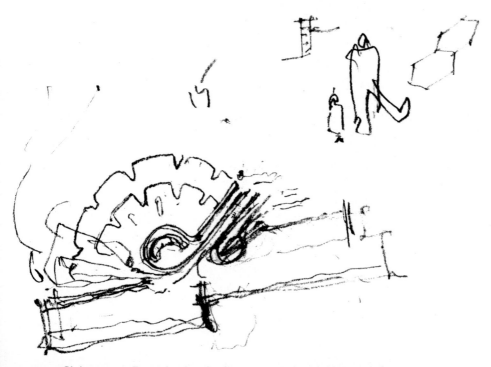

Civic centre, Rovaniemi – the library: Aalto's original *Ideenskizze*

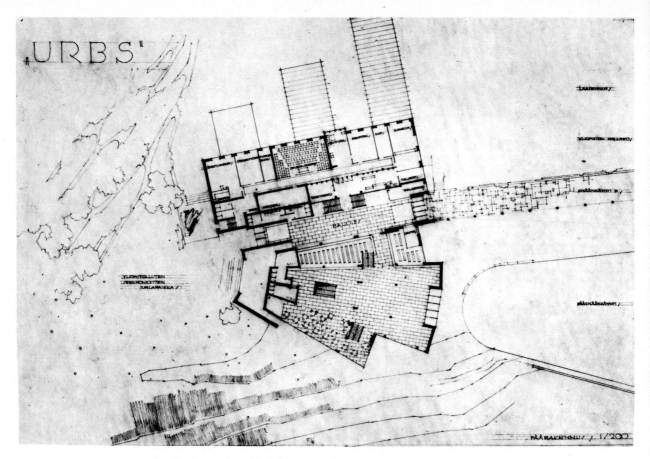

Pedagogical Institute (later University), Jyväskylä (1952–7): plan of central auditorium and lecture theatre complex (original competition entry "Urbs" of 1952)

familiar hallmark of his work in the 50s and 60s. First, the auditorium foyer at ground level rises up, back from the central vomitory in a series of steps cut out of acoustical tile 'planes'; this stepped space under the auditorium opens out to an approach road through a totally glazed rear wall. This glass wall, with its diagonal screw-rod door braces, is reminiscent of the Viipuri Library door-screen, and again its purpose is to 'admit' the external landscape into the interior space. As the auditorium is used by the city for community functions, this foyer becomes, in winter, the principal piazza in Jyväskylä. Thus, in a slightly disguised form, it is another incidence of Aalto's interior court. And leading off this 'court' is an internalised main street which gives access to the campus itself, literally a *field* which was designed to accommodate the college's outside sports activities. This 'street' also contains a monumental staircase, partially hidden behind a stepped wall, that leads to the lecture theatres which are reached from three mezzanine landings on three levels. The stair treatment recalls in a most direct manner the steps enclosed between walls of adjoining buildings that are a salient feature of Italian hill towns. Passing from one level to another one is in the transitional *passage* of the staircase, as at Säynätsalo town hall, which was being

Jyväskylä University: view of central auditorium and lecture theatre complex from within the campus, with (below) detail of rear entrance

Jyväskylä University: foyer of central auditorium complex

completed whilst the Jyväskylä stair was being designed.

Beginning with Tallin (1937), Aalto was to prepare designs for no fewer than seven museums, of which four were art museums of an international standard; and two of these came onto his drawing board in 1958. These were for two disparate physical and cultural climates: the one in Baghdad was not implemented; while that in Aalborg, the only one of the four to be realised, appropriately refined some of the ideas contained in the proposals for Tallin two decades earlier. But Aalto had still to wait fourteen years before these concepts took shape, for the North Jutland Art Museum, which he and Elissa designed in collaboration with Jean-Jacques Barüel, was not to be built until 1972.

Of the two designs, that for Baghdad has the most obvious similarities to the original Tallin design. These are apparent in two main features: (1) the stepping of the entrances to the galleries from the mall that cuts diagonally through the interior, linking the entrance hall with the foyer to the meeting room/auditorium and directly recalling the Tallin arrangement; and (2) the transfer of the sculpture garden (which in the Tallin design was the exterior extension of the 'mall') to the roof where it was sheltered by a giant louvre system which would reflect the sun as well as inducing the

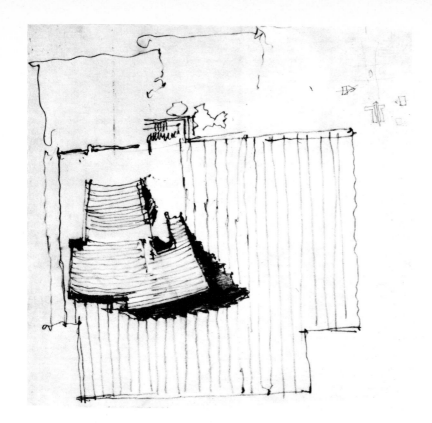

Art museum for Baghdad project: original *Ideenskizze* for roof terrace with fan-shaped amphitheatre (1958)

Baghdad art museum: original competition sections, showing the rooflight system to provide indirect natural lighting to the galleries, the roof-top amphitheatre and the horizontal *brise-soleil* to the roof garden

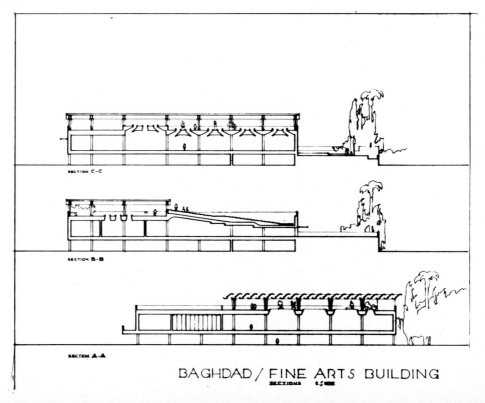

section C-C

section B-B

section A-A

BAGHDAD / FINE ARTS BUILDING

circulation of air. The roof garden and the roof-level amphitheatre (recalling the Otaniemi auditorium complex) would have given a distinctive profile to this building. As the galleries are top lit, the ground-floor walls are high and virtually windowless, which, allowing for the transfer of the Aalto 'courtyard' plan to roof level, gives the impression of a deep podium with the architecture starting at the first floor (as in the 'Forum Redivivum B' project). In addition to Aalto, Frank Lloyd Wright, Gropius and Le Corbusier were among other outstanding international architects commissioned to contribute designs for the Baghdad urbanisation programme, of which the art museum formed a part.

Although the Baghdad project and that for Aalborg have superficial similarities, these are confined to the plan profile of interlocking rectilinear volumes. In the Aalborg design there is a semi-basement containing storage, central heating and car parking, so that the gallery level is at the first floor on the approach side. On the rear side, which in the Baghdad design has a garden entrance providing an atrium to the auditorium foyer, there is a landscaped area which serves for outside gatherings and performances; this contains a terraced feature at an angle to the main building as well as a double-cusp amphitheatre. The first floor is tightly planned with large double-sided reflecting lanterns over the galleries, whilst the volume over the upper foyer and auditorium is shaped into a gently stepped pyramid. On closer examination the apparent similarity between the gallery level in the Baghdad and Aalborg designs disappears, the essential difference being that the linking diagonal 'mall' in the Baghdad project is replaced at Aalborg by an ambulatory that runs completely around the meeting room, which in the massing becomes the dominant volume in the composition.

The project for the Essen Opera House, commenced at the end of 1958 and submitted in an international competition early in 1959, is one of Aalto's most stunningly original projects. Its programme combined the problem of urban scale, presented by the major German industrial city, with a parkland setting. Our analysis has shown that this combination should provide an ideal context for Aalto's talents. His solution drew on a number of precedents already established in his own repertoire: these derive particularly from (1) the Vogelweidplatz Music and Sports Centre, Vienna, project (1953); (2) the House of Culture, Helsinki, (1953–8); and (3) Kiruna town hall, project (1958).

The House of Culture was Aalto's first asymmetrical auditorium and its form is clearly the inspiration for the Opera House plan, whilst the manner in which this auditorium form is 'suspended' within another, overall asymmetrical volume recalls the Vogelweidplatz project. In external form the Essen project is simpler and more monumentally volumetric than that for Vienna. Indeed, its synthesis of shape and mass in the achievement of a 'super-scale' recalls Aalto's thinking for the 'Drottning Torget' central station project for Gothenberg (1956, first prize but unbuilt), although its external expression clearly has more to do with the design of the 'snow-wall' in the Kiruna town hall project.

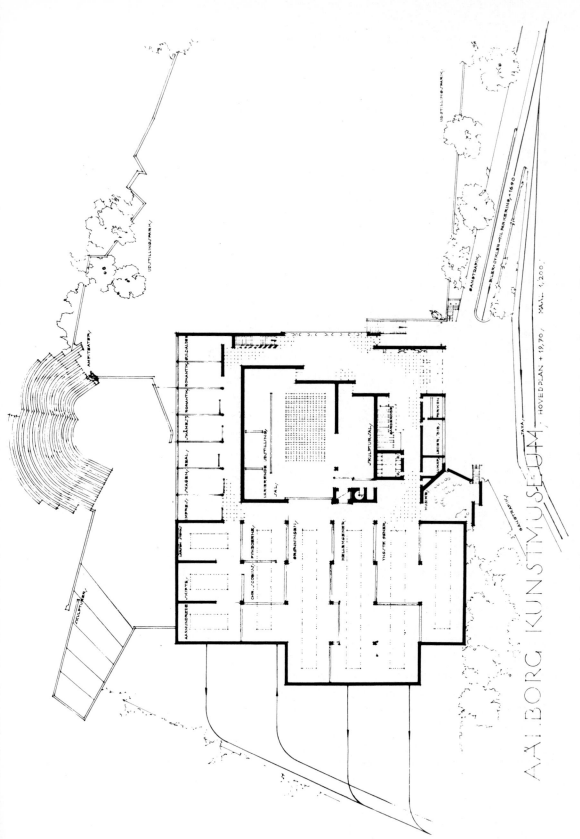

Art museum for Aalborg, original project (1958): plan, showing the galleries grouped not around an open court as in the Tallin project but around the lecture theatre

Aalborg art museum project: aerial view of model, showing the relationship of the museum's outline and massing to the amphitheatre

Internally, the vast scale of the Opera House auditorium called for a very different treatment from that of the Kultuuritalo. Faced with the requirement that it should accommodate smaller audiences as well as full capacity use, Aalto developed a great rear wall of *loges* and compartmental balconies which is intended to assume its architectural role whether full or empty. Certainly, the audience seated below in the stalls would be more aware of architectural qualities than its function. Clearly, Aalto called upon his experience in designing the great undulating display wall of the New York pavilion (1938–9) when he came to this related problem at Essen, and his sketches for the Opera House interior confirm this.

Revised designs for the Opera House were prepared in the Aalto office between 1961 and 1964, but the decision to go ahead was postponed on financial grounds. Further revisions were still being discussed at the time of Aalto's death in 1976, but still no commitment was made by the Essen municipality. It is clear that these

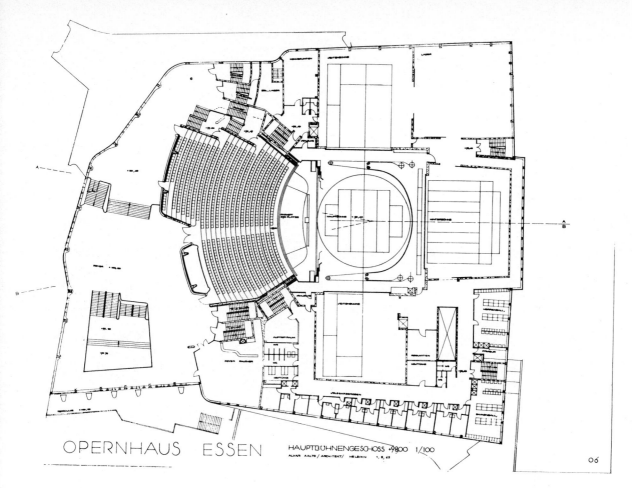

Essen Opera House project (original competition design 1958–9): plan at upper foyer level, showing main auditorium and stage (post-competition design, first proposal)

revisions in no way affected the spirit of the design but were essentially exercises in reducing the overall building volume in order to bring the cost down. Obviously the Essen authorities, well aware of the problems that had ensued from the commissioning of the Sydney Opera House, were more cautious than the Australians; but the price is that Essen still has no Opera House. The Essen authorities provisionally gave the go-ahead in the early summer of 1980, more than four years after Aalto's death. So, perhaps by the middle of the decade we may see that: '. . . dome-like room, kept in a deep blue colour (indigo) and so designed as to easily accommodate both absorbent and reflective acoustical surfaces (dark, neutral colours) . . . (*contrasted by*) the wall of *loges* in white marble, partly massive and partly broken up in a sort of filigree.'

In the long gestation period, during which Aalto himself was convinced that his ultimate auditorium design would never be realised, he incorporated some of his Essen ideas into the design for Finlandia House, built in Helsinki between 1967 and 1971 (see pp. 230–31).

Opera House for Essen project: original competition model

Essen Opera House: original study model for interior of the main auditorium (1960), showing the *loges* and bentwood treatment of side walls

There is, not surprisingly, a clear link between Aalto's designs for auditoria and those for his churches. This fits, of course, with his functionalist canon. What is surprising, perhaps, is the almost complete lack of connection between Aalto the ritualist (as evidenced by his designs for Malmi and Lyngby chapels, the Maison Carré and the 'Studio R-S', for example) and the five designs for churches of Aalto's mature period spread over more than a decade, beginning with Imatra (1956) and ending with Zürich-Altstetten (1967). The Riola design (1966) was not implemented until after his death, being completed (with the exception of the campanile, which was omitted from the contract) in 1978. Of these the most obviously functionalist, a simple wedge shape, was for the Wolfsburg suburb of Detmerode. The Detmerode plan is based on Aalto's original design for the Lahti church, with which he won first prize in 1950: this design was substantially modified in 1970 in preparation for construction, although the basic wedge shape was retained. A modification to the original design was an attached campanile in a more elaborate style than Aalto's 50s manner (e.g. Seinäjoki), and it was at Detmerode (built 1965–8) that he worked out this form of belfry. It consists basically of a number of vertical concrete planks to which subsidiary fins or louvres are attached at the actual belfry level. In fact the Detmerode design is much more refined, with the campanile probably standing as Aalto's best excursion into pure sculpture. The Lahti church was redesigned in

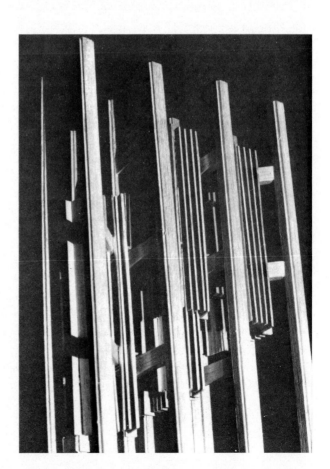

Detmerode parish centre project (1965): model of proposed form for campanile

Parish centre project for Detmerode district of Wolfsburg: model of proposed acoustic treatment for church ceiling

Aalto's last period when he was already in his seventies and the standard of concept and detailing was markedly in decline.

The other distinctive feature of the Detmerode church is the acoustical treatment of its interior. This consists of nineteen flat segmental 'domes', graduated up in five different sizes from the front of the church towards the rear. These 'cups' are suspended from the flat but raked ceiling. The pure, functionalist form of this treatment recalls much earlier Aalto motifs and seems more in character with the period from the Turun Sanomat building to the Viipuri Library, i.e., 1927–33.

Aalto's first major church design of his mature period was the commission in 1956 for Vuoksenniska in Imatra, eastern Finland. In this project, built between 1957 and 1959, he followed the new plastic expressionism which had been created in the design for the House of Culture, Helsinki (begun in 1955). The asymmetrical auditorium for the House of Culture becomes in the Imatra church a three-part shell form, also slightly asymmetrical, that allows the building to accommodate three different sizes of congregation. One third or two thirds of the church may be closed off by 'sliding walls', housed in the corresponding curved enclosures on the right hand side of the nave, that form the external walls. The ceiling is also shaped in the form of three distinct 'shells', developing a progressive undulation from altar to rear organ-loft that is reminiscent of the innovatory design for the Viipuri lecture room ceiling.

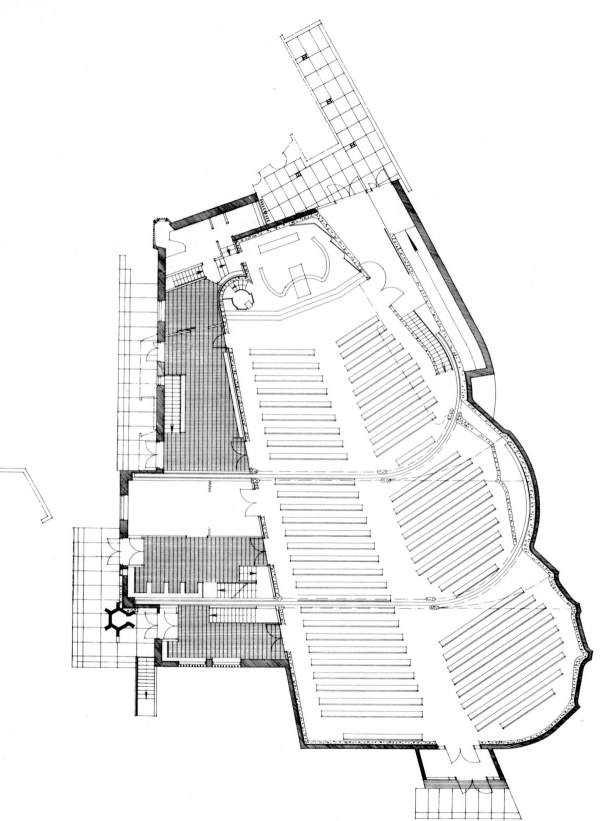

Church at Vuoksenniska, Imatra (1956–9): plan, showing the "moving wall" system of subdividing the interior according to the size of congregation

Vuoksenniska, Imatra: external view of the highly plastic form. The church was built in the heart of a forest but, shortly after its completion, a hurricane uprooted most of the trees in the vicinity

In the Imatra design Aalto provided the most convincing evidence of his ability to convert the plastic plan into a three-dimensional plasticity. The exterior of the church resembles a copper-roofed bunker or gun emplacement, while the faceted and finned detached campanile anticipates the Detmerode model by almost a decade. Inside the church Aalto's detailing of the transitions between the three 'compartments' of the nave demonstrates a total sense of coherence in the manipulation of complex geometries that is unequalled in Aalto's mature expression. But it is interesting to note that in 1959, just as the Vuoksenniska church was being completed, Reima Pietilä was stressing the plastic, free-form rhythms of his modular preoccupations in his Kaleva church design for Tampere.[30] Aalto's exploitation of the double-shell concept, first hinted at in the lanterns of the Pensions Institute (1952–6) and considerably developed in the House of Culture auditorium block (1955–8), reaches perfection in the Imatra church. This double-shell concept also forms a salient strategy in Pietilä's complex geometrics, as for example in the Finnish Embassy for New Delhi design of

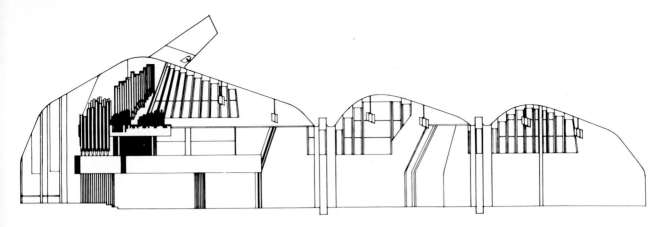

Section of church at Vuoksenniska, Imatra, showing internal form, the position of the moving walls and the rooflight at the east end

1963, the Malmi church competition entry of 1967 and the Monte Carlo Centre project of 1969.[31]

Aalto's Wolfsburg Parish Centre, designed in 1959 and built between 1960 and 1962, continues this plastic expressionism, although in this German example it is contained within the section alone, while the campanile takes a distinctly backward step also, with its primitive constructivist stepping of the parallel side walls. The most interesting achievement in this design is the grouping of church, parish centre and the presbytery around a hilltop *piazzetta*. His last two church designs provide, however, an interesting departure.

Vuoksenniska church, Imatra: interior view, showing the positions of the two moving walls and the windows located in the double-shell construction of the external walls

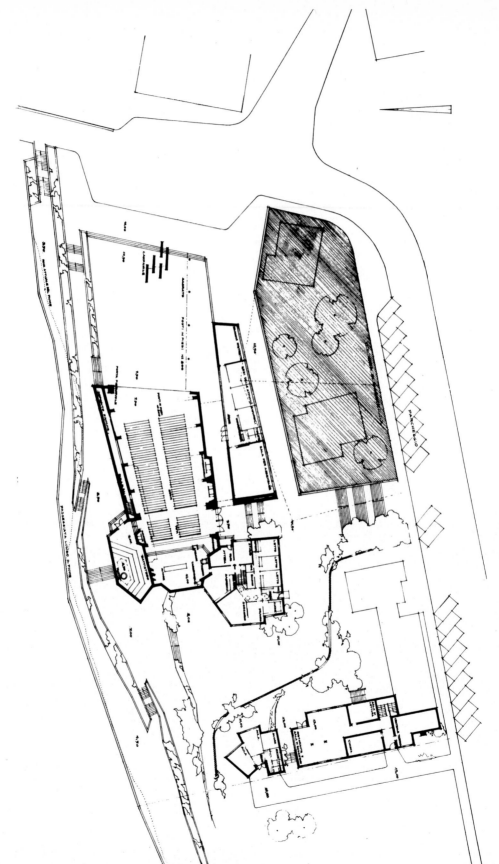

Parish centre at Riola, near Bologna: original plan (1966), showing the church, priest's house and parish hall

There are distinct similarities between the proposal for the Riola church and Parish Centre, near Bologna, commissioned in 1966, and that for the Altstetten district of Zürich of 1967. The geometry of these designs owes nothing to the mastery Aalto exhibited at Imatra; rather it has its origin in the forms of industrial sheds. It is interesting but disappointing that the path from Muurame (1926–9) should have led to Imatra and then to the anticlimax provided by these designs for Italy and Switzerland. In a sense his church designs provide the alpha and omega of Aalto's career. But the high point of this development is definitely to be found at Imatra. Regrettably the more cogent of these two final designs, that for Altstetten, was not built. Its combination of site treatment, particularly the formal approach by steps that are framed by a parapet wall and the campanile, with the tightly orchestrated massing of the church running west–east at the upper level and the parish hall (running east–west at the lower level) on either side of a 'street' recalls the compact urban imagery of the Pensions Institute and Säynätsalo. There is a distinct backward glance in this design also, to Viinikka church project for Tampere (1927), with its reference to an Italian hilltop piazza. The soft undulations proposed for the Altstetten roofline, and the overall coherence of the massing, including the sympathetic cut-off of the campanile walls angled at the top, are much more successful than those of the Riola design.

The section of the Riola church, with the serrated roof made up of half vaults supported on cranked portal frames, promises more than the completed interior of the building delivers. In fact, one is hardly aware of the vault system; the clumsy great frames dominate the nave and give it a distinctly industrial character. All the sensitivity of those early church interiors, of Jämsä (1925) and Muurame (1927–9), has gone, as has the confident, almost Baroque, plasticism of Imatra. And even the west front, where those half vaults are seen to best advantage, is a barren enough affair without the benefit of the sculptural campanile as a foil. But that campanile as proposed was not at all comparable in form and interest with either Detmerode or the Altstetten proposal. Also, the *batistero*, conceived by Aalto as a sunken projection at the end of the south aisle, thrusting out appropriately towards the river, has a curiously half-hearted lantern over the font. This lantern is certainly not the work of the man who designed those for the Pensions Institute (1952–6) or the new Academic Bookshop (1966–9). In fact there is no evidence, certainly not in the executed building, that Aalto had much to do with this design after the concept stage, especially when we consider that the design of the Academic Bookshop lanterns was exactly contemporaneous with the inception of the Riola. Surely Aalto, whose love of Italy was renowned, would have wanted to leave his mark on Italian soil more than any other than his own, Finnish soil.[32] But the execution was posthumous and the interior detailing owes little to the master's hand.

Even at the project stage the Altstetten design held more promise. In addition to the fine sense of urban compactness and complexity that this scheme has in the space between and around the building forms, the *Zwischenraum*, the interior promised

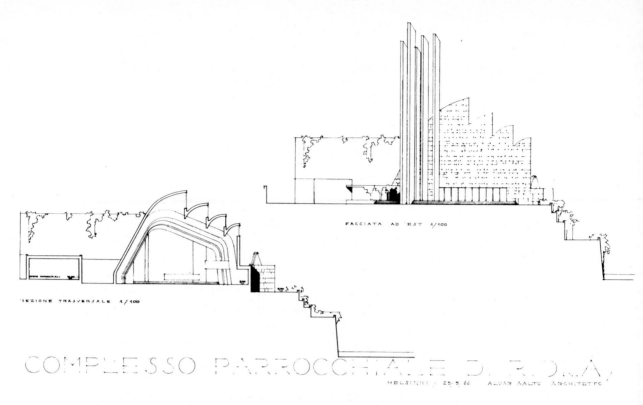

SEZIONE TRASVERSALE 1/100

FACCIATA AD EST 1/100

COMPLESSO PARROCCHIALE DI RIOLA

HELSINKI 25/5 66   ALVAR AALTO ARCHITETTO

Riola parish centre: original section and front elevation. The main body of the church was completed in 1978, without the campanile

Riola: interior view of completed church, showing dominance of arched frames

more variety and richness. In its section, the Zürich design also incorporates portal frames; but these are shaped and built into the ceiling so as to become more sculpture than structure. Also, the complex system of half vaults used at Riola, which attracts attention to the structural frame rather than adding richness, is replaced by the single natural vault created by the structure. The acoustic ceiling baffles consist of horizontal planes that thrust out from the frame, masking its junction with the north wall of the nave. Thus, most of the daylight is admitted through a clerestory and lower windows in the high south wall. This has the effect of dissolving, rather than highlighting, the structure on that side of the nave. The baffles then serve to enrich the interior rather than merely complicate it as do the half vaults at Riola. In fact, the entire section of the Altstetten project is more artful in its construction, with the parish hall at the lower level picking up the formal theme of the church itself and presenting in its stepped roof, a terraced garden to the street that runs through the scheme at the upper level. Indeed, the Altstetten design of 1967, made when the architect was almost seventy, potentially combines the plastic complexity of Imatra with that fine control of urban density which characterised the Pensions Institute and Säynätsalo.

Apart from the Hansaviertel block (1955–7), Aalto designed and built two other housing projects of significance during this mature period. These are the high-rise blocks for the Neue Vahr district of Bremen (1958–62) and the 'Schönbühl' development in Lucerne (1965–8).

Together with the auditorium block of the Wolfsburg Cultural Centre, the design of the Neue Vahr scheme, also begun in 1958, saw the emergence of the fully developed 'fan'-plan form. The logic of organising apartments in this fanned-out arrangement derived from the Baker Dormitory plan, completed more than a decade before; and although the Seinäjoki Library has a similar plan outline, the Neue Vahr block remains the most cogent use of its *gestalt*.

The deep apartment plans in the Bremen scheme fit precisely into this format, but, remembering Aalto's concern to give apartments some of the benefits of the private house, the Neue Vahr block clearly does not offer the same positive relationship of the rooms to the balcony to be found in the Hansaviertel scheme. What was so desirable in the single loaded corridor arrangement of the Baker Dormitory plan becomes something of a contrivance and certainly an inconvenience at Bremen. Once again the view is the paramount consideration. And balconies, of course, are less practical in a high-rise block. In the twenty-two storeys of the Neue Vahr scheme one cannot hope to achieve the same relationship of external to internal environment as in the mere eight storeys of the Berlin block.

There is no question, however, that Aalto's use of the Bremen site takes optimum advantage of the land form and the views. Also, in his articulation of the residential units, in their fan form, with the stepped rectilinear plan of the service core, Aalto produced one of the most elegant towers to emerge in post-war European archi-

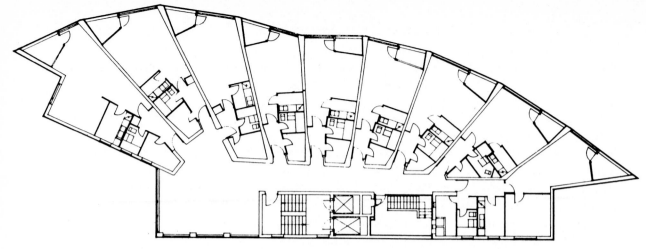

Neue Vahr apartment block: plan, showing the arrangement of the dwelling units in a fan formation with a linear service core

tecture. The planning of the individual apartments, which owes something to the deep-plan precedent of Le Corbusier's Marseilles Unité d'Habitation, is nothing short of ingenious. But the quality of the internal environment must still depend heavily on the sheer prestige of living there. The fenestration, with its slightly stepped

High-rise apartment block in the Neue Vahr district, Bremen (1959–62), showing the scuptural effect of the fan-plan in the massing of the building

arrangement of windows, assists in the modelling of the block by emphasising the horizontal layers of the fan. These large windows also bring the optimum amount of light into the deep interiors.

The 'Schönbühl' design is a hybrid, borrowing from both the Hansaviertel and the Neue Vahr precedents. In this sixteen-storey block the smaller apartments are arranged in a central core on each floor, sandwiched between more conventionally planned larger units at either end of the block. Also, its general plan configuration recalls the split-axis arrangement of the Hansaviertel design. There is less coherence between the front (apartment) facade and the rear elevation, while the clear articulation of these two elements in the Neue Vahr design is also lost at Lucerne. Thus, the Hansaviertel block remains Aalto's high point in apartment design from the planning point of view, whilst the Neue Vahr tower is more successful as pure form. Regrettably, Aalto was never asked to design housing of the quality of either block in his own country.

CHAPTER VII

Later Works and Projects

It is unusual for an artist to continue to produce his best work towards the end of his life. Failure of inspiration, or simply of the sheer energy required to sustain earlier momentum, is often a characteristic of an artist's final period. Many are spoiled by success and the attendant aggravations of *la bonne vie*, while most find it difficult to maintain the intensity of the intellectual and creative struggle that characterises the battle for recognition and the subsequent consolidation of ideas and reputation.

Aalto's post-war career matured between the late 40s and the mid-60s and although the work of his last decade is not without interest it is not at all comparable with that of either the 30s or 1947–66/7. It is difficult to draw a precise line which marks the beginning of this decline. After the Altstetten church project, however, his designs tend to make reference back towards earlier ideas and seem less assured and no longer as fresh.

Already in the student club house for the Västmanland-Dala 'nation' at Uppsala University there is evidence of this slipping of the creative cogs. This building, which was designed in 1961, the same year that Pietilä won the competition for the 'Dipoli' Student Centre at Otaniemi,[1] and built between 1963 and 1965, is technically inventive but weak in form. The problem presented by the need to subdivide the main first-floor hall into three smaller occasional meeting rooms is, after all, similar to that which confronted Aalto in the Vuoksenniska church, Imatra (designed 1956). But whereas Pietilä's design for Otaniemi is determinedly free in true 60s style, Aalto's Uppsala design has a functional formality that recalls his work of the early 30s. The cantilevering of the concrete 'cases' which contain the sliding doors used to subdivide the hall is bold and uncompromising, but as a gesture it simply does not add up to a total architectural statement. Indeed, Aalto's early perspective sketches suggest that he was depending upon the existing trees on the street frontage to mask the blandness of the Student House; but as these trees are deciduous, in winter all is revealed.

The Scandinavian House in Reykjavik, Iceland (1965–8), is another anomaly from the end of Aalto's mature period. Formally it anticipates the unresolved profile and massing of the 'Lappia' Theatre and Radio Centre in Rovaniemi (designed in 1969–70). Even the library of the Reykjavik building, although preserving a vestige of the sunken reading area, has none of the tranquillity of his other library designs. There is a nervousness in the ordering of space and form at both Uppsala and Reykjavik which suggests that Aalto is no longer in control of formal resolution.

The Royal Institute of British Architects was the first professional body to award Aalto its Gold Medal (1957) but following his sixtieth birthday in 1958 he received

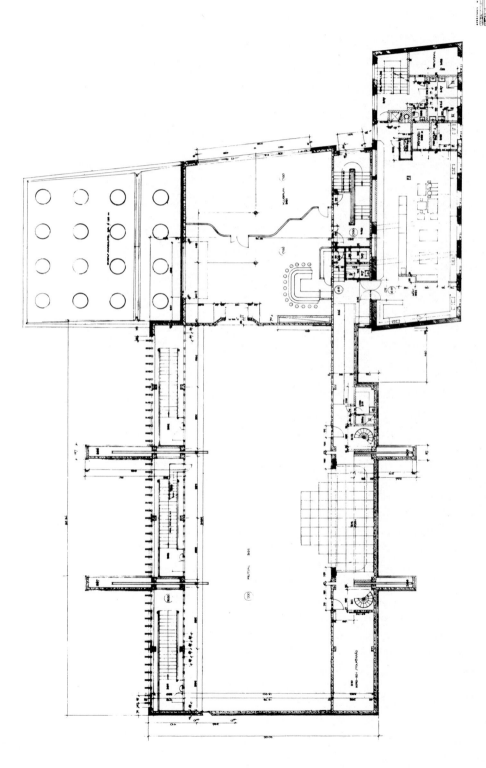

'Västmanland-Dala" student club house, Uppsala University (1963–5): plan of upper level, showing the main hall with the cantilevered boxes containing the sliding dividing-screens

"Västmanland-Dala" club house: exterior view, showing the columns and beams supporting the main hall, with the cantilevered boxes that receive the dividing-screens

many such tributes to his international stature. In 1958 he was made an Honorary Member of the Association of Finnish Architects (SAFA) as well as receiving the Association's Gold Medal. During the same year he was also made an Honorary Member of the Accademia delle Arti di Venezia and an Extraordinary Member of the Academy of Fine Arts in Berlin. Nineteen sixty saw him receiving an Honorary Doctorate from the Norwegian Institute of Technology in Trondheim; and in 1962 he was invited to the Soviet Union by the Academies of Architecture in Moscow and Leningrad, and lectured in both cities. Another Gold Medal followed in 1963, this time from the American Institute of Architects, and he travelled to the AIA Convention in Miami to receive it; and in the same year he was awarded the Cordon del Calli de Oro by the Mexican Society of Architects. Nineteen sixty-three also saw his election as President of the Finnish Academy. In 1964 he was honoured in his beloved Italy, receiving from the Faculty of Architecture at Milan University the *laurea honoris causa* in company with Louis Kahn and Kenzo Tange. He received a further South American honour in 1965 when he was made an Honorary Member of

Detail of glazed tiling in the foyer of the
"Lappia" building, Rovaniemi

the Collegio del Arquitetos del Peru. In the same year he received the Gold Medal of
the City of Florence and, in connection with the completion of his Uppsala student
house he was created an honorary member of the 'Västmanland-Dala nation' of that
university. Nineteen sixty-six brought him the Grande Ufficiale al Merito della
Repubblica Italiana; while in 1967 he travelled to the United States again, receiving
the Thomas Jefferson Medal from the University of Virginia in Charlottesville, then

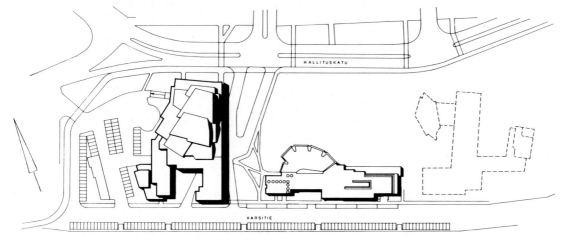

ROVANIEMEN TEATTERI- KONGRESSI- JA KONSERTTITALO

Civic centre, Rovaniemi: site plan, showing "Lappia" theatre and radio building (1969–75)
and library (1965–8), with the proposed city hall (dotted)

Civic centre for Jyväskylä (originally designed 1964): detail of curved concrete wall to police station (1976–8)

went on to San Francisco and lectured at Mount Angel Benedictine College, where he was building the new library (1965–70).

There is quite substantial evidence of degeneration in Aalto's work by 1964, when in his design for the administrative and cultural centre of Jyväskylä the forms he proposed for both the theatre and the council chamber border on the arbitrary. Aalto planned this extension to the existing town hall so that the administrative accommodation could be expanded in response to bureaucratic demands. The site is a rectilinear plot in the town's centre, which conforms to the grid-iron layout and is adjacent to a large square park containing Jyväskylä's principal church. This park extended on the other side of the road, onto the plot containing the town hall. Aalto's idea was to exaggerate the barrier of the street between the two sectors of the park by creating a raised piazza to run parallel to the street and linking the town hall and the proposed theatre. Against the axis of the street and this piazza he then extended the town hall into the site at one end and theatre block at the other. The extension to the theatre is in the form of the basically linear element of the police headquarters, thus linking, formally at least, the cops with the culture. This means that the project develops an 'L'-shaped frame for the park area to the rear of the town hall. At the time of writing only the police headquarters is completed, with its cultural

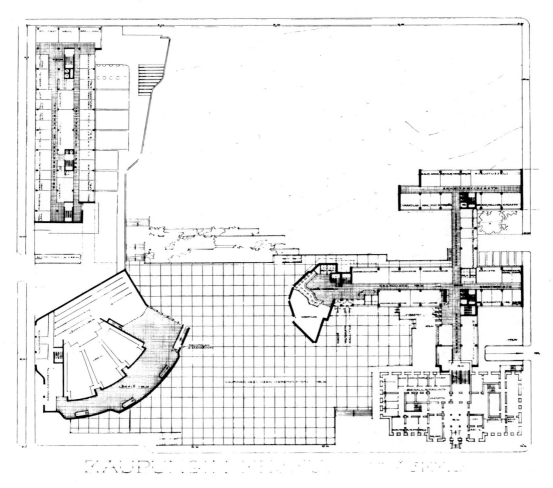

Civic centre for Jyväskylä: ground-floor plan, showing police station (top left), auditorium (bottom left), council chamber and administrative offices in relation to piazza

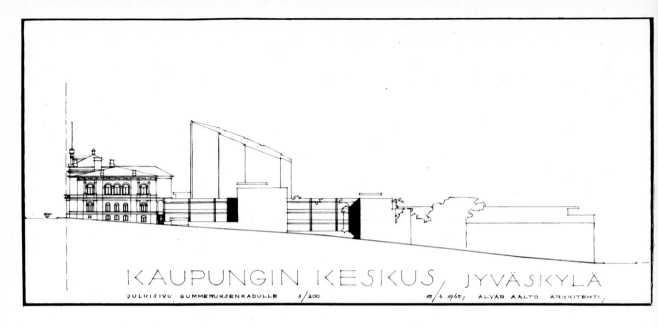

KAUPUNGIN KESKUS, JYVÄSKYLÄ

JULKISIVU·GUMMERUKSENKADULLE   1/200   15/6 1965,   ALVAR AALTO   ARKKITEHTI,

Jyväskylä civic centre: elevation, showing administrative offices and council-chamber tower in relation to existing town hall

—sculptural wavy wall extending towards the theatre, which came under construction in 1980.

The projected piazza at Jyväskylä is an irregular space cut out of a basic rectangle; the sculpted rear wall of the 'fan'-plan theatre (somewhat reminiscent of the House of Culture of 1955–8 in profile) backs onto the street from one end, whilst the council chamber juts out into the piazza at the end of an office 'arm' that is perpendicular to the spine which continues the short axis of the town hall into the site. Clearly, these two essentially sculptural elements not only break up the formality of the raised piazza but they are also intended to provide an interesting foreplay against the backdrop of the gently rising parkland beyond. But, as indicated in the original model, these two sculptural elements are really too far apart either to interact with each other or sufficiently restrict the flow of space between 'church park' and 'civic park'. The prevailing impression is that these plan forms are second-hand and have no particular significance in this place. There is even a striking resemblance between the tower form of the proposed council chamber and Reima Pietilä's Kaleva church at Tampere (designed in 1959 with construction commenced in 1964), with Aalto developing Pietilä's tube-like tower by truncating the volume at an angle of almost thirty degrees. Certainly, Aalto's tower for Jyväskylä promised to be every bit as startling as Pietilä's church, but apart from the effect of the angled truncation there is a distinct element of *déjà-vu*. Also, Aalto's tower lacks the careful modulation of Pietilä's Tampere design, with the resultant plan, a loose interpretation of the fan motif, having no functional basis in the actual arrangement of the council chamber.[2]

The disposition of elements in relation to the piazza in Aalto's competition entry for the design of the urban centre of Castrop-Rauxel in Germany (1965) reveals a clear reference to the Jyväskylä proposal. However, the reference to Pietilä's Tampere tube motif at Jyväskylä is abandoned at Castrop-Rauxel in favour of a backward glance to the massing of the auditoria of Aalto's Wolfsburg Cultural Centre, conceived in 1958 and begun in 1959. Thus, we see another instance, in the comparison of the council chambers at Jyväskylä and Castrop-Rauxel, of Aalto working as both 'modeller' (with plan-generated forms) and 'carver' (eroding forms suggested by the plan).[3] The general site planning centred on the piazza clearly provides a direct connection with the layout at Jyväskylä, repeating the long 'spinal' elements of that design. We can also see that both the Jyväskylä and Castrop-Rauxel designs have their origin in the 'Forum Redivivum B' project (1948) as far as the piazza element is concerned, whereas the spinal planning arrangement derives from the Otaniemi campus layout (1949). Both are also related to yet another urban centre project of the early 60s, the competition design for the Cultural Centre at Leverkusen, Germany, of 1962, where Aalto first combined piazza and park.[4] The Leverkusen design was unpremiated and Aalto's original model of the Jyväskylä project was so sketchy that it would be reasonable to expect substantial modification in its posthumous realisation. But the highly sculpted screen wall that already links the police headquarters with the incipient theatre appears to owe a substantial debt to Pietilä's geomorphic forms of the 60s.[5]

Whilst the 'Forum Redivivum B' design, which, it will be recalled, originally included a cultural sub-centre, probably remains as Aalto's strongest exercise in the use of the piazza, and the built form of the National Pensions Institute comes closest to its realisation,[6] Aalto's entry for the Siena Cultural Centre (1966) promised one of his most forceful and original contributions to urban design. The site chosen was the courtyard of a Baroque *fortezza* located almost due west of Il Campo beyond the City Stadium. This courtyard offered a truly Baroque scale, as the area within the ramparts of the *fortezza* could easily accommodate the entire Campo. These fortifications broke up the pattern of the mediaeval city on its western escarpment in the creation of this sharply angled *modern* bastion.

Aalto's basic concept for the Cultural Centre was to provide 'a clearly and boldly articulated architectural accent'[7] by creating a geometry that would be as strong and forceful as that of the *fortezza* ramparts. This he did by striking a diagonal axis almost along the dissection of the rectangular courtyard. He then developed his optimum use of the fan motif, by splitting the main elements of the composition – an amphitheatre and an auditorium – like two segments of an orange on either side of the amphitheatre stage.

The sense of arbitrariness that characterised the theatre plan form of both Jyväskylä (1964) and Castrop-Rauxel (1965) has disappeared in the Siena project and is replaced by the perfect logic of complementing the interior theatre with the exterior one about the axis of Aalto's Baroque geometry, imparting profiles which deliberately counter-mand those of the *fortezza*. The exaggerated spikiness of the fan-plan theatre with its four sectors (three for seating and the other wrapping the foyer around one end of the auditorium) is not only complementary but also a true antidote to the outer ramparts

Cultural centre for Siena: original Aalto *Ideenskizze* for the competition project (1966)

with their bold triangular bastions thrusting out from the four corners of the basic rectangular format of the castle. And a perfect, Platonic harmony was implied by contrasting the four-sector theatre (with only the three sectors of the auditorium expressed in the vertical massing) with the three-sector amphitheatre.

The result is a 'mirror' composition of three concave contrasted by three convex sectors (again the *carver* combining with the modeller) with the two elements held within a framework of seven sectors. Then, following the diagonal axial division of the site, the northern half of the remaining courtyard space is devoted to a piazza whilst the southern portion is given over to a park. Thus the whole design conspires to perfect Aalto's themes of amphitheatre (Epidauros/Otaniemi) and auditorium (fan motif) within the context of park and piazza, creating what was potentially his most taut urban composition since Säynätsalo, but with the added advantage of a truly-grand, Baroque scale. From all these points of view the Siena project seems to represent a summation of Aalto's thought in the mature period.

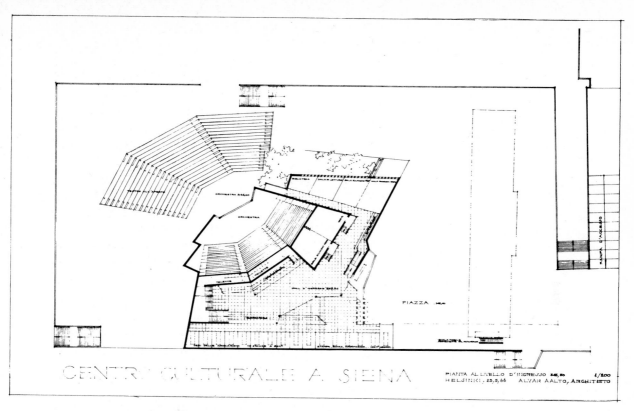

Siena cultural centre: plan at the piazza level of the competition entry

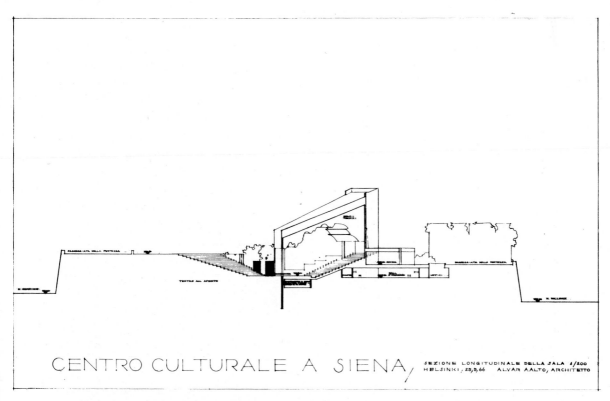

Cultural centre, Siena: section through the auditorium and complementary *amphiteatro* located within the original Baroque fortifications of the *fortezza*

Following on the original design for the North Jutland Art Museum at Aalborg in 1958, Aalto was commissioned in 1959 to build a regional museum for Central Finland in Jyväskylä. This is similar in function to the North Jutland example, housing a basic folklore collection and also intended to accommodate special travelling exhibitions of all kinds. In the Jyväskylä design, however, Aalto dispensed with the modular order of Aalborg, replacing this by a two-storey exhibition hall in the shape of a rectangle squeezed at one end that forms an 'L'-shaped plan with the entrance lobby wing which contains a cafeteria and administrative offices. The entrance to the offices and the permanent collection is at sub-basement level, taking advantage of the sloping wooded site. Access to the main exhibition hall and cafeteria above is by a staircase in the small entrance lobby. The slightly uncomfortable irregularity of plan form is partially a result of a tight site and the desire to keep all the trees. But the external form and massing also adds up to an arbitrary composition, with the entrance façade recalling the Cubist masses of 30s functionalism whilst the main volumes of the exhibition halls on the service side of the building recall Aalto's additions to the Varkaus sawmill of 1944–5. The Central Finland Museum, however, is of interest in the context of Aalto's small museum designs during his final period.

The better of these two projects is undoubtedly the unbuilt design for the Lehtinen private museum in Helsinki. Mr Lehtinen had been Finnish Consul in New York at the time of the 1938 World's Fair and was a member of the Fair Committee. To commemorate his association with that event the corrugated timber wall of Aalto's original pavilion was to have been partially reconstructed in the Lehtinen Museum. This museum was to have been located close to a Neo-classicist villa in a park bordering the sea on an island just outside Helsinki. Clearly, Mr Lehtinen's association with one of his early masterpieces stirred Aalto's memory with the result that this project attempts to capture in its plan some of the flowing movement of the original.

As in the New York Pavilion the exhibition space is two storeys in height with a gallery at first-floor level. The plan form consists basically of a triangular element (the fan motif lecture room) and a rectangular one, the latter being slightly cranked to facilitate a good connection between the two. As the museum was to house Mr Lehtinen's private collection but also be open to the public, Aalto created a small forecourt facing the villa, with the entrance vestibule giving direct access from this outside area to the lecture room, which in turn had French windows opening onto the forecourt. From the rear of the lecture room a staircase led up to the gallery, whilst the main exhibition space is stepped up away from the lecture room, changing axis subtly in the process. This stepping is reminiscent, of course, of Aalto's proposal for the Tallin Art Museum of 1937. The clarity of plan form recalls Aalto's confident handling of the Vuoksenniska church (1956–9) as does his treatment of the roofline, the eaves and the boldly stepped windows tucked immediately beneath them. For this reason the Lehtinen Museum design stands, together with three other unbuilt projects, as evidence of the late flowering of his genius: those other three designs are

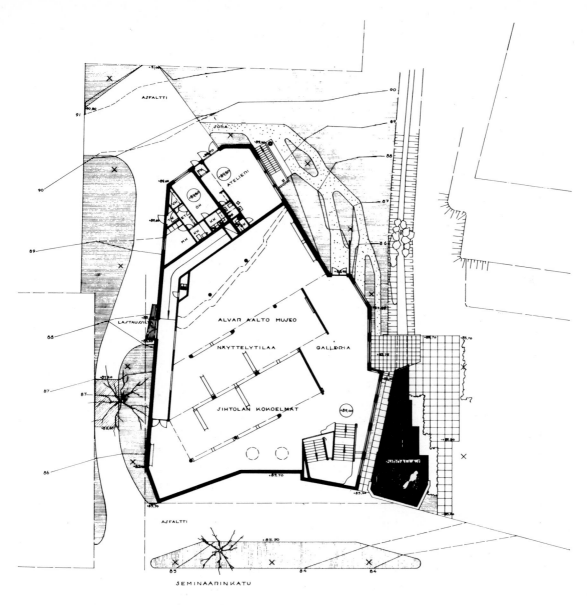

The Alvar Aalto Museum, Jyväskylä (1971–3): upper-level plan, showing the main gallery

(1) the Siena Cultural Centre (1966), (2) the church for Altstetten, Zürich (1966–7), and (3) the Art Museum for Shiraz (1970).

In recognition of his professional beginnings in the city and also his contribution to the growth of modern Jyväskylä through the design of the University master-plan and its main buildings, as well as his proposals for the Municipal and Cultural Centre, Aalto was asked in 1971 to design a further museum, adjacent to the Central Finland Museum and bearing his name. The Alvar Aalto Museum forms, together with the

Central Finland Museum, a cultural centre, sponsored by various corporate bodies and municipal authorities. It houses the Sihtola collection of Finnish and other paintings, and also has to be available for: (1) an Aalto exhibition at any time (in fact there is a semi-permanent one in place); and (2) in the summers to receive exhibitions associated with Jyväskylä's annual Festival of the Arts.

The plan morphology of this design is, frankly, baffling. Of course, as in the Central Finland Museum, the site is an extremely tight one. But whereas one might have expected Aalto to make a definitive last statement in this building, bearing his own name and built 1971–3, we find instead a curious *mélange* of old motifs done up into a clumsy parcel. The external envelope is arbitrary in the extreme and whereas the roof-light system of the first-floor gallery area is reminiscent of the coherence of the Aalborg Museum (built contemporaneously in 1972–3), Aalto's formal intention in this building, as in the Central Finland Museum, is unclear. It is perhaps tempting, therefore, to assign these two examples to Aalto's category of 'completely autonomous architecture'; but even this would be unfair to the master, as his sports hall for Otaniemi (1953) and his extension to the covered swimming pool at Jyväskylä University (1963) are both better examples of this genre of spontaneous expressionism.

In addition to all the other morphologies crammed into the Alvar Aalto Museum we find a version of the inclined, undulating wall of the New York World's Fair Pavilion incorporated uncomfortably into the exhibition space. And whereas that may well have been convincing within the gently undulating plan of the Lehtinen Museum it seems markedly out of place in the conflicting angles of the Aalto Museum's strange geometry.

Aalto's international reputation had become securely established in the 1950s; and from 1957, when he was awarded the RIBA Gold Medal for Architecture, he began to receive the world's highest honours in architecture and civic affairs. It was perhaps as an aftermath of this international acclaim, therefore, that he was to receive so many overseas commissions during his final decade. This was also fortunate because the talents of the new generation of architects in Finland, led by Reima Pietilä and including Mairja and Heikki Castrén, Kristian Gullichsen (son of Harry and Maire), Erik Kråkström, Osmo Lappo, Timo Penttilä, Keijo Petäjä, Aarno Ruusuvuori, and Kaija and Heikki Siren, had created considerable competition at home by the mid-60s.

Aalto's designs for the projected Villa Erica near Turin in 1967 again provide interesting evidence of his inconsistent intentions after 1966. The house was to be built on an abandoned golf course, and was to accommodate both quiet family living and extensive entertaining with house guests. But the biggest difficulty Aalto had to overcome was clearly the client, who, in the architect's own words 'had decided ideas of his own about certain functional relationships and about the nature of his future way of living'.[8] One can tell from Aalto's tone that at sixty-nine he was beyond the point of tolerating such strong-mindedness on the part of a client. Yet, more

The Alvar Aalto Museum: interior
view of the main gallery, showing the
Aalto furniture collection

Detail of the main entrance to the Alvar Aalto Museum

significantly, he gave in to the client's persistent interference with his intentions; and the result was a steady weakening of the design. It is therefore probably fortunate that it was not built. But, strangely, Aalto seems to have been fond of the design, for no less than ten pages are devoted to it in the third volume of Karl Fleig's *Collected Works*.

The Villa Erica began with one of Aalto's typically fresh notional sketches, that provided for the use of the fan motif plan growing from a linear spine. This fan element contained on the ground floor the dining room, the living room, the indoor swimming pool (between dining and living rooms!) and the library. All these rooms led off a wide, shaped entrance hall and each had, framed between projecting screen walls that separated the different functions, its own plot of garden and sector of the vista. Clearly, Aalto had entered quickly into the spirit of high Italian life-style. The rectilinear spine contained the servants' quarters and garages for four cars.

But all this essential Aalto charm and character was immediately eroded in the second and subsequent designs – there were four altogether – when the client dictated that the emphasis should be not on the good views but on the *good* indoor life. The result was that the swimming pool came to dominate the project, whilst the living area became a vast anteroom to the pool (in project number four) and the dining room was buried in the interior of the plan. It appears that Aalto tried in this final design to recall the plan morphology of the Villa Mairea, and the elevations are certainly reminiscent of the Noormarkku house. The general planning, however, shows the same formal weaknesses that characterise his Jyväskylä museums.

Aalto was once again confronted by the problem of providing an urban centre in rural surroundings when, in 1966, he designed the town hall and health centre for the west-central Finnish community of Alajärvi. This project, which was realised between 1967 and 1969, does not however bear any relation to the successful formula he invented for Säynätsalo. The Alajärvi building, which is much the same size as its Säynätsalo precursor, has a plan outline that is not dissimilar to that of the Lehtinen Museum (1965) but is based on a spinal corridor, double-loaded with administrative offices and lavatories, although the council chamber has the same place and similar form to that of the lecture room in the Lehtinen project. There is also a repetition of the street motif found in the contemporaneous Altstetten church (1966–7), an *allée* being created between the town hall and the separate health centre.

The intention of this linear design was clearly to draw attention by sight lines to the fine domed wooden Neo-classical church of Alajärvi. But Aalto's exterior treatment of the town hall is, in fact, a distraction. The random patterning of the windows, white-painted rendering and square blocks of granite, intended to draw attention to the council chamber itself, certainly does that; but in doing so the erosion of the building volume becomes totally disruptive. Clearly, this geometrical patterning has its origins in the courtyard at Muuratsalo, but its interpretation on the exterior walls of the Alvar Aalto Museum is much more coherent. And, in the final analysis, one is left wondering if another courtyard solution, echoing the *positive* volume of the

Town hall at Alajärvi (1966–9): the entrance façade, showing Aalto's most extreme erosion of the architectural form and mass in his detailing and use of materials

church dome by a *negative* interior space, the mass of the council chamber counter-pointing the church's detached campanile, might not have been a better response to Alajärvi's urban context. After all, the rural atmosphere of Alajärvi had already been tamed by the building of its Neo-classical church, and rather than building on the town's existing urbanity Aalto's design appears to undermine it. In fact the Alajärvi centre shows once again, as at Seinäjoki and Rovaniemi, that Aalto was always in danger with his urban compositions when he abandoned the tightly framed compositions, such as 'Forum Redivivum B', Säynätsalo and Wolfsburg Cultural Centre.

Although both the Villa Kokkonen at Järvenpää (1966–7) and the Villa Schildt at Tammisaari (1968) have the multi-axial, angled volumes that characterise much of Aalto's planning of the late 60s – a genre that can be traced back to the 'Studio R S' project of 1954 and reaches its most bizarre expression in the Aalto Museum of 1971 – Aalto is in fact looking back even further, to the Villa Mairea of 1937–9, in these designs. In the case of the Villa Kokkonen the image of the 'forest cottage', which had been achieved by partial timber cladding, and the truly rustic *porte-cochère* at Noormarkku, was extended by making the cladding continuous all round the house: this timber treatment was then carried into the house in the form of wide board panelling which is used throughout the interior. Almost the entire interior is of wood, with timber beams and a boarded ceiling. Some wall areas are, however, rendered or covered in natural linen, while the English parquet floors in the family room and the music studio are divided from each other by a travertine paved area which extends from the entrance lobby to create fireproof zones in front of the back-to-back fireplaces in both rooms. The somewhat free-form curves of this travertine zone are picked up by the canvas 'sail' that is suspended from the ceiling of the music studio, serving both to screen the light-fittings mounted directly on the boarding and also as an acoustic baffle.

Mr Kokkonen is a musician and composer, and Aalto's design for his villa is a finely tuned box; with subtle material and formal resonances, it is one of his most successful domestic interiors. In fact, allowing for the slightly inflated scale of the Maison Carré in consequence of its 'gallery' function and the non-realisation of the 'Studio R-S' the Villa Kokkonen is Aalto's finest house after the Villa Mairea, and in terms of the complete coherence of its details is in many ways the equal of its Noormarkku precursor. The plan form splits the axis of the house between a linear, mainly service wing and the living room and studio, which form a wedge shape responding to the shift of axis. There is a sort of buffer zone created between these two differently shaped elements by the master bedroom and the dining room. Also, there is a further 'split', this time an acoustic one, because the music studio is completely separated structurally from the living room to prevent the transfer of vibrations set up by the essentially wooden interior. At the point of intersection between the living room and the service wing a door from the Kokkonen dining room leads out under a stepped vine-clad pergola (recalling the entrance to Säynätsalo town hall) that descends to the sauna and swimming pool. Although much simpler in its exterior detailing than that at the Villa Mairea, the Villa Kokkonen sauna nevertheless recalls the Noormarkku example by its general disposition, its relation to the house and its earth roof. If further evidence of backward glancing on Aalto's part is required it is readily provided by the freely articulated sculpted roofline over the entrance door, which has its origins in his undulating forms of the 30s; for example in the Viipuri lecture room and the 'Savoy' vase, as well as the Varkaus sawmill extension (1944–5) and the fireplace of the Villa Mairea itself. In fact its application to this 'forest cottage' is very much in the cosmetic vein of Varkaus; but in the Kokkonen villa we have the effect without the cause. It seems to be very much an 'art statement', of which Aalto made free use in his final period, as for example in the 'cultural wall' that links the police headquarters with the theatre at Jyväskylä.

The *Ideenskizze* for the Villa Schildt (1968) recalls more the morphology revealed in the sketch plans for the Villa Erica (1967).[9] Although the Villa Kokkonen was being

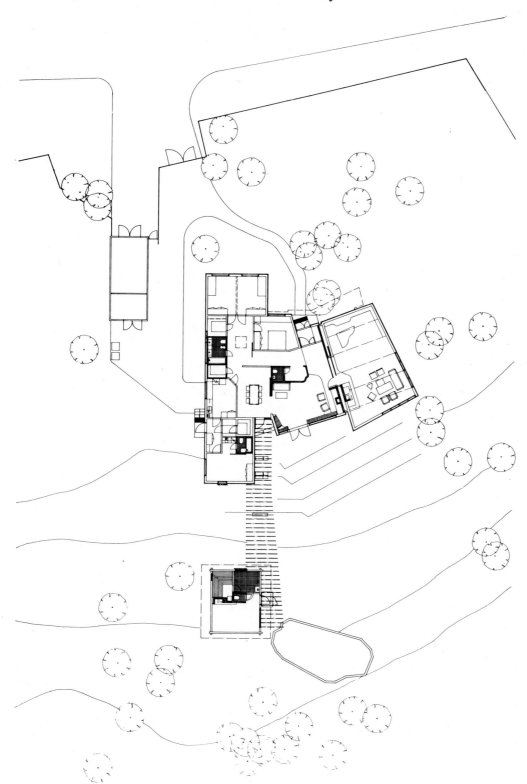

Villa Kokkonen at Järvenpää (1967–9): plan, showing the main structure, the separated music room, and the detached sauna linked by a covered way

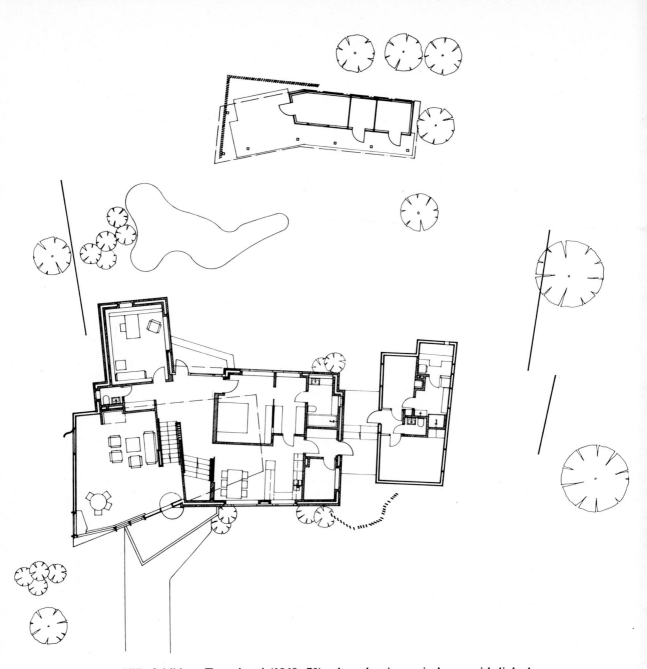

Villa Schildt at Tammisaari (1968–70): plan, showing main house with linked sauna

built (1967–9) at the time Aalto made the first sketches for the home of his friend, the Finnish critic Göran Schildt, the Schildt villa lacks the clarity of plan form achieved in the Kokkonen house. Once again we find the combination of linear element with triangular wedge that first appeared in the Lehtinen Museum project of 1965, with the guest room and sauna separated from the main house, while the garden pavilion and lily pond have no physical links with either. In the garden setting, however, Aalto has given the exterior massing a more dynamic expression which is reminiscent of a number of forerunners. For instance, the boarded living room and its balcony at first-floor level recall the studio of the Villa Mairea at first glance, whilst the detailing of the large wedge-shaped window refers to a more immediate predecessor, namely the administrative wing of the Alajärvi town hall. On the other hand, the single-storey 'L'-shaped wrap-around which contains Dr Schildt's study and the master bedroom with its painted brickwork, has a distinct echo of the kitchen side of Aalto's summer house at Muuratsalo. This mixture of established Aalto elements into a new cocktail is perhaps appropriate for a critic's house, and the effect is one of undeniable charm, nevertheless it all adds up, in external terms at least, to a much lesser work than the Villa Kokkonen. Charm is also a feature of the Schildt house interior, with its dominant feature a finely sculpted mantle to the brick chimney-breast of the fireplace. This feature again has its origin in the living-room fireplace at the Villa Mairea, going through a more restrained transition in the living-room fireplace of the Villa Kokkonen, and shows Aalto's genius with free form still alive and well at seventy! But the overall coherence of the Villa Kokkonen, generated of course by the singular image of the musical box, is missing from the more eclectic example, in terms of Aalto's own references, of the Villa Schildt.

The project for the Essen Opera House which Aalto had originally won in competition in 1959, was revised in 1961–4; and its continued revision, basically for budgetary reasons, was to occupy him during his final period and close to the end of his life. It is interesting, therefore, that quite contrary to his backward glances discussed above, Aalto used three other projects between 1963 and 1975 to work out his ideas for Essen. This process began with the invitation in 1963 to design the Edgar T. Kauffmann Conference Rooms on the top floor of the Institute of International Education in New York.[10] With this invitation came the stipulation from the Institute's building committee and the sponsoring commercial foundation, that the interior fittings and furniture had to be of Finnish manufacture. Furthermore, the clients requested special wall treatment in the lecture room to 'enhance the dignity of the Institute',[11] which allowed Aalto to introduce a simplified form of the bentwood elements which formed part of the mural relief in the main auditorium of the Essen Opera House as shown in the original model. Those elements, of course, had their genesis in the bent junctions of Aalto's characteristic chair legs and backs, which give a cohesion to the lecture-room design through the interaction between the sculptural reliefs on the wall and the Aalto furniture.

The original project for the Finlandia Concert Hall dates from 1962, whilst the contiguous Congress Hall was designed in 1970. This complex, the two parts being built in 1967–71 and 1973–5 respectively, is one of Aalto's least successful works. It is an enormous building and, without the boldness Aalto exercised in containing the similarly vast scale of the Essen project in one envelope, the result is a collection of monumental fragments. Of these the Congress Hall addition of 1973–5 is the most

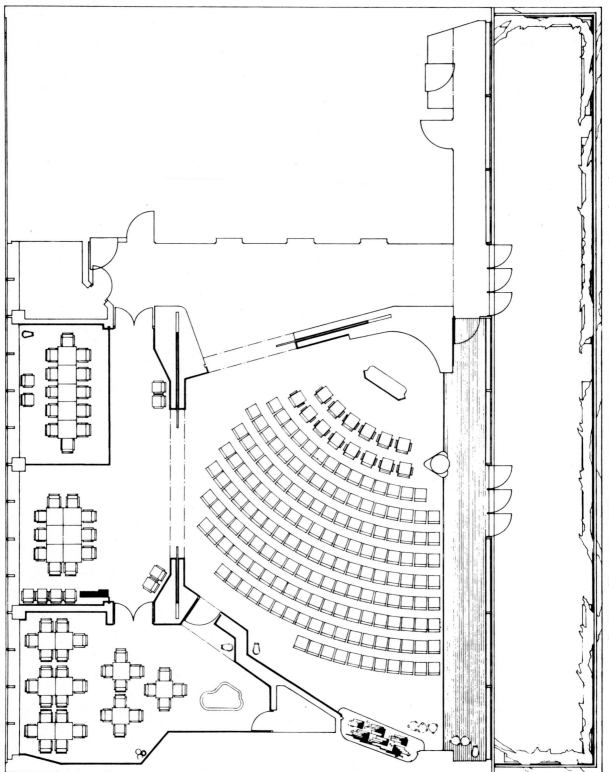

Institute of International Education, New York (1963–5): plan, showing disposition of meeting rooms and main lecture hall

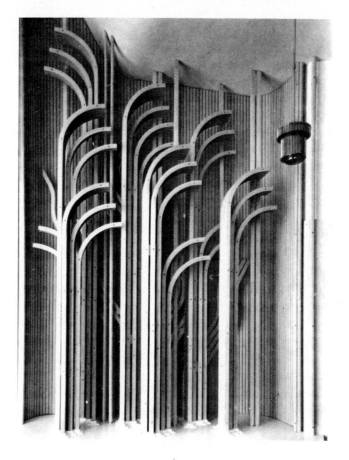

Institute of International Education: detail of lecture hall, showing recurrence of bentwood forms originally proposed for the Essen Opera House and here used as a freestanding sculptural element

interesting volume by far, although this is because in that portion of the building Aalto shakes off the straitjacket of a grossly inflated Lehtinen Museum plan format and makes direct reference to Reima Pietilä's first two important buildings, the Kaleva church in Tampere and the 'Dipoli' Student Centre at Otaniemi. The plan profile of the Congress Centre facing across the Mannerheimintie to Saarinen's National Museum leaves no doubt about the source of his inspiration. And it is entirely possible that, even subconsciously, Aalto, having taken on the mantle from Eliel Saarinen, used this unique opportunity of confronting the 'Old Man of Finnish Architecture' in his most romantic vein to indicate that there was only one Finnish architect worthy of carrying the baton for the next lap. Aalto was to the end a man proud of his reputation as the great pioneer and leader of modern architecture in Finland, and even arrogant in asserting this position;[12] but he did concede that Pietilä was the only other original force in Finnish architecture. This being the case, what would have been more natural than for Aalto, at the end of his career, to acknowledge Pietilä as his natural heir? After all, Pietilä had in his design for the Finnish Pavilion at the Brussels World Fair of 1958, paid *hommage* to Aalto's inspiration in the Otaniemi sports hall of 1953.

The cold Carrara-clad masses of the Concert Hall, once again echoing classicism,

City Centre development plan for Helsinki (1971–3), with the Mannerheimintie, running in from the right and the railway lines leading into Saarinen's Central Station (left). The Finlandia building provides the culmination of lakeside pavilion treatment (centre)

show that from 1967, when this part of the complex came under construction, Aalto lacked the mastery he had shown nearby in the Pensions Institute of 1952–6. Aalto's best buildings are undoubtedly his red-brick ones of the 1950s; and his later addiction to Carrara marble shows a return to the ideals of 'Italia la Bella', just as it was to prove a technical error also.[13] But the interior of the Finlandia Concert Hall provided Aalto with an opportunity to try out a version of his relief walls for the Essen auditorium at full size. This he did to great effect, creating the most successful auditorium of his career in the process. He adopted the same dark blue, painted wooden batten acoustical wall, incorporating elaborations of the bentwood forms he had introduced into the lecture room of The Institute of International Education. Against this indigo background the sharply angled Carrara-clad side balconies read like banks of Cubist clouds. The effect is rich, powerful and authentic, giving the Finlandia Concert Hall a permanent place in the catelogue of great twentieth-century auditoria. And from it we get a good idea of what the Essen Opera House might be like. At least the quality of information for the Essen project is much higher than for any other design remaining

Finlandia Concert and Congress Hall, Helsinki (1967–9): the main auditorium, showing Aalto's use of the bentwood treatment above the *loges* originally designed for the Essen Opera House

Finlandia Hall, the extension (1969–71): view from the Mannerheimintie, showing the undulating wall treatment reflecting a characteristic of Pietilä's planning rather than Aalto's

incomplete at Aalto's death. It is difficult enough to carry out an artist's design posthumously, as we have witnessed at Riola. But when the information is in short supply it could simply prove impossible. In the case of Essen, and on the 'Finlandia' evidence, we will see that the design is authentic even if we know that now there is only a ghost in the machine.[14]

In terms of planning, at least, in the competition project for the Wolfsburg Theatre, with which Aalto took only second prize in 1966, there was a further opportunity to develop the Essen version of the asymmetrical auditorium. But there are few clues here concerning the exterior treatment. This is bound to prove the major difficulty in creating an authentic envelope for the Essen Opera House. The translation of the rippling wall of timber, either the Lapua unstripped log version or the New York Pavilion example, both of 1937–8, into a sophisticated urban treatment is a problem on which Aalto's later designs shed little light. Certainly, we cannot look to those clumsy 'Finlandia' masses, that are in effect more redolent of Siren's Parliament Building than Saarinen's National Museum; and the modulated tile patterning on the Aalto Museum is of quite the wrong scale. In fact the council chamber at Seinäjoki had already proved that tiling is best limited to small-scale masses, or interiors. The Essen scale is much too large for metal profiles. This would seem to leave only concrete, and point the way back towards Pietilä's intentions for the Kaleva church in Tampere.[15]

It is indeed unfortunate that Aalto did not have more opportunities to design individual private houses in his final period. He was always happier at the more intimate scale that belonged to his Finnish experience; and the Kokkonen and Schildt houses clearly demonstrate that he retained into his seventies his unerring touch for reflecting individual life styles. Between 1966 and 1969 he did, however, produce three further unrealised projects for apartment buildings. These were: (1) the Gammelbacka housing estate for Porvoo (1966); (2) a second 'Schönbühl' development with a lakeside restaurant at Lucerne (1969); and (3) a satellite town for 12,500 inhabitants on the outskirts of Pavia, Italy (1966). The Gammelbacka housing is an interesting combination of the modular planning Aalto used in the Hansaviertel design for Berlin, and a more extended version of the fan plan found in both the Neue Vahr and 'Schönbühl I' towers; the difference being that the Gammelbacka scheme was limited to five storeys. Otherwise the scheme contained no new developments.

In the second 'Schönbühl' project both the restaurant and the terraced houses conformed to the fan motif, but whilst the restaurant form was decidedly in a post-50s (i.e., after Wolfsburg Cultural Centre) form, the terraced housing owes its origin to the engineers' houses at Sunila of 1937.

But the satellite town design for Pavia has an interesting feature based again on an earlier Aalto preoccupation. The main Rome–Milan *autostrada* runs more or less through the centre of the projected site. In avoiding direct views onto this motorway Aalto drew upon the planning *gestalt* of the Baker Dormitory at MIT, although the apartments in the Pavia scheme are fitted into snake-shaped plans with parallel rather

Housing development project, Pavia (1966): aerial view of model, showing serpentine block design of apartment blocks on either side of the *autostrada*

than radiating party walls. The façades are then stepped, and the deep balcony developed for the Hansaviertel block incorporated, to ensure that no room would face directly onto the busy *autostrada*. But regrettably this project makes no real contribution to urban design.

In 1974 Aalto had another opportunity to work on the smaller, village scale, when the Scandinavian–American Society invited him to design a 'Mid-Western Institute for Scandinavian Culture', to be located on a well-wooded hill in Wisconsin, with a unique view over the river valley below. His response to this programme, which combined an auditorium, library, exhibition space and artists' studios with a restaurant and outdoor recreations, a sauna and holiday cottages, was to return to the clarity and simplicity of the Villa Kokkonen plan (1966–7). Using the auditorium, this time a *symmetrical* one, as the fulcrum, he cranked the two linear wings, one on either side, with the central area combining the foyer and exhibition hall. From this central space one would come first, on the right, to the library and then to the artists' studios, looking down over the valley; while the entire left-hand wing is devoted to the restaurant. The library is small and has a linear arrangement rather than the typical Aalto plan with the sunken area as the 'core', but the sunken area is nevertheless retained as a room off the central circulation spine. This is a low-key building with several familiar Aalto characteristics – the library is of course top lit – and its restraint promised a better result than the more aggressively sculptural compositions of earlier cultural or civic centres, such as Jyväskylä. But he was now in his seventy-sixth year and this project does not have that unique stamp of earlier work.

In the Shiraz Art Museum project of 1969–70, however, designed when he was already seventy-two, the old fire was still burning brightly. Indeed, this design is unique because it combines the fan plan with the fan section for the first and only time in Aalto's work. The fan section we have noted, was invented for the Riola church, originally designed in 1966. Its striking use in the Shiraz project recalls the confidence

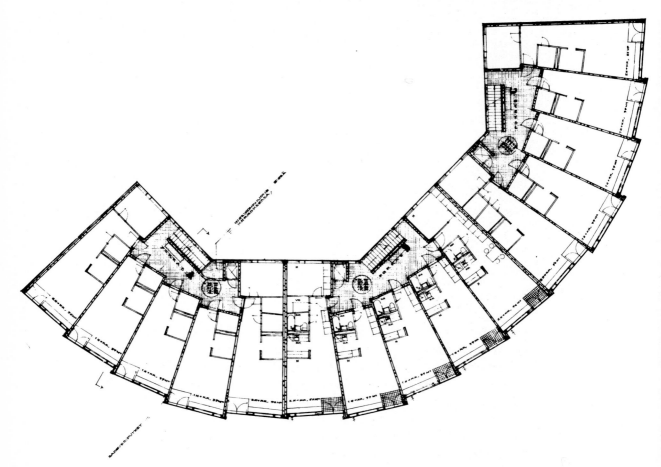

Housing project for Gammelbacka, Porvoo (1966): plan, showing the disposition of apartments in a modified fan-plan formation

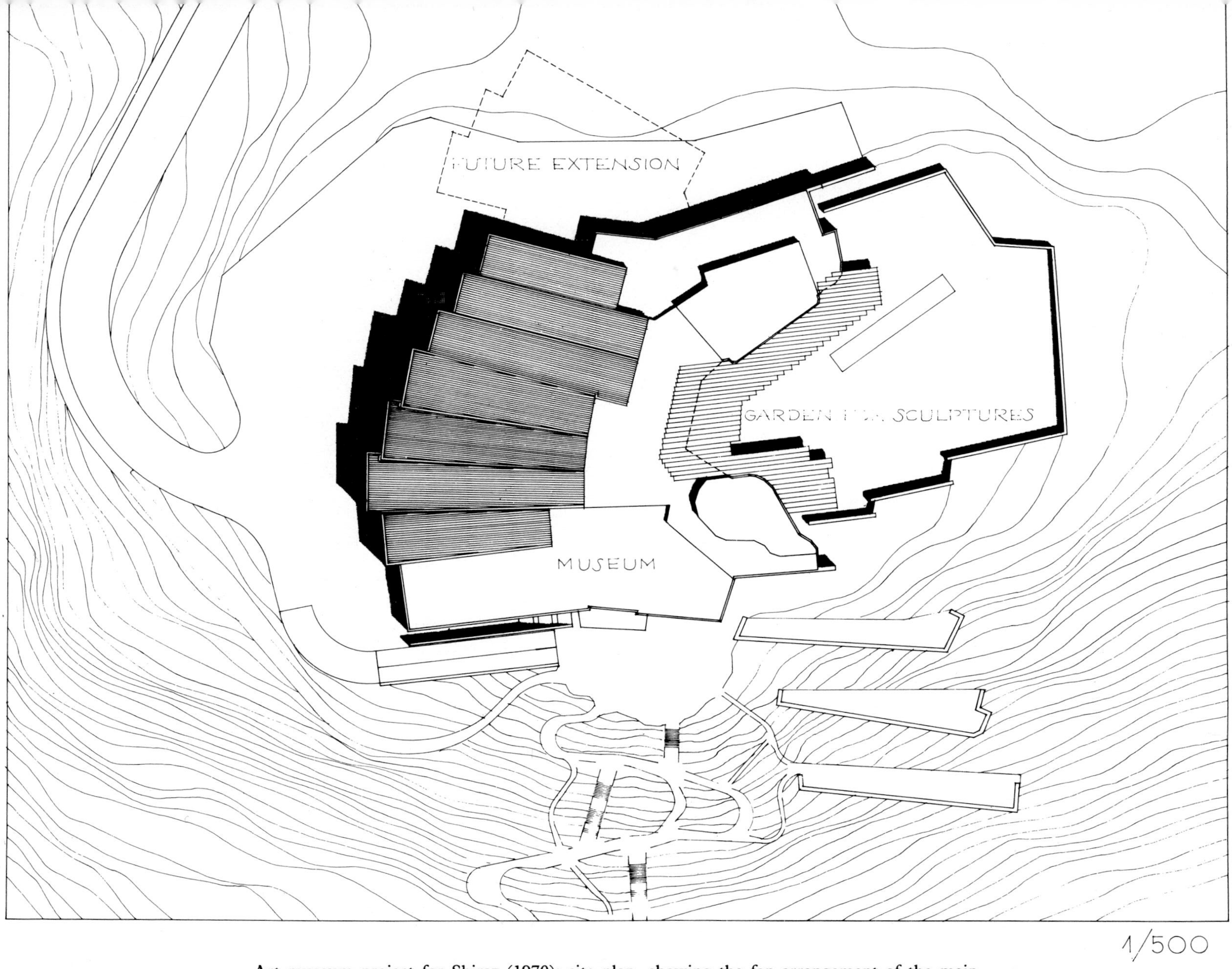

Art museum project for Shiraz (1970): site plan, showing the fan arrangement of the main galleries

1/500

FUTURE EXTENSION

GARDEN FOR SCULPTURES

MUSEUM

Shiraz art museum project: Aalto's original *Ideenskizze*, showing the formation of an organic acropolis within the landscape

of the Jyväskylä University main auditorium block but at a much more monumental scale. It is clear from his sketch of 10 October 1969[16] that he had seized on the commanding hilltop site to make a bold statement of massing and profile which would be visible for miles around. Apart from the reference through the use of the sculpture garden, which was to act as a forecourt to the main entrance, there is no concession to Islamic planning or formal models. But in terms of the long history of the area we can see Aalto's genius in providing a symbol for this site which speaks in the language of all hilltop settlements; a language, as we have seen, that was dear to him from the very beginning of his career.

Scale and magnitude are the central issues in Aalto's work and thinking; to understand him as an architect and designer we must first of all see his solutions to design problems in these terms. He became involved in the sphere of industrial design as early as 1928, when he helped produce a stacking chair used for the Jyväskylä Civil Guard Headquarters. This design combined a plywood seat and back with legs and frame of straight members in squared birch, a chair of extreme utility that is still in production. But through its adaptation in the 'Korhonen' chair of 1929 and refinement in the Paimio armchair of 1930–33 – indeed during all Aalto's subsequent experiments with wooden furniture of the 30s as well as in the post-war period (1947–66) – his interest was in the advantages of serial production where quality could be maintained by the relatively limited scale of manufacture and assembly.

Although standardisation remained a theme of his detailing it was never a feature of his planning, and the concept of mass production was anathema to him. This is borne out by the fact that the production of Artek furniture has never managed to keep pace with the demand for it in the post-war period.[17] As we have seen, the quality of architecture produced from Finnish offices is inextricably tied up with the small, tightly knit teams that work on its production, with the hand of the master necessarily always in control. Other offices, like those of Reima Pietilä and Timo Penttilä, which are engaged in an international programme of building, also work under constant strain because of this discipline. To be an artist of Aalto's calibre means a total dedication to architecture as a way of life.

The predominant evidence of Aalto's last works and projects is that, in this final period, he was happiest, both conceptually and in detailing, at the domestic or private scale. As we have seen, this is confirmed by the Villa Kokkonen (1966–7) and the Villa Schildt (1968), if not by the unhappy Villa Erica project. Although I have included the projects for the Siena Cultural Centre (1966) and the Shiraz Art Museum (1970) amongst the designs that demonstrate a late flowering of his genius, it is in two others – the Lehtinen Museum (1965) and the Altstetten church (1966–7) – that we can observe Aalto's true coherence of form and scale.

Early in his career, at the age of thirty-seven, he spoke of the importance of *variability*, explaining:

> [I mean] ways in which people can relate to their environment and the objects in it – that the *milieu* is able to meet psychology's demands for continuous renewal and growth. One normal way of easing the nervous pressure on modern man is a change of environment – after all, it is clear that man's immediate environment must be built so as to offer an almost automatic opportunity for constant change.[18]

Variability, therefore, in Aalto's terms, has to do with *experience, response* and the creation of *relationships* between man and his environment. He regretted:

> Though people acquire technically better housing and a more comfortable life – albeit in a limited form – in this way something is interrupted, and comfort is purchased at the expense of disharmony.[19]

And also that:

> ... people and families are allocated in a numerical way to millions of standardised buildings and stereotyped community units ... [with the result that] Instead of the physiological slum we produce what are psychological slum communities and a proletarianizing process that concerns some of man's most important conditions for life.[20]

We have noted with regret that, in terms of housing, Aalto was not given the opportunity to build apartments in Finland of the quality he achieved in the

Hansaviertel and Neue Vahr blocks. It is equally regrettable that he did not bring to fruition the ideas expressed in his projects for the Malmi funeral chapel, the 'Studio R S' and the Siena Cultural Centre. Because of his command of materials, his skill in furniture design and his lasting interest in producing interior environments of intimate scale and warmth, he ranks, together with Frank Lloyd Wright, as the outstanding humanising architect of the twentieth century (see Appendix).

CHAPTER VIII

'Life-Enhancing Charm'

In his obituary for the Swedish pioneer Gunnar Asplund, published in *Arkitekten – Arkkitehti* in 1940,[1] Aalto offers us an interesting insight into the complex eclecticism of his own architecture. He describes the new architecture as being no longer dependent upon purely historical reference, but mapping out terrain that connects man not only with accessible nature but also the primeval mysteries of his *environmental memory*. In much architecture, he says,

> ... the motivation for form derives from fragments – past ones – of architecture itself. But now there is another kind, which builds for man by taking man into account primarily as a social group, and making science and research its starting point. Yet in addition to these an even newer form has emerged which builds further, using socio-artistic methods, but extends them to include psychological problems – 'man the unknown' to the full. And this last has helped to show that architecture still has untapped resources and means open to it which draw directly on nature and on the reactions to the human psyche that written words are unable to explain.

Past fragments of architecture are, of course, those classical and Renaissance examples on which Aalto was brought up in the Technical University. His reference to building for man as 'a social group' describes one of the basic tenets of Modern Movement rationalism, the process of standardising for the 'big programme' and the concept of the 'mass client'. Meanwhile his description of the new architecture that uses 'socio-artistic methods' and 'draws directly on nature', with its concern for the 'reactions of the human psyche' presents his own programme – an argument for an amalgam of post-rationalist organic philosophy with references back to National Romantic forms and intentions.

His own work continued to manifest aspects of all three of these 'architectural attitudes' until the end. *Both/andism* or *pluralism* was the cornerstone of his architectural philosophy. This is what makes him so difficult to pin down and categorise because, although he was not subject to any particular influence at any one time, his abstract, socio-artistic method cut obliquely through the complex grain of many academically conventional formal sources. As he himself argued in his inaugural address upon election to the Finnish Academy in 1955:

> Whatever our task ... there is one absolutely vital condition that must exist

for its creation before it can take on the significance that makes it culture
... *In each and every case there must be a simultaneous reconciliation of*
opposites.

Whatever its source of inspiration, the concept of organic form for Aalto implied a
sense of 'wholeness'; in Alberti's terms, 'that certain consonance of diverging
elements'. Everything was grist to Aalto's mill if it fed something into the comprehensive cuisine from which he subsequently abstracted. In a discussion with Göran
Schildt, published in 1967, he said:

> Painting and sculptures are all part of my working method. So I wouldn't
> like to see them separated from my architecture ... I don't see paintings
> and sculptures as things in different professional spheres. ... to me these
> works are all branches of the same tree, the trunk of which is architecture.[1]

And this would seem to confirm Aalto's view of the comprehensiveness of the art of
architecture as essentially a Renaissance one. Also, as with the Italian Renaissance,
the rebirth of architecture of which Aalto was himself such a significant part must
draw upon the past as one of its resources in order to achieve its totality. As Aalto
wrote at the very beginning of his career, the year of his graduation, 1921:

> Nothing old is ever re-born. But it never completely disappears either. And
> anything that has ever been always re-emerges in a new form. It seems to
> me that at the moment we are striving towards a whole.[2]

He elaborated on this in the following year, in an essay entitled 'The Motifs of Past
Ages', viz:

> When we see how international and open-minded past ages have been
> without being untrue to themselves, we can accept influences from ancient
> Italy, Spain and the New World with open eyes. Our forefathers will always
> be our preceptors.[3]

It is difficult to imagine that, only five years after he wrote that, Aalto was well on
the way towards mastery of the new rationalism. During this important transitional
period he realised that to respond to modern functional requirements meant looking
beneath and beyond inherited formal solutions. What was required instead was some
kind of rational method, yet even in this Aalto depended more upon the logic of direct
experience than a detached form of scientific enquiry. In describing his design of the
Paimio Tuberculosis Sanatorium, he said:

> When I took on the planning I was ill myself, so I had a chance to do a few
> tests and find out what it was really like to be ill. It irritated me to lie
> horizontal all the time and the first thing I noticed was that the rooms were
> designed for people who spend their days in the vertical position, not for
> those who have to spend days on end in bed. Like moths around a candle

my eyes were constantly drawn towards the electric light. A room which is not designed specifically for people lying horizontal has no internal equilibrium or real peace. So I tried to design rooms for non-active patients which gave the bedridden a tranquil atmosphere.[4]

Naturally, such direct personal experience inclined him towards the human aspects of the problem and his fundamental quarrel with rationalism was that it fell short of this concern. He wrote with remarkable foresight in 1940:

The term 'rationalism' comes up in connection with modern architecture almost as often as 'functionalism'. Modern architecture has been rational-ised mainly from the technical point of view, just as technical functions have been given most weight. . . . in the purely rationalist period of modern architecture buildings were erected with an over-emphasis on rationalised technology and an under-emphasis on human functions . . . [but] . . . In itself rationalisation is not wrong in the first age of modern architecture, which we have now left behind. The fault is only that the rationalisation has not gone deep enough.[5]

Already in 1935 he had admitted that 'objects which can with justification be called "rational" lacked an essential "human quality"'. He found it significant that even the best rationalist achievements of modern architecture were incomplete in this sense. If we were to achieve a *built milieu* that was more friendly to man (and it is interesting to find this term 'built milieu' at least a quarter of a century before the hackneyed term 'built environment' came into use!) Aalto argued that we would have to extend our concept of rationalism. He compared all the various demands we are likely to make upon the quality of an object to a spectrum, which would always have to contain a complete range of responses to these demands. And he stressed the psychological factor, saying:

As soon as we take psychological demands into account or shall we say when we are able to do so – we have already extended our rational working approach so far that it is now easier to prevent inhuman results.

Again in his interview with Göran Schildt, published in 1967, Aalto complained that:

There is a great deal of architecture which never gets beyond the analysis level, though synthesis is what is actually needed.

But Aalto's concept of synthesis remained essentially within the sphere of abstraction, that is depending upon his ability to abstract intuitively. And intuition in Aalto's terms only operates when there is an adequate information-bank of experience to draw upon. In other words, the human factor must act as a filter and modifier within the rational process. As he wrote in 'The Humanising of Architecture', in 1940:

> The methods of architecture are sometimes reminiscent of those of science, the kind of research that natural science uses can also be applied to architecture. Architectural research may well be more methodical than before, but its essence can never be purely analytical. *Architectural research must always be more of an art and an instinct.*[6]

He reinforced this view in 1941, viz:

> A building is not a technical problem at all – it is an anti-technical problem. Thus a technical planning method cannot be applied to it. And any standardisation applied has to be archi-technical in character, too.[7]

And he further underlined it in his paper 'Art and Technology' of 1955, viz:

> In almost every task concerning form there are dozens, often hundreds, sometimes thousands of different contradictory elements, which are only forced to work in harmony with man's will. This harmony cannot be achieved in any way other than through art. Separate technical and mechanical elements only take on their final value in this way. A harmonious result cannot be achieved through calculations, statistics or probability theory.[8]

In the documentation prepared for the 1978 retrospective exhibition, Ragghianti's essay rightly draws our attention to the fact that:

> In his drawings and models Aalto often projects very clearly a sense of expansion created by powerful impulses avoiding empty, neutral space or one based on intellectual hypotheses and the abstract concepts of height, width and depth, replacing them with a living organism. This carries the spectator along with it, giving him an immediately powerful and uplifting sense of involvement with the springs of cosmic life ...

This seems to concur with Aalto's own credo, that:

> Our senses convey to us the raw material on which our thinking is based.[9]

Surely what Ragghianti describes is 'the theatre of environment'. Certainly, in referring to those powerful impulses that avoid empty neutral space or intellectual hypotheses, he appears to be describing Aalto's unique blend of Baroque turbulence and organic sensuousness, of which it is perfectly appropriate to use the term 'cosmic'. What is not so clear, however, is that although Ragghianti says he is talking about the 'drawings and models', the impression his description gives is that he is in fact reacting to the actual architecture itself. Of course, he does not speak about 'spectator' in the sense that we normally adopt in referring to people looking at paintings or drawings. The scale of the Aalto drawings and models, however, hardly corresponds with Ragghianti's impressions of them. That Aalto's drawings are the generators of the spatial forcefulness of his architecture is, nevertheless, undeniable.

It is for this reason that the Aalto sketches are of particular importance; because they take us behind the architectural scene and into the mind of the artist. Aalto's drawings demonstrate precisely his method of attack. The use of the term 'artist' is, of course, consistent with Aalto's frequent description of architecture as an art. His drawings exhibit the quality of freedom which he himself found in nature: they are 'systematic' only in this free sense, as any artist worthy of the name develops a thematic or systematic line of exploration. Also, they reflect what was his virtual contempt for so-called 'design method'. His sketches are, in the true sense, explorations: they move towards solutions not at all in a conventional methodic way but more in the free conceptual manner of the Baroque spatial tradition. Also, what is essential to Aalto's feeling out of spatial potentiality through these sketches is his sense of play. After all, he himself said that these early drawings 'are sometimes childlike compositions', and he described the early stages in the design of the Viipuri City Library, thus:

> ... I spent long periods getting my range, as it were, through naive drawings. I drew all kinds of fantastic mountain landscape, with slopes lit by many suns in different positions, which gradually gave birth to the main idea of the library building. The architectural framework of the library comprises various reading and lending areas stepped at different levels, while the administrative and supervisory centre is at the peak. *My childlike drawings were only linked very indirectly with the architectural idea, but in any case they led to an interweaving of the section and the plan shape, and to a kind of unity of horizontal and vertical construction.*[10]

Thus, he underlines the fact that the basic 'system' behind his free-ranging drawings is a systematic exploration of the plasticity of space and volume. And his method seems to have about it the same sense of joy that he wants to get built into the final product. Of his own experimental house at Muuratsalo, he wrote:

> ... though we are in the midst of an experimenting, calculating and utilitarian age, we still have to believe that play has a vital role in building a society for man, the eternal child. Surely, every responsible architect feels the same, in one way or another.[11]

I recall two observations concerning design method and planning from my conversations with Aalto that seem relevant here. They are:

1 'What's the point of a design method if you don't end up with a life-enhancing design?'

and

2 'The planning module should always be as small as possible, preferably not much more than a centimetre – and the modular element no bigger than a brick.'[12]

These observations do much to explain both his style of drawing and his sensitivity to detail. We have only to look at those exquisite wooden constructions, and the perfect matching of the material and the technology in the Artek furniture, to realise that Alvar Aalto's contribution was that of a Renaissance breadth and stature. He was endowed with the background and capabilities, and offered equally sensational opportunities, to become one of the greatest artists of the twentieth century. His constructions alone will surely give him a permanent place of honour in the history of art. To this we have to add his work in glass, the Artek furniture and quite outstanding and often distinctly oriental light-fittings, together with a sense of exterior form and interior space unsurpassed by any other architect during the past half-century.

Aalto's mastery of interior quality, however, appeared to stop short of the creation of a truly satisfactory religious space. In fact he seemed unable to permeate any of the churches he built with his sense of the cosmic and the mystical. Where one might have expected to find the intimate, reflective warmth we associate with the National Romantic spirit, or even the rough-hewn material immediacy of Karelian autonomous architecture, we find instead that Aalto's predilection for whiteness prevails. And this is true from the early example at Muurame, through those of Imatra, Seinäjoki and Riola.

The Vuoksenniska church at Imatra in particular appears to concentrate upon exterior form, while the elaborate functionalism of its plan, that permits three different spatial volumes to accommodate congregations of varying sizes, seems to dissipate any overall interior quality. In this respect the Imatra church reflects some of the cold impersonality of Engel's Great Church in Helsinki (now the Lutheran Cathedral). Yet the Vuoksenniska example is the most coherent of Aalto's realised church designs. The fact remains that an interior dialogue of light and shade, reflection and absorption, which experience of Säynätsalo Town Hall or even Rautatalo might suggest as the appropriate character for an Aalto church, a touch of what we might describe as Orthodox intangibility, is completely lacking. For such character one has to look instead at the churches of Sigurd Lewerentz, the only modern Swedish architect other than Asplund admired by Aalto. And even Sirén's chapel at Otaniemi, which is classical in outline only, achieves a more religious atmosphere through the handling of materials in the spirit of the National Romantic movement.

Ironically Aalto's secular interiors are more mystical than his religious ones. This is possibly because Finnish Lutheranism simply did not evoke a spiritual response in him. The promising indications of the exterior form at Imatra are simply not followed through inside. For instance, the double-skinned windows translate the forest rhythms Aalto first built into the Villa Mairea; but at Imatra they have their own existence between the exterior and the interior rather than making a specific contribution to the interior quality as such.

Aalto maintained his extraordinary dominance of Finnish architecture for almost half a century, and it is little wonder that he was both admired and envied by succeeding generations. Industrial expansion in Finland, as the country sought a new national identity following her independence from Russia, meant that Aalto's unique genius was required at home; unlike Saarinen he therefore did not need to emigrate to find work.[13] Although he had many overseas commissions, whether Aalto would have succeeded abroad on a continuous basis is extremely doubtful. He was, in spite of the complex eclecticism of his approach, essentially a son of Finland and he needed the programme of Finnish identity just as much as his country needed his genius: they were mutually interdependent. For this reason, after his early rationalist period, had he for any reason been transplanted to another Western culture he would clearly have been working directly against the *Zeitgeist*.

Even the strong Italian influence which Aalto always admitted to[14] must not be interpreted in too simplistic terms, neither in the context of the *cortile* in particular nor the organisation of external spatial and formal relationships in general. In this connection, Göran Schildt's passage, describing the Aalto family home at Jyväskylä, to where they moved around 1905, seems most illuminating:

> A few years later he [J.H. Aalto] bought what was at that time a typical town residence on the hill slope at Harjukatu 10, nowadays Yliopistonkatu 22. The site consisted of two terraces of yards and four separate wooden houses. The Aalto family lived in the largest section and rented out the smaller dwellings to families covering a very wide social spectrum.[15]

If one considers the spatial character of this group of buildings in relation to the traditional grouping of Finnish farm dwellings as described in Ranulph Glanville's article on 'Finnish Vernacular Farmhouses'[16] an interesting question is provoked. That is: 'Would not that particular configuration of buildings together with its *zwischenraum* have made a lasting impression on the young Alvar?' And if so, 'Does this not suggest a direct connection with the general morphology of his courtyard designs?'

Certainly, Aalto must have been struck by the essentially human scale of a number of related detached dwellings within a common yard. Glanville argues that:

> . . . As one moves from west to east across Finland, the external courtyard is gradually converted to become internal, and that the very existence of such courtyards both internal and external, in virtually every Finnish building, is the key to the 'Finnishness' of Finnish architecture.

There seems little dispute, at any rate, that this characteristic is *one* such key, and Aalto was extremely adept at manipulating the character and significance of the Finnish *cortile* or *atrium*. Also as Glanville points out, the example of farmhouse groupings would have become part of Aalto's stock-in-trade. There also seems little doubt that in his boyhood he would have been aware of such fine examples as the great farm at Pienmäki in Middle Finland, with its proximity to Jyväskylä. Another poignant observation made by Glanville concerns the essentially additive quality of indigenous Finnish architecture of the countryside, which is only planned in the loosest, schematic sense – with the projecting ends of timber members prepared ready for extension – then 'synthesised' according to developing needs.

From the point of view of courtyard design, looking across the whole spectrum of Aalto's life's work, the little town hall at Säynätsalo remains a consummate model of compositional resolution both from within and without. But one does not have to look far for evidence of an additive approach to design, in either the National Pensions Institute or the so-called 'House of Culture'. The treatment of corner junctions on the Pensions Institute has a distinctly additive character, as does the visual non-relatedness of the covered way to the auditorium mass at the front of the House of Culture.

Also, the entire planning concept of the Pensions Institute can be read as a progression of internal and external courts, while the former Pedagogical Institute (now University) of Jyväskylä has similar characteristics, with a distinct emphasis on the internalised 'courtyard' spaces derived from the fact that the University was designed for mainly winter use. Perhaps, therefore, given the courtyard tradition in the organisation of vernacular building groups and the additive nature of their realisation, it becomes more understandable how readily both classical and indigenous elements form a part of, and are so fluidly absorbed into, Aalto's work.

The ultimate flexibility of Aalto's particular blend of eclecticism therefore appears to stem from the broad scope of his source material and the sensitivity with which he was able to emphasise particular characteristics while playing down others. Thus, his architecture seems to depend upon the development not of a pure 'style' of expression but rather of a 'dramatic character' in providing a background for man's performance. In consequence, what must be emphasised in considering Aalto's approach and contribution to modern architecture is the great advantage of having been brought up in close contact with a vernacular tradition and also schooled in a strong academic discipline. It will perhaps help us to understand the present state of confusion in the art if we realise that these twin benefits are no longer available to us, and their lack must inevitably be reflected in the quality of much architectural design and execution. Authenticity in architecture, certainly as evidenced by Aalto, depends upon:

1 A thorough knowledge of materials and their related technologies.
2 An appreciative awareness of the immediate (and related) traditions within a society.
3 A developed framework of reference which links these first preconditions in postulating design solutions.

Aalto insisted that in design it was necessary 'to combine experimental work with the mentality of play, and vice-versa'.[17] For him, in the final analysis, form was:

... a mystery which eludes definition but makes man feel good in a way quite unlike mere social aid.[18]

And to give the master a last, if elusive, word on the meaning of his own work, perhaps his most cogent definition of architecture was that: '... Technology and economy must always be combined with a life-enhancing charm.'[19]

APPENDIX

Furniture and Interiors

In 1930 Frank Lloyd Wright enumerated the main principles that had given birth to his so-called Prairie Houses. The designs for these dwellings were characterised by long, low lines. This essential horizontality, linking the houses 'organically' with the ground, was mainly achieved by broad overhanging eaves. He listed nine points in his organic programme for those designs and, of those, the sixth and eighth are strongly reflected in Aalto's approach to form and detailing. In summary, Wright's two points were:

(1) the elimination of combinations of widely differing materials in favour of *monomaterial* as far as possible; and to use *no ornament that did not derive from the nature of materials*;

(2) to incorporate furnishings into organic architecture *making them all one with the building*, and designing them for machine work.

These two statements describe in essence Wright's philosophy of a modern architecture that is rooted in tradition whilst reflecting the impact of industrial production on building. But Wright was a traditionalist at heart and his view of the machine a romantic one. He saw the machine as a remote, abstract tool. In the eighth principle of the Prairie House he called for 'a perfect amalgam of structure and furniture'. His furniture, however, never transcended an awkward combination of rigid geometries and machine techniques, making it more a model for the sets of futuristic science-fiction films than the expression of twentieth-century industrial production. Wright's furniture is frequently uncomfortable to look at and to sit on. This is not at all the case with Aalto's designs. The Finnish master sought to make his furniture 'one with the building' but he did this from the position of a mastery of modern wood techniques in industrial production. In Aalto's case the realisation of material and geometric cohesion centred on the pleasing and comfortable curves that came not from the drawing board alone but also harnessed the technology of laminated bentwood construction. Wright described the interior decorator as being 'all curves and all efflorescence'. Aalto's interiors have the curves but these are rooted in a fundamentally modern use of wood. Laminated bentwood retains the traditional virtues of pleasing texture and natural warmth; but it is no longer simply cut and fitted, it is actually *moulded* into shape. The resulting harmonies go beyond the rigid abstraction of Wright and, in Aalto's hands, create an interior environment that blends the traditional with the new.

248

It was Wright's third principle of the Prairie House that 'the box form of room and volume should be eliminated', and we have seen that Aalto followed this tenet in all designs from that of his own house at Munkkiniemi (1934–6) onwards. We have also observed that Saarinen's design for Hvitträsk (from 1902) paralleled, in its ingenious plan arrangements, the transformations of domestic planning which Wright achieved in his Fricke House (1902), Cheney House (1904) and Robie House (1909), all in Oak Park, Chicago. The skilful changes of level achieved by Saarinen at Hvitträsk were a strong influence on Aalto's domestic interiors, as evidenced by the Villa Mairea and the Maison Carré as well as the designs for the Tallin Art Museum and the Finnish Pavilion for the 1937 Paris World's Fair. But Aalto also absorbed the planning characteristics of Wright's early Oak Park houses – the removal of traditional plan divisions, with the resultant free flow of space from room to room and the interpenetration of their merging volumes – and made these very much his own. Freedom of flowing line, form and space is a distinctive trademark of Aalto's interiors from the mid-30s onwards and it is in this context that we should view his furniture and related detailing.

Aalto's concept of making furniture 'one with the building' has to do more with his sense of *belonging* than mere *attachment* to the structure. It seems to be part of his concept of freedom that there should be some flexibility in the placement of furniture and furnishing. To him the architecture – the plan and its volumetrics – are the permanent form, and the disposition of furniture is variable, like that of figures in a landscape. *Built-in* furniture is, therefore, not a strong feature of the mature Aalto interior. The furniture of an Aalto interior has its *place*, and in small spaces this is more precisely defined and even *standardised*. But the sense of inevitability lies in the overall harmonic context more than in mere placement. Consequently, the Aalto interior is built up, *modelled* by a process of accretions and agglutination rather than being *carved* into the interior volume. This additive process can be traced back to the period 1927–30 with the formulation of the Paimio Sanatorium, Turun Sanomat and other related designs.

It is characteristic of the light fittings at Paimio, for example, that they are not *built in* or flush with the ceiling but added on to the surface. Similarly, the door handles to the patients' rooms, with the track for the lever-arm, are not *housed* in the door but *planted* on the surface. The idea of movable light-fittings, sliding along a continuous track, also emanates from the Turun Sanomat building and Paimio Sanatorium, so that although the technology is *built in* to the ceiling the fittings themselves remain as appendages.

Just as his early architecture was Neo-classical in inspiration, so Aalto's first furniture designs were based directly on Renaissance and Empire models. In the 1920s hand-made furniture in Finland cost the same whether copied from existing examples or an architect's drawing. Aalto exploited this fact and designed various pieces in the Neo-classical style for family and friends. In this way he learned not only stylistic points but also those of detailing and craftsmanship. He admired the work of those Finnish carpenters who had produced the eighteenth- and nineteenth-century variations of European Baroque churches, and he too became interested in interpreting the spirit of the past.

In the same way as he broke with Neo-classicism in the design of the Tapani System apartments for Turku (1927), he radically changed his approach to furniture when, in the following year, he made designs for the sacristy of the Muurame Church and some rooms in the Agricultural Cooperative Building in Turku. Among the joinery manufacturers to whom these designs were sent for estimates was the well-established Huonekalu-ja-Rakennustyötehdas company in Turku. The company's managing director, Otto Korhonen, was extremely experienced in the furniture field; moreover, he was a pragmatist who responded directly to the simple forms and straightforward detailing of the traditional country furniture with which he had been brought up. His concern was to switch from handicraft techniques to the more profitable industrialized production *without* sacrificing his firm's reputation for high quality. In this process Korhonen saw innovatory detailing as the key to the development of his business.

In his search for new approaches to furniture design Korhonen realised that when furniture was not wanted in a particular room its storage took a lot of space. He discovered that by placing the legs of chairs outside the limits of their seats, in other words projecting beyond the seat at the sides, the chairs could be stacked and therefore take up less space when not in use. This discovery was to prove as useful to him in the factory as it was in public buildings. Aalto was attracted by Korhonen's innovation and helped him refine this stacking chair. It was patented in Finland in 1929 and came into production in time to be used in the auditorium of the Association of Patriots ('Civil Guards') Building in Jyväskylä. This chair combined traditional solid wooden legs, back rails and seat rails with *formed* laminated plywood seats and backs. By becoming involved with Korhonen in this design for Huonekalu-ja-Rakennustyötehdas Aalto laid the foundations for two important characteristics of his later work: (1) the 'stacking' theme which was to become a hallmark of much of his furniture; and (2) the additive approach that gives the inimitable Aalto touch to many aspects of his designs – planning, massing, detailing and furniture.

Aalto continued this additive approach to the design of his furniture in the Korhonen chair of 1929 by combining an adaptation of the original Luterma moulded seat form to fit onto a tubular steel cantilever frame. And the design for the Korhonen chair was further refined in two chairs produced in 1929–30. In both of these later models the cantilever frame of the original Korhonen chair was retained but the seat itself, instead of being a simple 'L'-shaped plane of monolithic seat and back, had portions of the outside edges of that plane cut, and *folded* back to form arms. This device not only provided integral arms within the single moulded slab of plywood, it also created a more rigid structure by tying the back to the seat. Thus, the weakness of the original design, the sheer bending force at the junction of seat and back which produced cracking under the strain of leaning backwards, was overcome. It was in these refinements to the original Korhonen chair, therefore, that Aalto learned his

Stacking chair, Aalto's first exercise (1927) in furniture design, made for the Civil Guard Headquarters, Jyväskylä

first important lesson in laminated plywood design, which allowed him to progress beyond the earlier Thonet and Lutherma experiments with bentwood. For the secret Aalto discovered in producing his first playwood armchairs was that it is multi-planar *moulding* that gives the laminated material superior strength over the simple *bending* employed in the late nineteenth- and early twentieth-century models. This discovery was to influence the furniture designs of Marcel Breuer and Charles Eames and all who subsequently followed in Aalto's footsteps.

Curiously, Aalto never returned to this one-piece seat and arm formula, nor did he go on to exploit this means of cutting and counter-bending the single slab of plywood in his designs. His interest in this detail seems to have waned rapidly. It crops up again contemporaneously in two of his earliest experimental reliefs; but, after the design of the Paimio chair of 1931, and other all wood chairs of the same period, he concentrated on refining the design of the seat-and-back as one element and a combined legs-and-arms profile as the other. The technique of cutting, bending and splicing, which also occurs in those early experimental reliefs of 1929–33 and points the way towards a complex interweaving of laminations, did not recur in his work until after the Second World War; namely in the bi-axial chair and stool legs of the 1947 Artek series.

There are two variations on the original Korhonen design that still employ the

Armchair, combining tubular steel base with moulded plywood seat and arms in one piece

simple 'L'-shaped seat-and-back element. The first of these is also on a tubular steel frame but is a rectangular (rather than cantilever) form, with the base span cranked for extra rigidity; it is also a much lower chair, intended for informal sitting rather than at a desk or table, and had a quilted cover over the plywood seat-and-back. The second was also intended as an easy chair, of intermediate height between the other two versions, with the seat-and-back element inclined towards the rear of the chair for increased comfort and supported on a conventional frame held between two inverted-'U' leg-and-arm combination elements. This latter model was the most conservative design of Aalto's first serious period of furniture production, i.e., 1929–35.

Aalto's experimental relief constructions of 1930–33, prompted by his actual involvement in the technical problems of wooden furniture production, both in the workshop and factory, reveal his full genius for design and construction. In these exercises, undertaken in collaboration with Korhonen's workshops at the same time as he was consolidating his reputation as a leader of the international functionalist style, Aalto reveals many aspects of his complex *persona*. They vary from (1) a composition consisting of a knotty tree branch contrasted by a simulation of such a detail in bent and glued wooden dowelling; (2) two 'wheat-sheafs', again constructed from the wooden dowelling; (3) an abstract composition demonstrating a multi-axial bending of a rod made up of several dowel lengths; to (4) several studies that are simply full-size working drawings, i.e., sections of actual details of laminations, bends and connections. In their range and diversity they show his complete command of the aesthetic of wood and of modern timber technology in the early 30s; they reveal both the forestry background of his family on his mother's side (see Chapter I, p. 3) and his own extreme sensitivity as a designer and *artist*. None of his later paintings or sculpture ever exhibited the sureness, the quality and the control of these early constructions. They also contain important clues about his future predilections not only as a furniture designer but more importantly as an architect. For they are both restrained and explosive in their imagery; both technologically exact yet free-wheeling; both nervous and tentative yet immediately expressive; they are excitingly alive, like fingers seeking out the future of form; they are Aalto himself, portrayed abstractedly, yet instantly recognisable as the whole man. These constructions have an almost musical quality in their freedom of line, their counterpoint and their harmonic variations; they are highly strung chords, quivering with the energy of an archer's bow released. They show Aalto harnessing the natural strength of the forest into a new and powerful design force.

After these wild expressions of natural energy the sprung tension of the so-called Paimio chair (1931) fits perfectly into place in Aalto's development. It is not merely a further refinement of the one-piece seat-and-back Korhonen variations. For in the Paimio chair the seat-and-back is not simply *planted* onto leg elements. Instead, the leg assemblies, a continuous form that is basically a trapezoid of laminated plywood with a pronounced 'dent' at the front, rise to embrace the seat-and-back element. This element is also no longer a simple 'L'-shape but has scrolled ends that curve under the seat at the front and over the back, each end returning to the arm-leg-frames so that both the front and top of the seat-and-back element makes two secure connections with those frames. Thus, the seat-and-back-plane curves seductively to give a rhythmical counterpoint to the profile of the arm-leg-frames. In this way the Paimio chair is reminiscent of the space-time constructs of a Cubist painting: its planes are what they are but they seem to be both *more* and *less*. The Paimio chair, in its brilliant economy of material and form, succeeds in reducing the comfortable outlines and generous volume of the traditional, horsehair-stuffed armchair to the barest skeletal essentials. Indeed, in his long career as a furniture designer, spanning almost half a century from 1927, Aalto was not to surpass the elegant *bravura* of this early design, manufactured when he was only thirty-three, and much more daring than, say, Breuer's *Isokon* bentwood chaise-longue.

There were interesting variations of the 'Paimio' design, notably the three open cantilever frame designs for armchairs also originally executed for Paimio, and increasingly daring in their profile. In these designs, Aalto converted the tubular steel 'spring' armchair into plywood; but although the seats of these three chairs overcame the original weakness at the fold of the seat-and-back element, the compression produced by the severe bending stress on the lower inside angle of the leg-arm frame produced cracking under heavy use. However, in addition to their material and structural innovations, this whole series of chair designs by Aalto constituted the most elegant institutional furniture in use at the time. As the first realisation of the strategies outlined in his earlier experimental constructions, the geometry of these chairs already anticipates Aalto's architecture of the period from the Villa Mairea to the Imatra church; that is, from the mid 30s to the late 50s.

Other parallel developments in Aalto's furniture over the period 1929–35 were concentrated on the domestic and institutional markets, with many of the designs becoming initial items in the Artek catalogue. These designs included the celebrated three-legged stacking stool, the nest of three stacking occasional tables, the stacking double-topped coffee/occasional table, and the circular-seated cut-out back chairs and stools which spanned from a nursery chair to a high bar-stool with added foot-rest. All of these designs, in the unfussy simplicity of their construction, owe their original inspiration to the furniture Aalto designed for his own family's apartment in the South-Western Agricultural Cooperative Building, Turku (1927–8). In all but his design for a dining chair with a central, single-column cantilevered back-rest, however, the furniture of this period abandons the comprehensive totality of the Paimio design in favour of the characteristic additive approach to construction and form we have already noted. The hook-shaped leg elements that tuck under the seats are the main feature of this furniture. Webbing also makes its appearance as a seat-and-back membrane during this period, including in the designs for an armchair that once again separates the under-frame of the chair from the traditional splayed arms of eighteenth- and nineteenth-century origin. The exception to these trends in Aalto's designs towards the end of this first consequent period of his furniture is the brilliant tea-trolley (1933–5), in the one and two shelf models, the frame of which harks back to the arm-leg assemblies of the Paimio chair.

Between 1935 and 1939 bold innovation returned in Aalto's furniture designs, notably in the most daring and elegant of all cantilevered chaise-longues of the 1930s, which exploits the language of the Paimio chair and series, but now less with Cubist/constructivist perfection of form than sheer panache. The chaise-longue has webbing on an 'S'-profile rectangular frame. And the webbing is also used in another design that is a further variant on the Paimio cantilever armchair series. But only the chaise-longue equals the originality of Aalto's earlier Paimio armchair. This second period also included the design for the cantilevered bookshelves which were hung from triangular-profile bentwood brackets. And this bracket detail was also used in a cantilevered desk unit and a coat-and-hat rail, with the brackets moved to the underside of the units. The winged, upholstered high-backed armchair of this period is more conventional. But the cantilever-frame wide armchair is more daring again, with its arm-leg supports sweeping down at the back to achieve a better attachment to the edges of the upholstered 'L'-shaped seat-and-back element. The upholstered element is also strikingly original in its covering of *quartered* zebra skins. This quartering of the zebra skins follows naturally from Aalto's experiments with laminated plywood, the precise conjunction of the zebra stripes echoing the quartered grain effects of timber, only at a larger scale.

During this period (1935–9) Aalto also designed some outdoor furniture for the Villa Mairea in 1938, thus extending his interior imagery out to the terrace and garden. The table top for this set resembles a flower, with a circular centre piece surrounded by segmental boards that suggest petals; while the chairs have high, vertical slatted backs that derive from barrel staves. But these *rustic* designs, executed in conventional timber, with the backs of the chairs preformed for comfort, are but a pale shadow of the bent plywood examples. Waterproof marine plywood, as used for example by Ernest Race in his Cunard 'Oriana' deckchair was, of course, not available to Aalto in the late 30s.

It was the Gullichsens' commission to build the Villa Mairea that provided Aalto with his greatest opportunity to integrate the furniture with the structure. He took advantage of this by extending the treatment he had invented for his own house at Munkkiniemi (1934–6) in the Noormarkku design. This treatment, as developed in the Villa Mairea, literally *furnishes* the building form with wooden elements, so that the basic concrete structure which had been so proudly exposed in the Turun Sanomat building and at Paimio is now masked by the *environment of the room*, both the interior and the exterior room. We have seen (Chapter IV, pp. 85–90) how Aalto used wood, the natural *interior* of the forest, as the free-flowing material that passes through the house, linking the inside room with the outside room, furnishing both. The ceiling of the *porte-cochère* and the living room ceiling have similar boarding, the outside rough and the inside smooth. Those unstripped saplings that screen the outer porch under the *porte-cochère* recur in a refined form in the lobby approach to the living area. The interior columns are bound with horizontal strips of cane, while the staircase rising up from the living room again repeats the theme of the *porte-cochère* and lobby in its room-height balustrade (an early sketch shows that Aalto originally proposed to use bamboo poles for this balustrade).

It is the forest that furnishes this superb interior. Not always in its natural or near-natural state of course, for we have the sliding door, clearly influenced by the Japanese *shoji* screen, with its restrained oriental geometry; while on the first-floor landing the balustrade becomes a perforated plywood panel. Indeed, the Villa Mairea is virtually furnished by the timber elements of ceiling, wall and stair before the chairs, tables and tea-trolley are added. In none of his other domestic interiors does Aalto achieve the same degree of cohesion between structure and furniture, the same delicate balance of line, form and materials. Every detail is carefully put in place with superb craftsmanship; yet the result, the overall context, is soft and easy to live with. The interior of Villa Mairea, from the entrance throughout the living room, the entire ground floor, is artfully contrived so that, like the surrounding forest, it seems completely natural. In the words of Alberti, 'Nothing can be added or taken away except for the worse'. Even the sculptural treatment of the corner of the fireplace wall, reminiscent of Aalto's design for the architect Aalto Virtanen's gravestone in Helsinki (1935), is a necessary wearing away of that element, the soft contours of the modelling suggesting that the wind and rain had got at it.

Armchair, with moulded plywood seat and bent plywood legs and arms in one piece

(*Left and opposite*) Constructions based on examples of laminated jointing technique in plywood manufacture

Aalto's other two main periods of activity as a furniture designer belong to 1947 and 1954–6 respectively. As we have already observed, the first of these saw a further translation of the experimental relief constructions in the corner detailing of legs supporting chairs, stools and tables. This detail, unlike the additive formula developed in the early 30s, is a truly organic solution in that the head of the solid leg has laminations introduced into it which allows it to bend from the vertical to the horizontal rail. Two of these triangular section legs are then bonded together, so that their heads diverge at ninety degrees to each other, giving a branch-like form that is exposed at the corner by setting the seat or webbing back from the intersection. This corner detail, and the elegance of the constructional detailing as a whole, is seen to best advantage in the glass-topped occasional tables, where no part of the frame is hidden. In the chair the rear legs receive the continuation of the front leg-frame that becomes the seat-and-back. This detail, as in the early 'Civil Guard' chair, permits stacking. Apart from this range, with the 'branched' leg detail, most other models of 1947 are more conventional in appearance. They include upholstered high and low armchairs, easy chairs, and even a leather Ottoman type; but perhaps the most interesting detail is the binding of the arms either in cane (as in the Villa Mairea interior) or leather. There is also a fine stool from this period which combines the 'hooked' leg detail of the first period with a dished, circular plywood ring – a segment of a shallow cone in fact – that receives a loose seat of either cane or leather (in six segments, recalling the petal design of the garden table).

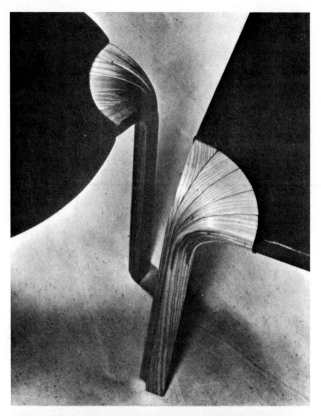

Stool and table design: detail showing laminated bentwood corner legs of fan shape

Construction, demonstrating the form potential of laminating bent wooden rods. This piece appears as a feature on the main staircase of the Council Chamber at Säynätsalo village hall

In his stool and table designs of 1954 Aalto further extended the branching image of the 1947 model to create a fan detail at the head of the legs. This detail is more constructional and less organic than the 'branch' design. Also, it is not continuous with the frame of the seat or table top. Instead, the fan-headed legs are fixed to sub-frames, which provides a less elegant and less convincing detail when exposed by the glass-topped tables but forms a perfect junction for the solid-topped stools and tables. Both stools and tables had a variety of tops – glass, birch, plywood, leather and laminated hardwoods – and the stools were square (with four fan-headed legs) and circular and triangular (with three legs). A three-legged variation of the laminated hardwood table was designed specially for the Maison Carré as part of the living-room furniture Aalto produced for that residence during 1956–8. The Carré furniture, however, is a distinct compromise between modern lines and the *substance* of French bourgeois taste and reflects the lines of the furniture Aalto designed in 1954–6 to be used in the executive suites and waiting areas of the National Pensions Building.

With the Villa Mairea Aalto made timber an essential element in his domesic interiors, just as in the Pensions Building he was to create a permanent place for wall tiling in his public buildings. But he was to return to the spirit of those early constructions in the interior treatments of public buildings between the late 50s and the early 70s. For whereas the Auditorium Building at Jyväskylä (1952–7) had as its main interior motifs the tiled walls and columns with the stepped acoustic ceiling of the entrance foyer, the Opera House at Essen, for which the first design dates from 1958–9, provided an opportunity for a large-scale relief in the auditorium. And the theme Aalto selected for these reliefs to cover the side walls at Essen relates to his early studies of bentwood connections and particularly the 'hook' leg motif of his first furniture period. This theme was repeated when he executed the seminar room for the Institute of International Education in New York in 1963–5, where the laminated hook motif is used in a playful, sculptural manner. And, whilst waiting for a decision at Essen, Aalto incorporated what is virtually the same design as originally proposed for the Essen walls into the main auditorium of the Finlandia building (1973–5).

Thus, between the late 50s and the mid 70s we see a development of Aalto's 'furnishing' of the Villa Mairea interior, with the timber elements that were designed for the walls of the Institute of International Education in New York and Finlandia in Helsinki actually being extensions of his early furniture experiments. It was in his approach to the detailing of wooden elements, in his seeking of a common ground for technology, structure and the pleasure to be found in natural materials that lay at the heart of Aalto's ability to make his furnishings 'one with the building'. For Aalto the *organic* was not simply a question of *material* or *geometry* but a sensibility that brought about form which could be felt.

Chronological List of Main Works

For a complete list of Aalto's designs the reader is referred to the official biography of the architect by Göran Schildt.

(Dates in brackets indicate construction period)

DATE	SITE/LOCATION	BUILDING/PROJECT	OFFICE BASE/ COLLABORATORS
1918	ALAJÄRVI	Porch addition to parents' house	
1918 (1919)	KAUHAJÄRVI	Addition of belfry to church	
1919	ALAJÄRVI	Youth Society Building	
1920	HELSINKI	Tivoli area, Finnish National Fair	Assistant in office of Carolus Lindberg
1921	HELSINKI	Diploma Project: Pavilion for Finnish National Fair	
1921–2	SEINÄJOKI	Building for Association of Patriots	
1922	TAMPERE	Industrial Exposition: main pavilion; snack bar pavilion; craft pavilion; band stand; and choral shell	
1923	HELSINKI	House of Parliament competition project	Jyväskylä
1923–4	JYVÄSKYLÄ	Railway employees' apartments	Jyväskylä
1923–4	JYVÄSKYLÄ	Workers' Club, 1st Prize, 1923	Jyväskylä
1923	JYVÄSKYLÄ	Multi-family house with shop	Jyväskylä
1924	ÄÄNEKOSKI ANTTOLA	Church restorations	Jyväskylä
1925	SEINÄJOKI	Building for Association of Patriots	Jyväskylä
1925	JÄMSÄ	Jämsä church competition entry	Jyväskylä
1925	VIITASAARI	Remodelling of church	Jyväskylä
1925	HELSINKI	Töölö church competition entry	Jyväskylä
1925		Competition entry for *Kasiteollisuus* furniture	Jyväskylä with Aino
1925	JYVÄSKYLÄ	'Casa Lauren', two-family house	Jyväskylä
1925–6	ALAJÄRVI	Villa Vainölä	Jyväskylä
1926	JYVÄSKYLÄ	Monumental plaza layout	Jyväskylä

DATE	SITE/LOCATION	BUILDING/PROJECT	OFFICE BASE/ COLLABORATORS
1926	GENEVA	League of Nations Head-quarters competition entry	Jyväskylä with Aino
1926–9 (1927–9)	MUURAME	Parish church	Jyväskylä and Turku (from summer 1927)
1926–9	JYVÄSKYLÄ	Association of Patriots Building (later Post Office). First competition success – 2nd prize	Jyväskylä
1927	ALAJÄRVI	Municipal hospital	Turku
1927	HELSINKI	Töölö church competition entry	Jyväskylä
1927	TAMPERE	Viinikka church competition entry	Jyväskylä
1927	JYVÄSKYLÄ	County Congregation's church, Taulumäkai	Turku
1927		Summer house competition entry for *Aitta*: 1st prize; 'Konsoli'; also 'Merry-Go-Round'	Turku
1927	PYLKÖNMÄKI	Church restoration and belfry	Turku
1927–8	TURKU	South-Western Agricultural Cooperative Building: first major open competition success	Turku
1927–9	TURKU	Standard, precast concrete apartment block for 'Tapani'	Turku
1927	VIIPURI	Municipal library competition entry: 1st design October 1927; 2nd design August 1928 (both on Aleksanterinkatu site); 3rd design 14 December 1933 (on new Torkkelinpuisto park site)	Turku and Helsinki (after summer 1933)
1928–9	TURKU	Offices and plant for *Turun Sanomat*	Turku
1928	HELSINKI	Independence monument competition entry	Turku
1928	KORPILAHTI	Restoration of church	Turku
1929 (1930–33)	PAIMIO	Tuberculosis Sanatorium	Turku
1929	TURKU	Turku's 700-Year Fair: choral shell	Turku, with Erik Bryggman
1929	HELSINKI	Church competition for Vallila area	
1929	KEMIJÄRVI	Restoration of church	Turku
1930	VIERUMÄKI	Institute for Physical Education competition: 3rd prize	Turku

DATE	SITE/LOCATION	BUILDING/PROJECT	OFFICE BASE/ COLLABORATORS
1930	TURKU	Water tower and treatment plant competition	Turku
1930	TURKU	Ideal Stadium and Sports Park competition	Turku
1930	HELSINKI	Tehtaanpuisto (later called Michael Agricola) church competition	Turku
1930	HELSINKI	Minimum Apartment Exhibition (Finnish Arts and Crafts Society)	With Pauli and Märta Blomstedt, Erik Bryggman and Werner West
1930	ZAGREB	University Hospital competition entry	With Pauli and Märta Blomstedt, Erik Bryggman and Werner West
1930–31	OULU	Cellulose factory at Toppila	With Pauli and Märta Blomstedt, Erik Bryggman and Werner West
1932	HELSINKI	Prototype house design for Insulite Company for Finland. Prototype weekend cottage design for Enso-Gutzeit Company (both in Nordic Building Conference Exhibition)	With Pauli and Märta Blomstedt, Erik Bryggman and Werner West
1933	HELSINKI	National (Olympic) Stadium competition	Turku/Helsinki
1933	PAIMIO	Housing for employees at sanatorium; terraced housing for doctors of the sanatorium	Hereafter, Helsinki
1933	STOCKHOLM	Redevelopment plan for Norrmalm	
1934	TAMPERE	Tampere Railway Station Competition	
1934	HELSINKI	Stenius housing development, Munkkiniemi	
1934	HELSINKI	National Exhibition Pavilion competition: 3rd prize	
1934	HELSINKI	Central Post and Telegraph Office competition	
1934–6	HELSINKI	Architect's own house and studio, Munkkiniemi	

DATE	SITE/LOCATION	BUILDING/PROJECT	OFFICE BASE/ COLLABORATORS
1935	MOSCOW	Finnish Embassy competition	
1935–7	SUNILA	Pulp mill	
1935	HELSINKI	ALKO plant and office block	
1936–7	PARIS	Finnish Pavilion for World's Fair: 1st prize, 'Le Bois en Marche'	Aino and Alvar plus Aarne Ervi and Viljo Rewell
1936	PARIS	Finnish Pavilion for World's Fair: 2nd prize, 'Tsit Tsit Pum'	Aarne Ervi and Viljo Rewell as main assistants
1937	TALLIN	Museum of Art	
1937	HELSINKI	Savoy Restaurant interior and glassware	With Aino
1937	HELSINKI	Extension to Helsinki University Library (original by Engel 1836–47) competition entry	
1937 (1938–40)	KAUTTUA	Development at Kauttua (Competition) stepped housing	
1937	KARHULA	Nordic United Bank	
1937–8	SUNILA	Director's house at pulp mills, Sunila	
1937–8	SUNILA	Two-storey housing for pulp mill workers, 1st and 2nd groups	
1937–9	NOORMARKKU	Villa Mairea for Harry and Maire Gullichsen	
1938	LAPUA	Forestry Pavilion for Agricultural Exhibition	
1938–9	SUNILA	Three-storey terrace housing for pulp mill workers, 1st and 2nd groups; four-storey housing	
1938	HELSINKI	Blomberg Film Studio, Westend, Helsinki, competition entry	
1938	NEW YORK	Finnish Pavilion for World's Fair; 1st prize: 'Maa, Kausa, Työ, Tulos'	With Stenius, Urpola and Bernoulli
1938–9	INKEROINEN	Elementary school	
1938–9	INKEROINEN	Anjala apartment buildings, 1st and 2nd groups	
1938–9	INKEROINEN	Housing for engineers	
1939–45	KARHULA	Apartment buildings for Ahlström Company	

DATE	SITE/LOCATION	BUILDING/PROJECT	OFFICE BASE/COLLABORATORS
1940	HELSINKI	HAKA housing development competition entry	
1940–41	HELSINKI	Erottaja Square competition for air-raid shelter and traffic plan (intersection of Mannerheimintie, Esplanaadi, Boulevardi): 1st Prize	
1941		Plan for a model town	This is the project Aalto produced with his students at MIT
1941	PORI	Master plan for Kokemäki river valley for Ahlström Company	
1942–3	KAUTTUA	Women's dormitory	
1942–3	OULU	Master plan for Oulujoki river valley	Bertel Strömmer the only other competitor
1942–3		Competition for Merikoski power plant	
1942–4	SÄYNÄTSALO	Village plan for Enso-Gutzeit	
1943	OULU	Town centre competition entry	
1944	AVESTA, Sweden	Town centre competition entry	With Albin Stark
1944	VAASA	Strömberg housing development	
1944	KAUTTUA	Extension of factory	
1944–5	ROVANIEMI	Master plan for the rebuilding and redevelopment of Rovaniemi	With 'planning team'
1944–5	KARHULA	Ahlström machine shop	
1944–7	VAASA	Strömberg meter factory and housing estate	
1944–5	VARKAUS	Sawmill extension for Ahlström Company	
1945	KAUTTUA	Engineer's house and sauna	
1945	HEDEMORA, Sweden	Artek factory exhibition pavilion	
1945–6	VARKAUS	One-family housing production	
1946	NYNÄSHAMN, Sweden	Heimdal housing development, seven-storey apartment blocks; competition project	With Albin Stark
1946	NYNÄSHAMN	Master plan competition entry	
1946	NYNÄSHAMN	Town hall design competition entry, 'Song of the Pines'	

DATE	SITE/LOCATION	BUILDING/PROJECT	OFFICE BASE/ COLLABORATORS
1946	NOORMARKKU	Sauna for Villa Mairea	
1946	PIHLAVA	One-family house	
1946–7 (1948–50)	CAMBRIDGE, Mass., USA	Baker House, senior dormitory at MIT	
1947	AVESTA, Sweden	Johnson Research Institute project	
1947	VAASA	Laundry and sauna for Strömberg factory	
1947–53	IMATRA	Regional plan for Imatra	
1948	HELSINKI	Commission for Engineers' Institute Building	
1948	HELSINKI	National Pension Bank Administrative and Cultural Centre Competition entry, 'Forum Redivivum': 1st prize (original site)	With Aino (their penultimate project)
1948	CAMBRIDGE, Mass., USA	Woodberry Poetry Room, Lamont Library, Harvard University	With Aino
1949	KARHULA	Ahlström factory warehouse	
1949	OTANIEMI	Helsinki Technical University general campus plan competition: 1st prize	With Aino (their last project)
1949–50	TAMPERE	Tampella housing	
1949	HELSINKI	Sea Harbour Facilities competition (motto 'Entrez en Paradis')	
1949	SÄYNÄTSALO	Town hall competition entry: 1st prize	
1949–54	OTANIEMI	Sports hall for Helsinki Technical University	
1950	LAHTI	Church and community centre competition entry: 1st prize	
1950	HELSINKI	Malmi Funeral Chapel competition entry: 1st prize	
1950	JYVÄSKYLÄ	Pedagogical Institute (later University) of Jyväskylä competition: 1st prize	
1950	HELSINKI	Kivelä Hospital competition	
1950–52	SÄYNÄTSALO	Town hall	Elissa Mäkiniemi acted as job captain

DATE	SITE/LOCATION	BUILDING/PROJECT	OFFICE BASE/ COLLABORATORS
1950–55	FINNISH LAPLAND	Regional plan for Lapland	
1951	KUOPIO	Theatre and Concert Hall competition: 1st prize	
1951–2	LYNGBY, Denmark	Cemetery master plan	
1951	HELSINKI	Erottaja Pavilion	
1951	KOTKA	Enso-Gutzeit paper factory	
1951	OULU	One-family house	
1951	INKEROINEN	Workers' housing	
1951	OULU	Typpi Oy sulphate factory	
1951–3	SUMMA	Enso-Gutzeit paper mill	
1951–4	CHANDRA-GHONA, Pakistan	Paper mill	
1951–4	SUNILA	Cellulose factory, Sunila, 2nd stage construction	
1951–4	SUNILA	Three-storey apartment houses, 3rd group	
1952 (1953–5)	HELSINKI	'Rautatalo' office and commercial building	
1952	KALLVIK	Enso-Gutzeit Club	
1952 (1958–60)	SEINÄJOKI	Church Competition entry: 1st prize	
1952–4	HELSINKI	Housing for personnel of National Pensions Institute, Munkkiniemi	
1952–6	HELSINKI	National Pensions Institute	
1952–7	JYVÄSKYLÄ	Pedagogical Institute, 1st stage	
1953	VIENNA	Sports and music centre competition; Vogelweidplatz competition: 1st prize	
1953	IMATRA	Imatra centre design project	
1953	MUURATSALO, Helsinki	Architect's own summer house	
1954	COMO, Italy	Studio R. Sambonet	
1954	HELSINKI	Housing AERO	
1954–5		Motorboat for Muuratsalo	
1955	MUNKKINIEMI, Helsinki	Architect's own office and studio	
1955	OTANIEMI	Design for main building, Helsinki Technical University	

DATE	SITE/LOCATION	BUILDING/PROJECT	OFFICE BASE/ COLLABORATORS
1955–7	GOTHENBERG, Sweden	City Hall and municipal offices competition	
1955	SUMMA	Urban design project	
1955	BAGHDAD, Iraq	Bank building competition	
1955	OULU	Theatre and concert hall project	
1955–7	BERLIN	Apartment block in the Hansaviertel for Interbau Exhibition	
1955–8	HELSINKI	House of Culture	
1955–64	OTANIEMI	Main Building, Helsinki Technical University	
1956	GOTHENBERG, Sweden	'Drottning Torget' Central Station, competition entry	
1956	OULU	Director's house for Typpi Oy	
1956	OULU	Master plan for University of Oulu	
1956	VENICE	Finnish Pavilion for Venice Biennale	
1956 (1957–9)	IMATRA	Church at Vuoksenniska	
1956–8	ILE DE FRANCE, France	Maison Louis Carré, Bazoches	
1956	NEW YORK	Metropolitan Opera House Competition	
1956–60	SEINÄJOKI	Church, Seinäjoki	
1957–8	STOCKHOLM, Sweden	Kampementsbacken housing development: 1st prize	
1957	MARL, Germany	Town hall, Marl, competition entry	
1957–61	ROVANIEMI	Korkalovaara housing development	
1957–61	AVESTA, Sweden	Sundh centre	
1958	KIRUNA, Sweden	Town hall, Kiruna, competition entry	
1958 (1972–3)	AALBORG, Denmark	North Jutland Art Museum, Aalborg, competition entry: 1st prize	With Jean-Louis Barüel
1958	BAGHDAD, Iraq	Art Museum, Baghdad, competition entry	
1958	BAGHDAD	Building for the Post Office Administration, Baghdad	

DATE	SITE/LOCATION	BUILDING/PROJECT	OFFICE BASE/ COLLABORATORS
1958–9	ESSEN	Opera House, Essen, competition entry: 1st prize	
1958 (1959–63)	WOLFSBURG, Germany	Cultural centre, Wolfsburg, competition entry	
1958 (1959–62)	BREMEN	High rise apartment block in Neue Vahr district	
1959 (1960–65)	SEINÄJOKI	Town centre, Seinäjoki, competition entry: 1st prize	
1959	HELSINKI	Bjornholm housing development	
1959–62	JYVÄSKYLÄ	Central Finland Museum	
1959 (1960–62)	WOLFSBURG, Germany	Parish centre	
1959–62	HELSINKI	Headquarters for Enso-Gutzeit	
1959–64	HELSINKI	Plan for central area redevelopment	
1960	SUOMUSSALMI	Finnish War Memorial (sculpture)	
1960–61	OTANIEMI	Shopping centre, Otaniemi student village	
1960–61	LIEKSA	Lieksankoski power station	
1960–63	OTANIEMI	Thermotechnical laboratory at Helsinki Technical University	
1960 (1962–5)	SEINÄJOKI	Town hall	
1961–2	ROVANIEMI	Office and apartment block	
1961–4	ESSEN	Opera House, Essen (2nd project)	
1962	HELSINKI	'Finlandia House' concert hall (original design)	
1961–2 (1962–4)	ESPOO	Group of apartment blocks, Tapiola	
1961–2	HELSINKI	Fennia-Patria office building competition: no prize	
1962	STOCKHOLM	Enskilda Bank building, Stockholm, competition entry: 2nd prize	
1962	LEVERKUSEN, Germany	Cultural centre competition entry	
1962–3	PIETARSAARI	Terrace housing	
1962 (1966–9)	HELSINKI	Stockmann department store expansion	

DATE	SITE/LOCATION	BUILDING/PROJECT	OFFICE BASE/ COLLABORATORS
1962–3	OTANIEMI	Heating plant at the Helsinki Technical University	
1962–3	ROVANIEMI	Housing development	
1962–4	HELSINKI	Administration building for the Scandinavian Bank	
1962 (1964–6)	OTANIEMI	Hostel for students, Helsinki Technical University	
1963	ROVANIEMI	Urban centre plan	
1963 (1964–5)	SEINÄJOKI	Library	
1963 (1964–6)	SEINÄJOKI	Parish house	
1963	JYVÄSKYLÄ	Extension to covered swimming pool, University of Jyväskylä	
1963	JYVÄSKYLÄ	Student Union Building, University of Jyväskylä	
1963	OTANIEMI	Master plan for Otaniemi village	
1963–5	NEW YORK	Edgar T. Kauffmann Rooms, Institute of International Education, New York	
1963–5	UPPSALA, Sweden	Student Association House for the nation 'Västmanland-Dala'	
1963–5	WOLFSBURG, Germany	'Heilig-Geist Gemeinde' kindergarten	
1964 (1976–8)	JYVÄSKYLÄ	Project for administrative and cultural centre	
1964	HAMBURG	BP administrative building, Hamburg, competition entry: 3rd prize	
1964	OTANIEMI	Wood technology laboratories, Helsinki Technical University	
1964–70 (1970–73)	HELSINKI	Administration building for the City Electric Company	
1964	PAIMIO	Extension to tuberculosis sanatorium	
1964–5	ROVANIEMI	One-family house	
1964–6	STENSVIK	Urban design project for Stensvik	
1964–7	TAMMISAARI	Tammisaari Savings Bank	
1964–9	OTANIEMI	Library of the Helsinki Technical University	

DATE	SITE/LOCATION	BUILDING/PROJECT	OFFICE BASE/ COLLABORATORS
1964–70	JYVÄSKYLÄ	Sports Institute, University of Jyväskylä	
1964	TURIN	Hotel, congress and office building	
1965	HELSINKI	Pohjola Insurance Office, 'Maiandros'	
1965	HELSINKI	Lehtinen private museum project	
1965–8	CASTROP-RAUXEL, Germany	Urban centre, competition project	
1965–8	REYKJAVIK, Iceland	Scandinavian House, Reykjavik	
1965–8	WOLFSBURG, Germany	Parish centre in Detmerode, Wolfsburg	
1965–8	LUCERNE, Switzerland	'Schönbühl' high-rise apartment house	
1965–70	MOUNT ANGEL, Oregon, USA	Library of the Mount Angel Benedictine College, Mount Angel	
1966	PORVOO	Experimental housing, Gammelbacka	
1966	PAVIA, Italy	Housing complex (straddling Rome–Milan *autostrada*)	
1966 (1967–9)	ALAJÄRVI	Town hall	
1966	SIENA, Italy	Cultural centre	
1966	WOLFSBURG, Germany	Theatre project, competition entry: 2nd prize	
1966–78 (1976–8)	RIOLA, near BOLOGNA, Italy	Church and parish centre for Riola	
1966–7	TURIN, Italy	Prototype warehouse and office buildings for Società Ferrero, Turin	
1966	KOKKOLA	Municipal library	
1966–9	HELSINKI	Academic Bookshop	
1967	ZÜRICH	Protestant parish centre, Zürich, Altstetten, competition: 1st prize	
1967–9	Near HELSINKI	Kokkonen house	
1967	Near TURIN, Italy	Project for Villa Erica	
1967–71 (1973–5)	HELSINKI	Concert and congress hall, 'Finlandia Hall'	

DATE	SITE/LOCATION	BUILDING/PROJECT	OFFICE BASE/ COLLABORATORS
1968–9	SEINÄJOKI	Theatre project	
1968–71	OTANIEMI	Water tower, Helsinki Technical University	
1968 (1969–70)	TAMMISAARI	Villa Göran Schildt	
1969–70	ALAJÄRVI	Parish centre	
1969	LUCERNE	Housing estate and lakeside restaurant, Schönbühl	
1969–70 (1970–75)	ROVANIEMI	'Lappia' theatre and radio building	
1970 (1971–3)	LAHTI	Church (2nd design)	
1970	ALAJÄRVI	Theatre	
1970	SHIRAZ, Iran	Art museum in Shiraz	
1970	JYVÄSKYLÄ	Administrative and cultural centre, 2nd design	
1970	JYVÄSKYLÄ	Police headquarters	
1971–3	HELSINKI	Master plan for central area redevelopment	
1971 (1971–73)	JYVÄSKYLÄ	Alvar Aalto Museum	
1973	BEIRUT	Sabbag Centre office building	With Alfred Roth (Zürich)
1973	SCHÖNBÜHL, Lucerne	Project for apartment tower	
1974	WISCONSIN	Project for Cultural Centre for Scandinavian–American Society	
1974–6	HELSINKI	Project to extend Enso-Gutzeit headquarters	
1975–6	REYKJAVIK Iceland	Planning of the University of Reykjavik	

Map of Finland, including principal sites of work by Alvar Aalto

Notes

INTRODUCTION

1 Beginning with the church at Seinäjoki (1956–60), Aalto used Carrara marble as an external material. Unfortunately, the Italian marble used on the exterior of the Enso-Gutzeit headquarters (1959–62) and Finlandia Hall (1967–71) was too thin, and has actually warped in the extreme exposure of the Finnish winter. Also the design of the fixings on the columns of the Enso-Gutzeit building and the length of the marble pieces are inadequate to overcome this hazard.

2 See Reyner Banham, 'The last of the few. The rise of Modern Architecture in Finland', *Architectural Review*, April 1957, pp. 243–59.

3 See Charles Jencks, *The Language of Post-Modern Architecture*, Academy Editions, London, 1978.

4 See John Boulton Smith, *The Golden Age of Finnish Art – Art nouveau and the national spirit*, Otava, Helsinki, 1975.

5 There are many stories told about Aalto's drinking habits and capacity, but most are apocryphal. When I visited him in New York in March 1978, James Johnson Sweeney, however, recalled an episode in Chicago, viz: 'Having spent three hours after lunch lying on the bed in his hotel room preparing for his lecture on housing in Lapland by staring at the ceiling, he spoke for 70 minutes without notes. Afterwards Sweeney conducted Aalto to the bar, where many of the local Chicago architects were awaiting him, and said: "You must be thirsty after that. What would you like to drink now?" Aalto thanked him and asked for two whiskies and two beers, which he then downed swiftly.'

6 For example, the courtyard house at Muuratsalo, and the architect's studio in Helsinki reflect the development at Säynätsalo and the Vogelweidplatz project for Vienna.

7 Christian Norberg-Schultz, *Meaning in Western Architecture*, Studio Vista, London, 1976, p. 400.

CHAPTER I

1 'My colleagues and I, in Finland, adhered to the theory that the nature of materials decides the nature of form. This was by no means an original thought; rather, it was a fundamental one. But this fundamental thought had for so long been buried beneath all kinds of accumulated stylistic nonsense, it was necessary to dig it out from its ornamental grave and reinstate it in its place of honesty. To do this, however, meant that one had to go backwards in time to a period when the employment of material was honest. Such a step was necessary to gain the necessary knowledge.' Eliel Saarinen, 1900.

2 Published in Helsinki, in Swedish only, in 1945.

3 Karelia is the easternmost province of Finland, the greater part of which was absorbed into Russia following the Second World War.

4 Both Professor Erik Kråkström and Elissa Aalto suggest that the classical influence upon Aalto's early work came most directly from the Swedish architect, Gunnar Asplund. But I believe this is again somewhat of a simplification, although certainly at the beginning of his career the young Aalto found Asplund's influence most accessible.

5 A suggestion supported by Elissa Aalto's remark that her husband was particularly

interested in the work of Francesco Borromini, made during a conversation with the author in Helsinki in February 1978.

6 It is precisely this coherence that is missing from the posthumously completed church at Riola de Vergato, near Bologna, where the detailing is decidedly not Aalto's own (see p. 203)

7 See Alvar Aalto, 'Architettura e arte concreta' ('The Trout and the Stream'), *Domus*, Nos. 223–5, 1947, pp. 103–15.

8 William J.J. Gordon, *Synectics*, Harper and Row, New York, 1962.

9 See Alvar Aalto, 'The Influence of Structures and Materials on Modern Architecture', a lecture given at the Nordic Building Conference in Oslo, 1938.

10 Ibid.

11 Ibid.

12 See Alvar Aalto, 'The Reconstruction of Europe reveals the central architectural problem of our time', *Arkitekten – Arkkitehti*, No. 5, 1941, pp. 75–80.

13 See Alvar Aalto, 'National Planning and the Goals of Culture', *Suomalainen Suomi*, Helsinki,1949.

14 See Alvar Aalto, 'Zwischen Humanismus und Materialismus', a lecture to the Austrian Architects' Association, Vienna, 1955.

CHAPTER II

1 This is the first issue of *Arkitekten*, which was edited by the architect Bertel Jung. He remained as editor until Wald Wilenius took over with effect from January 1906.

2 The article gave special emphasis to Butterfield's All Saints Church, Margaret Street, London, W1; St. Peter's, Ealing; and Norman Shaw's New Zealand Chambers and the Alliance Assurance Company in Pall Mall, in addition to discussing in some detail the work at Port Sunlight by Maxwell and Luke (Workers' Housing), Douglas and Fordham (School), and Grayson and Ould (the Post Office). There was also reference to E.W. Mountford's Northampton Institute in Clerkenwell.

3 Finland was annexed by the Swedes in 1362 and remained part of Sweden until 1809, when it passed under Russian domination as a result of the invasion by Alexander I in 1808.

4 See *Arkitekten*, March 1905.

5 Now the established industrial centre of Finland, and known affectionately by Finns as its Manchester.

6 Although Sonck himself was highly critical of the design in his later years, while he was engaged in the building of the St Michael Agricola Church in Helsinki (completed 1935) – a highly mannered brick structure which demonstrated Sonck's inability to work in the modern idiom.

7 See *Arkitekten*, October 1903.

8 See *Arkitekten*, October 1905.

9 See *Arkitekten*, December 1905.

10 Ibid.

11 See *Arkitekten*, March 1904.

12 When the studio in the main wing of the house was finished and Lindgren and Saarinen moved to their new quarters, the studio and workshop on the ground floor was converted into stables.

13 The partnership was finally dissolved in 1907 with the withdrawal of Gesellius, Lindgren having left two years earlier.

14 The *rya* is a deep-pile, handwoven and knotted rug traditionally used to decorate the interior walls.

15 Louis Sparre (1863–1964) was a Swedish noble, who had been an art student in Paris with Gallen-Kallela. As an enthusiastic amateur, on a visit to England in 1896 he met Charles Holme, who had just bought William Morris's former home, the Red House. Sparre brought English Arts and Crafts ideas back to Finland, and his 'Iris' factory was modelled on Morris's earlier example.

16 See *Arkitekten*, September 1904, p. 66, for original competition drawings.

17 See George Baird, *Alvar Aalto*, Simon and Schuster, New York, 1971, pp. 11–14.

18 See *Arkitekten*, February 1905, pp. 17–24, for this revised design.

19 See *Arkitekten*, October 1904, p. 70.

20 Ibid.

21 See *Arkitekten*, March 1908, pp. 34–5.

22 See *Arkitekten*, December 1908, pp. 122–31.

23 See *Arkitekten*, April 1909, p. 91, where Saarinen's pen-sketch perspective is published.

24 See *Arkitekten*, September 1909, pp. 124–5.

25 Completed in 1906 and restored in 1968 by Professor Aarno Ruusuvuori, it now serves as an exhibition space of the Helsinki City public relations department.

26 See above.

27 Although not as extreme as Furness's mannerism, there are strong affinities between Sonck's handling of façade elements and those of Furness, as for example in Furness's Bank in Philadelphia.

28 See Nikolaus Pevsner and J.M. Richards, *The Anti-Rationalists*, Architectural Press, London, 1973.

29 It is, for example, characteristic of Aalto not to give special importance or emphasis to the main entrance of a public building, as in the National Pensions Institute, or to virtually conceal it, as in the town hall at Säynätsalo and the House of Culture, Helsinki.

30 See *Arkitekten*, March 1908, pp. 29–30.

31 See *Arkitekten*, November 1911, pp. 119–20.

32 See *Arkitekten*, January 1913, pp. 3–5.

33 The Lahti town hall tower provided the model, in turn, for Saarinen's later Canberra design.

34 See *Arkitekten*, October 1914.

35 See *Arkitekten*, No.3, 1915, pp. 30–37.

36 See 'Den nya arkitetturen', *Arkitekten*, No. 9, 1916, pp. 103–8.

37 Keskuskatu or Central Street leads from the railway station square to the Swedish Theatre and Esplanade Street.

38 See *Arkitekten*, No. 3, 1917.

39 See *Arkitekten – Arkkitehti*, No. 3, 1921, pp. 7–12.

40 See *Arkitekten – Arkkitehti*, No. 6, 1922, pp. 81–5.

41 See *Arkitekten – Arkkitehti*, No. 7, 1922, pp. 97–104.

42 See *Arkitekten – Arkkitehti*, No. 2, 1923.

43 See *Arkitekten – Arkkitehti*, No. 4, 1923.

44 Now the Helsinki cathedral of the Lutheran Church.
45 See *Arkitekten – Arkkitehti*, No. 10, 1923, pp. 145–60.
46 See *Arkitekten – Arkkitehti*, No. 7 1923.
47 See *Arkitekten – Arkkitehti*, No. 6, 1923, pp. 82–96 (entire issue).
48 See *Arkitekten – Arkkitehti*, No. 7, 1924, pp. 85–98, for a review of the designs for the second Parliament competition.
49 See *Arkitekten – Arkkitehti*, No. 2, 1924, pp. 15–24.
50 See *Arkitekten – Arkkitehti*, No. 3, 1924.
51 See *Arkitekten – Arkkitehti*, No. 4, 1924, pp. 52–6.
52 See *Arkitekten – Arkkitehti*, No. 7, 1924, pp. 85–98.
53 See *Arkitekten – Arkkitehti*, No. 1, 1926, pp. 2 and 10–13. Aalto's plan form is similar to that of the Emmanuel Church in Helsinki (1904–5) by Eliel Saarinen.
54 See *Arkitekten – Arkkitehti*, No. 7, 1926, pp. 128–33.
55 See *Arkitekten – Arkkitehti*, No. 6, 1928, p. 80.
56 See *Arkitekten – Arkkitehti*, No. 8, 1928, pp. 117–19.
57 See *Arkitekten – Arkkitehti*, No. 2, 1928.
58 See *Arkitekten – Arkkitehti*, No. 3, 1929, pp. 42–6.
59 See *Arkitekten – Arkkitehti*, No. 6, 1929, p. 90.
60 See *Arkitekten – Arkkitehti*, No. 1, 1928.
61 See *Arkitekten – Arkkitehti*, No. 11, 1928.
62 See *Arkitekten – Arkkitehti*, No. 6, 1930, pp. 82–90.
63 See *Arkitekten – Arkkitehti*, No. 4, 1930, p. 63.
64 See *Arkitekten – Arkkitehti*, No. 8, 1930, pp. 121–4.
65 See *Arkitekten – Arkkitehti*, No. 5, 1930, pp. 71–2.

CHAPTER III

1 See *Arkitekten – Arkkitehti*, No. 2, 1923.
2 Alvar Aalto, *Sketchbook*, edited by Göran Schildt, Otava, Helsinki, 1972.
3 See P.D. Pearson, *Alvar Aalto and the International Style*, Whitney Library of Design, New York, 1978, pp. 84–7.
4 Ibid.
5 See Note 2 above.
6 See Alvar Aalto, 'Experimental House at Muuratsalo', *Arkitekten – Arkkitehti*, Nos. 9–10, 1953.
7 See Alvar Aalto, 'Zwischen Humanismus und Materialismus', a lecture to the Austrian Architects' Association, Vienna, 1955.
8 In these and all other references to Aalto's early furniture I am indebted to Dr Göran Schildt, who has allowed me to quote from his findings.
9 See also Appendix.
10 For example in the churches at Ruovesi, Saarijärvi, Pielpajärvi and Kemi (by Carl Ludwig Engel, 1827).

CHAPTER IV

1 Notably the Pyhäkoski power station near Oulu by Aarne Ervi (1950–58), and the

Hanasaari power plant in Helsinki by Timo Penttilä (1970–77).

2 Competition File in the Archives of the Museum of Finnish Architecture, Helsinki.

3 See P.D. Pearson, *Alvar Aalto and the International Style*, pp. 151–2.

4 Aalto submitted an alternative entry with the nonsense motto 'Tsit Tsit Pum', which was awarded the second prize. This entry was credited: 'Studio of Architect Alvar Aalto – main assistants Aarne Ervi and Viljo Rewell'. (Reference: Competition File in the Archives of the Museum of Finnish Architecture, Helsinki.)

5 See R. Glanville, 'Finnish Vernacular Farmhouses', the *Architectural Association Quarterly*, February 1978.

6 See G. Baird, *Alvar Aalto*, Simon and Schuster, New York, 1971.

7 This form can, in fact, be traced back to the shaped bandstand Aalto designed for the Itämeri restaurant in the South-Western Agricultural Cooperative Building, Turku, of 1930.

8 The disturbance of equilibrium and the imparting of a sense of instability was a favourite High Baroque and Mannerist device. See, for example, Giulio Romano's fresco in the Hall of the Giants at the Palazzo del Te, Mantua.

CHAPTER V

1 The Opera House for Essen in Germany, for which the original drawings were made in 1958–9, with the go-ahead for the revised design being given in the spring of 1980 (i.e., four years after Aalto's death), represents in its bold, simple volume what is potentially Aalto's finest achievement in terms of urban scale. In 1981 the decision to go ahead had, however, still not been confirmed.

2 See Chapter I.

3 Aalto was elected Chairman of SAFA in 1943 and remained so until 1948. He was therefore at the helm of his professional institute during one of the most critical periods of Finland's history.

4 See Chapter VI, pp. 144–5, for discussion of Aalto's first executed housing tower, the Hansaviertel block in Berlin.

5 See Chapter V, pp. 109–13, and Chapter VI, 149–50.

6 For a discussion of this period see P.D. Pearson, *Alvar Aalto and the International Style*, pp. 193–202.

7 See my article 'Après Aalto, une nouvelle vague?', *Architectural Design*, March 1980, pp. 22–38, where Ervi is discussed in the context of the post-Aalto generation of Finnish architects.

8 See Note 4 above.

9 'Munksnäs-Haga och Stor-Helsingfors: stadsplansstudier och förslag', Eliel Saarinen, 1915.

10 See my article 'The Urban Locus', *RIBA Journal*, February 1975.

11 Elissa Aalto confirmed this to be the case during a conversation with the author in Helsinki, February 1978.

CHAPTER VI

1 Aulis Blomstedt (1906–79) was probably the most important Professor of Architecture in

the Helsinki Technical University since the war. For a discussion of the post-Aalto generation of Finnish architects see my article 'Après Aalto, une nouvelle vague?', *Architectural Design*, February 1980.

2 Although this garden was in fact originally open to the public it never constituted a thoroughfare in the sense of the Smithsons' *piazzetta* of the London Economist Building, and the space is now reserved for the exclusive use of the employees. This action seems to have been taken to exclude alcoholics from the garden, an irony considering that this building is the bastion of Finland's social security programme!

3 Edited by Göran Schildt, Otava, Helsinki, 1972.

4 In his book *Alvar Aalto and the International Style*, P.D. Pearson refers (p. 218) to Säynätsalo, thus: 'At least one scholar has likened it to a Roman patrician's house' but, as he gives no reference, we must presume that this is a personal opinion.

5 In a conversation with the author in Helsinki in February 1979.

6 As I was driving with a Finnish architect from the airport into Helsinki in January 1978 he suddenly pointed out of the taxi window and said, 'What do you think of that Aalto housing over there?' I confessed ignorance of the project, although it appeared to have some Aalto characteristics. 'It's not *real* Aalto, of course,' my colleague added: 'only the details. You see it's by some former assistants. But he only ever teaches them to detail. So in this case the actual Aalto concept is missing.'

7 This shift in alignment, or *misalignment* of elements, in Aalto's compositions, may be traced back to his design for layout of the Turku 700-Year Fair of 1929.

8 See *The Collected Works of Alvar Aalto*, Volume I, edited by Karl Fleig, Girsberger, Zürich, 1963, the original archival survey of the master's work, p. 160.

9 Ibid.

10 In conversation with the author at Muuratsalo in July 1953. We have already observed how his home in Munkkiniemi was a similar kind of experiment.

11 From an essay entitled 'Discussion' which forms the preface to *Alvar Aalto* by Leonardo Mosso, Milan, 1967.

12 See my paper 'Pietilä's Progress', delivered at the Royal Institute of British Architects, 9 December 1980.

13 The local inhabitants viewed it as an oddity, for it appeared to have no windows at all from the exterior.

14 See *The Collected Works of Alvar Aalto*, Volume I, p. 168.

15 Ibid.

16 See Alvar Aalto, 'The Museum of Finnish Architecture', *Arkitekten-Arkkitehti*, 1954, p. 17.

17 See *RIBA Journal*, May 1957, pp. 254–64, for his speech of acceptance.

18 Unfortunately, when the author visited the house in November 1979 he found that Madame Carré, afraid of being alone with so many valuable paintings, had stripped the gallery bare. The patterns left by the paintings that had hung there were a sad commentary on Madame Carré's lone existence in the house Aalto had built for M. Carré and herself.

19 See *The Collected Works of Alvar Aalto*, Volume III, edited by Karl Fleig and Elissa Aalto, Artemis, Zürich, 1978, p. 74.

20 See Malcolm Quantrill, 'The Urban Locus', *RIBA Journal*, February 1975.

21 The Viipuri Library was damaged in the Finno-Russian War of 1940 and again later, during the Second World War, and was feared destroyed by the Russians. In fact it has been substantially restored to its original form by the Soviet authorities. These repairs

seem to have been effected in the late 60s or early 70s. The original Aalto furniture is no longer used, however. Aalto was in no way involved in this 'restoration', nor was his office consulted.

22 His least successful of this series is the 'Sähkotalo', the headquarters building for the Helsinki Municipal Electricity Company (1967–73). This design further reduces the ratio of glass to wall, with the cladding no longer of curtain-wall character but resembling the fenestration of a traditional masonry construction which has been copper clad.

23 It is interesting that, in comparing the Enso-Gutzeit *palazzo* with the Nordic Union Bank building, the latter turns out to be more truly Italianate in its proportional rhythms, recalling the flat pattern-making of Alberti's Palazzo Ruceliai. On the other hand, the Enso-Gutzeit building, with its use of thin planks of marble to face a deeply modelled exterior envelope, seems to contradict the material logic of the Venetian tradition as well as the formal discipline of modernism; yet its expression is rooted in an historical view of both periods. Returning to it twenty years after it was built (1960–62), one sees in it Aalto's anticipation of post-Modernist tendencies.

24 The Riola church was built posthumously in 1976–8 and remains incomplete (see p. 203).

25 Particularly J.M. (now Sir James) Richards and P. Morton Shand in the 1930s.

26 The quality control in Finnish architectural offices depends upon the maintenance of a small 'studio' with a closely coordinated team of hand-picked assistants working directly to the master's instructions. Such a group has an optimum number of between twenty and twenty-four. It is not the practice to take on more staff (in excess of those numbers) in response to an increased work load. Thus, a natural priority evolves in tackling the work in the studio at any one time, so that, as in a Renaissance painter's *atelier*, the most important commissions get most attention from the master and his draughtsmen.

27 See *The Collected Works of Alvar Aalto*, Volume III, pp. 96–103

28 Now restored and used as a permanent facility, currently by Portugal (1980).

29 See *The Collected Works of Alvar Aalto*, Volume I, p. 254.

30 See my paper 'Pietilä's Progress', delivered at the Royal Institute of British Architects on 9 December 1980.

31 Ibid.

32 One possible explanation is that Aalto, who was clearly delighted by the commission gave the impression that to receive it was a considerable honour. Whether this was misinterpreted by the Cardinal of Bologna is hard to say, but certainly the payment of professional fees was considerably delayed and the clients liked to convey the impression that the architect had donated his services. The matter was cleared up after the completion of the main church building in 1978, when Elissa Aalto was given a private audience by the Pope. But the priest's house, the resthouse and the nursery school, in addition to the campanile, remain unbuilt.

CHAPTER VII

1 See Malcolm Quantrill, 'Pietilä's Progress', an invitation lecture given at the Royal Institute of British Architects on 9 December, 1980.

2 Ibid.

3 See Chapter VI, pp. 177–81.

4 Of course the complete history of Aalto's treatment of the *park* and *piazza* nuclei goes back to Viipuri Library, the first design for which was pure *piazza*, whilst the built project is all *park*. The 'Forum Redivivum B' design remains his strongest statement of the *piazza* treatment; whilst the built form of the National Pensions Institute dissolves the interior *piazzetta* into a garden extension of the adjacent public park strip to the rear. It is not possible for an architect working within the framework of the Finnish town, and particularly in Helsinki, to avoid this confrontation with the dual emphasis of *park* and *square*.

5 See 'Pietilä's Progress'.

6 Aalto's project for a hotel, congress centre and office building of 1964, which is also a courtyard solution, owes a considerable debt to the form and layout of the National Pensions Institute.

7 See *The Collected Works of Alvar Aalto*, Volume II, Artemis, Zürich, 1971, p. 110.

8 See *The Collected Works of Alvar Aalto*, Volume III, pp. 34–5.

9 Ibid, pp. 35–6.

10 The remainder of the accommodation for this United-Nations-linked agency, which is situated on a site adjoining the UN Headquarters, was entrusted to W.K. Harrison.

11 See *The Collected Works of Alvar Aalto*, Volume II, pp. 84–7.

12 Helsinki remains, in the *fin de siècle* style, a great 'gossip shop'; and there are, as already mentioned, many apocryphal stories of Aalto's life and attitudes. This is one of the most biting: Aalto is on his deathbed and his assistants are gathered around him concerned about the future of the office. One asks him: 'Aalto, what are we to do? There's still no answer on Essen, and we have no more work in the office.' Aalto smiles benignly and, closing his eyes, answers: 'You know, you really mustn't worry about the lack of work because, after I've gone there'll be nobody to do it.'

13 The Carrara marble, used so extensively on the Enso-Gutzeit *palazzo* (1959–62) and subsequently on the Finlandia project, was employed in 'tiles' or 'planks'; but the thickness of these elements, approximately 20 mm, was insufficient to avoid buckling and distortion due to the extreme winter climate in Finland. Marble veneers of similar thickness used as external veneers in Italy are not, of course, subject to frost movement caused by temperatures of −20°C and more.

14 The popular sentiment amongst Finnish architects, particularly the anti-rationalists, is that it is not possible to keep an architect's spirit in his office after it has left his own body! Their verdict is that the office should die properly with the man.

15 The go-ahead for the revised design finally came in the early summer of 1980, after more than twenty years of indecision on the part of the Essen authorities. But at the time of writing this decision had not been confirmed.

16 See *The Collected Works of Alvar Aalto*, Volume II, p. 147.

17 Conversation with Åke Tjeder, Managing Director of Artek in his Helsinki office, October 1979.

18 See 'Rationalism and Man', a lecture at the annual meeting of the Swedish Crafts Association, Stockholm 1935, *Architectural Forum*, September 1937.

19 See 'The Reconstruction of Europe Reveals the Central Architectural Problem of Our Time', *Arkitekten–Arkkitehti*, Nos. 9–10 1941.

20 Ibid.

CHAPTER VIII

1 This discussion forms the Preface to Leonardo Mosso's book *Alvar Aalto*, Milan, 1967.

2 See Alvar Aalto, 'Painters and Masons', *Jousimies*, 1921.

3 See Alvar Aalto, 'The Motifs from the Past', *Arkitekten–Arkkitehti*, No. 2, 1922, pp. 24–5.

4 See Alvar Aalto, 'Zwischen Humanismus und Materialismus', a lecture to the Austrian Architects' Association, Vienna, 1955.

5 See Alvar Aalto, 'The Humanising of Architecture', *The Technological Review*, November 1940.

6 Ibid.

7 See Alvar Aalto, 'The Reconstruction of Europe Reveals the Central Architectural Problem of Our Time', *Arkitekten–Arkkitehti*, 1941.

8 See Alvar Aalto, 'Art and Technology', inaugural lecture as Member of the Finnish Academy, 1955.

9 See Alvar Aalto, 'Culture and Technology', *Suomi-Finland-USA*, Helsinki, 1947.

10 See Alvar Aalto, 'The Trout and the Stream', *Domus*, Nos. 223–5, 1947.

11 See Alvar Aalto, 'Experimental House at Muuratsalo', *Arkitekten–Arkkitehti*, 1953.

12 Aalto was extremely fond of this particular module/modular 'joke' and there are consequently several different versions. Pearson's account in *Alvar Aalto and the International Style* credits one of Aalto's assistants with the punchline and the 'centimetre' module is reduced even further, to that of a 'millimetre'.

13 Eliel Saarinen left his native Finland to emigrate to the United States in June 1923, just as the young Aalto was beginning work in his own architectural office in Jyväskylä.

14 See Alvar Aalto, 'The Trout and the Stream'.

15 See Göran Schildt, introductory essay to the documentation prepared for the Aalto retrospective exhibition, held in Finlandia House, Helsinki, January – February 1978 and transferred to the Royal Academy of Arts, London, in September – October 1978.

16 See Ranulph Glanville: 'Finnish Vernacular Farmhouses', *The Architectural Association Quarterly*, February 1978.

17 See Alvar Aalto, 'Experimental House at Muuratsalo'.

18 See Alvar Aalto, 'Zwischen Humanismus und Materialismus'.

19 See Alvar Aalto, 'Experimental House at Muuratsalo'.

Selected Bibliography

BOOKS, EXHIBITION CATALOGUES ETC.

Aalto, A., *The General Town Plan*, Helsinki, 1957.

Aalto, A., *Helsingen keskustasuunnitelma – Helsingfors centrumplan* (Plan for Central Helsinki), Helsinki, 1965.

Alvar Aalto (exhibition catalogue), Akademie der Künste, Berlin, 1963.

Alvar Aalto versus the Modern Movement, 1979. Alvar Aalto symposium, Jyväskylä, 1981.

Ålander, K., *Rakennustaide*, Werner Söderström Oy, Porvoo-Helsinki, 1954.

Artek Company Catalogue and supplement, 'Furniture Designs of Aalto', Helsinki, October 1941.

Baird, G. (Introduction), and Futagawa, Y. (Photographs), *Alvar Aalto*, Simon and Shuster, New York, 1971.

Banham, R., *A Guide to Modern Architecture*, Architectural Press, London, 1962.

Banham, R., *Age of the Masters: A Personal View of Modern Architecture*, Harper and Row, New York, 1975.

Becher, H.J., and Schlote, W., *Neuer Wohnbau in Finnland*, Kramer, Stuttgart, 1958.

Benevolo, L., *History of Modern Architecture*, MIT Press, Cambridge, Massachusetts, 1971.

Best, G., 'Method and Intention in Architectural Design', Broadbent and Ward (eds.), *Design Methods in Architecture*, Lund Humphries, Architectural Association Paper No. 4, pp. 147–65, London, 1969.

Borras, M.L., and Jaatinen, M., *Arquitectura Finlandesa in Otaniemi: Alvar Aalto, Heikki Siren, Reima Pietilä*, Ediciones Polygrafia, Barcelona, 1968.

Brawne, M., *Il museo oggi*, p. 75, Edizioni di Communità, Milan, 1965.

Dobbins, H., 'The Achievement of Finnish Architecture: Social Responsibility and Architectural Integrity', *Perspecta*, No. 8, pp. 3–36 (contains a portfolio of works by six Finnish architects).

Dober, R.P., *Campus Planning*, Reinhold Publishing Co., Cambridge, Massachusetts, 1963.

Dodi, L., Ponti, G., and Rogers, E.N., *Profilo di Alvar Aalto*, Pubblicazione del Politecnico, Milan, 1964.

Doflores, G., *Artificio e natura*, Einaudi, Turin, 1968.

Drew, P., *Third Generation: The Changing Meaning of Architecture*, Praeger, New York, 1972.

Finseven Inc., *Aalto Design Collection for Modern Living*, New York, 1955.

Fleig, K. (ed.), *Alvar Aalto*, Girsberger, Zürich, Vol. 1, 1963; Artemis, Zürich, Vol. 2, 1971, and Vol. 3, 1978.

Futagawa, Y. (ed. and photographs), Muto, A. (text), *Alvar Aalto: Church in Vuoksenniska and the City Centre in Seinäjoki*, Global Architecture Series No. 16, ADA Edita, Tokyo, 1972.

Futagawa, Y. (ed. and photographs), Muto, A. (text), *Alvar Aalto: La Maison Louis Carré*, Global Architecture Series No. 10, ADA Edita, Tokyo, 1972.

Futagawa, Y. (ed. and photographs), Muto, A. (text), *Alvar Aalto: Town Hall at Säynätsalo and the Public Pensions Institute*, Global Architecture Series No. 24, ADA Edita, Tokyo, 1973.

Giedion, S., *Aino und Alvar Aalto*, Kunstgewerbe Museum, Zürich, 1948.

Giedion, S., *A Decade of New Architecture*, Editions Girsberger, Zürich, 1951.

Giedion, S., *Mechanization Takes Command*, Oxford University Press, New York, 1948.

Giedion, S., *Space, Time and Architecture*, 5th edn ('Alvar Aalto: Irrationality and Standardization', pp. 618–67), Harvard University Press, Cambridge, Massachusetts, 1967.

Groak, S., Heinonen, R.L., Porphyrios, D., *Alvar Aalto*, Architectural Monographs No. 4, Academy Editions, London, 1978.

Grunigen, B. von, *Möbel aus Holz und Stahl: Alvar Aalto – Mies van der Rohe*, Gewerbemuseum, Basel, 1957.

Gutheim, F., *Alvar Aalto*, Braziller, New York, 1960.

Hamilton, S.D., Jr, *Alvar Aalto and the Architecture of Finland*, Architecture at Rice Series, No. 4, Houston, March 1962.

Hilberseimer, L., *Contemporary Architecture: Its Roots and Trends*, Paul Theobald, Chicago, 1964.

Hitchcock, H.R., *Architecture: Nineteenth and Twentieth Centuries*, Penguin Books, London, 1958.

Hoesli, B., ed., *Alvar Aalto Synopsis: Painting, Architecture, Sculpture*, Birkhauser Verlag, Basel, 1970.

Hofmann, N., and Kultermann, U., *Baukunst unserer Zeit*, Beukhard, Essen, 1969.

Hollatz, J.W., *Das neue Essener Opernhaus*, Essen, 1964.

Institut für Städtebau der Technische Hochschule, *Stadtebau in Finnland*, Stuttgart, 1966.

Jacobus, J., *Twentieth Century Architecture: The Middle Years, 1940–65*, Praeger, New York, 1966.

Jencks, C., *Modern Movements in Architecture* (Chapter 5 – 'Alvar Aalto and the Means of Architectural Communication', pp. 167–83), Anchor Press/Doubleday, New York, 1973.

Joedicke, J., *A History of Modern Architecture*, Praeger, New York, 1959.

Joedicke, J., *Architecture Since 1945: Sources and Directions*, Praeger, New York, 1969.

Jones, C., *Architecture: Today and Tomorrow*, McGraw-Hill, New York, 1961.

Kocker, A.L., and Breines, S., *Alvar Aalto: Architecture and Furniture*, Museum of Modern Art, New York, 1938.

Kultermann, U., *Der Schlüssel zur Architektur von heute*, Econ, Wein-Dusseldorf, 1963.

Labo, G., *Alvar Aalto*, Il Balcone, Milan, 1948. *L'opera di Alvar Aalto*, Edizioni di Communità, Milan, 1965.

Lindegren, Y., and Kråkström, E. *Helsinki Keskus*, Tilgmann Oy, Helsinki, 1955. Moderna Museet, *Alvar Aalto*, Stockholm, 1969.

Mairea Foundation, *Alvar Aalto as artist*, exhibition at Villa Mairea, catalogue (text by Göran Schildt), 1982.

Mosso, L., 'Alvar Aalto', Pehnt, W. (ed.), *Encyclopedia of Modern Architecture*, pp. 28–32, Harry Abrams, New York, 1964.

Mosso, L., *L'opera di Alvar Aalto – Catalogo della Mostra*, Edizioni di Communità, Milan, 1965 (Finnish edn, Otava, Helsinki, 1967).

Mosso, L., *Note storico' critiche sull' architettura finlandese, Introduzione a: Esempi di pianificazione edilizia in Finlandia*, Edizioni di Communità, Milan, 1960.

Museum of Finnish Architecture, *Suomi rakentaa – Finland Bygger (Finland Builds)*, 1953.

Museum of Modern Art, *Alvar Aalto, Architecture and Furniture*, New York, 1966.

Museum of Modern Art, New York, Exhibition Catalogue: *Architecture and Furniture: Aalto*, 1938.

Nasstrom, G., *Swedish Functionalism*, Bokforlaget Natur och Kulture, Stockholm, 1930.

Neuenschwander, E. and C., *Finnish Architecture and Alvar Aalto*, Praeger, New York, 1954 (edns in French and German also).

Norberg-Schulz, C., *Meaning in Western Architecture*, Praeger, New York, 1975, pp. 389–90, 398–9, 400 and 416.

Paullson, T., *Scandinavian Architecture*, Leonard Hill, London, 1958.

Pearson, P.D., *Alvar Aalto and the International Style*, Whitney Library of Design, New York, 1978.

Ray, S., *L'architettura moderna nei paesi Scandinavi*, Cappelli, Bologna, 1965.

Reid, H. *Art and Industry*, Faber and Faber, London, 1934.

Richards, J.M., *800 Years of Finnish Architecture*, David and Charles, Newton Abbot, 1978.

Richards, J.M., *A Guide to Finnish Architecture*, Hugh Evelyn, London, 1956.

Rogers, E.N., *Esperienze dell'architettura*, Einaudi, Turin, 1969.

Roth, A., *The New Architecture*, Verlag Girsberger, Zürich, 1940 (revised edn, 1975).

Ruusuvuori, A., *Omakotikirja, liusia pientaloja*, Helsinki, 1961.

Salokorpi, A., *Modern Architecture in Finland*, Praeger, New York, 1970.

Sanderson, W. (ed.), *International Handbook of Contemporary Developments in Architecture*, Greenwood Press, Connecticut, 1981.

Schildt, G., Mosso, L., and Oksala, T., *Alvar Aalto*, K.J. Gummerus Oy, Jyväskylä, 1964.

Schildt, G., *Alvar Aalto: Luonnoksia*, Otava, Helsinki, 1972.

Schildt, G., *Alvar Aalton Veistokset*, Helsinki, 1957.

Schildt, G., *Modern Finnish Sculpture*, Praeger, New York, 1970.

Schildt, G., *The Sculptures of Alvar Aalto*, Otava, Helsinki, 1967.

Scully, V., Jr, *Modern Architecture: The Architecture of Democracy*, Braziller, New York (revised edn), 1974.

Sharp, D., *Sources of Modern Architecture*, Lund Humphries, Architectural Association Paper No. 2, London, 1972.

Smith, J.B., *The Golden Age of Finnish Art*, Otava, Helsinki, 1975.

Smithsonian Institute, *Contemporary Finnish Architecture* (catalogue), Washington DC, 1955.

Suhonen, P., *Neue Architektur in Finnland*, Tammi, Helsinki, 1967.

Suomen Arkkitektiluto – Finlands Arkitekforbund (SAFA), *Commercial Architecture in Finland*, Helsinki, 1959.

Suomen Rakennustaiteen Museo, *Guide to Helsinki Architecture*, Fustannus Oy Otava, Helsinki, 1963 (updated in 1969).

Sveriges Arkitektur Museum, Moderna Museet, *Utstallningen på Finlands arkitektur-museum* (Exhibition by Finnish Museum of Architecture), Stockholm, 1969.

Tempel, E., *New Finnish Architecture*, Praeger, New York, 1968.

Venturi, R., *Complexity and Contradiction in Architecture*, Museum of Modern Art, New York, 1966.

Wickberg, N.E., *Architecture Finlandaise*, Exposition à Tunis, 1965.

Wickberg, N.E., *Finnish Architecture*, Otava, Helsinki, 1962 (Finnish edn, 1959; German edn 1963).

Zahle, E., *Scandinavian Domestic Design*, Methuen, London, 1963 (for the Museum of Industrial Art, Copenhagen).

Zevi, B., *Architecture as Space*, New York, 1957, pp. 157, 169, 226.

Zevi, B., *Verso Un'Architettura Organica*, Turin, 1945.

Zürich Kunstgewerbe Museum, *Aalto, Alvar and Aino*, Zürich, 1940.

ARTICLES

Aalto, A., 'Motifs From the Past', *Arkitekten-Arkkitehti*, No. 2, pp. 24–5, 1922.

Church at Jämsä, *Arkitekten-Arkkitehti*, No. 1, pp. 1–5, 1926.

Building for Civilian Reserve Organisation in Jyväskylä, *Arkitekten-Arkkitehti*, No. 7, 1926.

Töölö Church, *Arkitekten-Arkkitehti*, No. 5, pp. 57–8, 1927.

Aitta Summer House, *Aitta* (Helsinki), No. 5, 1928.

Viipuri Library, *Arkitekten-Arkkitehti*, No. 3, pp. 38–40, 1928.

South-Western Agricultural Cooperative Building, *Arkitekten-Arkkitehti*, No. 4, pp. 54–5, 1928.

Pylkonmäki Church, *Arkitekten-Arkkitehti*, No. 9, p. 130, 1928.

Paimio Sanatorium, *Arkitekten-Arkkitehti*, No. 3, pp. 42–4, 1929.

Turku Exhibition, *Arkitekten-Arkkitehti*, No. 5, 1929.

Various Aalto projects, *Arkitekten-Arkkitehti*, No. 6, pp. 9, 83, 90, 96–7 and 99–100, 1929.

Turku Exhibition, *Arkitekten-Arkkitehti*, No. 7, pp. 114–116, 1929.

Aalto, A., 'Residential area in an existing town-planning scheme', *Byggmästaren*, pp. 21–4, 1930.

Turun Sanomat newspaper plant, *Architectural Record*, Vol. 68, p. 510, December 1930.

Paimio housing, *Byggmästaren*, No. 2, p. 25, 1930.

Various Aalto projects, *Arkitekten-Arkkitehti*, No. 4, pp. 51 and 60–64, 1930.

Helsinki Sports Centre, *Arkitekten-Arkkitehti*, No. 5, p. 78, 1930.

Turun Sanomat, *Arkitekten-Arkkitehti*, No. 5, p. 78, 1930.

Two churches, *Arkitekten-Arkkitehti*, No. 7, pp. 103 and 106, 1930.

Michael Agricola Church, *Arkitekten-Arkkitehti*, No. 12, pp. 201–9, 1930.

Shand, P.M., 'The Work of Alvar Aalto', *Architectural Review*, p. 72, September 1931.

Factory at Oulu, *Arkitekten-Arkkitehti*, No. 12, pp. 188–93, 1931.

Goodesmith, W., 'Evolution and Design in Steel and Concrete', *Architectural Review*, pp. 206–7, November 1932.

Laine, Y., 'Typutstallningen', *Arkitekten-Arkkitehti*, No. 7, 1932.

Turun Sanomat, *Architectural Review*, pp. 234–5, November 1932.

Hospital in Yugoslavia, *Arkitekten-Arkkitehti*, No. 1, pp. 5–6, 1932.

Enso-Gutzeit summer cabin, *Arkitekten-Arkkitehti*, No. 3, p. 2, 1932.

Prefabricated house, *Arkitekten-Arkkitehti*, No. 4, p. 32, 1932.

Prefabricated house, *Arkitekten-Arkkitehti*, No. 5, p. 73, 1932.

Enso-Gutzeit summer cabin, *Arkitekten-Arkkitehti*, No. 6, p. 95, 1932.

Paimio Sanatorium, *Byggmästaren*, No. 12, pp. 80–83, 1932.

Factory at Oulu, *Casabella*, No. 50, 1932.

Hospital in Yugoslavia, *Casabella*, No. 51, pp. 67–73, 1932.

Dennison, B., 'From Angles to Body Curves', *Architectural Review*, pp. 70–72, August 1933.

Shand, P.M., 'A Tuberculosis Sanatorium in Finland', *Architectural Review*, pp. 85–90, August 1933.

'Standard Wooden Furniture at the Finnish Exhibition: A. Aalto Designer', *Architectural Review*, pp. 220–21, December 1933.

Paimio Sanatorium, *Arkitekten-Arkkitehti*, No. 6, pp. 79–80, 1933.

Stadium at Helsinki, *Arkitekten-Arkkitehti*, No. 6, p. 73, 1933.

'Tuberculosis Sanatorium, Paimio, Finland; A. Aalto, Architect', *Architectural Record*, Vol. 76, pp. 12–19, July 1934.

Tampere Railway Station, *Arkitekten-Arkkitehti*, No. 2, pp. 25–9, 1934.

Helsinki Exhibition Pavilion, *Arkitekten-Arkkitehti*, No. 3, p. 45, 1934.

Several Aalto projects, *Arkitekten-Arkkitehti*, No. 6, pp. 83–6, 1934.

Sanatorium in Paimio, Finland, *Das Werk*, pp. 293–300, October 1934.

International Architecture 1924–1934, Catalogue of the Centenary Exhibition of the Royal Institute of British Architects, London, 1934.

Toppila Sulphate Pulp Mill; Paimio Sanatorium for Consumptives, A. Aalto, Architect, *Architectural Forum*, pp. 180–81, September 1935.

'Portfolio of Applied Design: Pressed Plywood Furniture by A. Aalto', *Architectural Record*, p. 310, May 1935.

Municipal Library for Viipuri, *Arkitekten-Arkkitehti*, No. 10, pp. 145–58, 1935.

Paimio Sanatorium, *Casabella*, pp. 12–21, June 1935.

Shand, P.M., 'The Viipuri Library in Detail', *Architectural Review*, Vol. 79, pp. 107–14, March 1936.

'Library, Viipuri, Finland', *Architect's Journal*, Vol. 84, pp. 349–52, 10 September 1936.

Furniture, lamps, vases, *Architectural Review*, September 1936.

Paris Pavilion, *Arkitekten-Arkkitehti*, p. 99, 1936.

Paris Pavilion, *Casabella*, November 1936.

Viipuri Library, *Casabella*, No. 97, 1936.

Aalto, A., 'On Exhibitions', *Byggmästaren*, No. 32, pp. 355–6, 1937.

Aalto, A., 'Rationalismus und Mensch', *Form*, No. 7, 1935. Reprinted in English: *Architectural Forum*, September 1937.

Savoy Restaurant, *Architectural Review*, pp. 213–17, November 1937.

'Competition Project for Art Museum in Tallin', *Arkitekten-Arkkitehti*, No. 5, pp. 65–70, 1937.

'Aalto's own House, Helsinki', *Arkitekten-Arkkitehti*, No. 8, pp. 113–15, 1937.

'Finnish Pavilion, Paris World's Fair', *Arkitekten-Arkkitehti*, No. 9, pp. 137–44, 1937.

Paris Pavilion, *Byggmästaren*, No. 39, pp. 436–7, 1937.

Savoy Restaurant, *Arkitekten-Arkkitehti*, pp. 169–70, 1937.

Sunila Factory, *Arkitekten-Arkkitehti*, p. 42, 1937.

'Le Pavilion de la Finlande à l'exposition de 1937', *Cahiers d'art*, No. 8, pp. 269–79, 1937.

Sunila Factory, *Casabella*, October 1937.

Arteo Pascoe Inc., Exhibition Catalogue: *Furniture of Alvar and Aino Aalto*, New York, 1937.

Various Aalto projects, *L'architecture d'aujourd'hui*, No. 10, pp. 74–80, 1937.

'Exhibition, Museum of Modern Art', *Art News*, p. 14f., 2 April 1938.

'Alvar Aalto: Finland's Modern Master', *Architectural Forum*, April 1938.

'Aalto's own House near Helsingfors', *Architectural Review*, pp. 175–8, April 1938.

'Finnish Exhibit at the Fair', *Architectural Forum*, pp. 442–3, June 1938.

Mazzucchelli, A.M., 'Alvar Aalto', *Casabella*, September 1938.

Aalto, A., 'Influence of material and structure in modern architecture', *Arkitekten-Arkkitehti*, No. 9, pp. 129–31, 1938. Reprinted as 'The Influence of Construction and Material on Modern Architecture', *Alvar Aalto Synopsis* (Section B), pp. 12–14.

Floquet, P.L., 'Masters of New Architecture in Finland, Land of the Thousand Lakes – Alvar Aalto', *Batir*, October 1938.

Hanl, N.G., 'Alvar Aalto's International Exhibition', *Arkitekten-Arkkitehti*, No. 9, pp. 132–3, 1938.

'Extension to the University Library, Helsinki', *Arkitekten-Arkkitehti*, No. 6, pp. 86–96, 1938.

'Sunila Cellulose-Sulphate Factory', *Arkitekten-Arkkitehti*, No. 10, pp. 145–60, 1938.

Goldstone, H.H., 'Alvar Aalto', *Magazine of Art*, pp. 208–21 (portrait p. 194), April 1939.

Shand, P.M., 'Aalto', *Decoration*, Spring 1939.

'Sunila', *Focus*, Vol. 1, No. 3, pp. 13–26, Spring 1939.

'Sunila: Factory and Community', *Architectural Forum*, pp. 38–41, 382–5, May 1939.

Sunila, *Casabella*, May 1939.

'Sunila', *L'Architettura*, May 1939.

'Finnish Pavilion, New York Fair', *Architectural Review*, pp. 64–7, August 1939.

'Municipal Library in Viborg, Finland', *Arkitekten*, No. 2, pp. 24–8, 1939.

Stenius Housing, *Arkitekten-Arkkitehti*, p. 6, 1939.

'New York World's Fair', *Arkitekten-Arkkitehti*, No. 8, pp. 113–15 and 118–27, 1939.

'"Mairea", Maire and Harry Gullichsen's residence', *Arkitekten-Arkkitehti*, No. 9, pp. 134–7, 1939.

'Finland in New York, architecture; Aino and Alvar Aalto', *Byggmästaren*, No. 34, pp. 420–26, 6 November 1939.

Bunning, W.R., 'Paimio Sanatorium – an Analysis', *Architecture*, Vol. 29, pp. 20–25 (Sydney), 1 February 1940.

Kauttua Housing, *Casabella*, pp. 44–5, April 1940.

Aalto, A., 'Post War Reconstruction', *Magazine of Art*, p. 362, June 1940. Reprinted in *Alvar Aalto Synopsis* (Section B), pp. 14–15.

'Mairea, House in Norrmark; Workers' Houses and Pulp Mill in Sunila', *Architectural Forum*, pp. 401–3, 406–9, portrait p. 377, June 1940.

'Kauttua, architect Alvar Aalto', *Kentiku Sekai*, pp. 18–19, September 1940.

'Aalto at MIT', *Pencil Points*, Supp. 22, September 1940.

Aalto, A., 'The Humanising of Architecture', *The Technology Review*, pp. 14–16, November 1940. Reprinted in *Architectural Forum*, pp. 505–6, December 1940, and *Alvar Aalto Synopsis* (Section B), pp. 15–17.

Smith, G.E.K., 'Alvar Aalto', *American Scandinavian Review*, pp. 313–20, December 1940.

Aalto, A., 'E.G. Asplund in Memorium', *Arkitekten-Arkkitehti*, No. 11–12, p. 81, 1940.

Koppel, N., 'Villa "Mairea"', *Arkitekten*, Vol. 42, No. 7, pp. 93–9, Denmark, 1940.

Pagano, G., 'Due ville di A. Aalto', *Casabella*, No. 145, pp. 26–9, 1940.

'Breuer Replaces Aalto on Industrial Design Competition Jury', *Art Digest*, p. 16, 1 January 1941.

Aalto, A., 'The reconstruction of Europe is becoming the central problem facing present-day architecture', *Arkitekten-Arkkitehti*, No. 5, pp. 75–80, 1941. Reprinted in *Construzioni-Casabella*, p. 183, March 1943.

Aalto, A., *An Experimental Town*, student project at Massachusetts Institute of Technology School of Architecture, 1940. Reprinted as 'Research for Reconstruction: Rehousing Research in Finland', *Journal of the Royal Institute of British Architects*, pp. 78–83, 17 March 1941.

'Haka Housing', *Casabella*, pp. 46–7, May 1941.

'Designing Today's Furniture', *Interiors*, pp. 16–21, 40, 42 and 46, June 1941.

Aalto issue, *Arkitekten-Arkkitehti*, No. 1–2, 1941.

The Helsinki Centre Traffic Plan, *Arkitekten-Arkkitehti*, No. 1, pp. 9–10, 1942.

Aalto, A., 'Work of the Finnish Architects' Association towards standardisation', *Arkitekten-Arkkitehti*, No. 5–6, p. 41, 1943.

Aalto, A., 'Finnish standardisation in building', *Byggmästaren*, No. 1, pp. 1–7, 1943.

Avesta Town Centre, *Arkitekten-Arkkitehti*, No. 10, pp. 108–13, 1944.

Aalto, A., 'Rovaniemi rediviva', *Arkitekten-Arkkitehti*, No. 11–12, pp. 127–8, 1945.

'Rovaniemi Urban Development Plan', *Arkitekten-Arkkitehti*, No. 11–12, pp. 127–46, 1945.

'Aalto Rejoins Faculty at School of Architecture and Planning, MIT', *Architectural Forum*, p. 138, January 1946.

'Aalto returns to MIT', *Architectural Record*, pp. 118–20, January 1946.

'Rovaniemi', *Metron*, pp. 15–21, February 1946.

'Projekt für den Wiederaufhof von Rovaniemi in Finnisch Lappland', *Werk*, pp. 102–6, April 1946.

'Rovaniemi: Alvar Aalto, architect', *L'Homme et l'architecture*, pp. 51–8, July/August 1946.

Aalto, A., 'Fin de la Machine à Habiter' (The End of the Machine for Living), *Metron*, No. 7, pp. 15–21, 1946.

Aalto, A., 'Un Sanatorium pour toberculeux en Finlande', *L'architecture française*, No. 62, pp. 21–4, 1946.

Various projects, *Arkitekten-Arkkitehti*, No. 7–8, pp. 83–7, 91–4 and 120–21, 1946.

Nynäshamn Town Hall, *Byggmästaren*, No. 4, pp. 63–70, 1946.

'Avesta Town Centre', *Byggmästaren*, No. 23, pp. 434–6, 1946.

Aalto, A., 'Culture and Technology', *USA, Suomi-Finland*, No. 3, pp. 20–21, 1947.

Aalto, A., 'Architettura e arte concreta', *Domus*, No. 223–5, pp. 103–15, December 1947. Reprinted *Arkitekten-Arkkitehti*, No. 1–2, pp. 7–10, 1948; as 'L'oeuf de Poisson et le Sauman', *Werk*, pp. 43–4, February 1949; *I 4 Soli*, No. 3, 1965; as 'Abstract Art and Architecture', *Alvar Aalto Synopsis* (Section B), pp. 17–18, Basel, 1970.

'Rovaniemi: A Finnish Reconstruction Project', *Architect's Year Book*, No. 2, pp. 51–8, 1947.

'Aalto's Plan for MIT Dormitory: an Undisguised Expression of Function', *Architectural Forum*, p. 13, November 1947.

'Dormitory that Expresses New Ideas of Student Life', *Architectural Record*, pp. 97–100, December 1947.

Bill, M., 'Ausstellungen', *Werk*, March 1948.

Finseven Inc., *Aalto Designs*, New York, May 1948.

'New Designs for Chair and Stool', *Architectural Forum*, pp. 58f., June 1948.

Giedion, S., 'Über Alvar Aaltos Werk', *Werk*, pp. 269–75, September 1948.

Aalto, A., Foreword to *Eliel Saarinen* (by A. Christ-Janer), University of Chicago Press, 1948.

Blomstedt, A., 'Aino and Alvar Aalto', *Arkitekten-Arkkitehti*, No. 1–2, pp. 2–6 and 11–14, 1948.

Heiberg, B., 'Alvar Aalto's work – critical appreciation', *Bonytt*, Norway, No. 4, 1948.

Race, E., 'Trends in Factory-Made Furniture', *Architectural Review*, No. 617, p. 219, 1948.

'Aino and Alvar Aalto, 25th Anniversary', *Arkitekten-Arkkitehti*, No. 1–2, pp. 3–6 and 11–14, 1948.

'Siedlung in Nynäshamn, Finnland', *Werk*, p. 7, January 1949.

'Tuberculosis Sanatorium at Paimio, Finland', *Modern Hospital*, pp. 79–81, April 1949.

'MIT Senior Dormitory', *Architectural Forum*, pp. 61–9, portrait p. 54, August 1949.

Mumford, L., 'Monumentalism, Symbolism and Style', *Architectural Review*, No. 628, pp. 173–80, 1949.

Otaniemi plan, *Arkitekten-Arkkitehti*, No. 9–10, pp. 131–8, 1949.

Furniture, lamps, *Arkitekten-Arkkitehti*, No. 11–12, pp. 166–7, 1949.

'Finnische Möbel aus gepresstem Holz', *Architektur und Wohnform*, No. 4, pp. 77–80, 1949.

Baruel, J.J., 'Alvar Aalto', *Arkitekten-Manedsaefti*, No. 8 whole issue, Denmark, 1950.

Delafon, S.G., 'Mairea, une villa de l'architecte Finlandais', *Art et Decoration*, No. 18, pp. 9–12, 1950.

Giedion, S., 'Alvar Aalto', *Architectural Review*, pp. 77–84, February 1950.

Richards, J.M., 'The Next Step', *Architectural Review*, March 1950.

Sacks, L., 'Studentenheim des Massachusetts Institute of Technology', Cambridge, Mass., USA, *Werk*, Vol. 37, pp. 97–102, April 1950.

'Heimdal Housing, Sweden', *Architectural Review*, No. 640, p. 271, 1950.

'Forum redivivum', *Arkitekten-Arkkitehti*, No. 1–2, pp. 3–5, 1950.

'Lahti Church', *Arkitekten-Arkkitehti*, No. 3, pp. 33–5, 1950.

'MIT Dormitory and Otaniemi plan', *Arkitekten-Arkkitehti*, No. 4, pp. 53–66, 1950.

'L'oeuvre d'Aino et Alvar Aalto', *L'architecture d'aujourd'hui*, No. 29, pp. 1–36, supp. 1–3, April 1950.

Dunnet, H., 'Furniture since the War', *Architectural Review*, No. 651, pp. 151–66, 1951.

Rotzler, W., 'Der gedeckte Tisch', *Werk*, No. 12, pp. 373–9, 1951.

Santi, G., 'Il lungo commino di Alvar Aalto', *Domus*, pp. 9–12, January 1951.

'Malmi Funeral Chapel', *Arkitekten-Arkkitehti*, No. 1, pp. 11–15, 1951.

'Lagerhalle der Glasfabrik von Karhula, Finnland', *Werk*, pp. 112–15, April 1951.

Kivelä Hospital, *Arkitekten-Arkkitehti*, No. 8, pp. 101 and 108–9, 1951.

Schler, F., 'Europäische Architektur seit 1945', *Der Aufbau*, No. 6, pp. 213–34, 1952.

Veronesi, G., 'Alvar Aalto', *Emporium*, pp. 98–104, March 1952.

'Furnishing of M/S Finntrader', *Arkitekten-Arkkitehti*, No. 1, pp. 1–6, 1952.

'El arquitecto Alvar Aalto en las sesiones de critica de arquitectura celebrado en el mes de noviembre en Madrid', *Revista Nacional de arquitectura*, pp. 18–36, April 1952.

Aalto, A., 'On the Profession of a Director of a Building Department', *Arkitekten-Arkkitehti*, No. 2, pp. 1–8, 1953.

Aalto, A., 'The Decadence of Public Buildings', *Arkitekten-Arkkitehti*, No. 9–10, p. 148, 1953.

Various projects including Aalto's summer house, *Arkitekten-Arkkitehti*, No. 9–10, pp. 194–260, 1953.

'Furniture', *Die Kunst und das Schöne Heim*, pp. 198–9, February 1953.

'Sedie Moderne con Materiali Moderni', *Prospective*, No. 7, p. 43, 1953.

'Internationaler Wettbewerb für eine Sportshalle in Wien', *Werk*, supp. 233, December 1953.

Schildt, G., 'Alvar Aalto', *Casabella*, No. 200, pp. 4–17, February/March 1954.

'Alvar Aalto in the Finnish Forests: Civic Centre for Säynätsalo and Aalto's own experimental workshop and vacation home', *Architectural Forum*, pp. 148–53, April 1954.

Schimmerling, A., 'Pays nordiques: Finlande', *L'architecture d'aujourd'hui*, pp. 50–85 (Aalto's summer house, pp. 58–9; Säynätsalo Town Hall, pp. 72–5; Otaniemi, pp. 68–71; various other projects, pp. 66–7, 76), May 1954.

'Halle des sports de Vienne; project de concours, premier prix', *L'architecture d'aujourd'hui*, p. 72, July 1954.

'Community centre in Säynätsalo, Finland', *Arkitekten-Manedsaefti*, pp. 115–20, August 1954.

'Alvar Aalto in Zürich', *Werk*, supp. 240, October 1954.

Aalto, A., 'The Museum of Finnish Architecture', *Arkitekten-Arkkitehti*, No. 2, p. 17, 1954.

Aalto, A., '75 Years of the Academic Architects' Association', *Arkitekten*, p. 377, 1954.

Magnin, M., 'L'exposition de l'architecture cotemporaine de la Finlande', *Werk*, No. 2, pp. 55–6, 1954.

Pederson, J., 'The King's Funeral Chapel', *Arkitekten*, No. 19, pp. 145–51, 1954.

Roth, A., 'Finnland Baut', *Werk*, pp. 55–6, 1954.

'Exhibition at the NK store in Stockholm', *Arkitekten-Arkkitehti*, No. 3–4, pp. 51–4, 1954.

'Aalto's summer house, Muuratsalo', *Arkitekten-Arkkitehti*, No. 9–10, pp. 160f., 1954.

'Vogelweidplatz Wien', *Arkitekten-Arkkitehti*, No. 12, pp. 201–9, 1954.

'A visit to Alvar Aalto', *Bauen und Wohnen*, No. 3, pp. 119–24, 1954.

'Aalto's Conference Hall', *Byggekunst*, Vol. 36, pp. 1–7, 1954.

Thiberg, S., 'Competition for City Hall, Gothenberg', *Arkitekten*, pp. 356–7, 1955.

'Finland – Warehouse Building, Karhula Glassworks', *Architect's Year Book*, No. 6, pp. 165–7, 1955.

'Club à Kallvik, Finlande', *L'architecture d'aujourd'hui*, pp. 102–3, September 1955.

'Edificio per uffici e negozi "Rautatalo" a Helsinki', *Casabella*, No. 208, pp. 6–15, November/December 1955.

'Berlin-Ouest, exposition du bâtiment 1957 quartier Hansa; immeuble d'habitation', *L'architecture d'aujourd'hui*, p. 79, December 1955.

'Caisse d'allocations vieillesse à Helsinki', *L'architecture d'aujourd'hui*, p. 100, December 1955.

'Il padiglione finlandese alla Biennale di Venezia', *Sele Arte*, No. 24, 1955/6.

Schildt, G., 'Finland Builds', *Architectural Record*, pp. 161–8, February 1956.

'La villa Mairea di Alvar Aalto', *Domus*, No. 320, pp. 13–20, July 1956.

'Il padiglione finlandese alla biennale', *Domus*, No. 322, pp. 3–5, September 1956.

Aalto, A., 'Problemi de Architettura', *Quaderni ACI*, November 1956.

Aalto, A., 'Zwischen Humanismus und Materialismus', *Baukunst und Werkform*, No. 6, pp. 298–300, 1956.

Baruel, J.J., 'Construction form', *Arkitekten*, No. 1, pp. 1–5, Denmark, 1956.

Bloc, A., 'La Biennale d'Art de Venise', *Aujourd'hui, art et architecture*, No. 9, 1956.

Heid, G., 'Der Baumeister Alvar Aalto', *Baukunst und Werkform*, No. 6, 1956.

Schulten, M., 'Recent Architecture in Finland', *Architect's Year Book*, No. 7, pp. 79–99, 1956.

'Finnish pavilion, Venice Biennale' and 'Aalto in praise of wood', *Arkkitehti*, No. 6–7, 1956.

'Finnlands Haus im Hansaviertel', *Bauwelt*, No. 41, 1956.

'Il padiglione finlandese in Venezia', *Casabella*, No. 212, p. 72, 1956.

Harbers, G., 'Finnisches Glas', *Die Kunst und das Schöne Heim*, February 1957.

Royal Gold Medal for Architecture, 1957, *Royal Institute of British Architects Journal*, s.3, Vol. 64, p. 128, February 1957; and pp. 254–64, May 1957.

'Immeuble de bureaux à Helsinki', *L'architecture d'aujourd'hui*, pp. 70–73, February 1957.

'Alvar Aalto a Roma', *L'Architettura*, No. 17, p. 832, March 1957.

'Büro und Geschäftshaus "Rautatalo", Helsinki', *Werk*, pp. 102–8, March 1957.

Banham, R., 'The One and the Few: The Rise of Modern Architecture in Finland', *Architectural Review*, pp. 243–59, April 1957.

'Civic Group, Säynätsalo, and Insurance Office, Helsinki', *Architectural Review*, pp. 249–50 and 256, April 1957.

Aalto, A., 'RIBA – Annual Discourse, 1957', *Journal of the Royal Institute of British Architects*, pp. 258–64, May 1957. Reprinted in *Royal Architectural Institute of Canada Journal*, pp. 304–7, August 1957; and in *Alvar Aalto Synopsis*, pp. 21–4, Basel, 1970.

Veronese, G., 'Dalla Weissenhof all Interbau', *Communità*, August/September 1957.

Sears, H., 'Visit to Säynätsalo', *Royal Architectural Institute of Canada Journal*, pp. 340–42, September 1957.

'Milan Exhibition', *Interiors*, pp. 89–94, November 1957.

'Interbau 1957 in Berlin; zum Haus von Aalto', *Werk*, supp. 206, November 1957.

Sharp, D., 'Aalto and His Influence', *Architecture and Building*, pp. 476–9, December 1957.

'Finlande à Interbau', *L'architecture d'aujourd'hui*, pp. 10–11, December 1957.

Conrads, U., 'Revolution, Evolution, Convention', *Zodiac*, No. 1, 1957.

Mosso, L., 'Il nuovo studio di Alvar Aalto a Munkkiniemi; Edificio per l'assistenza statale ai pensionati; Kultuuritalo, Helsinki', *Casabella*, No. 217, pp. 7–27, 1957.

Westman, T., 'The Queen's Square in Goteborg', *Byggmästaren*, No. 6, pp. 133–4, 1957.

'Alvar Aalto 1957', *Architect's Year Book* (J. Wood ed.), No. 8, pp. 137–68, 1957.

Imatra regional plan, *Arkitekten-Arkkitehti*, No. 1–2, pp. 19–24, 1957.

Pensions Institute Housing, *Arkitekten-Arkkitehti*, No. 3, pp. 33–6, 1957.

Hansa Apartment Building, *Arkitekten-Arkkitehti*, No. 11–12, pp. 173–8, 1957.

Hansa Apartment Building, *Architektur und Wohnform*, No. 5, 1957.

Säynätsalo Town Hall, *Sele Arte*, No. 29, pp. 42–6 and 62, 1957.

Aalto, A., 'Henry van de Velde, in Memorium', *Arkitekten-Arkkitehti*, No. 11–12, p. 171, 1957.

'Der Wohnbau von Alvar Aalto an der Interbau Berlin 1957', *Werk*, pp. 9–12, January 1958.

'Central Bank for Pensioners in Helsinki', *Forum*, pp. 41–3 and 54–8, February 1958.

Vindigni, G., 'Tre nuove opere di Alvar Aalto in Finlandia', *L'Architettura*, No. 28, pp. 668–95, February 1958.

'Alvar Aalto baut Hochhaus in dem Bremer Vahr', *Neue Heimat*, No. 7, p. 48, July 1958.

Huber, B., 'Verwaltungsgebäude der stadtlichen Altersversicherung in Helsinki', *Werk*, pp. 221–6, July 1958.

Hansa Apartment Building, *Die Kunst und das Schöne Heim*, August 1958.

'Haus der Kultur in Helsinki', *Bauen und Wohnen*, pp. 310–11, September 1958.

Brawne, M., 'Looking up', *Architectural Review*, No. 740, pp. 161–70, 1958.

Carbonara, P., *Architettura Pratica*, No. 3, pp. 1305–12 and 1548 (various projects), Turin, 1958.

Heberbrand, W., 'Um die Marler Stadtkrone', *Bauwelt*, No. 14, pp. 315–27, 1958.

'Aalto's works, 1923–1958', *Arkitekten-Arkkitehti*, No. 1–2 (entire issue on Aalto), 1958.

'Imatra Church', *Arkitekten-Arkkitehti*, No. 6–7, p. 111, 1958.

'Entry for a Terrace House Competition in Mall', *Arkitekten*, No. 10, pp. 166–9, 1958.

North Jutland Museum, *Arkitekten*, No. 12, pp. 193–7, Denmark, 1958.

'Hansa Apartment Building', *Casabella*, No. 218, pp. 20 and 30–32, 1958.

'L'opera di Alvar Aalto de 1922 a 1958', *Casabella*, No. 222, p. 57, 1958.

'Hochhaus in Fächerform; der Stadthauliche Blickpunkt in dem Bremer Vahr von Alvar Aalto', *Neue Heimat*, No. 12, pp. 1–10, December 1958.

Aalto, A., 'Urban Design Project for Imatra', *Werk*, No. 11, pp. 400–403, 1959.

Burchard, J.E., 'Finland and Architect Aalto', *Architectural Record*, pp. 125–36, January 1959.

Huber, B., 'Projekt fur ein Kulturzentrum in Wolfsburg, Deutschland', *Werk*, supp. 142, July 1959.

Moser, W., 'Lutherische Kirche in Imatra, Finnland', *Werk*, pp. 289–93, August 1959.

Mosso, L., 'Lo spazio organico di Imatra', *Casabella*, No. 230, pp. 6–22, August 1959.

Schildt, G., Santini, P.C., 'Alvar Aalto from Sunila to Imatra: Ideas, projects and buildings', *Zodiac*, No. 3, pp. 26–82 (portrait p. 195), 1959.

'Vaults of Imatra, Aalto's New Church', *Architectural Review*, pp. 2–3, January 1960.

'Progetto per il museo a Aalborg, Danimarco', *Casabella*, No. 236, pp. 50–51, February 1960.

'Alvar Aalto – Finn without Borders', *Architectural Forum*, pp. 116–23, February 1960.

Mosso, L., 'Una casa di Alvar Aalto nei dintorni di Parigi: La Maison Carré', *Casabella*, No. 236, pp. 4–17, February 1960.

'Church at Imatra, Finland', *Architectural Design*, Vol. 29, p. 111, March 1960.

'Opernhaus Essen', *Werk*, pp. 312–14, September 1960.

'Fan plans: Aalto in Germany', *Architectural Review*, No. 765, pp. 318f., November 1960.

Giedion, S., 'Alvar Aalto', *Architectural Review*, Vol. 107, 1960.

Giedion, S., 'Alvar Aalto', *L'architecture d'aujourd'hui*, Vol. 20, 1960.

Mosso, L., 'La luce nell'architettura di Alvar Aalto', *Zodiac*, No. 7, pp. 66–115, 1960.

Pehnt, W., 'Aalto in Deutschland', *Zodiac*, No. 7, pp. 176–81, 1960.

Perrochet, M., 'La Maison Louis Carré de Alvar Aalto à Bazoches', *Werk*, pp. 417–22, December 1960.

Veronese, G., 'Une maison de Aalto en Île de France', *Zodiac*, No. 6, pp. 22–47, 1960.

'Vienna Sports Hall', *Architectural Review*, No. 758, p. 221, 1960.

'Maison Carré, *Architectural Review*, No.760, pp. 366–7, 1960.

'Aalto's Studio', *Arkitekten-Arkkitekti*, No. 1, p. 1, 1960.

Special issue on Aalto, *Arquitectura*, Vol. 13, No. 2, Madrid, 1960.

'Das Kulturzentrum in Helsinki', *Bau & Werk*, Vol. 13, No. 3, pp. 119–20, 1960.

Opernhaus Essen, *Bauwelt*, No. 5, pp. 128–30, 1960.

Special issue on Aalto, *Cuadernos de arquitectura*, No. 39, Madrid, 1960.

Schildt, G., 'L'Architecture à la Mésure de l'homme', *L'architecture d'aujourd'hui*, No. 93, pp. 1–15, 1960–61.

'Habitation près de Paris', *L'architecture d'aujourd'hui*, No. 93, pp. 1–15, 1960–61.

'Agence d'Alvar Aalto à Munkkiniemi', *L'architecture d'aujourd'hui*, Vol. 31, No. 93, pp. 6–9, December 1960–January 1961.

'Forma o verità? la Maison Carré', *L'Architettura*, pp. 6–9, May 1961.

Aalto, A., 'Il nuove centro di Helsinki', *Casabella*, No. 254, pp. 12–23, August 1961.

Brawne, M., 'Libraries', *Architectural Review*, No. 776, p. 248, 1961.

Ikonnikov, A., 'Finsky Arkitektor Alvar Aalto', *Arkitektura SSSR*, No. 7, 1961.

Tentori, F., 'Il piano di Alvar Aalto per il nuovo centro de Helsinki', *Casabella*, No. 254, pp. 12–23, 1961.

'New Centre for Helsinki', *Arkitekten-Arkkitehti*, 1961.

Helsinki Centre Plan and Maison Carré, *Arkitekten-Arkkitehti*, No. 3, pp. 33–66, 1961.

'Five Works by Alvar Aalto', *Kokusai-Kentiku*, No. 5, 1961.

'Finnische Architekten bauen', *Bauwelt*, No. 36, pp. 1014–1016, 1961.

'Nouveau centre d'Helsinki', *'L'architecture d'aujourd'hui*, pp. 68–71, April 1962.

Rubino, L., 'Processo ad un' grande architetto europeo: la ricerca incompiuta di Alvar Aalto', *L'Architettura*, No. 78, pp. 804–28, April 1962.

Geiger, M., 'Ausstellung, Keski-Suomen museo, Jyväskylä', *Werk*, supp. 243, October 1962.

Fiori, L., 'Alvar Aalto, i mobili più imitati del mondo', *Fantasia: revista Mensile della casa*, pp. 82–9, 1962.

Kuhne, G., 'Alvar Aalto baut in Deutschland', *Bauwelt*, pp. 1148–1151, October 1962.

Mosso, L., 'Storia dei mobili nell'architettura di un maestro: Alvar Aalto', *Arte Casa*, No. 38, pp. 35–40, 1962.

Mosso, L., 'Un inedito grafico di A. Aalto e di E. Bryggmann', *Pagina*, No. 1, 1962.

Rubino, L., 'Il centro culturale di Wolfsburg', *L'Architettura*, pp. 522–34, December 1962.

Schildt, G., 'L'architecture finlandaise d'aujourd'hui', *La Maison*, No. 9, 1962.

'Finn Grin: Aalto in Germany', *Architectural Review*, No. 790, p. 382, December 1962.

'Competition design for church at Humlebaek', *Arkitektur*, No. 8, pp. 162–3, 1962.

Pensions Institute, Helsinki, and Teachers' College at Jyväskylä, *L'Architettura*, No. 78, pp. 811–19, 1962.

'Headquarters for Enso-Gutzeit Company, Helsinki', *Arkitektur*, pp. 24–30, February 1963.

Mosso, L., 'Nel centro storico di Helsinki la sede Enso-Gutzeit di Alvar Aalto', *Casabella*, No. 272, pp. 4–25, February 1963.

Joedicke, J., 'Kulturzentrum der Stadt Wolfsburg', *Bauen und Wohnen*, No. 2, pp. 63–72, February 1963.

'Aalto's Recent Work in West Germany', *Architectural Forum*, pp. 120–25, March 1963.

Gutheim, F., 'Alvar Aalto Today', *Architectural Record*, pp. 135–50, April 1963.

Chiarini, C., 'A proposito della sede Enso-Gutzeit di Alvar Aalto' (with a reply by F. Tentori), *Casabella*, No. 276, pp. 1–11, June 1963.

'Sede dell'Enso-Gutzeit ad Helsinki', *L'Architettura*, p. 188, July 1963.

Gutheim, F., 'Alvar Aalto; AIA Gold Medalist – 1963', *American Institute of Architects Journal*, p. 85, July 1963.

Marconi, F., and Rubino, L., 'Polemica su Aalto', *L'Architettura*, p. 188, July 1963.

'Civic Wedge, Aalto's new centre for Helsinki', *Architectural Review*, p. 149, September 1963.

'Enso-Gutzeit, Aalto's new office block in Helsinki', *Architectural Review*, p. 149, September 1963.

'Der "Neue Vahr" in Bremen', *Bauen und Wohnen*, pp. 458–60, November 1963.

'Opernhaus Essen', *Bauwelt*, No. 25–6, pp. 722–4, 1963.

'L'église a Seinäjoki, Finlande, par Alvar Aalto', *L'architecture d'aujourd'hui*, No. 153, pp. 4–17, 1963.

'Enso-Gutzeit Building; New Centre for Helsinki; Cultural Centre for Wolfsburg', *Perspecta*, No. 8, pp. 5–14, 1963.

Aalto, A., 'Les ennemis de l'architecture', *Neuve d'Information de l'Union Internationale des Architects*, No. 25, pp. 22–5, February 1964.

'Centre culturel à Wolfsburg', *L'architecture d'aujourd'hui*, pp. 58–63, February 1964.

'Le lauree honoris causa conferite della facolta di architettura di Milano', *Casabella*, No. 286, pp. 54–5, April 1964.

'Work of Alvar Aalto: an exhibition at the Octagon', *American Institute of Architects Journal*, p. 50, April 1964.

Schildt, G., 'Alvar Aalto', *L'Architecture d'aujourd'hui*, pp. 112–17, April 1964.

Fasani, S., 'Alvar Aalto ed l'Enso-Gutzeit', *L'Architettura*, p. 112, June 1964.

'Zürich: Aalto-ausstellung', *Werk*, supp. 161–2, July 1964.

'Aalto, Kahn, Tange: laurea honoris causa, a Milano', *Domus*, No. 416, p. 16, July 1964.

'Hamburg, BP Administration Building', *Bauwelt*, pp. 710–11, July 1964.

Billeter, F., 'Zwei Steden mit Alvar Aalto', *Speculum Artes*, No. 4, 1964.

Norberg-Schultz, C., 'Architektur Heute', *Werk*, No. 3, p. 108, 1964.

'Stadtszentrum, Wolfsburg', *Deutsche Bauzeitschrift*, No. 3, pp. 273–80, 1964.

'Caisse d'allocations vieillesse à Helsinki', *L'architecture d'aujourd'hui*, December 1964 – January 1965.

Neue Vahr Apartments, *Lotus Architectural Annual*, pp. 72–5, 1964/5.

'Interviewing Aalto', *Progressive Architecture*, p. 48f., January 1965.

Smith, G.E.K., 'The Architecture of Alvar Aalto', *American Scandinavian Review*, Spring 1965.

'Development drawings: preliminary plan of church at Imatra', *Architectural Review*, p. 147, February 1965.

'Aalto in New York: Edgar J. Kaufmann Conference Rooms, Institute of International Education', *Progressive Architecture*, pp. 180–85, February 1965.

'Mittelpunkt des Baukunst: der Mensch', *Bauen und Wohnen*, No. 54, March 1965.

Elvin, R., 'Alvar Aalto in Retrospect', *Official Architecture and Planning*, Vol. 28, No. 4, pp. 551, 553 and 555, April 1965.

'University Building by a master hand: Aalto's new classroom complex for the Finnish Technical Institute', *Architectural Record*, pp. 169–76, April 1965.

Aalto, A., 'Discussions at the Congress on Nordic Urbanism', Congress Archives, Helsinki, p. 11, August 1965.

'Personality: the Individual in Architecture', *Progressive Architecture*, p. 176, September 1965.

'Exposition Alvar Aalto à Florence', *L'architecture d'aujourd'hui*, p. xxvi, September 1965.

'Interiors for the Edgar J. Kaufmann Conference Rooms of the Institute of International Education', *Architectural Review*, p. 238, October 1965.

Aalto, A., 'Le Corbusier, in Memoriam', *Progressive Architecture*, p. 236, October 1965.

Mosso, L., 'Letture di Aalto', *Critica d'Arte*, November 1965.

Hitchcock, H.R., 'Aalto versus Aalto: The Other Finland', *Perspecta*, Nos. 9 and 10, pp. 132–66, 1965 (reprinted in *Arkitekten-Arkkitehti*, No. 10–11, pp. 248–54, 1965).

Mendini, A., 'L'opera di Alvar Aalto', *Casabella*, Vol. 229, 1965.

Mosso, L., 'Alvar Aalto', *Sele Arte*, No. 76, pp. 12–24, 1965.

'The Plan for Central Helsinki by Alvar Aalto', *Arkitekten-Arkkitehti*, No. 3, pp. 30–33, 1965.

The work of Alvar Aalto, review of Florence Exhibition, followed by Aalto's article on architectural methods, *Casabella*, No. 299, pp. 40–61, 1965.

'Architettura Finlandese', *Chiesa e Quartiere*, Issue No. 36, 1965.

'Aalto a Firenze', *Marmo*, No. 4, pp. 7–51, 1965.

Heinonen, R.L., 'The Beginnings of Functionalism in Finland', *Arkitekten-Arkkitehti*, No. 11–12, pp. 162–70, 1966.

Marcolli, A., 'Incontro con Alvar Aalto, Firenze, 1965', *Arte-Oggi*, No. 25–6, pp. 50–64, 1966.

Mosso, L., 'Il Vogelweidplatz di Alvar Aalto', *Marmo*, No. 4, 1966.

Pica, A., 'La mostra di Alvar Aalto a Firenze', *Domus*, No. 435, pp. 1–10, February 1966.

Spring, B.P., 'Aalto Revisited', *Architectural Forum*, pp. 70–79, April 1966.

'Aalto on show at the Palazzo Strozzi in Florence', *Architectural Review*, pp. 323–4, May 1966.

'Exposition des meubles d'Alvar Aalto à Paris', *L'architecture d'aujourd'hui*, p. xiii, October 1966.

'Institute of Technology, Helsinki, Main Building', *Arkitekten-Arkkitehti*, No. 4, pp. 53–70, 1966.

Otaniemi Complex, *Architectural Design*, pp. 619–22, December 1966.

'Einkaufszentrum und Wohnhochhaus "Schönbühl" ', *Werk*, p. xxxii, December 1966.

'La Pisana della Maison Carré', *Lotus*, Vol, 3, No. 1, pp. 32–5, 1966–7.

'La chiesa italiana di Alvar Aalto', *Domus*, No. 446, p. vii; and No. 447, pp. 2–8, January 1967, February 1967.

'Church for Riola, Bologna', *Architectural Design*, pp. 233–4, May 1967.

'Three from Finland: recent show at Design Research of Finnish furniture design', *Industrial Design*, pp. 42–3, May 1967.

Santini, P.C., 'Alvar Aalto in Italia', *Ottagono*, pp. 91–5, October 1967.

Mosso, L., 'Alvar Aalto: Unité de l'homme et de l'oeuvre', *L'architecture d'aujourd'hui*, No. 134, pp. 1–13, October/November 1967.

Aalto, A., 'Town Planning and Public Buildings', *Arkitekten-Arkkitehti*, No. 3–4, pp. 35–8, 1967.

Aalto, A., 'Conversation with Göran Schildt', in Mosso, L., *Alvar Aalto: Works 1918–1967*, pp. 5–7, 1967.

Jencks, C., 'Alvar Aalto and some concepts of value', *Arena/Interbuild*, pp. 29–35, November 1967.

Kopp, A., 'Ville et Revolution', Editions Anthropos, Paris, 1967.

Moholy-Nagy, S., 'The Ageing of Modern Architecture', *Arkitekten-Arkkitehti*, No. 7–8, pp. 15–20, 1967.

Smithson, P., 'Alvar Aalto: The Second Generation Ethos', *Architectural Design*, December 1967.

'Stockmann's Book Shop', *Arkitekten-Arkkitehti*, No. 1–2, pp. 14–15, 1967.

'Church and meditation centre, Riola near Bologna', *Arkitekten*, Vol. 69, 1967.

'Town Centre at Castrop-Rauxel; Helsinki Centre Plan', *Arkitektur Wettbewerbe*, No. 52, pp. 28–32 and 50–56, 1967.

'Architectures nordiques', *L'architecture d'aujourd'hui*, Issue No. 134, 1967.

Aalto, A., 'Siegfried Giedion in Memorium', *Arkitekten*, No. 2, pp. 59–60, 1968.

Stephen, D., 'Institute of Technology, Otaniemi, Finland', *Architectural Review*, pp. 57–64, February 1968.

'Institute of Technology, Otaniemi, Finland', *Architectural Design*, Vol. 38, 1968.

'Alvar Aalto, Special Issue', *Arkitekten-Arkkitehti*, Vol. 65, 1968.

'Alvar Aalto', *Arkitekten*, No. 2, pp. 23–58f., 1968.

'Library Architecture', *Bauwelt*, Vol. 59, No. 21, pp. 647–58, 20 May 1968.

'Urban Design for Pavia', *Italia Nostra*, No. 59, pp. 8–10, 1968.

'Urban Design for Pavia', *Italia Nostra*, No. 61, pp. 13–14, 1968.

'Riola Church', *L'Architetto*, No. 6, pp. 8–12, 1968.

'Aalto on Lake Lucerne', *Progressive Architecture*, pp. 130–37, November 1968.

'Housing, Switzerland', *Werk*, Vol. 55, 1968.

Aalto, A., 'The Arts', *Alvar Aalto 1963–70*, Zürich, p. 12, 1969.

Joedicke, J., 'Bauen in Finland', *Bauen und Wohnen*, No. 4, pp. 111–19, 1969.

Llorens, J., 'The Work of Alvar Aalto', *Cuadernos da Arquitectura*, No. 72, pp. 8–24, 1969.

'Export Quality: Aalto's Architecture', *Architectural Design*, pp. 176–7, April 1969.

Special issue on Aalto, *Arkitektur*, April 1969.

Aalto, A., 'The Relationship between Architecture, Painting and Sculpture', from a discussion with Aalto in February 1969, in *Alvar Aalto Synopsis* (Section B), pp. 24–6, Basel, 1970.

'Alvar Aalto', *American Institute of Architects Journal*, pp. 59–64, February 1970.

'Alvar Aalto', *Architectural Record*, Vol. 125, 1970.

'Benedictins pas morts – III; La bibliothèque de Mount Angel', *Art d'Eglise*, Vol. 39, No. 154, pp. 146–53, January – March 1971.

'Aalto's Second American Building, Mount Angel Library, St Benedict, Oregon', *Architectural Record*, pp. 111–16, May 1971.

Zevi, B., 'Bricolage di Johansen ed Aalto informal', *L'Architettura*, pp. 142–3, July 1971.

Richards, J.M., 'Les styles divergents de l'architecture moderne', *L'architecture d'aujourd'hui*, No. 158, p. 58, October 1971.

'Mount Angel Library, Salem', *Architectural Design*, p. 645, October 1971.

Schildt, G., 'Protuberanzen der Architektur; ein Interview mit Alvar Aalto', *Bauwelt*, pp. 221–3, February 1972.

Pica, A., ' "Finlandia talo" a Helsinki: il nuovo centro musicale e un congresso Finlandia Hall, di Alvar Aalto', *Domus*, No. 508, pp. 12–16, March 1972.

Denison, J., 'Finlandia Hall: A Manager looks at Finlandia; and Abbey Library, Mount Angel, Oregon', *Architectural Review*, pp. 332–48, June 1972.

'Aalto again', *Architectural Review*, pp. 397–8, June 1972.

'Finlandia Hall: Helsinki's cause célèbre', *Progressive Architecture*, pp. 50–57, August 1972.

Reasoner, B., 'Alvar Aalto at Mount Angel Abbey', *Society of Architectural Historians Journal*, p. 224, October 1972.

Fogh, F., 'Aalto in Italia', *Arkitektur*, No. 1, pp. 24–32, Denmark, 1972.

Schildt, G., 'Alvar Aalto, a signpost', *Dansk Brugskunst*, pp. 225–32, December 1972.

'La Médaille d'or d'Alvar Aalto', *Academie d'Architecture Bulletin*, Vol. 61, pp. 183–97, 1972.

'North Jutland Art Museum, Aalborg', *Arkitektur*, No. 5, pp. 182–99,Denmark, 1972.

'Aalto in Italy: Riola', *Arkitektur*, No. 7, 1972.

Brawne, M., 'Aalto at Aalborg', *Architectural Review*, pp. 155–64, March 1973.

'A Milano per Alvar Aalto', *Domus*, No. 520, p. 42, March 1973.

'La luce di Aalto', *L'Architettura*, pp. 812–13, April 1973.

Abercrombie, S., 'Happy Anniversary, Baker House', *Architecture Plus*, pp. 58–65, July 1973.

Aalto, A. and E., Baruel, J.J., 'Architecture of Light for Objects of Art: The North Jutland Museum, Aalborg', *Architektur und Wohnwelt*, Vol. 81, No. 7, pp. 466–71, October 1973.

Mieczyslaw, P., 'Finlandia-talo', *Architektura*, No. 10, pp. 404–8 (Poland), 1973.

'Shopping centre (Alfred Roth) and Schönbühl Apartment Tower (Alvar Aalto)', *Architecture and Urbanism*, Vol. 3, No. 9, pp. 63–8, September 1973.

'Concert and Congress Hall in Helsinki: architect Alvar Aalto', *Arkitektur*, No. 4, pp. 133–44, Denmark, 1973.

Sabbag Centre Office Buildings, Beirut, Alfred Roth with Alvar Aalto, *Revue de la Construction*, Vol. 26, No. 256, pp. 3–9, December 1973.

'Alvar Aalto: Konzerthaus Finnlandia, Helsinki', *Werk*, No. 4, pp. 440–45, 1973.

'Mobili di Alvar Aalto', *Domus*, No. 532, p. 31, March 1974.

Special issue on Alvar Aalto, *Arkitekten-Arkkitehti*, No. 6, 1974.

'Concert and congress hall, Helsinki, by Alvar Aalto', *Architektur und Wohnwelt*, Vol. 82, No. 5, pp. 296–301, July 1974.

'Antiques', *Architecture Plus*, pp. 82–7, July – August 1974.

Miller, W.C., 'Alvar Aalto's Religious Architecture', *Faith and Form* (Journal of the Guild for Religious Architecture), pp. 10–13, Spring 1975.

'Finland honours four committed to planned towns', *Architectural Record*, p. 41, April 1975.

Herrera, P., 'The Maestro's late works', *Time*, vol. 106, No. 8, pp. 60–61, 25 August 1975.

'Beginning of the work on parish church of Santa Maria Assunta, Riola', *Parametro*, Vol. 6, No. 39/40, pp. 2–3, September/October 1975.

Boch, M., 'How Western ideology sees Alvar Aalto'; Barbieri, U., 'The death of poetic architecture'; Boekstaad, C., 'Critical debate on architecture'; *Wonen – TA/BK*, No. 15, pp. 11–23, 1976.

Price, M., 'The Nature of Finnish Design', *Industrial Design*, pp. 40–45, January/February 1976.

McQuade, W., 'The Enduring Work of a Great Finnish Architect', *Fortune*, pp. 120–27, March 1976.

Huxtable, A.L., 'A Master Builder who left Poetry and Art – not Monuments', *New York Times*, 23 May 1976.

'Man at the Centre', *Time*, p. 66, 24 May 1976 (obituary).

Obituary, *Architectural Record*, p. 33, June 1976.

Obituary, *American Institute of Architects Journal*, p. 77, June 1976.

'Alvar Aalto: 1898–1976', *The Architectural Review*, No. 953, July 1976.

Dixon, J.M., 'Alvar Aalto: 1898–1976', *Progressive Architecture*, pp. 7–8 and 24, July 1976.

Rambert, C., 'Alvar Aalto, le nordique', *Architectes*, No. 70, July/August 1976.

Mikkola, K., 'Aalto the Thinker', *Arkitekten-Arkkitehti*, No. 7 and 8, 1976.

Mosso, L., 'Alvar Aalto – internazionalismo e tradizione', *Casabella*, pp. 415–16, 1976.

Ellis, J., 'Aalto's Viipuri Municipal Library is still standing', *L'Architettura, Cronache e Storia*, Vol. 11, No. 7, p. 357, November 1976.

Flieg, K., 'Alvar Aalto zum Gedenken: Architektur war sein Medium', *Werk*, No. 10, 1976.

Gonzales, A., 'Alvar Aalto, racionalismo o racionalidad', *Cuadernos de arquitectura y urbanismo*, 113, 1976.

Norberg-Schulz, C., 'Alvar Aalto in memoriam', *Byggekunst*, No. 5, 1976.

'Alvar Aalto', *Arkitekten-Arkkitehti*, Vol. 73, 1976.

'Alvar Aalto 1898–1976', *Arkitekten*, No. 12, 1976.

'Alvar Aalto', *Bauen und Wohnen*, No. 6, 1976.

'Alvar Aalto', *De Architect*, No. 7, 1976.

Suhonen, P., 'Alvar Aalto and monumentalism', *Look at Finland*, No. 2, 1976.

Special Issue, *Space and Design*, pp. 3–212, January/February 1977.

Wrede, S., Rubinstein, M., 'A Survey of Aalto's Career', *Progressive Architecture*, April 1977.

'Furniture and furnishings. The integration of design and technology in Aalto's furniture and furnishing art by Finnish Society of Crafts and Design', *Progressive Architecture*, Vol. 58, No. 4, pp. 74–7, April 1977.

Baird, G., 'Reflections on Aalto's influence', *Canadian Architect*, May 1977.

Gresleri, G., 'Storia e imagine nel progetto di Riola', *Parametro*, Vol. 8, 1977.

'Alvar Aalto – his life, works and philosophy', *L'architecture d'aujourd'hui*, June 1977.

'Aalto überholt?', *Bauwelt*, Vol. 68, No. 40, 1977.

'The Invariants in Aalto's Language', *L'Architettura, Cronache e Storia*, Vol. 23, No. 2, pp. 66–7, June 1977.

'Zu Ehren von Alvar Aalto', *Möbelausstellung von Artek*, No. 2, 1977.

'Alvar Aalto: The secret of wood and the allegory of the senses', *Ottagono*, Vol. 12, No. 47, pp. 20–29, December 1977.

'Intervista ad Elissa Aalto', *Parametro*, Vol. 8, 1977.

Koening, G.K., 'Aalto – the last of the builders', *Parametro*, Vol. 8, No. 62, pp. 4–4573.

Niezabitowski, A., and Bielecki, C., 'Alvar Aalto 1898–1976: In Memoriam', *Architektura*, Vol. 31, Nos. 1–2, pp. 59–68 (Warsaw), 1977.

Tonelli, M.C., 'The Finnish Pavilion at the 28th Biennale of 1957 – A temporary building restored to become permanent', *Arkitektur*, No. 3, 1977.

Tonelli, M.C., 'Alvar Aalto', *Parametro*, Vol. 8, 1977.

Quantrill, M., 'An Architect of True Genius', *Sunday Times*, 3 September 1978.

Jones, P.B., 'Organic versus classic', *Architectural Association Quarterly*, No. 1, pp. 10–20, 1978.

Richards, J.M., 'The other Aalto', *Architectural Review*, October 1978.

Quantrill, M., 'Alvar Aalto: Themes and Variations', *Architectural Design*, Nos. 8–9, 1978.

Quantrill, M., 'Alvar Aalto and Post-Rationalism in Finnish Architecture'; Glanville, R., 'Detail and Totality, a style of completeness'; Miller, W.C., 'From Viipuri to Mount Angel: The evolution of the library in Aalto's work', *Architectural Association Quarterly*, No. 3, pp. 4–41, 1978.

'Aalto's new church near Bologna', *Domus*, No. 587, pp. 8–13, October 1978.

'Alvar Aalto', *Tegel*, No. 3, 1978 (Stockholm).

Santini, P.C., 'Alvar Aalto's church at Riola', *Ottagono*, No. 51, pp. 20–25, December 1978.

van Heuvel, V.W.J., 'Paimio sanatorium; Het sanatorium van Alvar Aalto en de invloed van architect Jan Duiker', *Baouwkunde wegen-en waterbouw*, 1978.

van Heuvel, W.J., 'Alvar Aalto's sanatorium and the influence of architect Jan Duiker', *Polytechnic di Tijdschrift*, Vol. 33, No. 12, pp. 755–9, December 1978.

'Parish Centre, Riola', *Architecture and Urbanism*, No. 1 (100), pp. 11–30, January 1979.

Abercrombie, S., 'Lamont Library, Harvard, Woodberry Poetry Room; a little-known 1949 design by the Finnish Master is a Harvard treasure', *Interiors*, Vol. 138, No. 7, pp. 74–5, February 1979.

Abercrombie, S., 'Aalto's second coming', *Portfolio*, Vol. 1, No. 5, 1979–80.

Clouten, N., 'Non-rectilinear spaces in Alvar Aalto's buildings in Finland', *Architecture and Urbanism*, pp. 3–6, February 1979.

van Heuvel, V.W.J., 'Aalto's experimenten in hout', *Houttechniek*, No. 1, 1979.

Hoffer, P., 'Aalto in Italy', *Architectural Review*, Vol. 165, No. 985, pp. 140–45, March 1979.

Honi, M., 'Alvar Aalto Symposium Jyväskylä', *Arkitekten-Arkkitehti*, Vol. 76, Nos. 5/6, pp. 24–9, 1979.

Abercrombie, S., 'Woodberry Poetry Room', *Society of Architectural Historians Journal*, Vol. 38, No. 2, pp. 120–22, May 1979.

Bell, D., 'Unity and aesthetics of incompletion in architecture', *Architectural Design*, Vol. 49, No. 7, 1979.

Morton, D., 'Aalto in Italy: the parochial church of Riola', *Progressive Architecture*, Vol. 60, No. 3, pp. 57–63, May 1979.

Porphyrios, D., 'The Burst of Memory: an essay on Aalto's typological conception of design', *Architectural Design*, Nos. 5/6, 1979.

'Church at Riola', *Architectural Review*, No. 985, 1979.

Blundell-Jones, P., 'Alvar Aalto Symposium', *Architectural Review*, Vol. 166, No. 990, p. 68, August 1979.

Kairamo, M., 'Are we destroying the heritage of Alvar Aalto', *Arkitekten-Arkkitehti*, Vol. 76, No. 2, pp. 38–9, 1979.

Kirkko, R., 'Church of the Cross, Lahti', *Arkitekten-Arkkitehti*, Vol. 76, Nos. 5/6, pp. 30–37, 1979.

Miller, W.C., 'Library of Mount Angel Benedictine College', *Architecture and Urbanism*, No. 10, pp. 3–38, October 1979.

'Aalto and After', *Architectural Design*, Vol. 49, No. 12, pp. 1–38 and 342f., 1979.

Groak, S., 'Aalto's House at Munksnas, 1934–36; Architect Alvar Aalto', *Architectural Design*, Vol. 49, No. 12, pp. 14–15, 1979.

Pearson, D., 'The legacy of Viipuri (Municipal Library); Architect Alvar Aalto', *Architectural Design*, Vol. 49, No. 12, pp. 6–13, 1979.

'Church of the Cross, Lahti; Architects Alvar Aalto and Elissa Aalto', *Arkitekten-Arkkitehti*, Vol. 76, No. 5/6, pp. 30–37, 1979.

Gresleri, G., 'Alvar Aalto's Church in Riola', *Kunst und Kirche*, No. 1, pp. 37–9, February 1980.

Peters, R.C., 'Aalto's luminous library in Oregon', *A.I.A. Journal*, Vol. 69, No. 11, pp. 72–3, September 1980.

Kliment, R.M., 'Alvar Aalto in Context', *Architectural Record*, Vol. 169, No. 12 (9), pp. 106–11, September 1980.

Suhonen, P., 'Aalto Literature: Architecture in Buildings and Ideas', *Arkitekten-Arkkitehti*, Vol. 77, No. 2, pp. 29–30 (English summary, pp. 65–6), 1980.

Sharp, D., 'After Aalto', *Building*, Vol. 239, No. 7168 (49), p. 30, 5 December 1980.

Keinanen, T., 'Glassware by Aino and Alvar Aalto', *Arkitekten-Arkkitehti*, Vol. 77, No. 8, pp. 48–54 (English summary, p. 60), 1980.

Photographic Sources

Copyright owners and photographers
Aalto Archives: xvi Valokuva Oy Kolmio
Museum of Finnish Architecture, Helsinki: 10 Thomas Rory Spence; 12 Rista; 18 Nyblin; 23 A. Salokorpi; 24 H. Havas; 36; 39 (above) Kari Hakli; 41, 43 (above and below) Gustaf Welin; 44 Paijänne; 50 (below); 53; 55 (below); 56, 57, 62 (above and below) Gustaf Welin; 65 Repro Heinonen; 66 Gustav Welin; 73, 76 H. Havas; 78; 79; 80 Gustaf Welin; 82 Repro Heinonen; 87 (above and below); 91; 95; 98 Gustaf Welin; 107 Foto Roos; 112, 119 Valokuva Oy Kolmio; 123; 125 (below); 126 (below); 129 P. Laurila; 131 Valokuva Oy Kolmio; 132 (above) E. Mäkinen; 132 (left); 132 (right) Valokuva Oy Kolmio; 135 H. Havas; 140; 147 H. Havas; 150; 152; 159 E. Mäkinen; 161 Teuvo Kanerva; 162, 171, 175 (above) H. Havas; 175 (below); 179; 180 (above and below) L. Mosso; 182; 184 P. Ingervo; 187 (above); 191 (above); 194 H. Havas; 196 (above), 196 (below), 197 P. Ingervo; 198; 200; 201 (below) H. Havas; 206 (below); 210 Rolf Dahlstrom: 212 Kari Hakli; 214; 221 (above) Kari Hakli; 223, 229 P. Ingervo; 230; 231 (above) A. Fethulla; 231 (below) Kari Hakli; 233 L. Mosso; 251 Kari Hakli; 252; 256 (above); 256 (below), 257 P. Ingervo; 257 Valokuva Oy Kolmio; 258 (above) H. Havas; 258 (above) Valokuva Oy Kolmio
Malcolm Quantrill: 9 (above, left and right), 55, 89 (above and below), 120, 124 (below), 126 (above), 151, 160, 166, 167, 183, 189 (above and below), 190, 204 (below), 211 (above), 221 (below)
The plans and drawings reproduced here were kindly supplied by Mrs Elissa Aalto and the Museum of Finnish Architecture. For permission to reproduce all the Aalto material thanks are due to The Aalto Foundation.

Index

Numbers in *italics* refer to illustrations